Intercultural Issues in the Workplace

Katerina Strani · Kerstin Pfeiffer
Editors

Intercultural Issues in the Workplace

Leadership, Communication and Trust

Editors
Katerina Strani
Languages and Intercultural Studies
Heriot-Watt University
Edinburgh, UK

Kerstin Pfeiffer
Languages and Intercultural Studies
Heriot-Watt University
Edinburgh, UK

ISBN 978-3-031-42319-2   ISBN 978-3-031-42320-8 (eBook)
https://doi.org/10.1007/978-3-031-42320-8

© The Editor(s) (if applicable) and The Author(s), under exclusive licence to Springer Nature Switzerland AG 2023

This work is subject to copyright. All rights are solely and exclusively licensed by the Publisher, whether the whole or part of the material is concerned, specifically the rights of translation, reprinting, reuse of illustrations, recitation, broadcasting, reproduction on microfilms or in any other physical way, and transmission or information storage and retrieval, electronic adaptation, computer software, or by similar or dissimilar methodology now known or hereafter developed.
The use of general descriptive names, registered names, trademarks, service marks, etc. in this publication does not imply, even in the absence of a specific statement, that such names are exempt from the relevant protective laws and regulations and therefore free for general use.
The publisher, the authors, and the editors are safe to assume that the advice and information in this book are believed to be true and accurate at the date of publication. Neither the publisher nor the authors or the editors give a warranty, expressed or implied, with respect to the material contained herein or for any errors or omissions that may have been made. The publisher remains neutral with regard to jurisdictional claims in published maps and institutional affiliations.

Cover credit: aelitta

This Palgrave Macmillan imprint is published by the registered company Springer Nature Switzerland AG
The registered company address is: Gewerbestrasse 11, 6330 Cham, Switzerland

Paper in this product is recyclable

Acknowledgements

We would like to thank the team of wonderfully patient contributors to this volume and all the colleagues who helped us assemble such a team.

We owe a debt of gratitude to Mairéad NicCraith and Jemina Napier, who provided wise, good-humoured guidance and practical advice from the beginning; to Agnes Tan for her input to the cross-cultural scenarios; and to the members of the Intercultural Research Centre writing group, who put up with us throughout.

The anonymous reviewers who commented on an early proposal gave valuable and constructive advice that helped shape the volume as it now stands. We would also like to offer special thanks to the colleagues at Palgrave who have worked with us on this project, and in particular Cathy Scott and Connie Li, who have shepherded us and this book from its inception.

Contents

1 **Setting the Scene: The Intercultural Dimension of the Contemporary Workplace** 1
Katerina Strani and Kerstin Pfeiffer

Part I Intercultural Communication

2 **Key Concepts for Cultural Communication in the Workplace** 15
Katerina Strani, Mairéad Nic Craith, Florian Scheuring, and Pedro Jesús Castillo Ortiz

3 **Multicultural Communication and Trust in the Contemporary Workplace** 31
Katerina Strani, Jane G. Bell, Panagiota-Penny Karanasiou, and Claudia Morais Castro

4 **Intercultural Perspectives of Work, Leisure, and Time** 49
Sara C. Brennan and Bernadette O'Rourke

Part II Cross-Cultural Leadership

5 **Leadership Across Cultures** 67
Daša Grajfoner, Lucy Bolton, and Ke Guek Nee

6 **Intercultural Coaching** 83
Silvia King, Daša Grajfoner, Lucy Bolton, and Ke Guek Nee

7 **Uncertainty and Trust in International Business Communication** 99
Yvonne McLaren-Hankin and Panagiota-Penny Karanasiou

Part III Economy

8 **Economy as Intercultural Challenge** 115
Ullrich Kockel

9 **Intercultural Issues in Finance** 133
Lina Fadel, Ken Brown, and Abdulkader Mostafa

10 **Currency, Identity and Trust: Cryptocurrencies, Central Bank Digital Currencies and the Case for the Bahamian Sand Dollar** 147
Dimitrios Syrrakos, Sophia Kuehnlenz, and Rory Shand

Part IV Language

11 **Global Englishes: Dialogue and Communication in the Workplace** 163
Mairéad Nic Craith, Philip McDermott, and Nicola Bermingham

12 **Multilingualism in the Workplace** 179
Bernadette O'Rourke and Sara C. Brennan

13 **Translation and Interpretation in Cross-Cultural Business Workplace Practices** 193
Min-Hsiu Liao, Pedro Jesús Castillo Ortiz, Jemina Napier, and Kester Newill

Part V Diversity

14 **Dignity and Diversity in the Workplace** 211
Jane G. Bell, Katerina Strani, and Jafar Ahmad

15 **Performing Gender in the Workplace** 227
Maryam Sholevar and Kerstin Pfeiffer

16 **Deaf People in the Workplace** 241
Mette Sommer Lindsay, Audrey Cameron, and Jemina Napier

Part VI Cross-Cultural Scenarios

17 **Cross-Cultural Scenarios** 257
Katerina Strani and Steven Glasgow

Glossary 275

Index 293

Notes on Contributors

Dr. Jafar Ahmad is an Iraqi-Canadian currently working as an analyst within the Middle-Eastern Relations Division at Global Affairs Canada. He completed his Ph.D. studies at Heriot-Watt University, Edinburgh in 2021 focusing on Shia-Sunni dynamics in Iraq. Prior to commencing his doctoral studies, he completed an M.Sc. in Arabic-English Translating and Interpreting at Heriot-Watt University. Dr. Ahmad was also awarded a Master of Arts in 2013 in the field of Conflict Analysis and Management at Royal Roads University, Canada.

Jane G. Bell studied anthropology before starting work at Heriot-Watt University as an assistant professor in English for Academic Purposes. Her research focuses on intercultural aspects of teaching and learning with a focus on neurodiversity. She is a member of the Intercultural Research Centre at the School of Social Sciences.

Dr. Nicola Bermingham is a senior lecturer in Hispanic Studies at the University of Liverpool. Nicola's research is situated at the intersection of sociolinguistics, educational linguistics and Hispanic and Lusophone linguistics, focusing in particular on the contexts of Galicia (Spain) and Cape Verde. She is the principal investigator on a British Academy funded project entitled "Monolingual Schools in Multilingual Societies: rethinking language and education in Cape Verde", which explores the ways that access to inclusive and equitable education can be ensured in multilingual, post-colonial contexts. Nicola is currently the editor of the Modern Languages Open Linguistics Section and Chair of the International Association for the Study of Spanish in Society.

Dr. Lucy Bolton is a chartered psychologist (BPS) and a registered occupational psychologist (HCPC), as well as a certified business coach (AC) and a trained occupational test user (BPS). She is an assistant professor in Business Psychology at Heriot-Watt University Dubai, leading the Master's in Business Psychology programmes globally. Lucy's area of speciality is business and coaching psychology, lecturing in the areas of coaching psychology, social and organisational change, diversity and research methods. Lucy has also conducted research in the areas of change management, workspace design, socio-technical systems, job design, employability and knowledge management, working with a number of global organisations including, Rolls-Royce, Bentley Motors, Marks and Spencer, the National Health Service (NHS), REED-NCFE and the UK Government Office of Science. Lucy has published her work and presented her research over the years at a number of international conferences.

Dr. Sara C. Brennan is an associate professor in the Département Langues et Cultures at the Université Toulouse Capitole in Toulouse, France. Based in critical sociolinguistics and linguistic anthropology, her research focuses on the links between minority language revitalisation and politico-economic developments, with a particular interest in social actors' engagement with minoritised languages in times of crisis. Sara's doctorate, completed at Heriot-Watt University (Edinburgh, 2017), examined the promotion and mobilisation of Irish as an economic resource for private sector businesses in the Republic of Ireland, with ethnographic fieldwork conducted in the wake of the post-2008 Irish economic downturn. Building on her work as a Sustaining Minoritized Languages in Europe (SMiLE) fellow at the Center for Folklife and Cultural Heritage of the Smithsonian Institution (Washington, D.C.) and a postdoctoral researcher at the Sorbonne Nouvelle (Paris), she is currently researching contemporary efforts to revitalise the Occitan language in southern France.

Ken Brown is an associate professor specialising in Finance at Edinburgh Business School, Heriot-Watt University. Ken plays a key role as the M.Sc. course leader and is a member of the On-campus Board of Studies. Ken joined EBS full time in 2000 and has experience of teaching Finance courses in many countries ranging from Mexico, to Australia and Uganda and Malaysia. His particular areas of interest in Finance are mergers and acquisitions, financial distress, risk management and finance in the oil and gas industry. He has an M.A. in Economics from the University of Edinburgh and an M.Sc. in International Banking and Financial Studies from Heriot-Watt University.

Dr. Audrey Cameron is a polymer chemist, who is deaf, and uses British Sign Language. Audrey is Chancellor's fellow in the School of Education at the University of Edinburgh, where she is conducting research on the benefits of using BSL for teaching science to deaf and hearing children, and is also the lead on the postgraduate programme for students studying to become chemistry teachers and teaches the Deaf Studies module as part of the M.Sc. Inclusive Education. From 2013 to 2015, she was a research fellow at the University of Edinburgh/NSPCC Child Protection Research Centre based and also worked as a research associate at Heriot-Watt University from 2017–2019 on the DESIGNS project focusing on deaf people's access to employment. Audrey is the chair of the University of Edinburgh's BSL plan working group and manages the Scottish Sensory Centre's BSL Glossary project, which has nearly 1,500 signs for science and maths with BSL definitions and examples. Audrey works with a team of 24 deaf scientists, mathematicians, teachers working with deaf children and BSL sign linguists since 2007.

Dr. Pedro Jesús Castillo Ortiz is an assistant professor in Translation and Interpreting at the University of Grenada, Spain. His research interests and expertise are in professional interpreting, with a focus on media interpreting.

Notes on Contributors

Dr. Lina Fadel is an assistant professor in Social Research Methods, and a member of the Doctoral Centre and the Intercultural Research Centre at the School of Social Sciences, Heriot-Watt University. With a background in critical literary theory, languages and intercultural studies, Lina's research is interdisciplinary and focuses on how we navigate sameness and difference in multicultural contexts. Her research interests include migrant narratives, representations of migration, critical theoretical, decolonial and literary perspectives on migration and autoethnographies of migration. A Syrian with a lived experience of migration, Lina is particularly interested in how people reconstruct their identities and engage in home-making following displacement, and she has done considerable work in recent years with Syrian refugees in Scotland and refugees in Calais. As well as publishing academic articles and in online media outlets including The Conversation, Lina performed a one-woman show at the Edinburgh Fringe in 2022, designed to expose the double standards that exist both at the UK border and in the media's portrayal of refugees. Lina is a creative writer and has recently joined *The Other Side of Hope*, the UK's first literary magazine of sanctuary, as their poetry co-editor.

Dr. Steven Glasgow is an assistant professor of Management at Heriot-Watt University, and is an associate head of the Management Department. Steven's research focuses primarily on how workplace inequalities in Scottish tourism are (re)produced, maintained and disrupted.

Dr. Daša Grajfoner is a Chartered Coaching psychologists (BPS), director of Coaching Lab at Heriot-Watt University and the past chair of the Division of Coaching Psychology at the British Psychological Society. Dasha is a visiting professor in Coaching Psychology at Sigmund Freud University in Vienna and an Assistant Professor at Heriot-Watt University, where she teaches and supervises in the areas of coaching, leadership and animal assisted interventions. She is a practitioner coaching psychologist and a researcher focusing on the theory and the application of coaching to improve mental health and well-being and to develop and improve leadership at workplace.

Dr. Panagiota-Penny Karanasiou holds a Ph.D. in Business Interpreting & Intercultural Communication from Heriot-Watt University in Scotland. She has been working at the University of Edinburgh for the last 6 years. She participated in various international conferences and published papers in English and Greek language. Dr. Karanasiou is also an entrepreneur in translation and interpreting. She is the owner and managing director of 15 translation agencies and employs 410 T&I professionals. She is an honorary president of the Hellenic Association of Qualified Translators, a member of the Chartered Institute of Linguists, the European Translation Studies and the Centre for Translation and Interpreting Studies in Scotland (CTISS).

Silvia King is a Positive Psychology coach with an M.Sc. in Applied Positive Psychology and Coaching Psychology. A Ph.D. candidate with Heriot-Watt University, Silvia explores Coaching Psychology in a Middle East context to enhance our understanding of coaching in cultural contexts. As a member of the Heriot-Watt University Coaching Lab and adjunct faculty, she supports the training of current and future coaches across the university's three campuses in Edinburgh, Dubai and Malaysia as well as the wider public. As a volunteer with the EMCC Global Research Centre for Excellence, Silvia supports the work of the EMCC to promote relevant research across coaching, mentoring and supervision and its implementation in the profession by non-academics and academics alike.

Prof. Ullrich Kockel is a professor of Creative Ethnology at the University of the Highlands and Islands. He taught at Leeds Polytechnic and NUI Galway before receiving his Ph.D. from the University of Liverpool, where he was appointed to the first-ever full-time post in Irish Studies at a British university. Ullrich also taught Geography at the University College Cork, and has held chairs in European Studies (University of the West of England), Ethnology and Folklife (University of Ulster) and Cultural Ecology and Sustainability (Heriot-Watt). He is a member of the Royal Irish Academy, a visiting professor at the Center for Social Anthropology, Vytautas Magnus University Kaunas, Lithuania and the Latvian Academy of Culture, and was the president of the International Society for Ethnology and Folklore (SIEF), 2008–2013.

Dr. Sophia Kuehnlenz is a senior lecturer in Economics at the Manchester Metropolitan University's Business School. She holds a Ph.D. in Economics from the Leeds University Business School, an M.Sc. and an undergraduate degree in Economics from the University of Bamberg. Sophia is a pluralist Macroeconomist interested in economic and financial crises. Her research aims to establish an improved Minsky—inspired theory and an overhaul of methodology (mainstream and heterodox) with regard to modelling crisis episodes specifically and capitalist production economies more generally. More recently, her research has expanded into the field of fintech, cryptocurrencies and CBDCs with an emphasis on implications for overall stability, governance and regulation. Sophia is a member of the Association for Heterodox Economics committee and various other academic organisations including the Post Keynesian Study Group (PKSG) and the Reteaching Economics Network.

Dr. Min-Hsiu Liao is an assistant professor in Translation and Interpreting Studies in the Department of Languages and Intercultural Studies at Heriot-Watt University, where she teaches Chinese-English translation, conference interpreting and research methods. Her broad research interests are intercultural communication, multimodality and discourse analysis. Her recent projects include research on the translation of museums and heritage sites, and multilingual urban landscape.

Dr. Philip McDermott is a senior lecturer in Sociology at Ulster University in Northern Ireland. Philip's research is concerned with the relationship between the state and the heritage of minority groups—especially migrant and linguistic minorities. He is particularly interested in the intersection between social policy and cultural policy as a space for empowerment. A further strand of Philip's work is in language policy and planning for (and by) migrant communities. He has an interest in the perception of migrant languages in public places, the ways that government and communities deal with such linguistic diversity and how multilingualism and bilingualism are dealt with in policy contexts. In 2022, he was awarded Ulster University's Distinguished Research Fellowship for the Faculty of Arts, Humanities and Social Sciences. He is currently the co-editor of the Irish Journal of Sociology and the Anthropological Journal of European Cultures (AJEC).

Dr. Yvonne McLaren-Hankin is an associate professor at Heriot-Watt University, Edinburgh, where she teaches and supervises in the areas of business communication, translating and interpreting. Her research interests lie in various aspects of business communication, in particular linguistic, textual and pragmatic features of corporate genres.

Claudia Morais Castro M.Sc., is an independent researcher. Her undergraduate studies were in International Business and Management and she decided to reroute her academic path to follow her passion for languages and cultures in the business context. Born and raised in Germany with Portuguese roots in a diverse environment inspired her to focus on intercultural differences. Claudia has researched the advantages and disadvantages of being bicultural in German small and medium enterprises and is planning on continuing this research at a larger scale.

Dr. Abdulkader Mostafa is a lecturer in Finance at the School of Social Sciences, Heriot-Watt University. His research interests are in real estate, investment and finance. Before moving into academia, Abdulkader had more than 20 years of work experience in both the commercial and investment banking. During his career in investment banking, he had extensive exposure to all types of transactions including Islamic finance, real estate funds, IPO, private equity, M&A and restructuring finance. He gained comprehensive experience in detailed financial modelling, fundamental financial analysis, financial due-diligence and corporate valuation. He also gained excellent experience in debt financing. He managed a large credit portfolio of corporate clients and participated in a large number of project finance transactions in both conventional and Islamic modes.

Prof. Jemina Napier is the chair of Intercultural Communication and a member of the SIGNS@HWU research group in the Centre for Translation & Interpreting Studies in Scotland in the School of Social Sciences at Heriot-Watt University. She is an interpreter researcher, an educator and a practitioner. She is accredited to work as an interpreter between British and Australian Sign Languages and International Sign. She conducts interdisciplinary linguistic, social and ethnographic explorations of direct and mediated communication in sign languages and has led various projects on interpreting in public service settings and the workplace. She was the Heriot-Watt University research lead along with other universities in a consortium for the European Commission funded DESIGNS project, which focused on deaf people's opportunities to access, maintain and progress in employment.

Dr. Ke Guek Nee is an associate professor in Psychology at Heriot-Watt University in Malaysia. Ke received her Ph.D. in Industrial and Organizational Psychology from the National University of Malaysia. She has secured various national and international research grants. Her research focus is on preventive measures of problematic online usage behaviours, cyber wellness, work and organisational psychology and leadership.

Kester Newill is a lecturer in Interpreting and Translation at the University of Stirling, with a focus on Mandarin. Kester's career in education has included working for schools, universities and NGOs across China and the UK in roles that involve teaching, teacher training and project management. Kester has developed scholarship in the areas of technology-enhanced learning, intercultural business communication and the teaching of Chinese as a Foreign Language. He has become more closely involved in the design and delivery of modules concerned with translation technologies and audiovisual translation. The latter, as it relates to media in China, is becoming a focus for future scholarship activities.

Prof. Mairéad Nic Craith is a professor of Public Folklore at the University of the Highlands and Islands (Orkney). She has previously held Chairs in Sociology at Ulster University and in Cultural Studies at Heriot-Watt University in Edinburgh. Mairéad held a DAAD Professorship at the University of Göttingen as well as an Honorary Professorship in Social Science at Exeter University. In 2018, Mairéad was a visiting scholar at the Celtic Studies Department, Harvard University. Throughout her academic career, Mairéad has published on the conceptual understanding of contemporary political-linguistic debates in Ireland and across Europe. Notable publications include *Europe and the Politics of Language: Citizens, Migrants, Outsiders* (Palgrave, 2006) and *Narratives of Place, Belonging and Language: An Intercultural Perspective* (Palgrave, 2012). Mairéad has worked with international bodies such as UNESCO and the European Centre for Minority Issues.

Bernadette O'Rourke is a professor of Sociolinguistics and Hispanic Studies in the School of Modern Languages and Cultures at the University of Glasgow. She was the chair of the EU COST Action IS1306 entitled New Speakers in a Multilingual Europe: Opportunities and Challenges (2013–2017). Her recent co-authored publications include New Speakers of Irish in the Global Context: New revival? (Routledge 2020) and the Palgrave Handbook of Minority Languages and Communities (Palgrave 2019) which won the British Association of Applied Linguistics (BAAL) Book Prize in 2020.

Dr. Kerstin Pfeiffer is an assistant professor of German and Cultural Studies at Heriot-Watt University. Her research centres on theatre, performance and heritage. She is particularly interested in the ways in which performances help to shape, maintain and challenge our notions of community and identity.

Dr. Florian Scheuring is an assistant professor at Edinburgh Business School in Heriot-Watt University's School of Social Sciences, and a member of the Centre for Logistics and Sustainability. He completed his Ph.D. in Business Management at Heriot-Watt University, exploring the influence of port community members on a port community's performance through a social capital lens. His research interests stretch across a range of topics, including performance management, stakeholder relationship management, logistics, supply chain collaboration as well as work-based learning. Florian is part of the Operations Management and Logistics subject group, engaged in Undergraduate, Postgraduate and DBA supervision, and has taught on Business Research Methods, Operations Management, Management in a Global Context and Freight Transport and Warehouse Management. He is the programme director of the M.Sc. Operations Management and manages the suite of Undergraduate Management Dissertations at Edinburgh Business School. Prior to his current role, he worked for Royal Mail in several management roles.

Dr. Rory Shand is a reader in Political Economy at Manchester Metropolitan University's Business School. His research interests are in public policy and management; sustainability and regeneration; governance frameworks and concepts.

Dr. Maryam Sholevar is an academic staff at Heriot-Watt University. She worked as a lecturer at the Department of Banking and Finance, Jimma University, Ethiopia. She earned her Ph.D. from SOAS University of London by proposing a new definition for financial literacy and inclusion while providing empirical evidence for the theoretical model proposed. She is now part of the Graduate Apprentice Programme at Edinburgh Business School. She completed the Aurora leadership programme offered by Advance HE.

Dr. Mette Sommer Lindsay (deaf, she/her) is an assistant professor in Languages and Intercultural Studies at Heriot-Watt University. She is a sociologist and obtained her Ph.D. at Heriot-Watt University in 2022, supervised by Professor Jemina Napier and Professor Kate Sang. She worked as a research fellow at the University of West of Scotland until summer 2022. Her research focuses on positionalities, epistemologies and power/oppression that shape deaf entrepreneurial motivations, behaviour and constructions. Her research interests include deaf and disability studies, sociology, qualitative research methods, minority entrepreneurship and employment, Bourdieu.

Dr. Katerina Strani is an associate professor and head of Cultural Studies at the Department of Languages and Intercultural Studies, Heriot-Watt University. She is leading the Migration theme at Heriot-Watt's Intercultural Research Centre and was a visiting professor at Adam Mickiewicz University in Poznań in 2021–2022. Katerina has a background in Languages and Politics and she has published research on intercultural dialogue, racism and hate speech, language and heritage as well as an edited volume on Multilingualism and Politics (Palgrave, 2020). Katerina has led international funded projects on racism and discrimination, linguistic and cultural inclusion of newly arrived migrants and refugees, and endangered languages. She has been leading a global course on Intercultural Issues in Business and Management, delivered on campuses in Edinburgh, Dubai and Malaysia, a Graduate Apprenticeship course, since 2016, as well as short CPD courses on Intercultural Awareness in the Workplace since 2022.

Dr. Dimitrios Syrrakos is a senior lecturer in Economics and Finance at Keele University's Business School. The key areas of Dimitrios's research include exchange rate economics, fiscal and monetary policy effectiveness, the eurozone debt crisis and international monetary relations. He has delivered a number of units ranging from Introductory Macroeconomics to Advanced Macroeconomics and Economics of European Monetary Union. During 2010–2015, he was invited numerous times as a featured Eurozone commentator on media including BBC World News, BBC News, BBC Radio 2, BBC Radio 5, BBC Radio Manchester and Radio Boston.

List of Figures

Fig. 2.1	Iceberg model of cultural layers, adapted from Schein (2010)	19
Fig. 8.1	Typical sources of "family" income earned by involvement in informal economy (after Kockel [1993])	123
Fig. 8.2	Two contrasting concepts of the individual -isolated (left) and socio-culturally embedded (right)	123
Fig. 11.1	Map of the British Empire (1920s) (*Source* https://commons.wikimedia.org/wiki/File:Map_of_the_British_Empire_(1920%27s).png)	164
Fig. 11.2	Three Circles of World Englishes (*Inner Circle Countries*: countries that represent traditional bases of the English language. *Outer Circle Countries*: regions where English has become strongly embedded as a second institutional language. *Expanding Circle Countries*: places where the influence of English as a foreign language is gaining ground. *Source* Adapted from Kachru [1992, 356])	165

List of Tables

Table 5.1	"Effective" and "Successful" leadership behaviours vs personality vs leadership styles vs Hofstede's dimensions	74
Table 5.2	"Ineffective" and "non-successful" leadership behaviours vs personality vs leadership styles vs Hofstede's dimensions	75
Table 5.3	The application of ABCDE model of coaching to leadership coaching case study	79
Table 11.1	Comparison between ELF and BELF approaches	172
Table 13.1	Translation strategies in the business context	195
Table 13.2	Examples of business contexts potentially requiring interpreters	196
Table 14.1	'Summary comparison of Asian versus Western understandings of dignity' (Lucas et al. 2012, 3)	214

Chapter 1
Setting the Scene: The Intercultural Dimension of the Contemporary Workplace

Katerina Strani and Kerstin Pfeiffer

> This introductory chapter presents the purpose of the volume, its scope and relevance in contemporary research and practice on global and intercultural workplaces. The book's nature and purpose are critical rather than prescriptive. It does not constitute a guide offering one-size-fits-all solutions to problems; instead, it serves as a tool for critique and in-depth understanding of workplaces in the global context. It also includes themes that are overlooked in existing workplace-related scholarship, such as multilingualism, translation and interpreting, cross-cultural understandings of workplace dignity, and deaf people in the workplace. These are critically discussed under the overarching themes of leadership, communication and trust.

1.1 Rationale and Scope of the Volume

This textbook focuses on culture and communication in the workplace. It looks at intercultural perspectives and issues in workplace communication with contributions from cultural studies, psychology, sociolinguistics, business management, economics, translation and interpreting studies. The interdisciplinary nature of this volume is its major distinctive strength. The book is not meant to be prescriptive, so it is neither a 'how-to' guide, nor does it offer one-size-fits-all solutions to problems in contemporary global workplaces. Instead, it constitutes a critical tool for in-depth understanding of the workplace in the global context and looks at themes that are

---

K. Strani (✉) · K. Pfeiffer
Languages and Intercultural Studies, Heriot-Watt University, Edinburgh, UK
e-mail: A.Strani@hw.ac.uk

K. Pfeiffer
e-mail: K.Pfeiffer@hw.ac.uk

© The Author(s), under exclusive license to Springer Nature Switzerland AG 2023
K. Strani and K. Pfeiffer (eds.), *Intercultural Issues in the Workplace*,
https://doi.org/10.1007/978-3-031-42320-8_1

often overlooked in business and management or intercultural communication scholarship, such as: the status of deaf people in the workplace, dignity in the workplace, intercultural perspectives of work, leisure and time, and the intersections between gender and culture in the workplace—in addition to previously studies themes of interculturality and the embedded economy, cross-cultural leadership and managing uncertainty.

The textbook also looks at a broad range of workplaces, for example health care, public services, museums and other cultural institutions, educational institutions, NGOs, charities, the retail sector, advertising, engineering, and businesses of different sizes. Contributors to the volume have expertise in different disciplines, industries, and geographical areas. Case studies are therefore drawn from Norway, China, Japan, the US, Russia, Saudi Arabia, France and other countries, and they include workplaces with deaf employees as well as deaf workplaces.

The volume is primarily addressed to students and academics. Practitioners would also find the book useful, as it tackles key issues and challenges in contemporary multicultural and multilingual workplaces. The book is also recommended for professional training, such as cultural awareness or working in culrturally diverse environments.

1.1.1 Current Trends in Research and Practice

Workplaces tend to undergo changes in line with socio-political and cultural shifts and trends. The world of work has always been inextricably linked to such developments and technological advances. Increasing global connectivity means that contemporary workplaces of various types are no longer confined to a single space; they are constantly evolving (Ladegaard and Jenks 2015; Cole et al. 2014) and becoming sites of cultural, linguistic, social and neuro- diversity. This means that workplaces can be considered as cultures themselves (Schein 2010), with their own rituals (Islam and Zyphur 2009; Kim and Strudler 2012), established norms, values, rules and practices that are prescribed, accepted or unacceptable. Such dynamic workplace cultures operate in international and cross-cultural contexts that may be different from their own. To maintain a competitive advantage, employees and workplaces need to be aware of intercultural relations and activities in different professional and geo-political contexts, as well as intercultural issues in the world of work at all levels, and learn to adapt their practices accordingly without losing their identity.

Academic literature on the world of work tends to come from the discipline of business and management, and issues regarding multiculturalism or cultural diversity are increasingly at the forefront of business and management studies given increasingly globalised business contexts and practices. Cultural diversity in such literature is largely regarded as a problem, a barrier, something to be addressed, tackled or managed. It is often described as a source of conflict (Martin 2014) and/or a costly aspect of global business (Stevens et al. 2008) due to the purported problems that it brings with it. The prevailing argument seems to be that if culture is managed and contained (or even suppressed) then this will lead to harmonious business relations, efficiency and productivity. For this reason, various models and approaches have been developed that espouse essentialist and fixed understanding of culture, and therefore attempt to categorise or group cultures according to their working practices, their values and approaches to work.

Despite resistance to this, both from critical business management literature and from other disciplines (see McSweeney 2002; Ladegaard and Jenks 2015), intercultural training for business and management based on these essentialist models has gained traction and developed into a (rather lucrative) industry of its own (see Szkudlarek 2009 on the ethics of intercultural training. The emphasis on intercultural training seems to be on cultural differences rather than similarities; on how to minimise or suppress these differences instead of capitalising on them or utilising them to achieve better results and more harmonious workplace relations (see Ladegaard and Jenks 2015, for a comprehensive critical account of this). Critical scholarship has emerged in recent years which is starting to question "dominating traditional (positivist) approaches" (Holmes 2017, 1). Alison Phipps puts this succinctly:

> When workers are managed as if they are machines, and cultures as if they are homogeneous and static, then the models of training created by those imaging human beings – individually and culturally – in this way, are bound to be models that permit no deviation, no place for critique, no space for divergence or difference. (Phipps 2010, 62)

The fact that concepts such as intercultural communication or intercultural training originated in "the metrocentres of the 'North'" (Holmes, 2017, 3) and are "typical of a certain Anglo-Saxon culture, discourse and worldview" (Kramsch 2002, 283) should be thematised and emphasised in all related research and discussion of norms and practices. Kramsch argues that if we do not revisit these concepts critically then they "can be easily highjacked [sic] by a global ideology of 'effective communication' Anglo-Saxon style, which speaks an English discourse even as it expresses itself in many different languages" (Kramsch 2002, 284). Kim and Strudler (2012), Shi-xu (2013), Du (2015), R'boul (2021) and others have introduced alternative concepts and models of interculturality that draw on Confucianism and on Islamic perspectives, respectively. However, there is still more work to be done in research, education and training that includes marginalised, disenfranchised and minoritised voices, to build "approaches that are inclusive, context-specific/sensitive, and understand human experience from the periphery and global 'South'" (Holmes, 2017, 3).

There is also a need to include disciplines such as anthropology, psychology, cultural studies and sociolinguistics in the critical discussion of contemporary intercultural workplaces. The world of work more often than not reflects social structures and cultural norms, and it is contingent upon human behaviour. The above disciplines have been researching intercultural dimensions in business workplaces through different lenses. Ferraro and Briody (2017) have been highly influential in their scholarship on international business from the perspective of cultural anthropology. Hayes (2021) also provides an overview of the anthropology of work and discusses processes of socialisation, enculturation, inequality and exclusion, as well as the role of language in workplace ethnography. Intercultural research, too, has looked at interculturality at work with an emphasis on excluded or marginalised groups as well as workplace dynamics from a nuanced cultural perspective in non-essentialist terms (see Kim and Bhawuk 2008). Moreover, sociolinguists have been studying language and multilingualism in workplace communication for decades (Clyne 1999; Meyer and Apfelbaum 2010; Angouri 2014; Lüdi et al. 2016). More specifically, Ilie and Schnurr (2017) have looked at discourse-based leadership across the overarching themes of power, management and gender. In addition, cross-cultural psychology and industrial, work and organisational psychology have studied workplace dynamics from an intercultural perspective (Triandis and Brislin 1984; Berry et al. 2002). The field of global finance and accounting has also studied the intercultural dimension with a focus on cultural finance (Nadler and Breuer 2019) and emancipatory critical accounting (Haslam et al. 2019).

These important discussions and research contributions have largely remained within the confines of their disciplines, however, and there is little cross-disciplinary work and understanding of the intercultural dimension in the world of work. There is therefore a gap in past and current approaches that tend to focus on a single disciplinary lens, which does not do justice to the complexity or range of intercultural aspects in workplaces. The contemporary research and practice context requires this interdisciplinary dialogue to move away from established monolithic notions of culture as a "scapegoat for disagreements, misunderstandings and clashes" in contemporary workplaces (Schnurr et al. 2017). Conflict also needs to be embraced not only as a fact of life in any workplace, but also as a constructive path to change, growth, creativity and innovation. This volume attempts to address these concerns by bringing together scholars from cultural studies, psychology, sociolinguistics, business management, translation and interpreting studies, to revisit previous studied themes and provide critical views on less studied ones. Before looking at these in detail, we provide some key definitions and assumptions.

1.1.2 Key Definitions and Assumptions

The concept of culture defies easy summary, as it has been defined in numerous ways from different epistemological and disciplinary lenses. In broad anthropological terms, we regard culture as a collective concept referring to the dynamic collection of shared meanings, which implies some degree of agreement on beliefs, values and practices without being essentialist or nation-based. We are not alone in rejecting the notion of 'national cultures' perpetuated by reductionist models of intercultural management (McSweeney 2002; Ladegaard and Jenks 2015 and others). Our work practices, preferences, attitudes and behaviours are shaped not only by our cultural background but also by our personality, our social class, our upbringing and educational background, and our life experiences including those of oppression, marginalisation or systematic exclusion.

Still, the degree of dynamicity and volatility of cultures is debateable. We cannot deny that there are shared understandings, socialised and standardised norms, rituals and traditions that remain unchanged through time and are also visible in the workplace. East Asian understandings of dignity and face, for example (see Oetzel and Ting-Toomey 2003; Okoro 2012), result in some level of predictability in workplace norms and attitudes or business practices in these areas. We therefore agree with Kecskes (2014, 5):

> We should strive for a compromise between the two approaches: one that acknowledges 'the possibility of ethnic or cultural marking in communicative behavior' but, at the same time, allows for the situational context to be salient and where participants co-construct (inter)cultures in situ.

The way in which we understand how the relationship between cultures work often influences the way we see cultures interacting. There are three key frameworks to consider in this respect:

> *Multicultural* refers to a workplace with multiple cultures, in which groups operate and work alongside each other but retain a cultural distinct identity. Multicultural workplaces can be seen as successful because they encourage groups to interact, but they can also be criticised for groups remaining too exclusive (see Modood and Meer 2012).
> *Intercultural* describes social or workplace situations in which cultural boundaries are fluid and people from different cultures interact together and enact change. Intercultural situations emphasise dialogue and the benefits of plurality (Modood and Meer 2012).
> *Cross-cultural* emphasises comparative relationships between cultures. Cross-cultural analyses look at how power features in relationships between cultures, and what happens when one culture is seen as 'dominant' (O'Sullivan et al. 1994).

Arguably, the basis of cultural conflict is judging another culture by the same standards, customs and values as our own. This ethnocentrism assumes that our culture (including organisational culture) is superior or should be seen as the standard. It also presupposes that if something is different, it is wrong. Ethnocentrism is partly due to lack of understanding of our own cultural identity. Only when we reflect on our own values, attitudes, norms and behaviour can we understand the culture of others. Without this self-critical and self-reflective work, we cannot see beyond the cultural differences at work and, instead of capitalising on them, we will always see them as barriers to minimise and overcome. What is more, the onus will always be on the 'other' (usually minority) group or individual to adapt to 'our' way and standards.

Overall, we espouse the business case for diversity and extend it to all workplaces. Researchers and practitioners have already demonstrated that multicultural workforces increase creativity and innovation with bringing new perspectives and ways of thinking (Gassmann 2001; Cseh 2003; Washington 2013). We also view leadership and management as distinct and often conflicting roles. A leader, as opposed to a manager, can be self-appointed and may in some cases work in opposition to established management to effectuate change and operationalise collective vision. Latest technological advances mean that aspects of management have been computerised and digitised, and managing tasks in global virtual teams can now be facilitated with shared apps that schedule meetings, set tasks and deadlines, track progress via Gantt charts, issue reminders, give penalties for missed deadlines or incomplete tasks and rewards for timely and full completion. The human aspect of leadership (and management) is of paramount importance, and the intercultural dimension has a central role in this respect.

1.1.3 Key Themes and Outline of the Book

The overarching themes that run through the entire volume are leadership (in the emancipatory and transformational way that appreciates and fosters interculturality), communication and its intercultural dimension, and trust. Trust is a crucial element of harmonious workplace relations and of successful performance in business and other industries, yet it is often overlooked. Trust can be rooted in human relationships or rules and procedures. Whichever is the case, when trust is broken or damaged, all aspects of a workplace suffer. Building trust in multicultural teams is more challenging than in monocultural teams (if these actually exist) because of contrasting norms and values. Due to the multi-facetedness and contingency of the concepts of trust, communication and leadership, especially in an intercultural context, these are embedded in all chapters and run as a thread throughout the book.

Against this backdrop, the textbook is divided into five thematic sections: *Intercultural Communication; Cross-cultural Leadership; Economy; Language; Diversity.* To ensure consistency between chapters so that the pedagogical framework is strong and consistent throughout the book, all chapters include the following set elements:

- 100-word overview preceding the introduction
- 1 or 2 case studies in text boxes
- 5 review questions
- 5 sources of recommended further reading in addition to the reference list.

Section I: Intercultural Communication consists of three chapters and draws largely on the disciplines of cultural studies, anthropology, sociolinguistics and management. Chapter 2 discusses key concepts in cultural communication in the workplace. Strani, Nic Craith, Scheuring and Castillo examine how culture and communication are intrinsic to our understandings of the workplace and provide core examples of how the workplace can be analysed both as a culture and as a communicative practice. The authors revisit established models with critical intent and emphasise the need to move beyond Anglo-Saxon understandings and frameworks. Overall, the chapter provides a critical theoretical framework around culture and communication for the volume's discussion on interculturality in contemporary workplaces, leaving leadership and trust for a more focused and explicit consideration in subsequent chapters.

Chapter 3 looks at multicultural communication in contemporary globalised workplaces. By critically revisiting and challenging established models and methods of analysis, Strani, Bell, Karanasiou and Morais Castro discuss power dynamics in multicultural workplaces, from competing cultures to a negotiated culture. They look at how this negotiated culture emerges, how trust is established, especially in a short timescale, and how multicultural teams function, negotiate and deal with conflict. They then move to key dimensions in cross-cultural interactions such as non-verbal, paraverbal and visual communication, politeness, turn-taking, cross-cultural negotiation and conflict. Trust is discussed from the perspective of team formation and teamwork, as well as the online dimension and how trust is developed in virtual teams. The chapter finishes with a critique of intercultural competence and proposes instead the concept of intercultural responsibility which is based on reflexivity, self-scrutiny and respect. It then gives recommendations on how to develop such intercultural responsibility in the workplace.

Chapter 4 looks at intercultural perspectives of work, leisure and time. After reviewing key definitions of these concepts, Brennan and O'Rourke look at cultural values before sketching out how such values influence understandings of work, leisure and time. They explain how punctuality and deadlines are perceived differently in different cultures, and how this may affect team cohesion and performance. A work meeting is then used to illustrate real-world implications of encounters between professionals with different culturally shaped perspectives on these concepts. The chapter ends with recommendations and insights crucial for successful leadership, communication and rapport-building in the contemporary workplace.

Section II: Cross-cultural Leadership consists of three chapters and draws on psychology, coaching and intercultural business communication. Chapter 5 focuses on leadership across cultures and critically revisits established models such as the GLOBE project. Grajfoner, Bolton and Guek Nee first discuss psychological models of leadership behaviour, before moving to cultural perspectives to leadership and emergent leadership styles. They look at leaders and groups and use insights from social identity theory to look at different aspects of leadership and follower perceptions before looking at ethnocentrism, prejudice, bias and discrimination. The chapter finishes with a discussion of executive coaching in the context of successful leadership. This provides a smooth transition to Chapter 6, which focuses on intercultural coaching. King, Grajfoner, Bolton and Guek Nee introduce coaching and coaching psychology in the workplace, discuss relevant coaching models and tools and explore ways in which students and trainees can develop their own intercultural coaching skills. The chapter argues that intercultural coaching can help address many of the cultural challenges that emerge in the workplace by virtue of the coaching process as well as the unique skillset required for coaching. Culture can be the focus of coaching conversations, while also informing the process. Given the level of complexity, coaches require broad expertise as well as high levels of intercultural sensitivity and literacy to fulfil their task.

Chapter 7 discusses uncertainty and trust in international business communication. McLaren-Hankin and Karanasiou examine this from an organisational and a workplace context. The organisational context focuses on crisis situations, specifically the crisis of trust in the world's banks and the role of social media in crisis communication. The workplace context looks at multilingual business negotiations.

Here, uncertainty and lack of trust can stem from different perceptions and expectations held by participants, as well as the undetermined nature of the relationships between them. The chapter also discusses rebuilding trust in the banking sector and looks at the case studies of Barclays bank, as well as the case study of Toyota when looking at crisis communication and the role of apologies.

Section III: Economy consists of three chapters and draws on economic anthropology, intercultural finance, political economy and international business. It may seem on the outset that a section on the economy is not strictly related to the intercultural dimension of workplaces or language and culture in the workplace. This is not the case, however, and in fact, a lack of awareness of the intercultural dimensions of economy and finance can cause communication breakdown, misunderstandings and conflict on the basis of disagreement on fundamental assumptions, values and norms. This can also be costly for businesses and organisations.

In Chapter 8, Kockel provides a historical and conceptual framework that is necessary to understand what is at play and what is at stake when discussing the economy as intercultural challenge. Kockel argues that, rather than a uniform global phenomenon, economy is culturally contingent, conditioned by historical, geographical, ecological, social and ideological factors. Contact between different cultural modes of economy can lead to friction, which may exacerbate crises, but it may also hold potential to find creative solutions for contemporary problems. Following a summary of historical, geographical and conceptual frameworks that help the reader understand economy as culture, the chapter examines a key trope of mainstream economics, the universally rational actor. It then considers the 'informal' economy, showing how cultural embedding works, before introducing alternative models of economy, many with religious foundations.

Chapter 9 then focuses on intercultural issues in finance. Fadel, Brown and Mostafa argue that an informed appreciation of cultural nuances and differences is central to global financial literacy and the establishment of trust, yet it is often overlooked. With this in mind, the chapter discusses how financial centres are operating in a globalised world and associated challenges, with a focus on London and New York. It then looks at money and mobile payments, drawing on the case of M-Pesa in Kenya, before moving to the cultural factors at work in the case of Islamic finance, and the risk-averse and culturally bound Japanese financial system. The chapter concludes that cultural literacy is essential for a comprehensive understanding of financial phenomena around the world.

Chapter 10 looks at the intercultural aspects of money and national currencies, which is perhaps the most overlooked aspect of intercultural issues in the world of work, and even in intercultural finance. Syrrakos, Kuehnlenz and Shand start their discussion by drawing on the historical evolution of the use of money during the last three centuries and assess the major developments since 1945. In doing so, the links between national money and identity are addressed by paying attention to the issue of trust. This is done from both an institutional and cultural perspective. Emphasis is also placed on latest developments involving a switch to international money, the advent of cryptocurrencies and the creation of Central Bank Digital Currencies. The latter is showcased via the Bahamian Sand Dollar and its implications for financial integration, national identity and work-based practices in the tourism industry.

Section IV: Language consists of three chapters and draws on sociolinguistics, cultural studies, sociology, translation and interpreting studies. Nic Craith, McDermott and Bermingham discuss dialogue and communication in the workplace through Global Englishes in Chapter 11. After contextualising the growth of English, they critically assess the role of English v. Englishes as 'the language of business' by considering its status in different continental locations. The chapter makes a distinction between English as a Native Language (ENL), English as a Lingua Franca (ELF) and Business English as a Lingua Franca (BELF). In doing so, it considers questions of ownership and appropriation in relation to the language itself, examining the implications of language choice in shaping how contemporary workplaces operate.

Chapter 12 then looks at workplace communication from the perspective of multilingualism, when linguistic diversity is evident and ELF or BELF may not be an option. Authors O'Rourke and Brennan argue that multilingualism can be both an asset and a challenge to be managed. After introducing the key concepts of multilingualism, 'new speakers' and lingua franca, O'Rourke and Brennan examine how language plays a critical role in contemporary workplaces, how multilingual individuals can leverage their language skills into professional and personal mobility, and how modern enterprises seek to manage their increasingly multilingual workforces. The chapter then focuses on the role of multilingualism in market development and customer service. Finally, it considers the rise of 'new speakers' (borrowed from the Galician *neofalantes*) as sociolinguistically diverse groups of great interest in workplace communication.

Chapter 13 focuses on translation and interpreting in cross-cultural business workplace practices. Liao, Castillo, Napier and Newill argue in this chapter that it is crucial for companies planning to expand into a different linguistic community to consider the relationship between language and culture, because the costs of making mistakes can be high. The chapter introduces the reader to the concepts and professional practices of translation and interpreting (T&I), different types of T&I activities and their significant role in business workplaces. They discuss ethics and client expectations, and then turn to business translation, looking at examples from promotional museum websites. They also look at sign language interpreting as an established workplace practice that is often overlooked (this is discussed in-depth in Chapter 16). The chapter also discusses computer-aided translation which constitutes an established practice among professionals and finishes with a checklist on conducting business through T&I.

Section V: Diversity consists of three chapters and draws on anthropology, cultural studies, migration studies, deaf studies and intercultural communication. Chapter 14 focuses on dignity and diversity in the workplace. While workplace diversity is a common theme in intercultural business and management literature, as well as intercultural communication, the concept of dignity and its cultural dimension is largely overlooked. Authors Bell, Strani and Ahmad introduce these key concepts and critically analyse key aspects of employee diversity. These include age, ethnicity, religion, race, class, gender, disability, impairment and neurodiversity. The chapter emphasises the difference between disability and impairment and advocates the social model of disability, rejecting the medical model. The authors use the case studies of Foxconn to illustrate the salient role of workplace dignity and its intercultural dimension, and a case study on diversity multicultural teams conducted by Deloitte. Employment law in relation to workplace discrimination is also examined, together with some international comparisons. The considerable benefits of an effectively led, diverse workforce are highlighted in relation to productivity, competitiveness and employee well-being. The chapter concludes with recommendations for employers.

Continuing the diversity theme, Chapter 15 focuses on performing gender in the workplace. Authors Sholevar and Pfeiffer examine how gender is practised and performed in the workplace. The chapter first outlines the key concepts of gender, performance and culture, before discussing dominant cultural stereotypes on how we 'do' gender in the workplace. Two case studies on women in computing and female entrepreneurs illustrate how people negotiate, (re)produce and challenge gendered cultures. The hotspots of the 'gender gap' are also discussed, providing insights into how workplaces and organisational culture(s) are shaped by socially accepted gender roles and can, in turn, reinforce and contest them.

Finally, Chapter 16 focuses on deaf people in the workplace. This goes beyond Translation and Interpreting practices and requirements for sign language interpreting in workplaces where employees are present—which is covered in Chapter 13. Instead, the chapter looks at the aspects of equality, diversity and inclusivity in workplaces, which requires consideration of deaf people's access to, and opportunities in, employment. Sommer Lindsay, Cameron and Napier explain that various accommodations can be made in the workplace, but with legal recognition of sign languages in many countries, and increasing media visibility, it is important to acknowledge the skills that deaf people bring to workplaces. The chapter provides a valuable and necessary piece in the puzzle of intercultural aspects of workplaces where we will learn about deaf people and sign languages, the challenges that deaf people can face at work (with a focus on the UK), the barriers to establishing trust, and the skills and strategies they use to navigate workplaces.

The last section of the book consists of **cross-cultural scenarios** and a **comprehensive glossary of key terms.** In Chapter 17, Strani and Glasgow bring together the overarching themes of the book and help to take stock of the challenges and opportunities inherent in intercultural workplaces through cross-cultural scenarios. Strani and Glasgow discuss seven scenarios. The first two scenarios focus on leadership, virtual teams, ethnocentrism, intercultural finance and gender in the workplace. Scenarios 3 and 4 focus on cross-cultural negotiation, and translation and interpreting. Scenarios 5 and 6 focus on trust, dignity and diversity and intercultural perceptions of work, leisure and time, and Scenario 7 discusses organisational culture and deaf people in the workplace. The glossary of key terms provides a necessary quick reference and revision tool for readers, as the terms are highlighted in bold and cross-referenced throughout the book.

References

Angouri, J. 2014. Multilingualism in the Workplace: Language Practices in Multilingual Contexts. *Multilingua—Journal of Cross-Cultural and Interlanguage Communication* 33 (1–2): 1–9.

Berry, J.W., P.R. Dasen, M.H. Segall, J.W. Berry, and Y.H. Poortinga. 2002. *Cross-Cultural Psychology: Research and Applications*. Cambridge: Cambridge University Press.

Clyne, M. 1999. *Variation in Communication Patterns and Inter-Cultural Communication Breakdown in Oral Discourse in Inter-cultural Communication at Work. Cultural Values in Discourse*. Cambridge: Cambridge University Press.

Cole, J., R. Oliver, and A. Blaviesciunaite. 2014. The Changing Nature of Workplace Culture. *Facilities* 32 (13–14): 786–800.

Cseh, M. 2003. Facilitating Learning in Multicultural Teams. *Advances in Developing Human Resources* 5 (1): 26–40.

Du, P. 2015. *Intercultural Communication in the Chinese Workplace*. London: Palgrave Macmillan.

Ferraro, G., and E. Briody. 2017. *The Cultural Dimension of Global Business*, 8th ed. London: Routledge.

Gassmann, O. 2001. Multicultural Teams: Increasing Creativity and Innovation by Diversity. *Creativity and Innovation Management* 10 (2): 88–95.

Haslam, J., N. Chabrak and R. Kamla. 2019. Emancipatory Accounting and Corporate Governance: Critical and Interdisciplinary Perspectives. *Critical Perspectives on Accounting* 63 (102094). https://doi.org/10.1016/j.cpa.2019.102094

Hayes, L. 2021. Language and Culture in Workplace Ethnography. *Oxford Research Encyclopedia of Anthropology*. https://doi.org/10.1093/acrefore/9780190854584.013.294.

Holmes, P. 2017. Intercultural Communication in the Global Workplace, Critical Approaches. In *The International Encyclopedia of Intercultural Communication,* ed. K. Young Yun, 1–16. New York: Wiley.

Ilie, C., and S. Schnurr. 2017. *Challenging Leadership Stereotypes Through Discourse: Power, Management and Gender*. Singapore: Springer.

Islam, G., and M.J. Zyphur. 2009. Rituals in Organizations: A Review and Expansion of Current Theory. *Group & Organization Management* 34 (1): 114–139.

Kecskes, I. 2014. *Intercultural Pragmatics*. New York, NY: Oxford University Press.

Kim, T., and A. Strudler. 2012. Workplace Civility: A Confucian Approach. *Business Ethics Quarterly* 22 (3): 557–577. https://doi.org/10.5840/beq201222334.

Kim, Y.Y., and D.P.W. Bhawuk. 2008. Globalization and Diversity: Contributions from Intercultural Research. *International Journal of Intercultural Relations* 32 (4): 301–304. https://doi.org/10.1016/j.ijintrel.2008.06.001.

Kramsch, C. 2002. In Search of the Intercultural. *Journal of Sociolinguistics* 6: 275–285. https://doi.org/10.1111/1467-9481.00188.

Ladegaard, H.J., and J.C. Jenks. 2015. Language and Intercultural Communication in the Workplace: Critical Approaches to Theory and Practice. *Language and Intercultural Communication* 15 (1): 1–12. https://doi.org/10.1080/14708477.2014.985302.

Lüdi, G., K. Hochle Meier, and P. Yanaprasart, eds. 2016. *Managing Plurilingual and Intercultural Practices in the Workplace: The Case of Multilingual Switzerland*. Amsterdam: John Benjamins.

Martin, G.C. 2014. The Effects of Cultural Diversity in the Workplace. *Journal of Diversity Management (JDM)* 9 (2): 89–92. https://doi.org/10.19030/jdm.v9i2.8974

McSweeney, B. 2002. Hofstede's Model of National Cultural Differences and Their Consequences: A Triumph of Faith—A Failure of Analysis. *Human Relations* 55 (1): 89–118.

Meyer, B., and B. Apfelbaum, eds. 2010. *Multilingualism at Work: From Policies to Practices in Public, Medical and Business Settings*. Amsterdam: John Benjamins.

Modood, T., and N. Meer. 2012. Interculturalism, Multiculturalism or Both? *Political Insight* 3 (1): 30–33.

Nadler, C., and W. Breuer. 2019. Cultural Finance as a Research Field: An Evaluative Survey. *Journal of Business Economics* 89: 191–220. https://doi.org/10.1007/s11573-017-0888-y.

O'Sullivan, T., J. Hartley, D. Saunders, M. Montgomery, and J. Fiske. 1994. *Key Concepts in Communication and Cultural Studies*. London: Routledge.

Oetzel, J.G., and A. Ting-Toomey. 2003. Face Concerns in Interpersonal Conflict: A Cross-Cultural Empirical Test of the Face Negotiation Theory. *Communication Research* 30: 599–624.

Okoro, E. 2012. Cross-Cultural Etiquette and Communication in Global Business: Toward a Strategic Framework for Managing Corporate Expansion. *International Journal of Business and Management* 7 (16): 130–138. https://doi.org/10.5539/ijbm.v7n16p130.

Phipps, A. 2010. Training and Intercultural Education: The Danger in Good Citizenship. In *The Intercultural Dynamics of Multicultural Working*, ed. by M. Guilherme, E. Glaser, and M. del Carmen Mendez Garcia, 59–77. Bristol: Multilingual Matters.

R'boul, H. 2021. "Alternative Theorizing of Multicultural Education: An Islamic Perspective on Interculturality and Social Justice. *Journal for Multicultural Education* 15 (2): 213–224. https://doi.org/10.1108/JME-07-2020-0073

Schein, E.H. 2010. *Organizational Culture and Leadership*, vol. 2. San Francisco, CA: Jossey-Bass.

Schnurr, S., A. Chan, J. Loew, and O. Zayts. 2017. Leadership and Culture: When Stereotypes Meet Actual Workplace Practice. In *Challenging Leadership Stereotypes through Discourse*, ed. C. Ilie, and S. Schnurr. Springer, Singapore. https://doi.org/10.1007/978-981-10-4319-2_5.

Shi-xu. 2013. Constructing New Forms of Intercultural Communication. In *Shi-xu, Discourse and Culture. From Discourse Analysis to Cultural Discourse Studies*, 377–393. Shanghai: Shanghai Foreign Language Education Press.

Stevens, F.G., V.C. Plaut, and J. Sanchez-Burks. 2008. Unlocking the Benefits of Diversity: All-Inclusive Multiculturalism and Positive Organisational Change. *The Journal of Applied Behavioral Science* 44 (1): 116–132.

Szkudlarek, B. 2009. Through Western Eyes: Insights into the Intercultural Training Field. *Organization Studies* 30 (9): 975–986.

Triandis, H.C., and R.W. Brislin. 1984. Cross-Cultural Psychology. *American Psychologist* 39 (9): 1006–1016. https://doi.org/10.1037/0003-066X.39.9.1006.

Washington, M. 2013. Intercultural Business Communication: An Analysis of Ethnocentrism in a Globalized Business Environment. *Journal of Business & Management* 1 (1): 20–27.

Part I
Intercultural Communication

Chapter 2
Key Concepts for Cultural Communication in the Workplace

Katerina Strani, Mairéad Nic Craith, Florian Scheuring, and Pedro Jesús Castillo Ortiz

Starting with a preliminary consideration of culture, communication, and the workplace in a global context, we examine how culture and communication are intrinsic to our understandings of the workplace, and provide core examples of how the workplace can be analysed both as a culture and as a communicative practice. We revisit established models with critical intent and emphasise the need to move beyond Anglo-Saxon understandings and frameworks. Overall, we provide a critical theoretical framework around culture and communication for the volume's discussion on interculturality in contemporary workplaces, leaving leadership and trust for a more focused consideration in subsequent chapters.

K. Strani (✉)
Languages and Intercultural Studies, Heriot-Watt University, Edinburgh, UK
e-mail: A.Strani@hw.ac.uk

M. Nic Craith
University of the Highlands and Islands, Inverness, UK
e-mail: Mairead.NicCraith@uhi.ac.uk

F. Scheuring
Heriot-Watt University, Edinburgh, UK
e-mail: F.Scheuring@hw.ac.uk

P. J. Castillo Ortiz
University of Granada, Granada, Spain
e-mail: pedrocastillo@ugr.es

© The Author(s), under exclusive license to Springer Nature Switzerland AG 2023
K. Strani and K. Pfeiffer (eds.), *Intercultural Issues in the Workplace*,
https://doi.org/10.1007/978-3-031-42320-8_2

2.1 Introduction

Culture, in its broadest sense, is a defining factor in the social relationships between people. It informs how we organise our lives and our work, what we consider meaningful, and who 'belongs' to our group. Culture is closely related to communication, which determines the very terms of these interactions, informs cultural precedent, and influences how we articulate ourselves, our social relationships and the world we inhabit. Supported by language, gesture, and silence, our communicative habits both express and construct how we see culture; indeed, our communicative systems might be considered 'cultures' themselves.

The contemporary workplace might be understood both *as* a culture and communicative practice, and as situated in broader local and global contexts. Today, employees and employers alike must negotiate the cultural and communicative demands of the workplace, alongside those of colleagues and competitors. This often gives rise to complex social relationships and amplifies dynamics of power and difference. Understanding the workplace primarily through the lenses of culture and communication allows us to analyse our workplaces better. It helps to identify differences and disputes that might otherwise appear inexplicable and highlight opportunities and potentials that otherwise would remain unseen.

With this in mind, this chapter discusses the key concepts of culture and communication in our understandings of the workplace in a global context. We look at communication across cultures and focus on intersubjectivity and shared meaning, before turning to organisational culture and how this affects the way we work alongside other forms of culture. We then discuss—and revisit with critical intent—established concepts and models of the cultural dimension of business. Hence, we wrap up by emphasising the need to move beyond Anglo-Saxon models of culture and communication, and to consider *diversity of cultures* instead of the overused term 'cultural diversity'.

2.2 Culture, Communication, and the Workplace

The concepts of culture and communication have been widely discussed across academic disciplines, including anthropology, political sciences, sociology, cultural studies and linguistics, and management. Consequently, there is no singular way to define them. However, across all over these disciplines, the 'cultural turn' that started in the 1970s has been influential in redefining how these concepts are viewed. The 'cultural turn' has encouraged scholars and disciplines to think about 'culture' and 'communication' not as static cultural 'artefacts', but as systems of meaning-making that are created over time through social interactions (Hall 1996; Kockel and Nic Craith 2004). This is important because it emphasises both 'culture' and 'communication' as living practices that are changeable and grounded in social dynamics.

It also emphasises the significance of *social relationships* between groups and individuals, and the structures and hierarchies involved therein—all of which are highly relevant to a consideration of workplace dynamics.

2.2.1 Culture

Sociologist Raymond Williams argues that in the twentieth century, the popular definition of 'culture' has changed (1985, 90). Where culture was previously understood as 'high Culture' and associated with 'the arts'—literature, philosophy, music, and language—today, culture is considered more as a part of everyday life. This shift is important, as it emphasises culture as a way of life that informs the many ways in which people interact with each other. While today culture can certainly be understood as something that is *creative*—and related to creative acts, such as storytelling, performance, language-use, and music—it can also be understood as something embedded in the *everyday*. Culture as *the everyday* informs the ways people greet each other or say goodbye; approach time and time-keeping; occupy space; talk to each other, argue, negotiate; eat together and provide for each other; understand the world and create systems of spirituality; or the ways people construct and understand gender .

In this respect, the category of culture can be understood as a particular way of doing things within a particular group. From a sociological perspective, Giddens suggests that the driving purpose of culture is to socialise people and provide a social template for their interactions (Giddens and Griffiths 2006, 163). Anthropologists have suggested that culture can be understood as preserving the heritage and memory of a people, and by doing so, is also instrumental in preserving the group itself (Nic Craith 2003). And cultural theorists have emphasised that because culture is concerned with relationships between people, groups, and society, the way in which it arranges, hierarchises, and maintains its categories is implicated in the political, both in a personal and in a public sense (Hall 1996).

Though these understandings of culture are informed by different disciplinary premises, one of the features that all agree upon (in different ways) is that the practice of culture is a way of creating systems of *meaning*, which creates systems of *belonging*. Through shared cultural practices, cultural points of reference, and cultural imagination, people feel that they are part of a collection of people with a similar purpose and history. These shared experiences of culture create what are known as **norms**: "sets of rules, standards and expectations that both generate and regulate social interaction and communication" (O'Sullivan et al. 1994, 158). Norms are morally constraining and binding and are best viewed as the *dos and don'ts* of a social situation or an institution. Over time, and through the practices of participants, norms establish a particular way of doing things and help maintain cultural identity. Cultures might be defined by norms of language (Nic Craith and Hill 2015), hospitality (Derrida and Dufourmantelle 2000; Phipps 2012; Hill 2016), behaviour, class, and economy (Kockel 2017), citizenship, gender, race, and ethnicity (Hill-Collins

2002; Ahmed 2012), among others. However, while they establish categories of belonging, cultural norms also create categories of exclusion that distinguish them from other cultures and have implications for the distribution of power (Butler 2011).

Cultural norms work alongside **cultural values**, which constitute part of our attitudes. Values are the result of cultural conditioning, which means that they differ between cultures and also between individuals. They also have a temporal dimension. In discussing the fluidity of values, Mackie and Strani (2023) note that "the values which might make actions meaningful today may be different from those which did so in the past, or indeed those which will in the future". Despite this, our own values are so much part of our consciousness that we believe them to be true and valid for everyone. If they are not shared by others, misunderstanding and communication collapse may occur.

2.2.2 Communication

Communication is the way we make ourselves understood within and across the groups to which we belong. It is also the way that people make meaning in the world, and as such is closely related to culture. Communicative systems consist of small units of meaning-making—from letters, to sounds, to gestures, or to images—that are organised into wider units of meaning. Communicative systems include oral, textual, visual, and signed languages, as well as other means of communication, such as gestures, body language, or behavioural activity or expression. Communication is also tied to a particular situation and is influenced by political, cultural, organisational, social, and situational contexts, as well as the environment and the medium in which it occurs (see Altheide's 1995 *Ecology of Communication*). A message cannot be detached from its communicative environment, or the people involved in the interaction, and should always be treated in context. For example, a message may have different intent and may be perceived differently, depending on who communicates it (e.g. their rank in their workplace, or their gender), the work environment, whether the message is written, signed, or spoken, whether it is online, face-to-face, or in a hybrid form, the political context of the country/ies at play, the topic of the message, and the personalities of those involved. And this is before we even discuss language or what is actually said.

The relationship between culture and communication is undisputed; however, the relationship is complex. A particular group's communicative *activity* might be considered a 'culture'. Equally, the particular *way* in which people communicate might be understood as 'creating culture'. At the same time, culture might be seen to influence how people communicate. Put another way, the relationship can be considered in three questions:

1. Does communication reflect or represent a cultural reality?
2. Does communication create a cultural reality?
3. Does culture create a communicative reality?

There is no fixed solution to the debate, but it is worth noting the different emphases that these questions place upon the relationship between culture and communication. Different approaches to this relationship may cause cultural clashes or misunderstandings.

2.2.3 Organisational Culture and the Workplace

How do the key concepts of culture and communication relate to the workplace? In the same way as a particular group's communicative activity, or the way people communicate, might be understood as a culture, a workplace may also be conceived *as* a culture. Scholars tend to describe workplaces *as* culture, arguing that in the same way that cultural practice informs peoples' everyday actions, cultural practices also inform business and workplace dynamics (Morgan 1986). The workplace can, therefore, be considered a culture because it establishes its own way of doing things and making them meaningful, from everyday rules of interaction to policies that establish an organisation's value proposition. As a culture, a workplace also establishes its own way of communicating, from the language(s) it expects employees to use (e.g. organisational acronyms), to the tone and style with which it 'speaks' to its customers, and the medium it uses to do so. An understanding of an organisation's culture and communicative practices allows us to analyse more comprehensively how an organisation works, to unpack its failures, and build upon its successes.

Scholarship that focuses specifically on organisational culture argues that to understand how a workplace operates, the activities of its employees, its mission statement, values, and priorities, the cultural patterns of the workplace must be established and analysed. Once this is done, workplace strengths can be nurtured, and its challenges can be addressed. Schein (2010) suggests thinking about organisational culture in three stages, according to the model below (Fig. 2.1). The model provides several reference points for each of the layers to engage in an organisational change process in the workplace. To begin with, there are distinctive layers of visibility. Schein (2010) distinguishes them as *artefacts, espoused beliefs and values,* and *basic underlying assumptions*.

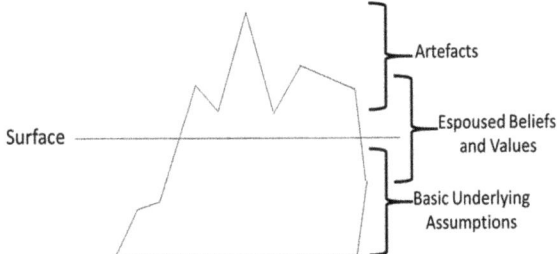

Fig. 2.1 Iceberg model of cultural layers, adapted from Schein (2010)

Artefacts can best be understood as objects or manifestations that can be observed or experienced when first engaging with a workplace. This includes aspects of the workplace that are readily identified and experienced, such as language, style of language (formality, tone, accent), architecture of buildings and offices. For example, an open-plan office communicates a different organisational culture—less hierarchical but perhaps one where visibility and monitoring are central—from a workplace with single offices and non-transparent doors. A workplace with performance graphs and a picture of the employee of the week on the wall expresses a different organisational culture from a workplace where there is artwork or motivational quotes on the walls, or indeed from a workplace where we see pictures of the CEO and senior leadership. Analysing how people use and engage with artefacts may help us understand how a workplace culture operates and how it may affect trust.

Espoused beliefs and values govern the day-to-day life of an organisation. These beliefs and values have been adopted by the respective organisation or its sub-groups, as they have proven to be beneficial for producing desirable results. Consider workplace rituals, for example (see Islam and Zyphur 2009) such as gift-giving, Friday drinks after work, office parties, rewards systems, or performance celebrations. Such rituals and practices may have been adopted for the purposes of team cohesion and sense of belonging. Development or change can occur when established values and beliefs no longer provide the benefits they once did. This refers to the temporal dimension and the fluidity of values that we discussed above (Sect. 2.2.1). Such change might be due to external factors e.g. policies, shift of client expectations, or internal disruption from changes in leadership. Espoused beliefs and values might also well be aspirations for the conduct of business in the organisation. However, these aspirations may often be different from the aspects that govern behaviour in the organisation and are experienced on a day-to-day basis. Importantly, organisational culture can vary significantly between departments or locations. Each of them represents a sub-culture that might be informed by the greater organisation's culture but also develops its own shared values, beliefs, and norms.

Consider a manager who has always pursued a low-cost strategy that may have included selling products of lesser quality. The organisation is now suffering from plummeting sales, and the manager decides to change their preferred strategy to a quality management approach. This results in the organisation improving the quality of their products, deviating from the traditional low-cost strategy. Sales are picking up once more, the organisation returns to being profitable. Employees' perceptions of the organisation shift, thus re-establishing trust in the organisation, in the product, and in the manager's leadership. And due to its recorded success, quality management becomes an embedded *shared value* of the organisation, and the espoused belief becomes 'high quality equals high performance'. If quality management continuously proves to work in favour of the organisation, it may transform into an *assumption*. This assumption would directly be linked to the organisation's performance.

Basic underlying assumptions are the hardest facets of organisational culture to detect and uncover. They represent the subconscious ways of *"doing things"* in the organisation. Very often, these were originally espoused beliefs and values that have proven their validity and applicability—such as the quality management example above. They might be found in an organisation's mission statement, which clarifies the organisation's purpose and defines the scope of its operations and aspirations.

Though beliefs, values and assumptions might structure the way in which a workplace functions at all stages, this is not to say that they are necessarily adopted by all who are part of the organisation. When this happens, cultural norms can act as a source of friction.

> **Case study 1: Google France**
> Google believes that its success is largely the result of a strong organisational culture. Part of that culture involves giving employees lots of positive feedback. When Google moved into France, it learned that in that country, positive words are used sparingly, and criticism is provided more strongly. One French manager told me, "The first time I used the Google form to give a performance review, I was confused. Where was the section to talk about problem areas? 'What did this employee do really well?' The positive wording sounded over the top". But Google's corporate culture is so strong that it often supersedes local preferences; the French manager added, "After five years at Google France, I can tell you we are now a group of French people who give negative feedback in a very un-French way".
> Source: Meyer, E. 2015. "When culture doesn't translate". *Harvard Business Review*. https://hbr.org/2015/10/when-culture-doesnt-translate

Employees identifying with the core organisational values and belief systems develop a shared understanding, feel more comfortable in their line of work and are understood as being higher performing in their job (Alvesson 2012). Kristof (1996) understands this person/organisation fit as at least one party gaining something they desire from the other . This alignment of fundamental values which are at the core of the organisation is also an integral part of assessments during the hiring process of new employees. Scholars further suggest that non-conformity with organisational or sub-culture values, particularly with the basic underlying assumptions, severely affects the settling in process and reduces the likelihood of the new member of the group to become a part of the team (Bauer and Erdogan 2011). An employee not adapting to the philosophy of the focal organisation may find themselves excluded.

Overall, organisational culture theory provides a starting point to examine how the workplace might be considered in cultural terms. It emphasises the roles that norms and values play in establishing how an organisation works and provides several tools with which the cultural context of a workplace can be analysed. However, the focus largely remains on the internal systems of a workplace and not any external factors or contexts. For this reason, organisational culture needs to be looked at within the broader social, political, situational, and communicative contexts discussed above.

2.3 Communicating Across Cultures: Intersubjectivity and Shared Meaning

It is often said that communication is the act of sending and receiving information in a linear and reciprocal manner. This is a grossly simplistic view that does not do justice to the intricacies of communication processes, especially in an intercultural business context. Any behaviour, including the absence of action, could be interpreted by other people as having meaning. A colleague who is silent throughout a meeting or a negotiation, an airline passenger who sits with headphones on and eyes closed, a company CEO who always wears jeans and T-shirts, they are all communicating something. As Austrian-American philosopher and communication theorist Paul Watzlawick put it, "one cannot not communicate".

Understanding is a complex cognitive process that involves great uncertainty, yet it is fundamental in communication. It is also taken for granted or tends to be assumed too quickly. What is crucial in achieving understanding is **intersubjectivity** (Habermas 1987; Strani 2010). This refers to a distinct common world shared by people when they communicate. Individuals may have their own worldviews and their own experiences, assumptions, values, and meanings that *they* consider "common sense" and *they* take for granted (e.g. that the manager is always right, that the manager is always a man, that your colleagues are also your friends, etc.). But to reach understanding and communicate meaningfully and constructively, we need to move beyond our own subjective world into a shared, intersubjective world, which consists of shared meanings and interpretations.

If understanding is a shared process, then it involves a considerable degree of uncertainty. For example, after a business negotiation, participants assume they have understood each other but their individual interpretations may be quite different. Understanding in this case is a "fictional coupling of expectations" (Grant 2003, 108). These complexities and contingencies exist in monolingual, monocultural environments, as well as multilingual and multicultural ones. Meaning is never absolute; it is not something static that exists a priori, but it constitutes a selection process (Strani 2010, 134), whereby it is filtered through past selections such as assumptions, norms, values, or contexts. The **negotiation of meaning** (Gumperz 1982) is one of the main aspects of intercultural communication. Once meaning is negotiated and agreed, an intersubjectively shared space is created for people to communicate 'on the same page'. In this way, meaning is both a *process* and *product* or result of communication.

Even if intersubjectivity and a shared meaning are achieved, there are still barriers to overcome. Pan, Scollon and Scollon (2001, 14) tell us "whether it is personal or professional, many people expect information to be presented in a clear, concise and sincere manner". Professional communication practice has shown, however, that this norm is rarely followed. We discussed above that there are various contexts to consider, which act as a frame of reference for assumptions, implications, and interpretation of the message (socio-political, cultural, organisational, situational, and conversational contexts).

2.4 Revisiting Established Models of the Cultural Dimension of Business

In 1980, Dutch social psychologist Geert Hofstede published an influential volume suggesting ways of measuring 'national cultures' and looked at how cultures might work differently in different contexts. Based on a large-scale survey of IBM employees worldwide, Hofstede concluded that 'national cultures' can be reflected in the way businesses work. He initially developed four and later six dimensions of 'national cultures' that reflect the way businesses work—acknowledging that, since culture is a collective concept, these dimensions apply at national and not at individual level, and individual behaviours may differ from what the cultural dimensions prescribe. These six dimensions are:

1. *Power Distance*: the extent to which less-power groups accept unequal distribution of power. In cultures with low power distance, efforts are made to minimise unequal power relationships, while cultures with high power distance are more tolerant of inequality.
2. *Uncertainty avoidance:* the sense of threat or stress that is felt when faced with uncertainty, ambiguity, or the unknown.
3. *Individualism v. collectivism:* in highly individualistic societies, people assume responsibility for themselves rather than expecting the state to look after them. In collectivist societies, there is a strong sense of family and community, and people are integrated into primary groups. In individualistic cultures, ambition, rewards, responsibilities and penalties are directed at individuals, whereas in collectivist cultures these apply at collective or group level.
4. *Masculinity v. Femininity:* this dimension does not refer to men and women. Cultures with a high score in 'masculinity' are meant to be more assertive, whereas a high score in 'femininity' means that cultures are more caring.
5. *Long-term v. Short-term orientation:* long-term orientation, sometimes also referred to as *Confucian Dynamism,* places greater emphasis on perseverance where the short-term approach is more interested in speedy results.
6. *Indulgence v. restraint*: the gratification versus restraint related to life, social norms and freedoms (Hofstede 2011).

Hofstede assigned scores for each of these dimensions to countries (the assumption is that each national culture corresponds to a country) and developed a country comparison tool where countries' scores can be compared against each other. Another such model was developed by Fons Trompenaars and Charles Hampden-Turner. In

1997, they conducted a large-scale study of managers and organisation employees from 49 countries, which led them to identify 5 dimensions of human relationships which influence cross-cultural business communication—not only when it comes to *doing* business, but also managing people and facing moral and ethical dilemmas (Trompenaars and Hampden-Turner 2012, 10). These dimensions are: universalism v. particularism (or rules v. relationships); individualism v. communitarianism (similar to Hofstede's third dimension above); neutral v. affective (referring to whether emotional expressiveness is encouraged or frowned upon); diffuse v. specific (indirect communication, rich in cultural references and assumptions v. direct communication); and achievement v. ascription (meritocratic v. non-meritocratic and hierarchical societies).

Even though Hofstede's cultural dimensions theory is highly cited and constitutes a very popular paradigm in cross-cultural management, it has been strongly criticised for its static view of culture and the rigid distinctions between what he sees as 'national' cultures. Critics have highlighted methodological flaws to the development of the six cultural dimensions on the basis of a one-company approach (McSweeney 2002; Jones 2007) and the difficulty in replicating Hofstede's study and achieve the same results (Eringa et al. 2015). We agree with critics who have strongly criticised the basic premise of Hofstede's and Trompenaars and Hampden-Turner's models that 'national cultures' exist, that they are homogeneous and static, and that they can be broken down into distinct dimensions that are quantifiable, measurable, and comparable (see Brannen 2009). Given that culture is learned and not something with which we are born, it is difficult to assume that cultures have fixed traits that can be generalizable to such an extent, let alone immutable and static. In twenty-first-century globalised workplaces, where national borders have little relevance and people's experiences and backgrounds are increasingly enriched and varied, we should be moving away from essentialist, nation-based conceptualisations. Instead, we should distinguish between established social norms and etiquette, which refers to "cultural marking in communicative behaviour" (Kecskes 2014, 5) from culture as a whole.

We share Holden's (2002) premise that established models that see "culture-as-difference and culture-as-essence" are neither helpful nor do they reflect the reality of today's globalised workplaces (in business and beyond). Indeed, as Ladegaard and Jenks (2015, 6) highlight, "the '*cultural awareness*' industry appears to exacerbate cultural differences rather and stereotypes rather than alleviate them". And when culture is presented as a problem, Holden argues, this can ruin business relationships (2002, 58). He proposes looking at culture as a *knowledge resource*, which companies can use as a competitive advantage instead of a problem to be managed (258). Chapter 14, which looks at dignity and diversity in the workplace, expands on this through the business case for diversity.

2.5 Cultural Diversity or Diversity of Cultures? Beyond Anglo-Saxon Models

Overall, when communicating across cultures, we must overcome two dominant assumptions: first, that cultures are homogeneous; and second, that cultures are equal. There is no unity in any given culture. While norms, practices, rituals, etc. exist, any idea of uniformity is misleading. We have explained how attempts to categorise national cultures have been fiercely criticised by scholars. It is more useful to recognise such categories as potential explanations of different attitudes and practices in the workplace, rather than providing oversimplified stereotypes about nationalities and cultural groups. Clausen puts it succinctly: "national origin serves as the point of departure for managers as a source of values, meaning and norms, but is not determinant with respect to behaviour or communication outcomes" (2007, 318). Furthermore, power relations between different cultural groups are never equal in contemporary workplaces. Indeed, relations between more and less powerful cultures in the workplace are at the heart of multicultural analysis.

It becomes clear, therefore, that we should not try to standardise professional communication practices around the world. This is neither possible nor wise, since there is in fact no such thing as a "standard" (Pan, Scollon and Scollon 2001, 3). There have been attempts, particularly in business management, to establish the so-called Anglo-Saxon "standard". Such standardisation would inevitably mean suppression of cultural practices within groups and forced assimilation, homogeneisation, and uniformity. This would seriously undermine creativity, innovation, and problem-solving capabilities and would eventually lead to an alienated workforce.

Case study 2: Daniel

Daniel, a Hong Kong Chinese student, writes an email to his teacher in the autumn of 2012:

> In a Western mindset, it's good to be expressive and vocal, to communicate directly, and to engage in close relationships. However, as you know, many Chinese people think the opposite … There is a contradiction between two assumptions we seem to make in class: (1) There is no such thing as 'good' and 'bad' culture; and (2) Most of the models we adopt in class are based on a Western mindset, and according to these models, our indirect approach to communication is bad. Is there any way out of this dilemma? Please correct me if I'm wrong.

Source: Ladegaard and Jenks (2015, 3).

Here, it is obvious that assumptions of what is a good communicator, a confident student, or professional are not universal and should be regarded as such. On this example, the performance of confidence is challenged through Eastern understandings of respect and hierarchical relationships of education and work.

The practice of imposing Western business and communication parameters is as old as the Western dominance through imperialism (most notably Spanish and

British). The way big Anglo-Saxon powers (the USA and the UK) and their multinationals have understood 'multiculturalism' is by imposing their way of doing business as the standard, leaving the rest of the world, particularly those areas where raw materials and workforce come from, as undeveloped. It should not be forgotten that certain business cultures and relations are intrinsically rooted in centuries-old relations of colonialism, imperialism, slavery, and exploitation. This means that many of the individuals coming from areas or countries with a past under these systems may also bring a more or less aware cultural background of the 'oppressed' and being the 'other' (cf. Freire 1996; Galeano 1973). Consider the cases of the US sugar trade in Latin America in the nineteenth and twentieth centuries, most notably in Cuba and other Caribbean areas. The imposition of US-style business meant that "in Cuba, sugar became the master key for US domination, at the price of [...] the relentless impoverishment of the soil" (Galeano 1973, 81).

Furthermore, most of the multicultural business in the world neither involve Western cultures in the workplace nor do they have the West as the centre of the business (Shohat and Stam 2008). And yet, "intercultural communication is still being hijacked by global ideologies of effective, proactive, direct, upfront communication Anglo-Saxon style" (Ladegaard and Jenks 2015, 4). Truly global managers and leaders are aware of such dynamics and aim to adapt in accordance with the practices and norms of local, organisational and workplace cultures. Formulating "locally grounded, globally minded and historically conscious frameworks" (Shi-xu 2009, 29) is key to establishing harmonious relationships while respecting local cultural identities and norms. The next chapter discusses the challenges of multicultural communication and trust in contemporary workplaces.

Review Questions

1. Think back over the themes of culture, communication, and the workplace introduced in this chapter. How might we consider the workplace a culture? What is the role of communication in this relationship?
2. What categories does Schein (2010) suggest can be used to analyse organisational culture? How useful do you think these categories are?
3. To what extent do you think it is useful to think about 'cultures' in national terms? What are the advantages/disadvantages of this approach?
4. How does the concept of intersubjectivity challenge linear models of communication? How is this helping our understanding of cultural communication at work?
5. Do you agree with attempts to standardise and universalise business practices? Why/Why not?

Recommended Further Reading

- Brannen, M.Y. 2009. Culture in Context: New Theorizing for Today's Complex Cultural Organizations. In *Beyond Hofstede*, ed. C. Nakata, 81–100. London: Palgrave Macmillan. https://doi.org/10.1057/9780230240834_5
- Holden, N. 2001. Towards redefining cross-cultural management as knowledge management. A synopsis prepared for a showcase presentation for the International Management Division American Academy of Management Meeting, Washington, August 2001. Available at: https://core.ac.uk/download/pdf/17277505.pdf
- Jameson, D. 2007. Reconceptualising Cultural Identity and Its Role in Intercultural Business Communication. *Journal of Business Communication* 44 (3): 199–235.
- Ladegaard, H.J., and C.J. Jenks. 2015. Language and Intercultural Communication in the Workplace: Critical Approaches to Theory and Practice. *Language and Intercultural Communication* 15 (1): 1–12. https://doi.org/10.1080/14708477.2014.985302.
- Nic Craith, M. 2012. Cultural Patterns and Belonging. In *Narratives of Place, Belonging and Language: An Intercultural Perspective*, 126–148. London: Palgrave.

References

Ahmed, S. 2012. *On Being Included: Racism and Diversity in Institutional Life*. Durham: Duke University Press.
Alvesson, M. 2012. *Understanding Organizational Culture*. London: Sage.
Altheide, D.L. 1995. *An Ecology of Communication: Cultural Formats of Control*. United States: Aldine de Gruyter.
Bauer, T.N., and B. Erdogan. 2011. "Organizational Socialization: The Effective Onboarding of New Employees" Culture in Context: New Theorizing for Today's Complex Cultural Organizations. In *Beyond Hofstede*, ed. C. Nakata, 81–100. London. Palgrave Macmillan. https://doi.org/10.1057/9780230240834_5
Butler, J. 2011. *Gender Trouble: Feminism and the Subversion of Identity*. Oxford: Routledge.
Clausen, L. 2007. Corporate Communication Challenges: A 'Negotiated' Culture Perspective. *International Journal of Cross Cultural Management* 7 (3): 317–332. https://doi.org/10.1177/1470595807083376.
Derrida, J. and A. Dufourmantelle. 2000. *Of Hospitality: Anne Dufourmantelle Invites Jacques Derrida to Respond*, trans. R. Bowlby. Stanford: Stanford University Press.
Eringa, K. et al. 2015. How Relevant Are Hofstede's Dimensions for Inter-Cultural Studies? A Replication of Hofstede's Research Among Current International Business Students. *Research in Hospitality Management* 5 (2): 187–198.
Galeano, E. 1973. *Open Veins of Latin America*. New York: Monthly Review Press.

Giddens, A., and S. Griffiths. 2006. *Sociology*. Cambridge: Polity Press.
Grant, C.B. 2003. *Rethinking Communicative Interaction: New Interdisciplinary Horizons*. Netherlands: John Benjamins Publishing Company.
Gumperz, J.J. 1982. *Discourse Strategies*. Cambridge: Cambridge University Press.
Freire, P. 1996. *Pedagogy of the Oppressed*. New York: Penguin Group.
Habermas, J. 1987. *The Theory of Communicative Action. Lifeworld and System: A Critique of Functionalist Reason*, vol. 2. Cambridge: Polity Press.
Hall, S. 1996. The Question of Cultural Identity. In *Modernity: An Introduction to Modern Societies*, ed. S. Hall, D. Held, D. Hubert, and K. Thompson, 595–634. London: Blackwell Publishing.
Hill, E. 2016. Welcoming Nations? Hospitality as a Proxy for National Identity: A Consideration of British and Scottish Contexts. In *Public and Political Discourses of Migration: International Perspectives*, ed. A. Haynes, M. J. Power, A. Dillane and J. Carr, 193–206. Plymouth: Rowman & Littlefield.
Hill-Collins, P. 2002. *Black Feminist Thought: Knowledge, Consciousness, and the Politics of Empowerment*. London: Routledge.
Hofstede, G. 2011. *Dimensionalizing Cultures: The Hofstede Model in Context. Online Readings in Psychology and Culture*, Unit 2. Retrieved from http://scholarworks.gvsu.edu/orpc/vol2/iss1/8
Holden, N. 2002. *Cross-Cultural Management: A Knowledge Management Perspective*. United Kingdom: Financial Times Prentice Hall.
Islam, G., and M.J. Zyphur. 2009. Rituals in Organizations: A Review and Expansion of Current Theory. *Group & Organization Management* 3491: 114–139.
Jameson, D. 2007. Reconceptualising Cultural Identity and Its Role in Intercultural Business Communication. *Journal of Business Communication* 44 (3): 199–235.
Jones, M. 2007. Hofstede—Culturally Questionable? In *Oxford Business & Economics Conference*. Oxford, UK. https://ro.uow.edu.au/commpapers/370
Kecskes, I. 2014. *Intercultural Pragmatics*. New York, NY: Oxford University Press.
Kockel, U. 2017. *Culture and Economy: Contemporary Perspectives*. Bern: Springer.
Kockel, U., and M. Nic Craith. 2004. *Communicating Culture*. Münster: LIT Verlag.
Kristof, A.L. 1996. Person-Organization Fit: An Integrative Review of Its Conceptualizations, Measurement, and Implications. *Personnel Psychology* 49 (1): 1–49.
Ladegaard, H.J., and C.J. Jenks. 2015. Language and Intercultural Communication in the Workplace: Critical Approaches to Theory and Practice. *Language and Intercultural Communication* 15 (1): 1–12. https://doi.org/10.1080/14708477.2014.985302.
Mackie, A., and K. Strani. 2023. On the Soft Power of Values: The Scotland Is Now Campaign. In *The Routledge Handbook of Soft Power*, 2nd ed., ed. N. Chitty, L. Ji and G. Rawnsley. London: Routledge.
McSweeney, B. 2002. Hofstede's Model of National Cultural Differences and Their Consequences: A Triumph of Faith—A Failure of Analysis. *Human Relations* 55 (1): 89–118.
Meyer, E. 2015. When Culture Doesn't Translate. *Harvard Business Review*. https://hbr.org/2015/10/when-culture-doesnt-translate
Morgan, G. 1986. *Images of an Organization*. London: Sage.
Nic Craith, M. 2003. *Culture and Identity Politics in Northern Ireland*. Bern: Springer.
Nic Craith, M., and E. Hill. 2015. Re-locating the Ethnographic Field: From 'Being There' to 'Being There.' *Anthropological Journal of European Cultures* 24 (1): 42–62.
O'Sullivan, T., J. Hartley, D. Saunders, M. Montgomery and J. Fiske. 1994. *Key Concepts in Communication and Cultural Studies*. London: Routledge.
Pan, Y, S.W. Scollon, and R. Scollon. 2001. *Professional Communication in International Settings*. Malden, MA: Wiley-Blackwell.
Phipps, A. 2012. Voicing Solidarity: Linguistic Hospitality and Poststructuralism in the Real World. *Applied Linguistics* 33 (5): 582–602.
Schein, E.H. 2010. *Organizational Culture and Leadership*, vol. 2. Hoboken, N.J: Wiley.
Shi-xu. 2009. Reconstructing Eastern Paradigms of Discourse Studies. *Journal of Multicultural Discourses* 4 (1): 29–48. https://doi.org/10.1080/17447140802651637

Shohat, E., and R. Stam. 2008. Culture Debates in Translation. In *The Postcolonial and the Global (NED-New Edition)*, ed. R. Krishnaswamy and J. C. Hawley, 124–133. Minneapolis: University of Minnesota Press. https://doi.org/10.5749/j.ctttszqx.14

Strani, K. 2010. 'Communicative Rationality and the Challenge of Systems Theory': Beyond Universal Pragmatics: Studies in the Philosophy of Communication. In *Beyond Universal Pragmatics: Studies in the Philosophy of Communication*, ed. C.B. Grant, 123–148. Oxford: Peter Lang.

Trompenaars, F., and C. Hampden-Turner. 2012. *Riding the Waves of Culture: Understanding Diversity in Global Business*. London: Nicholas Brealey.

Williams, R. 1985. *Keywords: A Vocabulary of Culture and Society*. Oxford: Oxford University Press.

Chapter 3
Multicultural Communication and Trust in the Contemporary Workplace

Katerina Strani ⓘ**, Jane G. Bell, Panagiota-Penny Karanasiou, and Claudia Morais Castro**

> In increasingly globalised workplaces, there is an urgent necessity for good intercultural communication skills. The ability to work together harmoniously and successfully in a multicultural environment challenging but vital to the success of a workplace. Sharing a common "negotiated culture" is of paramount importance. But how does this negotiated culture emerge, how is trust established, especially in a short timescale, and how do multicultural teams function, negotiate and deal with conflict? How do we then develop intercultural competence in the workplace? We attempt to respond to these questions by critically revisiting and challenging established models and methods of analysis.

3.1 Introduction

The contemporary international workplace is also a multicultural workplace. An increasingly global business environment means that employees and managers are constantly negotiating a common working culture that is also in line with the culture of the organisation so that people can work together in a smart, harmonious and

---

K. Strani (✉)
Languages and Intercultural Studies, Heriot-Watt University, Edinburgh, UK
e-mail: A.Strani@hw.ac.uk

J. G. Bell
Heriot-Watt University, Edinburgh, UK
e-mail: Jane.G.Bell@hw.ac.uk

P.-P. Karanasiou
University of Edinburgh, Edinburgh, UK
e-mail: info@pkcommunicate.co.uk

C. Morais Castro
Independent researcher, Krefeld, Germany

© The Author(s), under exclusive license to Springer Nature Switzerland AG 2023
K. Strani and K. Pfeiffer (eds.), *Intercultural Issues in the Workplace*,
https://doi.org/10.1007/978-3-031-42320-8_3

purposeful way. We begin our discussion with power dynamics in multicultural workplaces, before looking at key dimensions in cross-cultural interactions. We then focus on building trust in global multicultural teams, and critically revisit the concept of intercultural competence by challenging its Anglo-centric premises.

3.2 Power Dynamics in Multicultural Workplaces: From Competing Cultures to Negotiated Culture

Intercultural encounters in the workplace more often than not involve power differentials. There is usually one or more dominant culture(s), which may or may not overlap with the organisational culture. Scholars have broadly identified processes of *acculturation, assimilation* and *integration* when cultures interact for a prolonged period. We revisit these categories with a critical lens.

Acculturation, which has been studied extensively by cross-cultural management scholars, refers to the process of learning a new culture (usually the dominant culture) through immersion and adopting its values and practices. Acculturation is not a one-way process, but an interactive one, which is why it may lead to change in both cultures through continuous contact. Phinney et al. (2006, 72) describe acculturation both as a process and as "phenomena which result when groups of individuals having different cultures come into continuous first-hand contact, with subsequent changes in the original culture patterns of either or both groups". Communication is central to this process. Depending on the dominant culture, different levels of *acculturative stress* may arise. This does not mean that the other two processes—assimilation and integration—are stress free. Rather, people are less likely to experience acculturative stress if they have a closer relationship with the majority culture (Tadmor et al. 2009) or if this dominant/majority culture is supportive and receptive to change.

We see acculturation as a multi-directional *process* rather than a result or an end state. It is multi-directional because it constitutes a learning process for all parties (minority, dominant and organisation) and it requires adjustments, major or minor, at all these levels. Also, on an individual level, the adaptation process is very versatile. The purpose of developing models to describe this process is unclear. These models can neither be descriptive, as they cannot capture the contingency and complexity of such multi-directional processes, nor can they be prescriptive for the same reasons—it is neither possible nor desirable to have a blueprint to acculturation, for instance (although various scholars have attempted it).

Next, **assimilation** suggests that each cultural group is being absorbed into the dominant culture. This is also called *subtractive multiculturalism* (Triandis 1994, 241) because individuals are forced to abandon some of their own cultural principles in favour of the dominant cultural identity (e.g. assimilation of migrants in a host country). Assimilation is also sometimes called 'mainstream acculturation' (Jurcik et al. 2013)—a problematic term, which implies that the dominant or 'mainstream' culture is the norm, and minority cultures are **'othered'** and considered deviant by default. Assimilation refers to the "melting pot" model in migration studies (Steinberg 2014). The result resembles a fusion of various cultures molten into one, where individual cultures are not distinguishable, but the one culture that has absorbed all others is. Surprisingly, Barker (2017, 291) notes that assimilation is the predominant acculturation approach for reasons of cultural preference: "undesirable but deemed necessary for maintaining successful careers in the host country". This is partly because of the "powerful role played by the dominant group in influencing the way in which acculturation would take place" (Berry 2005, 706).

Finally, **integration** describes a possible end result of the process of acculturation. Integration may be described as *additive multiculturalism* because the acquisition of the dominant culture occurs without losing one's own cultural identity (cf Barker 2017). However, again, as in the case with acculturation, integration needs a fertile ground in the form of an open and inclusive dominant culture. Like acculturation, integration is a multi-directional process, and it is not the responsibility of the minority culture alone. It is also important to remember that acculturation processes may not always lead to integration if the dominant culture does not encourage or foster it, or if there are government, legal or systemic mechanisms that prohibit it.

The key to balancing hierarchical power dynamics in a multicultural workplace and establishing **trust** is communication in the form of **intercultural dialogue**. This involves interaction, dialogue and contact between cultures beyond simple co-existence or mere tolerance, towards recognition of dynamic identities, promotion of respect and shared values (see McDermott et al. 2016). Multicultural groups with the most harmonious relations are those whose members do not feel that their identity is threatened (Browaeys and Price 2011, 294). Intercultural dialogue is instrumental in implementing the aims of interculturalism, such as fostering understanding and empathy with others. Acculturation processes based on intercultural dialogue may lead to the shift from competing cultures to a **negotiated culture**, which is "an ongoing, emergent, working arrangement of imperfectly shared rules and routines" (Brannen et al. 2006, 45). A negotiated culture involves new meanings, new understandings and, ultimately, a new culture altogether (Clausen 2007).

While acculturation may help the emergence of a negotiated culture through mutual change and adaptation, a negotiated culture is unlikely in cases of assimilation. Integration helps, but it is not a prerequisite for the emergence of a negotiated culture.

Case Study—Alleo

Alleo was founded in 2007 to design, promote and develop German-French cross-border train services. It is a joint subsidiary of SNCF (French national rail) and Deutsche Bahn (German national rail) with headquarters in Strasbourg. Described as "two Goliaths", these two national giant companies have distinct organisational cultures. A willingness to find solutions through binational pairs ('dyads') working together and exchanging knowledge and contacts has contributed to the **emergence of a negotiated culture**.

> Building interpersonal as well as organisational relationships was key to this process. For example, the high-speed trains' on-board service used to switch at the French/German border. The proposal was to introduce a French-German joint binomial train service from the beginning to the end. But it wasn't just a case of the French attendant dealing with French passengers, tickets and queries and the German attendant dealing with the German passengers. Attendants were given language and team development training, which "helped to develop solidarity and common identity". Today, the German and the French attendants stay together during the whole trip, offering a bilingual (or trilingual) joint service to the passengers. "DB's and SNCF's train attendants complement each other very well, and as a result we got better customer evaluations" (French interviewee). In these interactions, a new negotiated culture emerged as a mix between professional cultures and corporate cultures, after trust was established as a result of sustained and meaningful intercultural interactions.
> Adapted from Barmeyer and Davoine (2019).

3.3 Key Dimensions in Cross-Cultural Interactions

Having looked at power dynamics, competing cultures and negotiated culture, this section looks more closely at dimensions of cross-cultural interaction at work.

3.3.1 Nonverbal and Visual Communication

Visual communication includes clothing, jewellery, colours and symbols that colleagues wear or use. A hijab, turban or a cross, are common examples of visual communication of someone's religion, for example. The choice of formal v. informal clothing, specific logos and symbols or even hairstyles can communicate people's beliefs and attitudes. This communication may be intentional or unintentional.

In addition to this, sometimes people use contextualisation cues to show how the content of our utterances should be interpreted and avoid misunderstandings. **Nonverbal communication** may include such contextualisation cues, such as body language, facial expressions, gestures, movement, posture, eye contact and proximity. Again, these may be intentional or unintentional, but they all carry and communicate meaning. Based on Edward Hall's proxemics, Gabbott and Hogg (2001, 6) identify four categories of nonverbal communication:

a. *Proxemics*. Also referred to as 'personal space', proxemics refers to the amount of physical space that people feel appropriate or necessary to exist between themselves and others.

b. *Kinesics* refers to body movements and gestures.
c. *Vocalics.* Aspects such as pauses, volume (speaking loudly or softly), intonation, speed, stress and pronunciation. This category is also called **paraverbal communication.**
d. *Oculesics* refers to eye behaviour such as gaze and movement, e.g. rolling your eyes, staring or making eye contact in general. In many Asian cultures, for example, direct eye contact is prohibited between persons of differing status. Some employees on the autistic spectrum may avoid eye contact, finding it stressful or invasive, or may overcompensate by attempting to mimic 'neurotypical' interaction (Trevisan et al. 2017).

There are other categories of nonverbal communication, such as *haptics*, which refers to touch. Some cultures are more tactile than others, e.g. in some cultures kissing or hugging friends regardless of gender, while in others it is offensive to touch someone (especially their hair) who is not a relative. Some forbid physical contact between genders, which would prohibit handshakes for example.

3.3.2 Politeness

Politeness is associated with socially accepted good manners and it is culturally bound. What is considered polite in one country or context may not be considered polite in another, for example, kissing on the cheek. The purpose of politeness is to show respect, to be accepted by our peers, to have a good working relationship with our colleagues, or, sometimes, to get our point across in a negotiation.

Politeness strategies are influenced by power relationships, and the degree to which these are hierarchical; and by distance, in the sense of how well two people know each other. A large power difference may exist between an employee and employer in a hierarchical organisation, but a small distance, in the sense that they work together every day and know one another quite well. Power differences are acknowledged in many cultures through use of titles or through use of informal or more formal personal pronouns (e.g. *anta* versus the more formal *antom* in Arabic or *tu* and *vous* in French). However, use of informal titles or personal pronouns to a stranger may be interpreted as insulting or aggressive in some cultures, while formal titles may seem awkward in more relaxed US or UK-style organisations.

3.3.3 Turn-Taking

Turn-taking refers to the length of time people normally wait before responding to the other person in a conversation ('taking their turn to speak'). Conventions on turn-taking vary considerably across cultures, resulting in ample scope for misunderstanding. For example, Northern Europeans are more likely to wait until the other person finishes their 'turn' before responding, while people from Mediterranean cultures may be more tolerant of overlapping, interruptions, increase in volume, rising intonation or even simultaneous speech. This is sometimes called **turn appropriation** (Clyne 1999).

Studies in Conversation Analysis have shown how the lengths of time that count as silence may be calibrated differently across cultures. Such studies have shown that South Asians in general tend to be more comfortable with silence than Europeans, for example, largely because these cultures tend to be more hierarchical, and turn appropriation would be avoided out of respect (Clyne 1999).

3.4 Building Trust in Global Multicultural Teams

Taking the complexity of these cultural and communicative dimensions into consideration, we now turn to how cross-cultural interactions are then managed in global teams, how trust is established and how a negotiated culture emerges. The role of global teams is important, not only in completing tasks, increasing efficiency and providing 24-work rotation, but also in establishing and maintaining relations with external partners, such as suppliers or salespeople. Global teams work in multiple locations across multiple time zones, and often speaking multiple languages—so they are also multicultural. Building trust is crucial to this process. Trust within organisations is, according to Mayer et al. (1995), the belief of a party in another to carry out a desired action without being able to influence the trustee. This is especially important—and challenging—in a diverse workforce.

3.4.1 Forming the Team

In global multicultural teams, team development stages are longer in time and more complex. Browaeys and Price (2011, 290) observed that during the forming stage, which is the time when team members are meant to get to know each other and start building a long-lasting relationship, those with **task-oriented working practices** spent little time getting to know each other, while those with **relationship-oriented working practices** spent much more time establishing a personal relationship.[1] Team bonding is, therefore, less important for certain cultures that would prefer to focus more on the task at hand.

---

[1] Trompenaars and Hampden-Turner's model, which introduced the distinction between task-oriented and relationship-oriented "cultures", was discussed and extensively criticised in Chapter 2 of this volume, where we cautioned against established notions of "national cultures" that focus on differences rather than harmonious working relationships. While we reject the assumption that these categorisations can be applied to essentialist, reductionist and homogeneous conceptualisations of cultures, the categories themselves can be useful in identifying approaches, preferences and behavioural trends in the workplace.

In relationship-oriented, particularistic practices, for example, trust is built on the basis of the personal relationships, bonding and cohesion developed in the forming stage. In task-oriented, universalistic approaches, trust is built on the basis of ground rules being established early and clearly and consistency being applied (Trompenaars and Hampden-Turner 2012; also see Chapter 2 of this volume). This distinction more often than not refers to personality traits or personal preferences. At the crucial early stages of team formation, there may also be tensions between "self-categorisation, social identity formation and stereotyping on the one hand, and emotional arousal on the other" (Kaar 2010, 102). Recognising and interpreting such differences and "affective states" (ibid.) early on is important, as it affects the way trust is built in the team.

3.4.2 Team Meetings

A considerable amount of time in a team's life cycle is spent in meetings. Meetings reveal cultural differences, as well as differences in power and social status in an organisation or project. But they are also crucial to the cohesion of the team, and a source of trust-building or breaking. Aspects of team meetings that affect trust range from organisational issues such punctuality, seating position of attendees, or agenda control, to emotion display.

Punctuality is crucial in team meetings and performance in general, but there are different interpretations of punctuality across cultures, and this includes organisational cultures. Task-oriented personalities, or cultures, would not trust people or teams who were not punctual according to their own standard. Chapter 4 on Intercultural Perspectives of Time explains how punctuality and deadlines are perceived differently in different cultures, and how this can have a detrimental impact on team cohesion and performance.

Regarding seating position of attendees, rectangular or oval board-meeting style tables are often used for meetings, in which the team leader (CEO, manager, etc.) sits at the top or middle of the table with the hierarchy moving downwards. The common assumption is that round tables are better for teamwork, as they create a more equal environment and encourage the participation of all members in the group. Pan and Scollon (2001) challenge this assumption and give the example of a Chinese colleague who stayed silent throughout such a meeting and did not engage at all. The colleague later explained that sitting at a round table reminded her of family dinners where children were expected to be silent (ibid.).

Additionally, when participating in a multicultural meeting, it is important to observe who is doing the talking, who keeps the meeting moving along and whose views seem to matter. In Japan, for example, meetings are formal, and it is those with a higher rank in the company (usually older male) who have the agenda control and whose opinion is valued most (Clausen 2007). In the US, meetings are more relaxed, with brainstorming a common and necessary process to generate ideas. Still, a hierarchy based on nationality, race or status may be observed, and actions and decisions made in meetings are usually written down and communicated to all team members.

Emotions and emotion display also seem to play an important role in the development of trust and in assessing trustworthiness. Kaar (2010) discusses how different cultures have different emotion display rules, as well as "trust-eliciting behavious and actions signalling trustworthiness" (101) which are learned, internalised and socialised. These are mostly evident in cross-cultural negotiations and situations of conflict, both of which are discussed below.

3.5 Cross-Cultural Negotiation

Negotiation is a process where people of conflicting interests deliberate to decide on a joint action agreed upon by everyone. During negotiations, the parties are trying to convince each other that their own interests are also the interests of the other party, or that a request they may be making is not really in their interest. Some of the most effective negotiators are those who succeed in persuading the other party that what the first speaker wanted all along was in fact the other speaker's idea—and that everyone benefits from the outcome.

Australian linguist Michael Clyne, who conducted studies on intercultural communication at work in the 1990s, distinguishes between symmetrical and asymmetrical negotiation, depending on the dynamics of the group. Symmetrical negotiation is more equal in terms of turn-taking, while in asymmetrical negotiation one person dominates the discussion, takes long turns and does not leave much opportunity for response (Clyne 1999). Clyne also found that cultural styles of negotiation vary considerably. According to his 1999 study, Southeast Asian employees were more subservient and did not like conflict. The study also observed that Southeast Asian employees "negotiate as little as possible" (120) and "cooperate by saying what they think they are expected to say" (ibid.). Similarly, Brew and Cairns (2004, 339) hypothesised that the communication styles of East Asian employees from more collectivist cultures might be less confrontational and more accommodating than their more individualist European counterparts. But they also found that context and the power relationship between colleagues were often more influential factors. Conversely, Warren (2012, 485–486) found that, typically, "Western negotiators are solely concerned with the best outcome for their organization, whereas the Chinese have two competing needs: to promote their organization's interests and to promote and protect the nation's interests". While such an essentialist approach may not be helpful, and the label "Western" negotiators is reductionist considering the diversity within this category, it is useful to be aware that Chinese collectivism does imply that the nation's (or the state's) interests are always at play in business negotiations.

Indirectness is another aspect worth considering. It may be an expression of politeness, e.g. 'perhaps this avenue should be considered' instead of 'we must do this'. It may also be an indication of defensiveness, in which the speaker does not want to explicitly express a view they may later wish to retract. However, it can also be used to seek rapport. For example, a Japanese colleague may find the use of 'no' too face-threatening, and try to express refusal in a more positive manner; so "one never says 'no', but listeners understand from the form of the 'yes' whether it is truly a 'yes' or a polite 'no'" (Tannen 1984, 269).

No two negotiators operate the same way even if they come from the same country, company or even department. National boundaries do not determine someone's culture or negotiation characteristics, so negotiators should not assume that their counterparts share common negotiation characteristics due to their geographical location. Furthermore, business negotiations often involve an interdependent network. Interpreters also become part of that network (Karanasiou 2016) and should not be treated by the negotiators as mere language facilitators. They are active members of the communicative process that can affect and be affected by it. The role of translators and interpreters is discussed at length in Chapter 13.

3.6 Intercultural Conflict

Conflict is a fact of life in any team, and in some cases, it is a necessary process for meaningful change and growth—if we consider the *forming, storming, norming, performing* pattern of team formation and performance. Culture can be a critical determinant of conflict and can be considered both a source of the conflict and the means for its resolution. Emotion display is an important dimension in this process, which is sometimes sidelined in relevant research. Relevant to this is the concept of **face**, which originated in Chinese culture and is now used across cultures to describe the concern for our own public dignity and that of others. Face is generally associated with respect, honour, status, reputation, credibility, competence, family/network connections, loyalty and trust (Oetzel et al. 2001, 237).

Face is hugely important across Asia. It is known as *lian* or *mianzi* in Mandarin, *mentsu* or *taimen* in Japanese and *chae myon* in Korean. In China, *lian* refers to the moral character of a person, while *mianzi* refers to the social status achieved through success (Oetzel et al. 2001, 236). In Japan, *mentsu* refers to someone's moral character, while *taimen* refers to the image one presents to others (ibid.). The latter is close to Western concepts of face, which generally focus on our image.

In conflict situations, people try to save face and preserve their image, integrity, honour and status by using various strategies, which vary cross-culturally. For example, apologies and forgiveness are often key aspects of conflict resolution, and forgiveness is linked to willingness to cooperate (Ayoko 2016). However, conceptions of forgiveness vary cross-culturally as do expectations of apologies or forgiveness. These may be perceived as a sign of weakness rather than a collegiate act. Or people from collectivist cultures with a greater emphasis on social harmony may place greater value on apologies and forgiveness and be more willing to forgive than those from more individualist cultures (Hook et al. 2009).

American Professor Mitchell R. Hammer, who worked with NASA to analyse cultural aspects of conflict between astronauts, developed an **Intercultural Conflict**

Style Model (ICS) in 2005. The model distinguishes between direct and indirect approaches to conflict resolution, and emotionally restrained versus emotionally expressive approaches. Direct conflict styles according to Hammer's model focus on problem-solving and value individual expression and assertiveness, whereas indirect styles focus on relationship repair, nonverbal and paraverbal communication for hints and contexts and value tact and diplomacy. Unsurprisingly, emotionally expressive conflict styles value "emotional authenticity" (Hammer 2005) in the sense of expressiveness and externalisation of emotions, while they tend to distrust emotional restraint. Similarly, emotionally restrained conflict styles value calm and preservation of 'face' and tend to distrust confrontation and lack of emotional control. What is particularly interesting in Hammer's model is that emotional expressiveness is interpreted as sincere and trustworthy by people with emotionally expressive conflict styles, but as insecure and untrustworthy by people with emotionally restrained conflict styles. For example, Mills and Grainger (2016) argued that Americans consider directness to be associated with power whereas indirectness is akin to dishonesty as well as subservience (269).

An obvious limitation of Hammer's 'conflict inventory' is that a person's choice of style or strategy may vary according to context, influenced by features such as power relations or the speakers' relationship. There are also many degrees of emotional expressiveness. If considerations of power relations and context are included, this may still be a useful conceptual tool, perhaps not for intercultural, but for *interpersonal* conflict in the workplace. As we have emphasised throughout this chapter, and indeed throughout the volume, we should avoid the tendency to attribute individual behaviours to cultures, and to assume that individuals are representatives of (their) entire cultures at work.

3.7 Trust and the Online Dimension

The online dimension is increasingly becoming a constitutive feature of multicultural teams, whether global or not. Considering time zone differences and national and religious holidays when scheduling meetings is a first step towards inclusivity and cohesion in a virtual global team. But elements of team meetings such as seating position, agenda control, formality, turn-taking, nonverbal and visual communication, as well as negotiation and conflict involve different challenges when such organised encounters are conducted online. For example, only the manager/CEO may have their camera on, their image may be "pinned" to employees' screens, and employees may be required to have their cameras on or off as a rule. A meeting held online with no cameras is a different speech event compared to the same meeting held in-person because word use, speaking speed and visual cues would be different. Turn appropriation may be more difficult in online meetings but meeting hosts may have the authority to 'mute' members. The ability to respond appropriately to these social cues impacts communication flow, understanding, trust and relationship-building.

The initial stages of team formation are crucial in trust-building, particularly in online environments where relationships are more difficult to develop or establish. Agreeing on expectations and clarifying team member roles early is key to ensure transparency, shared vision and facilitate harmonious relations at work. These roles and expectations should cover both synchronous (meetings, conference calls) and asynchronous communication (e-mails, discussion boards, shared documents). Williams (2008) argues that "it requires greater skill to use e-mails to foster trust or repair trust once it is broken" (164). This is because visual and nonverbal cues are removed from communication, which makes it harder to interpret meaning in messages, and establish intersubjectivity as well as trustworthiness on the basis of the aspects discussed in the previous section. Paralinguistic aspects, such as intonation or stress, and nonverbal cues (gestures, facial expressions), are immediately perceived in face-to-face interactions but lacking in email or other written communication (e.g. corporate discussion boards).

For these reasons, Cagiltay et al. (2015, 13) recommend using "richer communication channels" such as video or audio rather than "lean communication channels" such as text, at least in the initial stages of team formation. Other scholars go as far as suggesting that an initial face-to-face meeting of all team members is advantageous in building and establishing trust before moving online (Staples and Zhao 2006, 402). Jarvenpaa and Leidner argue that "trust might be imported, but is more likely created via a communication behavior established in the first few keystrokes" (1999, 811). Indeed, while communication focused on the task(s) is necessary to maintain trust, "social communication that complements rather than substitutes for task communication may strengthen trust" (ibid.). For this reason, leaders need to "develop special skills for leading in cyberspace" (Williams 2008, 164). One of these skills is intercultural competence.

3.8 Intercultural Competence

3.8.1 Developing Intercultural Competence

Intercultural competence is usually defined as the ability to communicate 'effectively' in a variety of cultural contexts. However, the term 'effective communication' is vague. Success and effectiveness have different meanings for universalistic and particularistic, achievement and ascription, individualist and collectivist working practices. Does effective communication mean that the task is done successfully, that everyone is respected, that no misunderstandings occur, or that the manager's view prevails? This depends on the objectives set by the organisational or negotiated culture.

Various Intercultural Competence models have been developed over time. American sociologist Milton Bennett's **Development Model of Intercultural Sensitivity (DMIS)** (1993) illustrates the stages of people's adjustment with "the newness" and describes the ways people experience cultural difference. The DMIS ranges from the ethnocentric to the ethnorelative, with the latter stages achieved after prolonged periods of living and working with other cultures. Culture shock is then relative to a person's developmental stage on the DMIS continuum. The three ethnocentric stages in sequential order are 'Denial', 'Defense' and 'Minimization', and the three ethnorelative stages are 'Acceptance', 'Adaptation' and 'Integration'.

British linguist and intercultural education expert Michael Byram's (1997) model of intercultural communicative competence is based on five forms of knowledge or 'savoirs' (from the French for knowledge). These are:

1. *Savoir*: knowledge of self and other
2. *Savoir être:* self-critique, interpretive and relational skills
3. *Savoir comprendre:* interpreting and relating to the other culture
4. *Savoir apprendre/faire:* discovering and interacting
5. *Savoir s'engager:* critical cultural awareness (adapted from Byram 1997, 34).

Based on Byram's model, Glaser et al. (2007) proposed a transformational model for developing intercultural competence as part of the EU-funded ICOPROMO project (Intercultural Competence for Professional Mobility). As in the case of Byram's model, "awareness of self and other, getting to know oneself, reflecting upon one's culture-bound upbringing and standpoint and analysing in depth one's norms, values, beliefs and behaviours" (Glaser et al. 2007) are at the core of the ICOPROMO transformational model. More importantly, both models emphasise the importance of reflexivity and self-critique as well as acquiring information on cultural others. There is clearly a focus on the process which results in transformation of the self, of perspectives, of attitudes and behaviours rather than just the resulting skill sets. Taking Byram's critical cultural awareness (*savoir s'engager*) further, Glaser et al. propose that the development of intercultural competence involves learning and unlearning processes of such attitudes, behaviours and perspectives.

Finally, Matveev and Nelson's (2004) cross-cultural communication competence model is business and task based. It includes interpersonal skills (without an indication on how to develop these skills), team effectiveness (which enlists desirable abilities that have little cultural relevance), cultural uncertainty and cultural empathy. The latter two aspects are important; indeed, the focus on **empathy** is paramount for intercultural competence. Scholars have particularly emphasised empathy as a key skill for and practice of intercultural dialogue. For Houghton (2012), "intellectual empathy" means a bottom-up process and cognitive skill that necessitates the suspension of prior knowledge and values in favour of basing one's understanding only on the information provided by the interlocutor. As such, the practice of intellectual empathy results in a decentring one's own cultural positioning that "seems to help reduce the resistance to the ideas of others" (Houghton 2012, 97).

3.9 Beyond Intercultural Competence

Overall, what is central to intercultural competence is the ability to move away from ethnocentrism and its perils. Competence in this case focuses on the ability to transform and adapt to new cultural contexts. Ironically, intercultural competence literature can be largely ethnocentric itself.[2] Parmenter's (2003) work is an exception to this, as it offers a much-needed international perspective of intercultural competence, beyond an Anglo-centric focus. Parmenter provides insights from Japan, China and Korea in her discussion of intercultural competence and discusses Confucian influences on culture, the importance of relationships, face, self-improvement and self-development. She concludes that the link between intercultural competence and citizenship education "may need to be redefined in societies where citizenship of a nation is based above all on cultural and ethnic (rather than legal and territorial) definitions of the nation and national identity" (Parmenter 2003, 131).

Overall, there is a plethora of non-academic resources discussing, problematising and attempting to give solutions to possible pitfalls of cross-cultural negotiations. These resources, which claim to educate their readers on how to do business with people from different nationalities or cultures, are quite popular with people doing business abroad and serve as their first point of reference for getting to know the cultural characteristics of their interlocutors. The way that they approach cultural identity and cultural characteristics is mainly based on anecdotal experiences of their authors, as well as from popular perceptions that are intertwined with that specific culture. Such resources tackle issues, such as popular culture, behavioural patterns, greetings and salutations, and even dietary preferences of people of differing nationalities.

The main objection to the 'how to' literature is that it creates a patronising view of people and does not leave room for flexibility or for analysing the idiosyncrasies and background of each person in question. British linguist and UNESCO Chair in Refugee Integration through Languages and the Arts, Professor Alison Phipps, warns against the quick fixes and surface-level approaches of intercultural training. Even the term intercultural competence implies a fixed end state or an attained goal. Once we reach it, there is nothing left to do. Phipps adds a sixth *savoir* to Byram's model: *savoir se transformer*, knowing to change oneself (Phipps 2010), which emphasises the self-transformational aspect of the intercultural journey. Guilherme (2012) also moves beyond the static notion of intercultural competence and proposes the concept and principle of **intercultural responsibility** in the workplace. Guilherme defines intercultural responsibility as "a conscious and reciprocally respectful, both professional and personal, relationship among the team/group members, assuming that they have different ethnic backgrounds, whether national or sub-national" (ibid.).

---

[2] Consider: 'ICC is still being hijacked by global ideologies of effective, proactive, direct, upfront communication Anglo-Saxon style, which replicates Western discourses even when the language and the context are Chinese' (Ladegaard and Jenks 2015, 4).

The building blocks of intercultural responsibility according to Guilherme are coherence, understood here as agreement that expectations and responsibilities are mutual and reciprocal, empathy and solidarity.

Overall, only when we try to learn and scrutinise our own culture, beliefs, assumptions and worldviews can we begin to understand other perspectives. Our self-assessment should also include how our personal perceptions and biases influence our own interactions and relationships in the workplace. Stepping outside our cultural boundaries and changing perspective is not an easy task, but it is a first step to recognition of difference and establishing relationships at work and beyond.

Chapter Review Questions

1. What is a negotiated culture and how does it emerge?
2. Consider the meaning of the following gestures cross-culturally: thumbs-up, smiling, tapping on shoulder, kissing and bowing.
3. How do you build trust in a multicultural team?
4. How is the online dimension affecting the work of global multicultural teams?
5. What is intercultural responsibility and how can we develop it?

Recommended Further Reading

- Clausen, L. 2007. Corporate Communication Challenges: A 'Negotiated' Culture Perspective. *International Journal of Cross Cultural Management* 7: 317–332.
- Cui, V., Vertinsky, I., Robinson, S., and O. Branzei. 2018. Trust in the Workplace: The Role of Social Interaction Diversity in the Community and in the Workplace. *Business & Society* 57 (2): 378–412. https://doi.org/10.1177/0007650315611724
- Oetzel, J., Tink-Toomey, S. Masumoto, T., Yokochi, Y., Pan, X. Takai, J., Wilcox, R. 2001. Face and Facework in Conflict: A Cross-Cultural Comparison of China, Germany, Japan, and the United States. *Communication Monographs* 68 (3): 235–258.
- Parmenter, L. 2003. Describing and Defining Intercultural Communicative Competence–International Perspectives. In *Intercultural Competence*, ed. M. Byram, 121–147. Strasbourg: Council of Europe. https://rm.coe.int/16806ad2dd
- Primecz, H., Romani, L., and S. Sackmann, eds. 2011. *Cross-Cultural Management in Practice: Culture and Negotiated Meanings*. Edward Elgar Publishing.

References

Ayoko, O.B. 2016. Workplace Conflict and Willingness to Cooperate: The Importance of Apology and Forgiveness. *International Journal of Conflict Management* 27 (2): 172–198. https://doi.org/10.1108/IJCMA-12-2014-0092.

Barker, G.G. 2017. Acculturation and Bicultural Integration in Organizations: Conditions, Contexts, and Challenges. *International Journal of Cross Cultural Management* 17 (3): 281–304. https://doi.org/10.1177/1470595817712741.

Barmeyer, C., and E. Davoine. 2019. Facilitating Intercultural Negotiated Practices in Joint Ventures: The Case of a French-German Railway Organization. *International Business Review* 28 (1): 1–11. https://doi.org/10.1016/j.ibusrev.2018.06.001.

Berry, J.W. 2005. Acculturation: Living Successfully in Two Cultures. *International Journal of Intercultural Relations* 29 (6): 697–712.

Brannen, M.Y., C. Gómez, M.F. Peterson, L. Romani, L. Sagiv, and P.C. Wu. 2006. People in Global Organizations: Culture, Personality and Social Dynamics. In *The Blackwell Handbook of Global Management*, ed. H.W. Lane, et al., 26–54. Oxford: Wiley-Blackwell.

Brew, F.P., and D.R. Cairns. 2004. Do Culture or Situational Constraints Determine Choice of Direct or Indirect Styles in Intercultural Workplace Conflicts? *International Journal of Intercultural Relations* 28: 331–352.

Browaeys, M.J., and R. Price. 2011. *Understanding Cross-Cultural Management*. Financial Times/Prentice Hall.

Byram, M. 1997. *Teaching and Assessing Intercultural Communicative Competence*. Clevedon: Multilingual Matters.

Cagiltay, K., B. Bichelmeyer, and G. Kaplan Akilli. 2015. Working with Multicultural Virtual Teams: Critical Factors for Facilitation, Satisfaction and Success. *Smart Learning Environments* 2 (1): 1–16. https://doi.org/10.1186/s40561-015-0018-7.

Clausen, L. 2007. Corporate Communication Challenges: A 'Negotiated' Culture Perspective. *International Journal of Cross Cultural Management* 7: 317–332.

Clyne, M. 1999. Variation in Communication Patterns and Inter-Cultural Communication Breakdown in Oral Discourse. In *Inter-Cultural Communication at Work. Cultural Values in Discourse*, 90–159. Cambridge: Cambridge University Press.

Gabbott, M., and G. Hogg. 2001. Non-Verbal Communication in Service Encounters: A Conceptual Framework. *Journal of Marketing Management* 17 (1): 5–26.

Glaser, E., M. Guilherme, M. Méndez García, and T. Mughan. 2007. ICOPROMO, Intercultural Competence for Professional Mobility, Council of Europe. http://archive.ecml.at/mtp2/ICOPROMO/ICOPROMO_WEB/Lucru/Files/ECML%20ICOPROMO%20mainE.pdf.

Guilherme, M. 2012. Critical Language and Intercultural Communication Pedagogy. In *The Routledge Handbook of Language and Intercultural Communication*, ed. J. Jackson, 366–380. Abingdon: Routledge.

Hammer, M.R. 2005. The Intercultural Conflict Style Inventory: A Conceptual Framework and Measure of Intercultural Conflict Resolution Approaches. *International Journal of Intercultural Relations* 29 (6): 675–695.

Hook, J.N., E.L. Worthington Jr., and S.O. Utsey. 2009. Collectivism, Forgiveness, and Social Harmony. *The Counseling Psychologist* 37 (6): 821–847.

Houghton, S.A. 2012. *Intercultural Dialogue in Practice: Managing Value Judgment Through Foreign Language Education*. Clevedon: Multilingual Matters.

Jarvenpaa, S.L., and D.E. Leidner. 1999. Communication and Trust in Global Virtual Teams. *Organization Science* 10 (6): 791–815.

Jurcik, T., R. Ahmed, E. Yakobov, L. Solopieieva-Jurcikova, and A.G. Ryder. 2013. Understanding the Role of the Ethnic Density Effect: Issues of Acculturation, Discrimination and Social Support. *Journal of Community Psychology* 41: 662–678. https://doi.org/10.1002/jcop.21563.

Kaar, A. 2010. Emotional Management: Expressing, Interpreting and Making Meaning of Feelings in Multicultural Teams. In *The Intercultural Dynamics of Multicultural Working*, ed. M.

Guilherme, E. Glaser and M. del Carmen Mendez Garcia, 95–108. Bristol, Blue Ridge Summit: Multilingual Matters. https://doi.org/10.21832/9781847692870-009.

Karanasiou, P. 2016. Public Service Interpreting and Business Negotiation Interpreting: Friends or Foes? In *Challenges and Opportunities in Public Service Interpreting*, ed. T. Munyangeyo, M. Rabadan-Gomez, and G. Webb, 191–211. London: Palgrave Macmillan.

Ladegaard, H.J., and C.J. Jenks. 2015. Language and Intercultural Communication in the Workplace: Critical Approaches to Theory and Practice. *Language and Intercultural Communication* 15 (1): 1–12. https://doi.org/10.1080/14708477.2014.985302.

Matveev, A.V., and P.E. Nelson. 2004. Cross Cultural Communication Competence and Multicultural Team Performance: Perceptions of American and Russian Managers. *International Journal of Cross-Cultural Management* 4 (2): 253–270. https://doi.org/10.1177/1470595804044752.

Mayer, R.C., J.H. Davis, and F.D. Schoorman. 1995. An Integrative Model of Organizational Trust. *Academy of Management Review* 20 (3): 709–734.

McDermott, P., M. Nic Craith, and K. Strani. 2016. Public Space, Collective Memory and Intercultural Dialogue in a (UK) City of Culture. *Identities* 23 (5): 610–627. https://doi.org/10.1080/1070289X.2015.1054828.

Mills, S., and K. Grainger. 2016. *Directness and Indirectness Across Cultures*. Basingstoke: Palgrave Macmillan.

Oetzel, J., S. Tink-Toomey, T. Masumoto, Y. Yokochi, X. Pan, J. Takai, and R. Wilcox. 2001. Face and Facework in Conflict: A Cross-Cultural Comparison of China, Germany, Japan, and the United States. *Communication Monographs* 68 (3): 235–258.

Pan Y. and W. Scollon. 2001. Analyzing Communication in the International Workplace. In *Professional Communication in International Settings*, ed. Y. Pan, S.B.K. Scollon and R. Scollon. Malden, MA: Blackwell Publishers.

Parmenter, L. 2003. Describing and Defining Intercultural Communicative Competence–International Perspectives. In *Intercultural Competence*, ed. M. Byram, 119–147. Strasbourg: Council of Europe. https://rm.coe.int/16806ad2dd.

Phinney, J., J.W. Berry, and P. Vedder. 2006. The Acculturation Experience: Attitudes, Identities and Behaviors of Immigrant Youth. In *Immigrant Youth in Cultural Transition: Acculturation, Identity and Adaptation Across National Contexts*, ed. J.W. Berry, J. Phinney, D.L. Sam, and P. Vedder, 71–116. Mahwah: Lawrence Erlbaum.

Phipps, A. 2010. Training and Intercultural Education: The Danger in Good Citizenship. In *The Intercultural Dynamics of Multicultural Working*, ed. M. Guilherme, E. Glaser and M. del Carmen Mendez Garcia, 59–77. Bristol: Multilingual Matters.

Staples, D.S., and L. Zhao. 2006. The Effects of Cultural Diversity in Virtual Teams Versus Face-to-Face Teams. *Group Decision and Negotiation* 15: 389–406. https://doi.org/10.1007/s10726-006-9042-x.

Steinberg, S. 2014. The Long View of the Melting Pot. *Ethnic and Racial Studies* 37 (5): 790–794. https://doi.org/10.1080/01419870.2013.872282.

Tadmor, C.T., P.E. Tetlock, and K. Peng. 2009. Acculturation Strategies and Integrative Complexity: The Cognitive Implications of Biculturalism. *Journal of Cross-Cultural Psychology* 40 (1): 105–139.

Tannen, D. 1984. The Pragmatics of Cross-Cultural Communication. *Applied Linguistics* 5 (3): 189–195.

Trompenaars, F., and C. Hampden-Turner. 2012. *Riding the Waves of Culture: Understanding Diversity in Global Business*. London: Nicholas Brealey.

Trevisan, D.A., N. Roberts, C. Lin, and E. Birmingham. 2017. How Do Adults and Teens with Self-Declared Autism Spectrum Disorder Experience Eye Contact? A Qualitative Analysis of First-Hand Accounts. *PLoS ONE* 12 (11): e0188446.

Triandis, H.C. 1994. *Culture and Social Behavior*. New York: McGraw-Hill.

Warren, M. 2012. Professional and Workplace Settings. In *The Routledge Handbook of Language and Intercultural Communication*, ed. J. Jackson, 481–494. Oxford and New York: Routledge.

Williams K. 2008. Effective Leadership for Multicultural Teams. In *Effective Multicultural Teams: Theory and Practice. Advances in Group Decision and Negotiation*, vol. 3, ed. C.B. Halverson and S.A. Tirmizi, 135–172. Dordrecht: Springer. https://doi.org/10.1007/978-1-4020-6957-4_6.

Chapter 4
Intercultural Perspectives of Work, Leisure, and Time

Sara C. Brennan and Bernadette O'Rourke

> In the increasingly globalised, multicultural workplaces of the twenty-first century, it is essential to understand the diversity of perspectives on three concepts that fundamentally shape professional practices and relationships: work, leisure, and time. After reviewing key definitions of these concepts, this chapter discusses cultural values before sketching out how such values influence understandings of work, leisure, and time. A work meeting is then used to illustrate real-world implications of encounters between professionals with different culturally-shaped perspectives on these concepts. Students will thus be equipped with insights crucial for successful leadership, communication, and rapport-building in the contemporary workplace.

4.1 Introduction

The topic of "work-life balance" has in recent years received much attention in the media and has been the subject of countless self-help books. Particularly in the wake of the COVID-19 pandemic, during which many people around the world found themselves working from home, the nature of this balance is a matter of lively public debate and scholarly study (see Palumbo 2020). Developing a healthy work-life balance is usually seen as something to strive for…but what might not be as apparent is that this concept implies a division between two distinct and separate realms, "work" and "life", with time spent on "life" being added in to counterbalance the

S. C. Brennan (✉)
Université Toulouse Capitole, Toulouse, France
e-mail: sara.brennan@ut-capitole.fr

B. O'Rourke
University of Glasgow, Glasgow, UK
e-mail: Bernadette.ORourke@glasgow.ac.uk

necessary (and potentially overwhelming) time spent on "work". In a globalised, multicultural workplace in which people from different backgrounds interact on a constant basis, however, not everyone necessarily shares the same view of work and life, or of time for that matter. The diversity of views on the often taken-for-granted concepts of "work", "leisure" (as an element of non-work "life"), and "time" will thus be the focus of this chapter, together with their applications in the workplace.

4.2 Key Concepts

While often taken at face value, work, leisure, and time are in fact concepts that escape easy definition. Academic research has indeed highlighted their profound complexity and the vast array of perspectives that have been taken on their meanings at different times, in different societies and places, and within different fields (Klein 2009; Provis 2009; Purrington & Hickerson 2013). This section will thus provide a preliminary discussion of the many challenges involved in arriving at a basic understanding of these concepts.

4.2.1 Defining "Work", "Leisure", and "Time"

A traditional definition of *work* would normally centre on the notion of "paid employment", but would it also include 'extra unpaid hours, the time taken to travel to and from work and the more intractable problems of farmers, hoteliers, and others who work from home and where the border between home and work is very porous' (Guest 2002, 261–262)? New technologies, Guest (2002) further argues, have facilitated increased opportunities for working from home, thereby blurring the boundaries between work and home, and thus the balance between work and life. As the perceived opposite of work, life could thus be seen as "the rest of life", with free time and leisure both constituting dimensions of non-work time. While free time involves no commitments, *leisure* can be differentiated and defined as 'the pursuit of a specific activity' (Guest 2002, 263)—and more specifically, an 'activity chosen in relative freedom for its qualities of satisfaction' (Kelly 2012, 3). Such a definition of leisure, however, points to the subjectivity at the core of its meaning: whereas one person might find cooking to be a relaxing, satisfying leisure activity, another might find it a stressful, time-consuming chore that distracts from the leisure opportunities of non-work life. Similarly, while activities such as painting, writing, or once again cooking could be enjoyed as non-work leisure activities by bankers, teachers, and taxi drivers, they would constitute the core of work activities for professional painters, journalists, and chefs. Moreover, while a professional painter might consider watercolours to be their life's work, their relatives might still ask a dreaded question at every family gathering: "When are you going to get a real job?" Painting might thus seem like a waste of time to the extended family, while the watercolourist would likely see themselves as investing time in their craft. This familial controversy therefore also points to the great diversity in perceptions of *time*. While time in contemporary Western society is generally thought of as 'a kind of linear progression measured by the clock and calendar' (Whitrow 2003, 1), time, like work and leisure, is a concept that can be very divergently conceptualised from different perspectives, including cultural ones.

4.2.2 Cultural Values: A Necessary Concept for Understanding Intercultural Perspectives on Work, Leisure, and Time

A further central notion for this discussion of varying approaches to work, leisure, and time is that of *cultural values*. Defined as 'shared, abstract ideas about what a social collectivity views as good, right and desirable', cultural values represent 'the broad goals that members of the collectivity are encouraged to pursue' and which guide individuals' judgements and justifications of their own and other people's behaviour (Sagiv and Schwartz 2007, 177). When considering cultural values, it is important to avoid broad brushstrokes and to be wary of overgeneralising and essentialising different cultures. While overgeneralisation refers to the extension of observations about one part of a society's population to the entire society, essentialism relates to a perspective on culture as a fixed, unchanging attribute of a group of individuals. These processes can effectively position certain (mental, physical, etc.) traits as going 'hand in hand' with a particular nationality, reducing a culture to a finite collection of stable characteristics (Piller 2009, 319–320). It is thus crucial to keep in mind that cultures are dynamic and diverse and that individual people and their beliefs are not necessarily or automatically determined by their cultural background.[1] Successful intercultural communication, however, can sometimes depend at least in part on an effort to understand our own and others' cultural values, and this chapter aims to foster a sensibility to the importance of taking these notions into consideration in the contemporary workplace.

4.3 Intercultural Perspectives of Work

Fully acknowledging the blurriness of the concept of work, particularly under the technologically flexible conditions of the globalised economy, we opt here for a basic definition of work as "paid employment" so that we may begin discussing different cultural understandings of work and its relationship to non-work life.

---

[1] Editors' note: See Chapters 1 and 2 on this.

4.3.1 Cultural Values and the Meaning of Work: The Example of Individualistic and Collectivist Perspectives

Many scholars of intercultural communication have pointed to how the meaning of work to the life of an individual is shaped—though not entirely determined—by cultural values. Understanding such values as 'the bases for the specific norms that tell people what is appropriate in various situations', the functioning of societal institutions (including the economic system, the family, religion, etc.), as well as their objectives and their modes of operation, can be seen as shaped by and expressing the priorities of that society's cultural value system (Schwartz 1999, 25). An individualistic society that prioritises the well-being of the individual over that of the group, for instance, is likely to approach the organisation of social life in a way that is different from a collectivist society, which prioritises the group over the individual (see Chapter 2). Decades of research have highlighted how the individualistic or collectivist orientation of a given society can fundamentally shape business practices, management approaches, investment strategies, corporate governance, and other key dynamics of economic activity (see, for instance, Mai et al. 2020; Kyriacou 2016; Hofstede et al. 2010; Power et al. 2010).[2] Individual success, ambition, and autonomy tend to be prized in the often highly competitive workplaces of individualistic cultures, in which employees 'are expected to act rationally according to their own interest, and work should be organized in such a way that this self-interest and the employer's interest coincide'; collectivist cultures, meanwhile, prioritise the cultivation and maintenance of a cohesive in-group, with employees expected to remain loyal to and to 'act according to the interest of this in-group, which may not always coincide with his or her individual interest' (Hofstede 2001, 235; Schwartz 1999).

Beyond such broad observations, the study of collectivist versus individualistic cultural values in the workplace has revealed how the impact of different conceptions of and approaches to work far exceeds the confines of the office. To give but one example also relevant to this chapter's discussion of time and leisure, research has illustrated how cultural values shape the meaning of work in relation to the worker's family. Within a cultural value system that prioritises collectivism, an individual's work is often seen as a means of supporting the family. Instances of imbalance between work and life are thus accepted as inevitable elements of efforts to provide for the family. In more individualistic societies, meanwhile, work tends to be seen as the achievement of the individual, who is striving towards the fulfilment of their own potential through paid employment and success in the workplace. Work thus comes to be seen as distinct from the worker's familial roles and obligations, with a work-life imbalance seen as damaging to the individual's efforts to pursue their own professional and personal development (Haar et al. 2014, 363).

It should be noted that collectivism and individualism are not the only cultural values that can shape local understandings of work. Research by Aryee et al. (1999,

---

[2] Editors' note: For a discussion of individualism v. collectivism, see Chapter 2 and the Glossary of Key Terms at the end of this volume.

260–261) on workers in Hong Kong illustrates how a range of values co-exist and enter into tension with each other while influencing the local understanding of work in relation to the family. Noting the Chinese foundations of Hong Kong society, the authors observe that Confucianism has traditionally strongly influenced daily life in Hong Kong. As these philosophical traditions prioritise the family over individuals as the fundamental unit of society, the maintenance and preservation of the family are seen as the primary aims of the individual. At the same time, however, contemporary Hong Kong is a modernised economic hub with high levels of productivity, earning, and costs of living. This situation can generate a tension between more traditional and more modern dynamics, which Aryee et al. (1999, 261) describe as being resolved through 'an orientation to work whereby work is perceived primarily as an instrument for obtaining the economic means to maintain the family'. Blurring the lines between work and family roles, the strong commitment to work often displayed by Hong Kong Chinese employees can, therefore, be seen as linked to the traditional importance of ensuring the family's (financial) well-being. Aryee et al.'s (1999) research thus highlights how not only nationality, but also religion and historical socioeconomic dynamics impact the values that shape the meaning of work.

> **Case Study 1: One Country, Two Cultures: Navigating Deadlines in Belgium**
>
> Pant's (2016) recollection of his attempt to schedule meetings in Belgium exemplifies how diverse cultural values can translate into markedly different business practices, even within the same country. As an Amsterdam-based employee of an American electronics company, Pant was asked to present a broadcasting system to both the French- and Flemish-speaking media outlets of the Belgian government. His initial inclination to schedule one joint demonstration for representatives from the two services was strongly discouraged by the government aides with whom he was liaising, so he agreed to schedule two separate meetings, one with the Flemish representatives at 10:00 and one with the French representatives at 14:00 that same day.
>
> The reasoning behind this strategic advice was soon evident. As recounted by Pant, the two meetings progressed in profoundly different manners. His first meeting, with the Flemish, made clear the importance placed within their culture on respecting deadlines:
>
> > At 9:58 AM on the day of the demos, no one had arrived. At 9:59 AM the members of the Flemish delegation entered the room almost en masse. Flemish culture, I learned, highly valued punctuality. This trait was reflected in their precise technical questions, which were primarily centered on how the equipment could improve time efficiency over their current methods.
>
> His assumption that the French meeting would follow the same norms, however, was soon proven misguided:
>
> > At 1:58 PM there was no one in the room. "They'll all show up at two", I thought, but when 2 PM rolled around the room remained empty.

> At 2:06 PM members of the French-speaking service slowly trickled in, laughing and conversing with each other. The demo didn't officially start until after 2:15 PM, and unlike their Flemish counterparts, the French delegation wasn't concerned with time efficiencies of the equipment so much as its ability to enable team synergies and creativity.
>
> In foregrounding the contrasting Flemish and French prioritisations of deadlines and time efficiency, Pant's experience aptly illustrates both how varying cultural values can manifest themselves in divergent business practices, and how important sensitivity to such differences can be for successful professional interactions.

Beyond influencing individuals' priorities in relation to work, cultural values also impact the understanding of appropriate behaviour in the workplace. Research has pointed to the perceived appropriateness of pauses and small talk during workplace meetings as two interactional dynamics that often highlight difference in intercultural communication (Hua 2014; Spencer-Oatey and Xing 2003). While native English speakers can tolerate approximately three seconds of silent pause in a business meeting discussion, for example, Aboriginal Australians are accustomed to long silences during an interaction. Meanwhile, meetings in Spain often begin with up to half an hour of small talk while meetings in Germany tend to begin without any small talk at all. The normal topics of such small talk also seem to vary across cultures: English colleagues generally stick to "neutral" topics like the weather and general well-being during small talk, but in Taiwan new co-workers might immediately ask each other personal questions about family and finances (Hua 2014, 34–35).

4.4 Intercultural Perspectives of Leisure

Just as perspectives on work can vary from culture to culture, so too can perspectives on a major component of non-work life: leisure. As the following discussion will illustrate, there is no single accepted definition of leisure, despite nearly a century of research on the concept (for reviews of the literature, see Newman et al. 2014; Iso-Ahola 1979). In his analysis of the challenge of defining leisure, Sager (2020, 5) notes that the concept 'describes a state of freedom from necessity', and that 'to be at one's leisure is to be free to pursue activities of value'. While still nebulous, this cautious characterisation offers a starting point for examining the complexity of intercultural perspectives on leisure, a concept both highly subjective and closely shaped by cultural values.

4.4.1 Situating Leisure Within Economic Systems, Social Relations, and Cultural Dynamics

As noted by Régi (2012, 3), leisure is 'embedded in the context of other cultural morals, social rhythms or economic desires'. In many Western cultures, for example, leisure is linked to freedom and seen as a reward for work. As the crucial ingredient of the work-life balance, leisure is often associated in Western cultures with 'the good life' and is thus something to be celebrated (Rojek 2010, 1–2). Western cultures, however, are not uniform in their approaches to leisure. To illustrate but one dimension of divergence, researchers have connected diverse positioning on leisure among Western countries to the ways that different countries' forms of capitalism influence and are influenced by social relations. As argued by Henzler (1992), more socialist European capitalism favours greater concern for the quality of life of a given society and thus accords leisure an important place in social life, while more individualistic American capitalism is more oriented towards the market and thus emphasises work and productivity, thereby minimising the room left for leisure. A concern for the quality of life of one's fellow members of society in European contexts can be seen as linked to an economic system in which citizens pay more taxes, but in return have access to the more varied opportunities for leisure supported by the government: subsidised cultural and performing arts centres (museums, theatres, etc.), subsidised public transportation systems facilitating visits to such centres and to parks, more holiday time, shorter working days, etc. (Gratton and Taylor 2004; Henzler 1992). In the more individualistic, market-oriented United States, meanwhile, an aversion to taxes and government intervention and a prioritisation of productivity and material gain can be seen as associated with shorter holidays left to the discretion of employers, less availability of public transport, longer working hours, etc.

Beyond questions of economic systems and social organisation, the amount of space accorded to leisure in workers' lives can be linked to other dimensions of different peoples' social and cultural dynamics. Schor (1996), for instance, has observed that leisure time has declined while productivity has increased in the United States. Noting that increases in income have not corresponded with decreases in working hours or increases in leisure, she argues that this paradoxical situation reflects the American "cycle of work and spend": unlike in Western Europe, where increases in productivity have led to reductions in working hours, Americans tend to channel increased income into increased consumption (Schor 1996, 12). Whereas leisure time might be more readily seen as the reward for work in Western Europe, Americans may view increased purchasing power as the reward for their longer hours in the office.

4.4.2 Keeping in Mind the Diversity of Perspectives on Leisure

Again, it is important to keep in mind that such observations tend to overgeneralise and essentialise cultures: not every European spends their free time wandering through subsidised art museums, while not every American works 100 hours per week and spends their rare non-work time buying and Instagramming shiny new things. This discussion is not meant to neatly categorise and define cultures and their fixed, shared approaches to leisure; rather, it is meant to highlight divergences in general tendencies with respect to leisure that vary from region to region, country to country, city to city, etc.

Thus far, we have only drawn on Europe and the United States as examples, as non-Western perspectives on leisure have historically gone under-researched (Ito et al. 2014). In recent decades, however, a growing body of literature has highlighted the diversity of positionings on leisure found throughout the non-Western world. In China, for example, the concept of leisure is highly influenced by Taoism and Confucianism. Diverging from the European and American focus on consumption, the Chinese perspective on leisure instead emphasises harmony with nature (Liu et al. 2008). A survey of the Luo ethnic community of Kenya, meanwhile, suggested that they perceived leisure as 'behaviors or activities that give people happiness or bring back or soothe the heart or spirit' (Chick 1998, 117).

4.5 Intercultural Perspectives of Time

Time flies, time will tell, time is money, time is ripe, time heals all wounds, time is running out, time marches on…even just from these clichéd phrases that people use all the time without necessarily thinking about them, it is clear to see that time is something that can be understood from a multitude of perspectives, including cultural ones. Research on globalised management has indeed put forth the notion of 'time visions' to encapsulate the diverse perceptions of the concept 'based on different ethnic and national orientations about time' that develop along multiple dimensions, including continuity, linearity, and chronicity (Saunders et al. 2004, 19–20). To begin to develop a consciousness of the many ways of understanding time, this section discusses three perspectives on time that tend to vary from culture to culture: (1) the strict or relaxed accountability of time; (2) a sequential or synchronic perspective on time; and (3) a focus on the past, present, or future.

4.5.1 Precise Punctuality or Fashionable Lateness? Strict Vs. Relaxed Accountability of Time

Turning to the first perspective, cultures often diverge in how closely or loosely they adhere to schedules, timetables, deadlines, and other fixed points in or durations of time. As a world centre for watchmaking, for example, Switzerland is a country known for its punctuality: the trains generally run precisely on time, as do business meetings. Drive two hours from Geneva across the border into France, however, and you could visit Lyon, a city known to run on its own time: *le quart d'heure lyonnais* ('the Lyonnais fifteen minutes') is often casually invoked to explain or excuse a slight (or not so slight) delay in arrival or start time. The expression 'time is money' is a common one in the United States, meanwhile, where the punctual and effective use of time is a central feature of productivity—and thus of money-making. American lawyers, for instance, tend to bill clients by the quarter or tenth of an hour, thus submitting charts detailing every 15 or 6 minutes of their work, respectively. In the Middle East, meanwhile, the passing of time is often considered less important than the building and maintenance of social relationships: the fact of having a meeting can be seen as more important than adherence to the time at which it was scheduled to start or end. Cultures can, therefore, vary widely in their perspectives on punctuality and the rigidity of schedules, and thus in their willingness to spend (or conversely, waste) time on social relations (Fulmer et al. 2014; Bluedorn 2002).

4.5.2 One at a Time or All at Once? Sequential Vs. Synchronic Perspectives

Taking up the second perspective, Trompenaars and Hampden-Turner (1997, 120) observe that while some cultures perceive time as sequential and thus as 'a series of passing events', others see time as synchronic, 'with past, present, and future all interrelated so that ideas about the future and memories of the past both shape recent action'.

> **Case Study 2: Diverse Perspectives of Time in a Butcher's Shop**
> Trompenaars and Hampden-Turner (1997) illustrate these notions by taking the reader on a visit to two butchers' shops, one in the Netherlands and one in Italy. In the Dutch butcher's shop, the orderly sequence of time and thus of action means that there is a time and place for everything and everyone:
>> In the Netherlands you could be the Queen, but if you are in a butcher's shop with number 46 and you step up for service when number 12 is called, you are still in deep trouble. Nor does it matter if you have an emergency; order is order. [...] the butcher calls a number, unwraps, cuts and rewraps each item the customer wants, and then calls the next number. (Trompenaars and Hampden-Turner 1997, 123–124)

In cultures like that of the Dutch that perceive time as sequential, schedules would be respected, meetings would closely follow agendas, and tasks would be tackled one at a time. In Italy, meanwhile, a more synchronic perspective on time could be observed in a butcher's shop, where the butcher managed several activities at the same time:

> In a butcher's shop in Italy [the authors] once saw the butcher unwrap salami at the request of one customer and then shout 'who else for salami?' The sequential idea is not entirely absent. People still pay in turn when they are finished, but if a customer has all she wants, she might as well pay and leave earlier than someone wanting additional cuts. The method serves more people in less time. (Trompenaars and Hampden-Turner 1997, 123)

In cultures with a more synchronic perception of time like in Italy, multitasking would carry the day, with a less rigid adherence to order and scheduling being seen as a more efficient way of accomplishing tasks.

4.5.3 Look to the Past, Focus on the Present, or Plan for the Future?

To conclude with a discussion of the third perspective, Kluckhohn and Strodtbeck (1961) propose that cultures can be seen as orienting their perception of time towards the past, the present, or the future. A past orientation would draw heavily on past experience to guide the present and would focus on the preservation and maintenance of traditional wisdom. Operating within this perspective, entrepreneurs would be likely to rely on what worked in the past to tackle the challenges of the present. A present-oriented culture, meanwhile, would instead focus on 'the here and now', prioritising spontaneity and in-the-moment experience. Present-oriented business plans would thus likely be geared towards current demands and goals, with relatively short-term horizons for future actions and outcomes. Future-oriented cultures would then invest great importance in planning ahead, working towards long-term goals and benefits even if that entails sacrifice in the present or innovating away from the ways of the past. Enterprises operating within this perspective would frame current action within longer-term plans and objectives.

4.6 Bringing It All Together: Negotiating Intercultural Perspectives on Work, Time, and Leisure in a Business Meeting

While the themes explored in this chapter cover a wide swath of human life and activity, they could all potentially come into play throughout the course of an average day of work. Within the linguistically and culturally diverse workplaces of the globalised economy, there is a strong chance that intercultural perspectives on work, leisure, and time could become relevant in any gathering of people coming together to address a shared objective or work collaboratively on a task. Providing but one possible example of the interplay of these perspectives in the workplace, we will now walk through a hypothetical business meeting between representatives from two advertising firms to illuminate how diverse concepts of work, leisure, and time can enter into even the most mundane activity.

4.6.1 First Things First: When and How to Start the Meeting?

Differing perspectives on time might be evident even before the meeting starts. Say the meeting was scheduled to start at 16h: the question then becomes, who will actually be there at 16h? One firm might be shaped by cultural values that prioritise punctuality and strict adherence to schedules, so their representatives would likely arrive at least a few minutes before 16h to ensure they were on time for the start of the meeting. The other firm, however, might be informed by cultural values that orient more towards a looser adherence to timetables and deadlines that prioritises relationship development over punctuality (see Chapter 3 on task-versus relationship-based trust). Not having wanted to cut short an earlier meeting with a client that ran over schedule, which would have affected their relationship as a basis of their trust, the representatives from this firm might arrive at 16h15 for their next meeting. Such a situation might start the meeting off on the wrong foot if the two firms do not consider the cultural backgrounds of all the parties involved, their task- versus relationship-based approaches to trust, and how their perspectives on time and punctuality might differ.

The beginning of the meeting might then reveal different cultural perspectives on work and what is considered appropriate work behaviour. For the representatives of one firm, it might be customary to begin a meeting with five or ten minutes of small talk to break the ice, get to know each other, and build rapport. For the other firm, however, small talk might be deemed inappropriate or seen as a waste of time (Bubel 2006; Meierkord 2000; Spencer-Oatey 2000). This divergence of positionings on small talk might be further exacerbated by the topics of discussion: for the first firm, it might be completely natural to ask their new business colleagues about their family lives, or how much their bonuses were this year. If the representatives of the second firm are unaware of the cultural acceptance of such topics, they might feel uncomfortable or even off-put because of this line of questioning. Some understanding of the different cultural perspectives on small talk among colleagues might thus be essential for ensuring the smooth progression of the meeting.

4.6.2 Getting Down to Business: Intercultural Perspectives on Drawing Up a Plan

If the two firms' representatives manage to make it past the start of the meeting, different perspectives on time might then complicate their efforts to draft a joint business plan. Say one of the advertising firms is informed by cultural values that orient towards the present: their representatives might then push for a plan for an advertising campaign for a client that draws on the most current pop culture references and maximises short-term profit, aiming to capitalise on the trends of the moment. Moreover, this firm might have a more synchronic perspective on time, and thus want to launch multiple advertising initiatives at the same time. The other firm, however, could be shaped by cultural values that prioritise the future. In this case, the second firm might gravitate towards a less topical advertising campaign that adheres more closely to the long-term development of the client's brand. With an eye on the future benefits of a coherent brand image, this firm would likely be willing to sacrifice the profit potential of jumping on current trends to focus more on long-term objectives. With a more sequential perspective on time, this firm would also likely prefer to focus on one advertising initiative at a time, seeing each one through to completion before starting on the next. Once again, an awareness of diverse cultural orientations towards time would potentially prove crucial for the two firms' collaboration on successfully developing a joint campaign.

4.6.3 All Good Things Must Come to an End…Mustn't They? Wrapping Things Up While Working Interculturally

As it takes some time for the two firms to work through their culturally informed, divergent perspectives on the shape of the campaign, they finally begin making progress right as the clock strikes 18h 30, which is when the meeting was scheduled to end. The question then becomes: Who stays, and who goes? For one firm, productivity might be prioritised over leisure and thus staying past the end of the working day to finish a project is completely normal and may in fact be the norm. In Japan, for instance, a majority of employees work notably long hours. This phenomenon has been attributed to various factors in Japanese society, such as a sense of group awareness that makes people reluctant to leave the office before their boss or co-workers, or an orientation towards input, rather than output, that values the number of hours or years worked and the demonstration of loyalty and commitment to the company (Ono 2018). The representatives of a firm shaped by such cultural values would thus likely assume that the meeting should continue until the details of the campaign have all been hammered out. For the other firm, however, a greater concern for work-life balance might foster a workplace environment in which staying late at the office is not the norm, allowing employees to juggle work and leisure more easily. The representatives of this firm might then be more inclined to schedule a follow-up meeting for another day and go home to their families at the regular hour that evening. Their preference for ending the meeting midway through the planning, however, might then be interpreted as a lack of initiative by the other firm's representatives. To provide but one example, research has highlighted the potential for tension between an emphasis in the Chinese business society on sacrificing one's personal or family time to finish all of the day's tasks, and an appreciation for work-life balance among Indonesian business leaders (Bildstein et al. 2013). Thus, from the start to the finish of this meeting, recognition of divergent intercultural positionings on the concepts of work, leisure, and time emerges as a critical component of efforts to manage collaborative work in the globalised, multicultural workplace.

4.7 Concluding Remarks: Work, Time, and Leisure in the Twenty-First Century

As technological advances and managerial developments continue to evolve, more and more people will encounter new modes of working and diverse perspectives on the meaning of work itself, on the relationship between work and leisure, and on the notion of time that informs these understandings. Adapting to and succeeding in the globalised, increasingly digital and multicultural workplace will require an acute awareness of the potential for divergent viewpoints on how to conduct work and balance it with the rest of life. This chapter has thus introduced and fostered critical reflection about key questions that will only become more essential to navigating professional relationships and practices in the workplaces of the twenty-first century.

Chapter Review Questions

1. In what ways can 'work' and 'leisure' be very challenging concepts to define and delimit?
2. How do collective and individualistic cultural values influence perspectives on work? What other culturally shaped perspectives on work can you think of?
3. How can different cultural perspectives on leisure be linked to different economic models?
4. What are some strengths and weaknesses of sequential and synchronic approaches to time?

5. What kinds of cultural values might impact employees' decisions concerning working hours?

Recommended Further Reading

- Adeclas, J., Hur, T., and Kim, S. 2021. An Exploration of Leisure Motivation as Cultural Practices: A Cross-Cultural Approach. *Leisure Sciences.* Available at: https://doi.org/10.1080/01490400.2021.1985662
- Brislin, R.W. and E. S. Kim. 2003. Cultural Diversity in People's Understanding and Uses of Time. *Applied Psychology: An International Review* 52 (3): 363–382.
- Haugh, M., and V. Sinkeviciute. 2021. The Pragmatics of Initial Interactions: Cross-Cultural and Intercultural Perspectives. *Journal of Pragmatics* 185 (special issue): 35–39.
- Jameson, D.A. 2007. Reconceptualizing Cultural Identity and Its Role in Intercultural Business Communication. *Journal of Business Communication* 44 (3): 199–235.
- Tsaur, S.H., and C.-H. Yen. 2018. Work–Leisure Conflict and Its Consequences: Do Generational Differences Matter? *Tourism Management* 69: 121–131.

References

Aryee, S., V. Luk, A. Leung, and S. Lo. 1999. Role Stressors, Interrole Conflict, and Well-Being: The Moderating Influence of Spousal Support and Coping Behaviors Among Employed Parents in Hong Kong. *Journal of Vocational Behavior* 54 (2): 259–278.
Bildstein, I., S. Guldenberg, and H. Tjitra. 2013. Effective Leadership of Knowledge Workers: Results of an Intercultural Business Study. *Management Research Review* 8: 788–804.
Bluedorn, A.C. 2002. *The Human Organization of Time: Temporal Realities and Experiences.* Stanford: Stanford University Press.
Bubel, C. 2006. ' How Are You?' 'I'm Hot': An Interactive Analysis of Small Talk Sequences in British-German Telephone Sales. In *Beyond Misunderstanding*, ed. K. Bührig and J. D. ten Thije, 245–260. Amsterdam and Philadelphia: John Benjamins.
Chick, G. 1998. Leisure and Culture: Issues for an Anthropology of Leisure. *Leisure Sciences* 20 (2): 111–133.
Fulmer, C.A., B. Crosby, and M. J. Gelfand. 2014. Cross-Cultural Perspectives on Time. In *Time and Work, Vol. 2. How Time Impacts Groups, Organizations and Methodological Choices*, ed. A. J. Shipp and Y. Fried, 53–75. London: Psychology Press.
Gratton, C., and P. Taylor. 2004. The Economics of Work and Leisure. In *Work and Leisure*, ed. J.T. Haworth and A.J. Veal, 85–106. London and New York: Routledge.

Guest, D.E. 2002. Perspectives on the Study of Work-Life Balance. *Social Science Information* 41 (2): 255–279.

Haar, J.M., M. Russo, A. Suñe, and A. Ollier-Malaterre. 2014. Outcomes of Work–Life Balance on Job Satisfaction, Life Satisfaction and Mental Health: A Study Across Seven Cultures. *Journal of Vocational Behavior* 85 (3): 361–373.

Henzler, H.A. 1992. The New Era of Eurocapitalism. *Harvard Business Review* 70 (4): 57–68.

Hofstede, G. 2001. *Culture's Consequences: Comparing Values, Behaviors, Institutions and Organizations Across Nations*, 2nd ed. Thousand Oaks and London: Sage.

Hofstede, G., G.J. Hofstede, and M. Minkov. 2010. *Cultures and Organizations: Software of the Mind*, 3rd ed. New York: McGraw Hill.

Hua, Z. 2014. *Exploring Intercultural Communication: Language in Action*. Oxford and New York: Routledge.

Iso-Ahola, E. 1979. Basic Dimensions of Definitions of Leisure. *Journal of Leisure Research* 11 (1): 28–39.

Ito, E., G.J. Walker, and H. Liang. 2014. A Systematic Review of Non-Western and Cross-Cultural/National Leisure Research. *Journal of Leisure Research* 46 (2): 226–239.

Kelly, J.R. 2012. *Leisure*, 4th ed. Urbana, IL: Sagamore Publishing.

Klein, W. 2009. Concepts of Time. In *The Expression of Time*, ed. W. Klein and P. Li, 5–38. Berlin and New York: Mouton de Gruyter.

Kluckhohn, F.R., and F. Stodtbeck. 1961. *Variations in Value Orientations*. New York: Row, Peterson.

Kyriacou, A.P. 2016. Individualism–Collectivism, Governance and Economic Development. *European Journal of Political Economy* 42: 91–104.

Liu, H., C.K. Yeh, G.E. Chick, and H.C. Zinn. 2008. An Exploration of Meanings of Leisure: A Chinese Perspective. *Leisure Sciences* 3095: 482–488.

Mai, S., S. Ketron, and J. Yang. 2020. How Individualism–Collectivism Influences Consumer Responses to the Sharing Economy: Consociality and Promotional Type. *Psychology & Marketing* 37 (5): 677–688.

Meierkord, C. 2000. Interpreting Successful Lingua Franca Interaction: An Analysis of Non-Native/Non-Native Small Talk Conversations in English. *Linguistik Online* 5 (1). https://doi.org/10.13092/lo.5.1013

Newman, D.B., L. Tay, and E. Diener. 2014. Leisure and Subjective Well-Being: A Model of Psychological Mechanisms as Mediating Factors. *Journal of Happiness Studies* 15: 555–578.

Ono, H. 2018. Why Do the Japanese Work Long Hours? Sociological Perspectives on Long Working Hours in Japan. *Japan Labor Issues* 2 (5): 35–49.

Palumbo, R. 2020. Let Me Go to the Office! An Investigation into the Side Effects of Working from Home on Work-Life Balance. *International Journal of Public Sector Management* 33 (6/7): 771–790.

Piller, I. 2009. Intercultural Communication. In *The Handbook of Business Discourse*, ed. F. Bargiela-Chiappini, 317–329. Edinburgh: Edinburgh University Press.

Pant, B. 2016. Different Cultures See Deadlines Differently. *Harvard Business Review* 23. Available at: https://hbr.org/2016/05/different-cultures-see-deadlines-differently

Power, D., T. Schoenharr, and D. Samson. 2010. The Cultural Characteristic of Individualism/Collectivism: A Comparative Study of Implications for Investment in Operations Between Emerging Asian and Industrialized Western Countries. *Journal of Operations Management* 28 (3): 206–222.

Provis, C. 2009. On the Definition of Work. *Labour and Industry* 20 (2): 123–137.

Purrington, A., and B. Hickerson. 2013. Leisure as a Cross-Cultural Concept. *World Leisure Journal* 55 (2): 125–137.

Régi, T. 2012. Tourism Leisure and Work in an East African Pastoral Society. *Anthropology Today* 28 (5): 3–7.

Rojek, C. 2010. *The Labour of Leisure: The Culture of Free Time*. London, Thousand Oaks, CA, New Delhi, and Singapore: Sage Publications.

Sager, A. 2020. Philosophy of Leisure. In *Routledge Handbook of Leisure Studies*, ed. T. Blackshaw, 5–14. London and New York: Routledge.

Sagiv, L., and S.H. Schwartz. 2007. Cultural Values in Organisations: Insights for Europe. *European Journal of International Management* 1 (3): 176–190.

Saunders, C., C. Van Slyke, and D.R. Vogel. 2004. My Time or Yours? Managing Time Visions in Global Virtual Teams. *The Academy of Management Executive* 18 (1): 19–31.

Schor, J.B. 1996. Work, Time and Leisure in the USA. In *Work, Leisure and the Quality of Life: A Global Perspective*, ed. C. Gratton, 6–21. Sheffield: Leisure Industries Research Centre.

Schwartz, S.H. 1999. A Theory of Cultural Values and Some Implications for Work. *Applied Psychology* 48 (1): 23–47.

Spencer-Oatey, H., ed. 2000. *Culturally Speaking: Managing Rapport through Talk Across Cultures*. London and New York: Continuum.

Spencer-Oatey, H., and J. Xing. 2003. Managing Rapport in Intercultural Business Interactions: A comparison of two Chinese-British welcome meetings. *Journal of Intercultural Studies* 24 (1): 33–46.

Trompenaars, F., and C. Hampden-Turner. 1997. *Riding the Waves of Culture: Understanding Cultural Diversity in Business*. London: Nicholas Brealey Publishing.

Whitrow, G.J. 2003. *What Is Time? The Classic Account of the Nature of Time*. Oxford and New York: Oxford University Press.

Part II
Cross-Cultural Leadership

Chapter 5
Leadership Across Cultures

Daša Grajfoner⊙, Lucy Bolton⊙, and Ke Guek Nee⊙

> What do the following leaders have in common? Barrack Obama, Mother Theresa, Nelson Mandela, Sheryl Sandberg, and Ghandi? They are all recognised across different countries, and through their cross-cultural awareness, they shaped cultures and values. Against the backdrop of globalisation, there is increasing demand for such leaders who are capable of transforming workplace cultures and values. Leaders do not exist on their own, however; leadership is a behaviour. Leaders interact with their environment and their followers, co-creating organisational dynamics and cultures. In this chapter, we discuss research in psychology that demonstrates links between leadership and culture at various levels.

5.1 Psychology of Leadership and Culture

Leadership has been defined in many ways. Despite these many definitions, few key approaches are recognised by most scholars as accurately reflecting what it is to be a leader. Two early approaches to leadership theories are the **Trait Approach-Great Man** theories, focusing on innate qualities and characteristics, and the **Behaviour Approach**, focusing on what leaders do and how they act. But what is psychology of

---

D. Grajfoner (✉) · L. Bolton · K. G. Nee
Heriot-Watt University, Edinburgh, Scotland, UK
e-mail: D@Grajfoner.com

L. Bolton
e-mail: L.Bolton@hw.ac.uk

K. G. Nee
e-mail: G.N.Ke@hw.ac.uk

D. Grajfoner
Faculty of Applied Business and Social Studies, DOBA Business School, Maribor, Slovenia

© The Author(s), under exclusive license to Springer Nature Switzerland AG 2023
K. Strani and K. Pfeiffer (eds.), *Intercultural Issues in the Workplace*,
https://doi.org/10.1007/978-3-031-42320-8_5

leadership and how is it different from the study of leadership? If we define leadership as influencing the behaviour and actions of others, then understanding the psychological processes behind the ability to exercise this influence, and the mechanisms that prompt individuals to follow their leaders, is crucial. We must acknowledge that such influence does not only exist between the leader and the followers, but it is mediated by the context. Social, organisational, and cultural situational factors play a role in effective leadership style (Haslam et al. 2011).

Successful leadership can be defined as the ability to create and facilitate groups of followers that will be motivated for working towards achieving organisational vision and goals. Therefore, the leader is essentially creating a stimulating culture that will bring individuals together in the commitment towards mutually agreed common goals. This is of course conditioned not only by individual leadership behaviours and styles, but also by the psychological makeup of the followers, as well as the context, including culture. A culturally intelligent leader can recognise and identify cultures within the organisation and in a broader social context, and communicates these effectively, at the right time, using the correct channels.

Haslam et al. (2011) identify the factors that influence a leader's capacity or ability to influence others.

- First, **the culture of the leader's group**; this can be a department, a team, an informal group in one or multiple locations.
- Second, the **culture of the organisation** and the type of leadership that is adopted by that institution.
- The third factor influencing leadership effectiveness is workplace **diversity**: how many leaders are men, how many women, how are other minority groups represented in the leadership structure? The focus of psychology of leadership is therefore to understand the "mental glue" that binds leaders and followers together in the pursuit of shared vision or goals.

Looking at the psychology of leadership, we consider both "old" perspectives of leadership and the "new" perspective. The "old" perspectives focus on the individual; they are leader-centric and emphasise a leader's traits and behaviour as the main contributor to effective leadership. The "new" perspective on leadership defines leaders as "one of us." The actions the leader takes are in the interests of the group, and therefore the leader is in fact promoting the group's interests. For this reason, this new psychology of leadership underlines both the identity of the leader and of the group that is being led. Leaders are expected to be actively involved in shaping the identity of the group as well as representing the group's values, ideas, and priorities. Throughout the chapter, we emphasise the importance of the interaction between the leader, followers, and the context, which includes organisation or environment and culture.

Psychology is crucial for our understanding of how leaders and followers function across cultures and how to develop good practices for leadership. Cross-cultural perspectives on leadership contribute to our understanding of how leaders are defined in different cultures, what their desired traits and behaviours are, how leaders perceive themselves and how they are perceived by others. This is particularly important in global workplaces. Organisations today are expecting their leaders to have the skills and competencies for leading global teams, an awareness of cultural differences and the ability to adapt their leadership style and behaviours accordingly.

To examine cross-cultural perspectives on leadership, this chapter refers to one of the largest studies that has researched this topic—GLOBE 2004 (Global Leadership and Organisational Behaviour Effectiveness) founded by Robert House in 1991 (House et al. 2001, 2004). The global quantitative survey study, which ran for ten years, compared leadership traits and behaviours that are desirable in different parts of the world and in different cultures. It utilised a questionnaire to investigate the mechanism underlying leadership behaviours, traits, and skills across cultures. It found that leaders' attributes are closely associated with their cultural values (Javidan and Dastmalchian 2009) and broadened the realm of the desired behaviours of effective leaders. Additionally, the GLOBE CEO Study (House et al. 2014) involving 24 countries, found that leaders' behaviours reinforce organisational outcomes and cultural expectations and that leadership behaviours were an important element for organisational success.

5.2 Leadership Behaviour and Its Learning

The current debate about leadership behaviour and its effects can be illustrated through three classical human learning theories.

5.2.1 *Classical and Operant Conditioning*

In a Psychology context, human behaviour starts with learning. Basic human learning theories have important applications in leaders' work.

Classical (Pavlovian) Conditioning is learning about one's environment. Classical conditioning often occurs unintentionally, as the repeated exposure to a stimulus elicits a response, even if it is unconscious. For example, in an organisation, the windows are washed before senior management is about to pay a visit. Eventually, lower-level employees associate the windows being washed with an upcoming visit from senior management and act accordingly.

Operant Conditioning is learning the outcome of behaviours. These processes involve leaders learning to take or refrain from certain actions in order to avoid undesired outcomes or to bring about desired ones. Reinforcement and punishment both become conditioned to the outcome, that is the consequences of response or behaviour determine the likelihood of it being repeated.

Operant conditioning is popular for organisational performance and varies in different cultures. In collectivist cultures, reward in the form of praise is preferred to be given to the team rather to a particular individual, but the same cannot be said for individualistic cultures, where employees prefer to be praised individually (see Chapter 2). In terms of punishment, status-conscious cultures (in Asian countries, for example) are likely to be motivated to perform better if punished with demotion; however, punishment will likely demotivate employees in different cultures.

5.2.2 Cognitive Behavioural Approach

Given that leaders' behaviours contribute to effectiveness and organisational success, we take a critical look at these behaviours and to their contributing factors. The "Cognitive Behavioural Approach" aims to understand the reasons why individuals assess a particular situation the way they do and how this assessment makes them feel. American Psychologist Aaron T. Beck developed the concept of **Cognitive Behavioural Therapy (CBT)**, which builds on the assumption that thinking processes are influenced by emotional and behaviour responses (Beck 1976). For instance, a leader may experience partial or negative thinking, when confronted with a difficult situation in the workplace. Their thoughts about the situation lead them to experience certain emotions, which, in turn, influence their behaviour and their response to the situation. The triggers for the cycle of reaction lie on "thinking;" the risk of negative thought is explained by numerous types of thinking errors (Bennett-Levy et al. 2004), which can create bias in the leader's thinking. Leaders' thinking patterns associate closely with their core beliefs, and these core beliefs are generated from their cultural context.

5.2.3 Personalities and Traits

Leader personality traits are also an important factor for leadership effectiveness and organisational success. These traits can be defined as individual differences in characteristic patterns of thinking, feeling, and behaving. The most prominent personality framework is the *"Big Five" model*, which consists of: extroversion, agreeableness, conscientiousness, neuroticism, and openness.

- *Extroverted* leaders are sociable, assertive, energetic, and articulate, as opposed to introverted leaders, who are calm, quiet, and thoughtful.
- Leaders with *Agreeable* personality, tend to be altruistic, trusting, modest, humble, kind, and considerate.
- Leaders who are high in *Conscientiousness* are persistent, ambitious, self-disciplined, resourceful, persevering, and hard working.
- *Neuroticism* indicates traits of emotional instability. High neuroticism is associated with being awkward, pessimistic, jealous, fearful, anxious, unconfident, insecure, and oversensitive
- *Openness* can be described as the willingness to listen, accept, and try new methods or ideas. Some basic behaviours for openness are curiosity, creativity, insight, and imagination. For instance, "open" leaders encourage learning, engage in creative marketing strategies, and prefer meeting new people.

5.3 Cultural Perspectives on Leadership

Leadership is strongly influenced by cultural variation. It is therefore important to recognise different cultural perspectives, or "lenses" that influence leadership. The core cultural perspectives are introduced below, with considerations of how these can influence leadership behaviours, approaches, and styles.

5.3.1 Cultural Dimensions

Chapter 2 of this book critically discussed Hofstede's cultural dimensions and suggested more nuanced understandings of culture. Whilst the quantification of culture in this way does not capture cultural diversity within a country, or deviations from a stereotype, and cannot be representative of how a nation behaves, nevertheless the dimensions themselves may be helpful in explaining a behaviour after it has occurred (see Clausen 2007). These cultural dimensions may also reflect societal viewpoints that stabilise norms over long periods of time, consequently impacting leadership across regions. Culture can influence the degree of leadership commitment, morale, and cooperation. This leads to different leadership styles and practices in terms of formality and hierarchy i.e., "Power-Distance" (PD). For example, within a country with high PD, such as Malaysia, a leader is likely to adopt a more autocratic leadership style, engaging infrequently with lower-level employees. Leaders operating within a lower PD culture, however, will place more trust in their subordinates (Hofstede 2001).

5.3.2 Organisational Culture

As we saw in Chapter 2, organisational culture leads to shared meanings between members. These shared meanings are influencing values, regulations, processes, and performance success. Organisations will also be framed by societal cultural values and practices. Organisational practices will be learned through socialisation, being reinforced by leaders in a company. Organisational factors (e.g., industry, size) will influence leadership behaviours in the shape of company values, practices, ethics, and the direction and aims of the company through policies and processes. For example, more flexible leaders may introduce "dress down Fridays." There may also be subcultures within organisations, based on tasks and/or departments.

5.3.3 Individual Personality

Individual personalities are important in understanding the perceptions and manifestations of leadership behaviours. Individuals will be socialised into their own culture, resulting in the internalising of attitudes, thereby shaping their managerial strategies e.g., individual preference to help others, being directive, supportive, or participative (French 2015). This influence will also be based more on individual experiences e.g., upbringing, religion, gender etc. This individual level of analysis varies greatly between leaders and shapes the interactions between "national" and organisational culture. **Personality theory** argues that our individual trait differences are made up of five factors in the "Big Five" model (see Sect. 5.2.3 above): extraversion, agreeableness, conscientiousness, neuroticism, and openness (McCrae and John 1992). For example, individuals high on extraversion tend to show low need for a supportive environment and high workaholism. High levels of conscientiousness, openness to experience, and extraversion are amongst the most prominent of these traits that make an effective leader. Each trait represents a continuum on which individuals can be placed anywhere.

There are likely to be conflicts and interactions between different cultural perspectives, especially with companies now operating internationally across countries. This places increased importance on individual leadership skills, where leaders must appreciate the situational factors, as well as follower expectations and individual differences. An organisation operating in the Middle East is likely to have different values compared to Britain, for example, regardless of the leader's nationality or cultural background.

This integration of cultural factors around environments and individuals results in different memberships and identities, which may result in significant cultural differences within organisations and teams. Individual leaders will need to demonstrate skills and leadership styles to manage these different cultural perspectives effectively.

5.4 Emerging Leadership Styles

In the twenty-first century, leadership research focuses on emerging leadership approaches which emphasis the *process of leadership*. Emerging leaders are collaborative, do great teamwork, and are excellent communicators. These qualities are demonstrated by authentic leadership, spiritual leadership, servant leadership, adaptive leadership, and transformational leadership.

The *contingency model of leadership*, introduced by Fiedler (1964), reflects the reciprocal nature of culture, suggesting that leaders will be more effective when they are able to choose appropriate behaviours and styles *across* situations. This approach emphasises the situational and relationship influences faced by a leader, viewing culture as a contingent factor. Leaders' belief systems will lead them to work independently without collaboration from others (Aktas et al. 2016). Creation of control-oriented organisation may survive through stable business environments; however, this management orientation experiences high-risk operation continuity in globalisation. In global business environments, these leaders and the team are unable to handle rapid changes, where inflexible environments become more turbulent.

With this, we emphasise the importance of *"Learning-Oriented Leadership"* (Schein 2010). This highly effective type of leadership uses the skill of "Humble Inquiry," whereby leaders seek help from employees, are supportive of the learning efforts of others, acknowledging one's own limitations (Schein 2010). Under Learning-Oriented Leadership, leaders must become learners themselves, then recognise and reinforce learning behaviour. Organisational learning directly and positively influences knowledge management. In turn, transformational leadership positively and indirectly influences organisational innovation through organisational learning and knowledge management.

There are a number of contemporary perspectives on leadership that have developed through the lens of culture. One example is *servant* leadership, elements of which have been shown to be important across different cultures. The GLOBE project indicated that what we consider dimensions of servant leadership, such as egalitarianism, moral integrity, empowering, empathy, and humility are often linked to effective and desired style of leadership. For instance, findings indicate that leaders from European cultures strongly relate to egalitarianism and empowering as compared to Asian cultures.[1] Nevertheless, the study supported that leaders from Asian cultures emphasise heavily on empathy and humility as compared to European cultures. GLOBE provided empirical evidence on how a country's culture affects leadership practised. For example, Takahashi et al. (2012) showed that Japanese leadership practices and behaviour have strong roots in Japanese culture and differ from styles practised in the West. The research outcomes of three cross-country CEOs by Gutierrez et al. (2012) revealed that despite different culture contexts, India, China, and Western countries, shared similar leadership competencies, namely results-oriented or achievement-driven, and forward-thinking.

Nonetheless, this research sheds light on the distinctive competencies across these three cultures. In business decisions, Indian CEOs considered national welfare, China CEOs prioritised mutual benefits, and Western CEOs applied interpersonal understanding and talent management (Gutierrez et al. 2012). Based on Chan and Mak's study (2014) on the People's Republic of China, findings indicate that trust in leaders mediated the relationship between servant leadership and subordinates' job satisfaction.

Overall, certain leadership behaviours are likely to be preferred in a given culture, yet some argue that there should be universal structures that leaders must align with in order to be effective, regardless of cultures. The GLOBE study determined six global leadership behaviours: effective leadership behaviours are being charismatic, team-oriented, humane-oriented, participative; and ineffective leadership behaviours are autonomy (in the sense of individualism) and being self-protective. For instance, autonomous leaders reflect independent and individualist leadership. In addition, unsuccessful leader behaviour demonstrates more visionary,

---

[1] The GLOBE project refers to "Asian Cultures" in general and makes rather sweeping distinctions overall. This is one of its many limitations.

Table 5.1 "Effective" and "Successful" leadership behaviours vs personality vs leadership styles vs Hofstede's dimensions

Effective and successful leader behaviours	Personality traits	Leadership styles	Hofstede's dimensions
Team-oriented, Humane-oriented, and Participative = *Trustworthy/ Positive/ Encouraging*	Openness Curious Creative Insightful Imaginative Intellectual Agreeableness Altruistic Trusting Modest Humble Kind Considerate	Authentic Leadership Servant Leadership Spiritual Leadership Adaptive leadership Transformational Leadership Democratic Leadership	Uncertainty-Avoidance Masculinity–Femininity
Charismatic = *Foresighted/ Builds confidence/ Intelligent/ Decisive/Plans ahead*	Conscientiousness Persistent Ambitious Resourceful Persevering Energetic Planner Extroversion Sociable Assertive Socially Energetic Articulate Outgoing	Charismatic Leadership Transformational Leadership Democratic Leadership	Individualism–Collectivism Uncertainty-Avoidance

performance-oriented decisions. To summarise and compare these findings, Table 5.1 illustrates the mapping of leadership behaviours, personality traits, leadership styles against Hofstede's dimensions (Table 5.2).[2]

5.5 Leaders and Groups

Different theories exist on leaders, followers, and groups and how they interact with each other, using insight from social psychology. These are discussed below considering their influence on leadership approach and the management of work groups.

---

[2] Editors' note: The GLOBE research project and the mapping against Hofstede's dimensions are provided here for recognition purposes only and not advocated, in line with the spirit of the volume. Both GLOBE and Hofstede's models have been strongly criticised for their neglect of intra-cultural variations and of the organisational context and culture (see Dorfman 2003). Schnurr et al.'s study of actual workplace practices in Hong Kong questioned "whether it is at all possible to make (general) claims about leadership [...] without acknowledging and differentiating between different professions, industries and workplaces" (2017, 100).

Table 5.2 "Ineffective" and "non-successful" leadership behaviours vs personality vs leadership styles vs Hofstede's dimensions

Ineffective and non-successful leader behaviours	Personality traits	Leadership styles	Hofstede's dimensions
Autonomy = *[Dictatorial/ Ruthless]* Being self-protective = *Egocentric/Non Cooperative/ Nonexplicit*	Neuroticism Awkward Pessimistic Jealous Fearful Anxious Unconfident Insecure Oversensitive	Transactional Leadership Authoritarian Leadership Task-Orientation Style	Power-Distance Long-term–Short-term Orientation Individualism–Collectivism

5.5.1 Social Identity Theory (SIT)

According to **Social Identity Theory (SIT)** (Tajfel and Turner 1992; Turner et al. 1987), an individual's uniqueness projects self-esteem and defines their individual norms. For example, a leader would naturally believe in their own uniqueness and self-identity, including their culture, language, and nationality norms (Banaji and Prentice 1994). An individual's self-identity is likely to influence their leadership style (Ellemers et al. 2004), and how they perceive workplace behaviours by others.

Personal and social identity play a vital role in the formation of **in-groups and out-groups** in the workplace, based on gender, age/life stage, religion, economic background, as well as race, nationality, and ethnicity. An in-group is a social group with which an individual psychologically identifies as being a member; whereas, by contrast, an out-group is a social group with which they do not identify (Tajfel and Turner 1992). Different groups may have distinctive norms, values, and patterns of behaviour to differentiate them from other groups. For example, there are likely to be cultural groups with differing attitudes about authority, communication, and independent working (French 2015).

5.5.2 Prototypical Leadership

One possible way for leaders to boost their self-esteem is by their own personal achievements or affiliation with well-known and groups of individuals with similar attributes (i.e., in-groups). Prototypical leadership occurs when a group perceives the leader as more effective as compared to a non-prototypical leader; a prototype being a set of attributes e.g., attitudes and behaviours (Hogg et al. 2012). Research connecting leadership and groups has supported the view of in-group favouritism and group achievement in boosting self-esteem (Mackie and Smith 2015). In addition, leaders who use negative stereotypes to derogate members of stereotyped groups, or perhaps out-groups, made them feel superior (Fein and Spencer 1997). Consistent with the SIT of leadership, Hogg et al. (2012) highlighted positive associations between prototypical leaders and groups. Research findings show that prototypical leaders generally have more influence over group members and are perceived more positively by them (DeRue and Ashford 2010).

Leader-member exchange (LMX) theory is also important in understanding the formation of in-groups and out-groups. This theory focuses on the relationship between a leader and members of their team, stating that in-group members often receiving more support and attention from the leader as compared to out-group members (Graen 1976; Graen and Cashman 1975). In particular, cultural in-groups and out-groups can determine how people engage with and respect each other, influencing relationships between leaders and their followers, with some followers receiving certain privileges from leaders (Alimo-Metcalfe 2013). For example, in Asian cultural contexts, collectivist leaders are more valued for their connectedness in a group with their personal identity, than an individualist leader with increased independence from the group. Members of the group who identify with a collectivist leader would develop more engaging, trusting relationships with their leader, as compared to those who value individualistic leadership qualities, who may receive less support and one-on-one time with the leader.

5.5.3 Follower Perceptions

Cultural variations in leadership will also influence *perceptions* of what makes a good and effective leader. Research shows that followers determine how culture affects leadership, more so than leaders using their own will. For example, Japanese leaders are *expected* to be humble, which may override a leader's individual personality. On the other hand, where there is high individualism over collectivism, leadership itself would be viewed as an independent characteristic that a person could acquire. It can therefore be useful to consider culture at an aggregate and collective level, beyond a leader's personality and values.

A study by Chen and Kao (2009), for example, found that paternalistic leadership positively affected psychological health within Chinese workers, yet had a negative effect in non-Chinese workers. Therefore, although it is clear that some leadership styles are universally accepted by followers, there are some specific approaches to leadership that would be particularly effective within certain cultures and to followers from specific groups.

Overall, leaders should ensure that they have a positive impact on the organisation, avoiding strengthening in-groups and out-groups and thereby leading to cultural segregation, stereotyping, and discrimination, and generally being detrimental to working relationships (Burns et al. 2013). This can result in social distancing, harassment, bullying, and the risk of physical and psychological health problems in victimised individuals e.g., low self-esteem, depression (Einarsen et al. 2013).

5.5.4 Ethnocentrism, Prejudice, and Discrimination

Stereotyping, due to perceptual selection and over-generalising, can lead to perceptual distortions and bias. This failure to recognise and respect the unique perspectives of others becomes a major barrier to leadership and can lead to discrimination—the negative distinction or exclusion on the basis of the identity of an individual or group (e.g., sex, race, nationality, religion, disability) (Colella et al. 2017). Attitudes emerging from individual differences, such as ethnocentrism, prejudice, or discrimination, will negatively affect work relations, acceptance, and ultimately job satisfaction and performance. Furthermore, trust between leaders and followers would be broken, subsequently impacting altruism and organisational commitment. A cycle is then reinforced as ethnocentrism and prejudice affects how leaders and their values influence their followers, which then becomes strengthened throughout the wider organisational culture. This ultimately prevents us from appreciating each individual and their qualities. A truly effective and skilled leader cannot avoid these issues, as difficult as that may be, especially if they are on the receiving end of ethnocentrism and prejudice behaviours.

For example, a woman in certain countries would not be accepted at a leadership level, hitting the "**glass ceiling**," an invisible barrier which inhibits women's progression due to implicit views of their roles at work (Ryan and Haslam 2006, 2007). As cross-cultural working increases, it is vital for leaders to have a commitment to developing *all* employees, embracing diverse views, challenging exclusion, and thereby allowing multicultural teams to flourish.

5.6 Becoming an Effective Leader Using Executive Coaching

Coaching interventions, based on psychological evidence, can address a variety of issues and can assist with developing desirable leadership skills and competencies. Coaching can help with both leaders' existential and identity-related issues and with practical skills and competencies (Grajfoner et al. 2022). For example, during the coaching process, leaders can identify and modify thinking and behavioural patterns, explore their identity, increase their self-awareness and awareness of others, explore emotional and cultural intelligence, strengthen their vision, goals, and work on communication skills. These interventions can have a significant impact on organisational leadership development and how an organisation manages cultural issues. It comes as no surprise that elements of coaching, like SMART goals (Specific, Measurable, Achievable, Relevant and Time-Bound) or GROW (Goals, Reality, Options, Way forward) model of coaching are widely integrated in organisational leadership structures (Palmer and Whybrow 2007).

Very often in the coaching process, the emphasis is on the one-to-one relationship between the coach and coachee. More recently the inclusion of other relevant elements, followers, and situations, has encouraged the development of a more comprehensive models of leadership and executive coaching, which are based on a variety of leadership theories and coaching frameworks. Sometimes this complexity is referred to as systemic leadership coaching (Lee 2003).

Leadership coaching can broadly be categorised in three areas: (1) Developing self as a leader, (2) Developing others, and (3) Context of leadership, for example environment and situations. The latter is particularly important for identifying and developing effective leaders in culturally diverse organisations. A coach can therefore focus on the leader as an individual, the role of organisation (environment and situation), and the role of followers (team members). These elements are overlaid by relationships, of particular importance when considering cultural component. Consequently, leadership coaching typically involves some aspects of self-awareness, coaching for thinking, behaviour and mood/emotional change, learning, enhancing creativity, individual's capacity to step back, see the bigger picture, and reflect on organisational culture, values, and vision—things that may have been taken for granted.

> **Jasmine: Leadership Coaching**
>
> Jasmine is a female leader at a global organisation, based in Germany, with branches round South and East Asia. She has recently been promoted to a senior position to lead team, consisting of senior managers, predominantly males in Germany and India.
>
> Jasmine has been referred to a coach as she is experiencing high levels of anxiety related to her new leadership role. Since she started, she feels lack of support and initiative from her team, and she also feels that they are not taking her seriously. She believes that men in her new team have difficulties accepting a female leader. This situation has led her to become distrusting towards her team and she is experiencing high levels of anxiety before team meetings. She also feels very irritated by her male team members.
>
> Her goals for coaching are to identity and adopt tools to deal with her anxiety, to understand where her team members are coming from, and to improve the communication with her team and strengthen her leadership position.
>
> How would you approach this situation and how would apply coaching to address the issues Jasmine is facing in her leadership role?
>
> The most important aspect of leadership coaching is to formulate the case, using a coaching tool such as ABCDE (Palmer and Whybrow 2007), based on Cognitive Behavioural Therapy (Beck 1976).
>
> Use Table 5.3 to identify one of your leadership issues or issues that you are experiencing when working in groups. Do a role play with one of your colleagues/peers, ask them to take the role of a coach and go through the ABCD process. Draw a similar table. Once you are done, swap roles.

5 Leadership Across Cultures

Table 5.3 The application of ABCDE model of coaching to leadership coaching case study

Stage of the Model	Coachee's response	Coach's observation/approach
A: Activating event What is the issue, or cause for concern?	Avoiding team meetings and being snappy towards her male team members	
B: Belief What is Jasmine telling herself about this situation? Jasmine explores her believes and thoughts that may influence her avoidance and self-deprecating thoughts	"They think I am an imposter. They do not take me seriously. They do not thin a woman could lead them." "Maybe I am just not equipped for this role, and should quit."	Coach acknowledges there may be some negative thinking patterns and aims to raise Jasmine's awareness of those thoughts and how unhelpful they can be
C: Consequences What are the resulting behaviours, emotions, and physiological reactions?	"I have withdrawn and I am avoiding meeting with my team. I do not trust them, which gives me palpitations every time I have to chair the meeting."	Jasmine is experiencing avoidance behaviours, she is stereotyping her male team members, is experiencing a negative emotions, which let to palpitations. The coach helps her to connect those elements and increase her self-awareness
D: Disputing How could Jasmine dispute her self-believes that affect her thoughts, feelings, and behaviours?	"Maybe I should ask them about what they think about this new set up and how they feel having me a leader. I should also show them that I know my job, that I can do it. As I am not feeling very confident at the moment, I should perhaps take some leadership development courses to help me getting the skills and competencies that I need."	Jasmine is encouraged to look at the situation from different angle and focus on positive aspects of the work that she has done with the team
E: Effective new approach How can Jasmine move forward? What options does she has?	"I can try to get a proper feedback on my role from the team. I am scared, but I should listen to what they have to say. If necessary I can bring in a coach to facilitate this. The coach can also help us with some team building and looking at our goals, regardless of our background and where we are based."	Jasmine is asked to look ahead and the actions she can take to move forward. She is also encouraged to be aware about her thoughts, emotions, and behaviours whilst going through the process. And how can she modify them to achieve those common goals

The next chapter focuses on Intercultural Coaching and its increasingly central role in the workplace.

Chapter Review Questions

1. Do you agree with Haslam et al.'s (2011) factors that influence a leader's capacity or ability to influence others? Why (not)? Can you think of others?
2. Based on behavioural science theories from the field of Psychology, how could leaders encourage their team to enhance individual and team performance?
3. Think about leaders you have experienced in the workplace. How have different cultural perspectives influenced their leadership style? Which aspects of leadership have been the most influential?
4. Think about some strategies that a leader could adopt to reduce bias, prejudice, and favouritism towards followers that they may be inclined to make. Can you identify some potential barriers to these?
5. How would you describe leadership coaching and which situations would you use coaching in an organisation?

Recommended Further Reading

- Ellam-Dyson, V., D. Grajfoner, A. Whybrow, and S. Palmer. 2018. Leadership and Executive Coaching. In *Handbook of Coaching Psychology: A Guide for Practitioners*, 2nd ed., ed. S. Palmer and A. Whybrow, 439–452. London: Routledge.
- Grajfoner, D., C. Rojon, and F. Eshraghian. 2022. Academic Leaders: In-Role Perceptions and Developmental Approaches. *Educational Management Administration & Leadership* 0 (0).
- Gutierrez, B., S.M. Spencer, and G. Zhu. 2012. Thinking Globally, Leading Locally: Chinese, Indian, and Western Leadership. *Cross Cultural Management: An International Journal* 19 (1): 67–89.
- Haslam, S.A., S.D. Reicher, and M.J. Platow. 2011. *The New Psychology of Leadership: Identity, Influence and Power*. Hove: Psychology Press.
- House, R.J., P.W. Dorfman, M. Javidan, P.J. Hanges, and M.F.S. De Luque. 2014. *Strategic Leadership Across Cultures: The GLOBE Study of CEO Leadership Behavior and Effectiveness in 24 Countries*. Thousand Oaks, CA: Sage Publications.
- Javidan, M., and A. Dastmalchian. 2009. Managerial Implications of the GLOBE Project: A Study of 62 Societies. *Asia Pacific Journal of Human Resources* 47 (1): 41–58.

References

Alimo-Metcalfe, B. 2013. A Critical Review of Leadership Theory. In *The Wiley-Blackwell Handbook of the Psychology of Leadership, Change, and Organizational Development*, ed. H.S. Leonard, R. Lewis, A.M. Freedman, and J. Passmore, 13–47. Hoboken, NJ: Wiley.

Aktas, M., M.J. Gelfand, and P.J. Hanges. 2016. Cultural Tightness–Looseness and Perceptions of Effective Leadership. *Journal of Cross-Cultural Psychology* 47 (2): 294–309.

Banaji, M.R., and D.A. Prentice. 1994. The Self in Social Contexts. *Annual Review of Psychology* 45 (1): 297–332.

Beck, A.T. 1976. *Cognitive Therapy and the Emotional Disorders*. New York: Penguin.

Bennett-Levy, J.E., G.E. Butler, M.E. Fennell, A.E. Hackman, M.E. Mueller, and D.E. Westbrook. 2004. *Oxford Guide to Behavioural Experiments in Cognitive Therapy*. Oxford: Oxford University Press.

Burns, G.N., L.M. Kotrba, and D.R. Denison. 2013. Leader-Culture Fit: Aligning Leadership and Corporate Culture. In *The Wiley-Blackwell Handbook of the Psychology of Leadership, Change, and Organizational Development*, ed. H.S. Leonard, R. Lewis, A.M. Freedman, and J. Passmore, 113–128. Hoboken, NJ: Wiley.

Chan, S.C., and W.M. Mak. 2014. The Impact of Servant Leadership and Subordinates' Organizational Tenure on Trust in Leader and Attitudes. *Personnel Review* 43 (2): 272–287.

Chen, H.Y., and H.S.R. Kao. 2009. Chinese Paternalistic Leadership and Non-Chinese Subordinates' Psychological Health. *The International Journal of Human Resource Management* 20 (12): 2533–2546.

Clausen, L. (2007). Corporate Communication Challenges: A "Negotiated" Culture Perspective. *International Journal of Cross Cultural Management* 7 (3): 317–332. https://doi.org/10.1177/1470595807083376.

Colella, A., M. Hebl, and E. King. 2017. One Hundred Years of Discrimination Research in Journal of Applied Psychology: A Sobering Synopsis. *Journal of Applied Psychology* 102 (3): 500–513.

DeRue, D.S., and S.J. Ashford. 2010. Who Will Lead and Who Will Follow? A Social Process of Leadership Identity Construction in Organizations. *The Academy of Management Review* 35 (4): 627–647.

Dorfman, Peter. 2003. International and Cross-Cultural Leadership Research. In *Handbook for International Management Research*, ed. Betty Jane Punnett and Oded Shenkar, 265–355. Ann Arbor: University of Michigan Press.

Einarsen, S., A. Skogstad, and L. Glasø. 2013. When Leaders Are Bullies: Concepts, Antecedents and Consequences. In *The Wiley-Blackwell Handbook of the Psychology of Leadership, Change, and Organizational Development*, ed. H.S. Leonard, R. Lewis, A.M. Freedman, and J. Passmore, 129–153. Hoboken, NJ: Wiley.

Ellam-Dyson, V., D. Grajfoner, A. Whybrow, and S. Palmer. 2018. Leadership and Executive Coaching. In *Handbook of Coaching Psychology: A Guide for Practitioners*, 2nd ed., ed. S. Palmer and A. Whybrow, 439–452. London: Routledge.

Ellemers, N., D. De Gilder, and S.A. Haslam. 2004. Motivating Individuals and Groups at Work: A Social Identity Perspective on Leadership and Group Performance. *Academy of Management Review* 29 (3): 459–478.

Fein, S., and S.J. Spencer. 1997. Prejudice as Self-Image Maintenance: Affirmation the Self Through Derogating Others. *Journal of Personality and Social Psychology* 73 (1): 31–44.

Fiedler, F.E. 1964. A Contingency Model of Leadership Effectiveness. *Journal for Advances in Experimental Social Psychology* 1 (12): 149–190.

French, R. 2015. *Cross-Cultural Management in Work Organisations*. London: Kogan Page.

Graen, G.B. 1976. Role-Making Processes Within Complex Organizations. In *Handbook of Industrial and Organizational Psychology*, ed. M.D. Dunnette, 1201–1245. Chicago: Rand-McNally.

Graen, G.B., and J. Cashman. 1975. A Role-Making Model of Leadership in Formal Organizations: A Developmental Approach. In *Leadership Frontiers*, ed. J.G. Hunt and L.L. Larson, 143–216. Kent, OH: Kent State University Press.

Gutierrez, B., S.M. Spencer, and G. Zhu. 2012. Thinking Globally, Leading Locally: Chinese, Indian, and Western Leadership. *Cross Cultural Management: An International Journal* 19 (1): 67–89.

Haslam, S.A., S.D. Reicher, and M.J. Platow. 2011. *The New Psychology of Leadership: Identity, Influence and Power*. Hove: Psychology Press.

Hofstede, G. 2001. Culture's Recent Consequences: Using Dimension Scores in Theory and Research. *International Journal of Cross-Cultural Management* 1 (1): 11–17.

Hogg, M.A., D. van Knippenberg, and D.E. Rast III. 2012. The Social Identity Theory of Leadership: Theoretical Origins, Research Findings, and Conceptual Developments. *European Review of Social Psychology* 23 (1): 258–304.

House, R.J., P.W. Dorfman, M. Javidan, P.J. Hanges, and M.F.S. De Luque. 2014. *Strategic Leadership Across Cultures: The GLOBE Study of CEO Leadership Behavior and Effectiveness in 24 Countries*. Thousand Oaks, CA: Sage Publications.

House, R., P. Hanges, M. Javidan, P. Dofman, and V. Gupta. 2004. *Culture, Leadership and Organizations*. Thousand Oaks, CA: Sage.

House, R., M. Javidan, and P. Dorfman. 2001. Project GLOBE: An Introduction. *Applied Psychology* 50 (4): 489–505.

Javidan, M., and A. Dastmalchian. 2009. Managerial Implications of the GLOBE Project: A Study of 62 Societies. *Asia Pacific Journal of Human Resources* 47 (1): 41–58.

Lee, G. 2003. *Leadership Coaching: From Personal Insight to Organisational Performance*. Kogan Page Publishers.

McCrae, R.R., and O.P. John. 1992. An Introduction to the Five-Factor Model and Its Applications. *Journal of Personality* 60 (2): 175–215.

Palmer, S., and A. Whybrow, eds. 2007. *Handbook of Coaching Psychology: A Guide for Practitioners*. London: Routledge.

Ryan, M., and A. Haslam. 2006. What Lies Beyond the Glass Ceiling? The Glass Cliff and the Potential Precariousness of Women's Leadership Positions. *Human Resource Management International Digest* 14 (3): 3–5.

Ryan, M.K., and S.A. Haslam. 2007. The Glass Cliff: Exploring the Dynamics Surrounding the Appointment of Women to Precarious Leadership Positions. *Academy of Management Review* 32 (2): 549–572.

Schein, E.H. 2010. *Organizational Culture and Leadership*. San Francisco: Jossey-Bass.

Schnurr, S., A. Chan, J. Loew, and O. Zayts. 2017. Leadership and Culture: When Stereotypes Meet Actual Workplace Practice. In *Challenging Leadership Stereotypes Through Discourse*, ed. C. Ilie and S. Schnurr. https://doi.org/10.1007/978-981-10-4319-2_5.

Smith, E. R., and Mackie, D. M. (2015). Dynamics of Group-Based Emotions: Insights From Intergroup Emotions Theory. *Emotion Review* 7 (4): 349–354. https://doi.org/10.1177/1754073915590614.

Takahashi, K., Ishikawa, J., and Kanai, T. October 2012. Qualitative and quantitative studies of leadership in multinational settings: Meta-analytic and cross-cultural reviews. *Journal of World Business* 47 (4): 530–538. https://doi.org/10.1016/j.jwb.2012.01.006.

Tajfel, H., and J.C. Turner. 1992. "Social Psychology of Intergroup Relations" Qualitative and Quantitative Studies of Leadership in Multinational Settings: Meta-Analytic and Cross-Cultural Reviews. *Journal of World Business* 47 (4): 530–538.

Turner, J.C., M.A. Hogg, P.J. Oakes, S.D. Reicher, and M.S. Wetherell. 1987. *Rediscovering the Social Group: A Self-Categorization Theory*. Oxford: Basil Blackwell.

Chapter 6
Intercultural Coaching

Silvia King⬤, Daša Grajfoner⬤, Lucy Bolton⬤, and Ke Guek Nee⬤

> Intercultural coaching can help address many of the cultural challenges that emerge in the workplace. It does so by virtue of the coaching process as well as the unique skillset required for coaching. Culture can be the focus of coaching conversations, yet it also informs the process. Given the level of complexity, coaches require broad expertise as well as high levels of intercultural sensitivity and literacy to be effective. In this chapter, we introduce coaching and coaching psychology in the workplace, discuss relevant coaching models and tools and explore ways in which you can develop your own intercultural coaching skills.

6.1 Introduction

Workplaces across the globe are complex systems with visible and invisible hierarchies, interdependent processes and structures that intend to allow organisations to function. The people in the workplace need to navigate these internal systems but also interact with the world outside, like their clients and customers. However, increasingly remote and distributed teams in global organisations add an external dimension

---

S. King (✉) · D. Grajfoner · L. Bolton · K. G. Nee
Heriot-Watt University, Edinburgh, Scotland, UK
e-mail: sk2091@hw.ac.uk

D. Grajfoner
e-mail: d@grajfoner.com

L. Bolton
e-mail: L.Bolton@hw.ac.uk

K. G. Nee
e-mail: G.N.Ke@hw.ac.uk

© The Author(s), under exclusive license to Springer Nature Switzerland AG 2023
K. Strani and K. Pfeiffer (eds.), *Intercultural Issues in the Workplace*,
https://doi.org/10.1007/978-3-031-42320-8_6

to what were traditionally internal structures. Effective communication, trust between individuals and skilled, inspiring leaders are integral parts of successful organisations and functioning workplaces. Yet sometimes, communication can break down, trust can be damaged, leaders may be derailed or employees may struggle. Coaching is a process that can support individuals and teams in intercultural workplaces to prevent, address and reduce such workplace challenges.

In this chapter, we will first explore what coaching and coaching psychology (CP) are, the role they play in the workplace and the role of culture in coaching. Second, we introduce coaching-related theories, models and frameworks that incorporate cultural aspects and consider how they may influence expectations from and efficacy of coaching in the workplace. Third, we will share some practical tools that may be useful in intercultural coaching.

CP is an applied psychological science; thus, we aim to make this chapter practical with questions that invite you to reflect on your reading as well as case studies to illustrate practical intercultural coaching challenges.

6.2 What Are Coaching and Coaching Psychology?

Coaching is often defined as a process that offers support to an individual, which is performance-focused and goal-centred resulting in action (Law et al. 2007). CP on the other hand is a scientific study of behaviour, cognition and emotion within coaching practice (Grant 2008; Passmore et al. 2010) with the purpose of enhancing well-being and performance in personal life and work domains, underpinned by models of coaching (Grajfoner 2020). Those models are grounded in either established adult learning theories or different schools of thought in psychology (Palmer and Whybrow 2019). Although this chapter focuses on the distinction between coaching and CP, and in most part uses coaching to denominate both terms, it is informative to highlight that there is a wider discussion around this issue (Passmore and Lai 2019). Being a coach is clearly distinguished from being a mentor. Both coaching and mentoring are seen as being learner-centred and driven, but a mentor is predominantly a critical friend who oversees the development of another (Hay 1999). These pragmatic definitions are not merely pedantry, as they instead enable both coaching and mentoring to interact with relevant psychological theory, particularly in respect to learning and development.

A coach works with individuals called coachees and organisations as clients on what is possible, using imagination, vision and motivation as resources; looks for bridges to the future; connects what *is* to what *might be*; links inner purpose to outer work; inspires others to be more effective as leaders, teams and networkers; models the way ahead and trains coachees towards that model. Additional roles of coaches include:

- guiding clients to high performance and optimal quality of life, questioning the status quo and seeking creative, transformative results,

- advocating, criticising and extending corporate culture and wisdom and fostering emerging scenarios with a long view and a short action plan,
- endorsing and sponsoring others without having power of control over them,
- facilitating professional development and organisational systems development,
- supporting clients and organisations through necessary transitions, encouraging networking through alliances and linkages with common goals and acting as a catalyst for renewal and resilience,
- motivating, seeking deeper results, exploring new directions, innovating and investing in the future,
- helping identify key social roles and promoting successful performance in all of these within a balanced daily schedule,
- facilitating change in a person or organisation by clarifying values, beliefs and purpose in personal and work lives,
- locating any emergent developmental challenges that might exist, and inventing vital learning agendas for clients, when these seem appropriate (Palmer and Whybrow 2019).

6.3 The Role of Coaching in the Workplace

Workplace coaching as a learning and development intervention for leaders, employees and teams, has become increasingly popular since its beginnings in the 1980s and with executive or leadership coaching in the 1990s. Executive coaching has been defined as a formal one-on-one intervention with the targeted aim to help executives develop purposeful, positive change in their leadership behaviours and to support their personal development (Athanasopoulou and Dopson 2018; Grant 2012). Benefits of executive coaching include the coachee having a clearer understanding of their own style, improved communication and engagement skills and more effective stress management strategies (e.g., Grant et al. 2009; McCarthy and Milner 2013). Challenges include leaders finding time for the coaching sessions and the expense of such interventions (Dagley 2006).

John Whitmore became renowned as the initiator of the modern coaching movement and as a co-creator of one of the most-used coaching models globally, the GROW model (Whitmore 1992, 2017). GROW stands for Goals, Reality, Options and Way Forward, and provides a four-stage, sequential coaching model. Its flexible and user-friendly nature promoted its popularity beyond the business coaching world.

Initially, coaching was organised and paid for by the sponsoring organisation and was exclusive to *individuals at the top*: leaders and executives who are expected to develop not only themselves, but also those they lead and closely work and engage with. As workplace coaching began to develop, more targeted coaching solutions were offered, such as skills coaching to address a specific skills deficit of the coachee, or development coaching and career coaching to support a person's professional and career development, amongst others. Today, coaching is typically offered across all organisational hierarchies, though still mostly in the Western world; however, this is changing.

A more recent shift is away from coaching by coaches towards "*managers as coaches*". Underlying this trend is a realisation that trusting relationships are at the core of both the coaching process and leadership, with extra care required as managers form dual relationships with their subordinates. "Managers as coaches" are trained and equipped with similar levels of coaching skills as coaches, like listening, perception, providing feedback and supportive encouragement of those they lead through transparent communication. Until more research is available to understand the "manager as coach" practice across regions and cultures, insights from general coaching practice (see Sect. 6.4.3) need to be applied here. Nevertheless, in multicultural environments, additional skills that "managers as coaches" require are cultural awareness and emotional intelligence (see Sect. 6.5.2) to heighten the quality of their intercultural working relationships and leadership.

Coaching can also include entire teams instead of individuals. *Team coaching* involves initiating and facilitating team discussions focused on improving skill development (e.g., cross-cultural communication) and team processes, increasing individuals' self-awareness and appreciation of others; it has also been found to enhance innovation effectiveness and performance through team learning. Team coaching, for example across geographic locations or departments, can help to break down silos between different parts of an organisation, enhance team functionality and maturity whilst team goals are understood at the team instead of individual level. With globally dispersed teams becoming the norm, intercultural team coaching is likely to gain more relevance.

6.3.1 The Role of Culture in Coaching

In this chapter, we understand culture as the "generally accepted beliefs, conventions, customs, social norms and behaviours" of a group with which an individual self-identifies (van Nieuwerburgh 2016, 450). So, culture can be any group with any combination of characteristics, which can defy generalisation or (national) stereotyping. Because coaching is a relational, social process driven by the coachee, coaching offers, by definition, opportunities to overcome stereotyping or biases and focus on the whole individual in their diversity of personal, cultural and biological characteristics instead. Culture can feature in coaching and CP in two ways: as the object of and an influence on coaching.

6.3.1.1 Culture as the Object of Coaching

Culture can be the object of a coaching process when cultural aspects play a role in achieving the coachee goal and enhance the organisation on systemic levels. For example, a company creates a project team with experts from across the organisation (i.e., different locations and departments) who face communication challenges; or a manager hires a new team member who seems to struggle to blend into the team culture. Part of the coaching process may then be to develop an understanding for cultural differences and ways to adapt, as illustrated in Case Study 1.

> **Case Study 1**
>
> A North American, highly skilled, subject expert came to coaching when he struggled to replicate his previous success in Asia. As a quick thinker and problem-solver, his role in a global organisation was to pull together rapid-response teams from across the company and lead the development of bespoke client solutions. Since both time and quality were of the essence, he tended to push other team members on deadlines and expected high-quality contributions from everyone. Given time pressure, he didn't waste time on the relationship with colleagues and focused on tasks. His communication was clear and direct. Because of his excellent results with clients, he was transferred to China to replicate the success there but struggled. Based on internal 360° feedback and a personality profile, he understood where the problems might be. His coaching goal was to develop strategies to help him address the identified challenges and bring his career back on track.
> What do you think may have been the biggest challenges for this person based on what you know so far?
>
> During coaching it emerged, that his communication style and task focus had been an issue already in North America, resulting in relationship and trust challenges with some colleagues. The transfer to China brought the challenges from his personality into sharper contrast where he was perceived as rude and impatient. Since addressing communication could show the most immediate effect for the coachee, the sessions focused on this area first. Later, the sessions explored ways to build relationships and trust longer-term.
>
> Taking a cognitive-behavioural coaching (CBC; Palmer and Szymanska 2008) approach, the coach followed an ABCDE structure: First, **A**ctivating events (i.e., the situations where communication had gone wrong) were identified. Second, the coachee explored his **B**eliefs (i.e., thoughts and beliefs around these situations) and third, the **C**onsequences (e.g., resulting emotions or behaviours). Fourth, in conversation, the coachee **D**isputed his beliefs around the topic. Lastly, alternative perspectives emerged that allowed the coachee to develop **E**ffective new approaches (e.g., trying out different behaviours and ways to communicate). Between sessions, the coachee kept a journal to check when, if and how these strategies worked. In the following session, these behavioural strategies could then be refined, or better fitting ones developed.
>
> For example, to build trusting relationships with colleagues, the belief of relationships being a waste of time was disputed. The coachee understood that respectful relationships that respected hierarchy and maintained harmony in the

> group were important for his Asian colleagues and that, in turn, relationships were important for him to succeed in his role. Time management and agenda setting strategies were explored to deliberately create time for relationship building. As an immediate change, the coachee added time at the start of meetings for this purpose.

6.3.1.2 Culture as Influence on Coaching

CP and coaching practice have their roots mainly in Europe and North America. Psychology and related disciplines, like counselling, have recognised the need for the inclusion of cultural considerations, by creating the field of cross-cultural psychology or through practitioner guidelines, for example by the American Psychological Association or the European Mentoring and Coaching Council. However, different views exist on whether the goal should be to create a single, universal psychology and guidelines for everyone on the planet or if we may need different "psychologies" for different groups or parts of the world. The latter has led to the exploration of so-called indigenous psychologies (Adair 2006) that draw on culture-specific values, norms and indigenous forms of coaching traditions (see Sect. 6.4.3). The next section will take a closer look at these and some "universal" cross-cultural coaching frameworks.

6.4 Cultural Frameworks and Perspectives for Coaching

A variety of terms are used to describe culturally influenced encounters, specifically cross-cultural, intercultural and multicultural (see Glossary). Despite their differences, these terms are often used synonymously in coaching literature, beginning with cross-cultural coaching (CCC). This term first gained wider recognition with Rosinski's book *Coaching across Cultures* (2003), yet no single definition has emerged. Instead, related terminologies have been introduced that share with CCC the common concern of a cross-cultural element in the coaching object and/or an intercultural facet in the coaching relationship, like interculturally-sensitive coaching (van Nieuwerburgh 2016), global coaching (Rosinski 2010) or intercultural coaching (Rosinski and Abbot 2010). In this chapter, we use these terms synonymously due to their underlying commonalities.

6.4.1 Bennett's Model Applied to Coaching and Coach Development

Coachees with cultural challenges in the workplace are likely to seek ways to develop cross-cultural competence. Yet, intercultural coaches will need to develop their own intercultural sensitivity and skill first before they can support their coaching clients in this. Such a developmental coaching process may start—for both—at different levels of intercultural sensitivity.

As seen in Chapter 3, Milton Bennett created and repeatedly updated a developmental model for intercultural sensitivity, defined as the "ability to have (a) more complex personal experience of otherness" (Bennett 2017, 2). Key to the development of this intercultural competence according to Bennett is learning and creation of meaning through perception/experience, communication and language. A connected concept is that of cultural literacy (Wilson 1974) which originally described an understanding of a person's own culture as well as an "ability to work effectively with people who are culturally different and to demonstrate the skills this requires" (p. 86). A recent literature review (Shliakhovchuk 2021) revisited the construct in its original sense in business contexts and identified unclear delineations to other constructs, like cultural intelligence (CQ) or intercultural competence and literacy. Nevertheless, the review suggests a set of competencies and skills for a global, multicultural workforce that correspond with other culture frameworks which are subsumed under an updated cultural literacy model (Shliakhovchuk 2021, 242):

- cultural mindfulness (cultural self-awareness + local cultural awareness + intercultural sensitivity + empathy),
- critical thinking,
- curiosity,
- being a change agent leader/influencer (includes patience).

Whilst only one example, Bennett's and the cultural literacy models suggest that the intercultural coaching process may involve a variety of different skill and competence developments for the coachee, depending on their starting point from ethnocentric to ethnorelative perspectives. It also gives an indication of what types of coaching competencies coaches may need to develop in themselves for successful intercultural coaching. Last but not least, such capabilities may also support intercultural researchers in their endeavour to identify and potentially mitigate biases stemming from cultural influences on the research. In Sect. 6.5 of this chapter, we will look at tools that can help us develop and work with these competencies.

6.4.2 Intercultural Coaching Across Contexts

Several CCC models have been proposed to support intercultural coaches, such as Plaister-Ten's (2013) Cross-Cultural Coaching Kaleidoscope, a three-stage model that views the coaching relationship as an adaptive system of factors that together form culture, or Passmore and Law's (2009) Universal Integrated Framework, a five dimensions model which seeks to integrate a range of coaching models and includes, as one dimension, cross-cultural emotional intelligence, consisting of the four competencies of EQ.

Rosinski (2003, 2010) developed the Coaching Across Cultures model, which includes the Cultural Orientations Framework (COF) and assessment. Similar to Hofstede but more granular, the COF provides a set of 17 cultural dimensions that aim to offer coach and coachee a language to discuss cultural challenges and an assessment for the coachee to situate themselves within their cultural environment. Whilst these models take a more universal view in that they may be adaptable to many cultural contexts and approaches, the onus to apply the tool in a culturally appropriate manner lies with the coach.

6.4.3 Indigenous Coaching Approaches

Indigenous psychology (IP) generally tends to involve "obtaining a descriptive understanding of human functioning in cultural context" through the study of "knowledge, skills, and beliefs people have about themselves and how they function in their familial, social, cultural, and ecological context" (Kim et al. 2006, 4). Several IPs exist along different culture lines, for example CP for coaching, or Islamic psychology with the integration of Muslim perspectives into psychology (e.g., Rothman and Coyle 2018).

Coaching and CP-specific research outside North America and Europe is very limited, thus restricting the conclusions that can be drawn for intercultural coaching. Whilst no specific coaching IPs appear to have developed, cultural coaching-like traditions have been highlighted and some coaching models developed. One commonality across Asia and the Middle East appears to be more mentoring-like relationships between a coach, guide, teacher or mentor who imparts knowledge to a pupil, mentee or coachee (King et al. 2021).

In the Middle East, for example, informal mentoring-type relationships have been described in society as well as in organisations, including, for example, role-modelling in career development and therapy. Coachees seem to expect that coaches teach and direct them (Dodds and Grajfoner 2018), and may not distinguish between mentoring, role-modelling, teaching and coaching. Instead, they may expect coaches to fulfil all these roles (King and van Nieuwerburgh 2020). In Malaysia, coaching has seen rapid growth in the past 15 years, driven by the support from government-linked agencies. Coaching training providers, associated with global industry bodies like the International Coaching Federation, have sprung up alongside national coaching associations (e.g., the Malaysian Association of Certified Coaches). Research, for example on how to enhance leadership capabilities through executive coaching for organisational performance (Gan and Chong 2015), is emerging alongside.

Coaching has established itself in China, for example in HR as a development approach, as a peer coaching process for customer support teams or as executive coaching. Coaches are expected to possess intercultural leadership coaching skills and high sensitivity to cultural issues. Women's contributions to senior management are highly valued, and many Chinese female top executives receive formal coaching to further develop their careers. In Thailand, creating a coaching atmosphere in small and medium-sized enterprises is one example of empirical-based coaching practices for talent development and business performance that were observed. In India, modern adaptations of the *guru* (teacher) and *shishya* (pupil) tradition into a mentor–mentee dyad in management contexts have been proposed as a basis for coaching in national cultural contexts (Raina 2002).

In Africa, the paradigm of *Ubuntu* has found increasingly formal integration into coaching practice, training and research (Geber and Keane 2013). Ubuntu is often translated as "I am because you are" and could be said to reflect a value system that is systemic, collective and humanistic. Similar to traditions in Asia or the Middle East, Ubuntu recognises hierarchies and collective ownership of outcomes, for example, which may influence expected coaching behaviours as well as the coaching process. In the next section, we will explore ways to coach in such diverse culture and value systems.

6.5 Coaching with Intercultural Sensitivity and Skill

When coaching interculturally, we may need to understand what is happening in us and our coachees when we encounter "difference" in verbal or non-verbal behaviour. Culture appears to shape our psychology and behaviour and activate brain processes and interpretations of social interactions, which may trigger biases and negative emotions. Some coaching tools can be especially helpful to address such challenges, for coach, coachee as well as researcher. They also correspond with competencies for cultural literacy and intercultural sensitivity mentioned earlier, and further support the establishment of trust. By recognising the importance of creating a trusting coach–coachee relationship from the outset of the process, individuals will be more motivated to use such coaching tools to reduce bias that can lead to judgement.

6.5.1 Cultural Intelligence

Cultural intelligence (CQ) describes the capability to function effectively in various intercultural contexts and appears correlated to cultural adaptability, performance, lower emotional exhaustion, better relationships and leadership outcomes. Since its initial introduction, other categorisations under the term CQ and related concepts (see cultural literacy above) have emerged which also aim to capture the many qualities that enable such effective intercultural functioning. This indicates that coaches have a broad field to work in, depending on where the particular challenges for the coachee may be. It also suggests that intercultural coaches may need high levels of CQ themselves, including self-awareness, to identify the cultural elements at play in a particular context as well as a broad toolkit to choose the appropriate approach for the coachee, and to apply it in a culturally sensitive manner to establish trust.

6.5.2 Emotional Intelligence and Mindfulness

Emotional intelligence (EI/EQ) describes an individual's ability to perceive, use, understand and manage emotions, in the self and others (Goleman 1995; Salovey and Mayer 1990). Due to the complex emotional responses that cross-cultural encounters may produce, EQ can play an important role for intercultural communication and interaction. Mindfulness and self-awareness in coaches can support EQ. Introduced by Jon Kabat-Zinn (2003), mindfulness describes a state of complete focus on the experience in the moment in an open and non-judgemental manner. This experience can include emotions and thoughts.

When using EQ cross-culturally, more recent research in neuroscience suggests that contrary to traditional suggestions of universal emotional expressions, the facial expressions relating to different emotions can vary across cultures (Barrett et al. 2019). EQ therefore may require the parallel development of intercultural sensitivity and cultural literacy through exposure to other cultures plus contextual awareness.

6.5.3 Systemic Coaching

As we saw in Sect. 6.4.3, some cultures may take a more systemic, collectivist view of the person, for example in Ubuntu. Thus, systemic coaching (Whittington 2012) may offer a helpful addition by visualising patterns, hidden dynamics and relationship elements through *relational maps*. These maps are created by coachees through placement of objects on a surface. Coaches act only as facilitators, for example by asking questions about distance between or sizes of objects. Apart from allowing insights for the coachee, system maps also create the basis for the exploration of culture-specific meanings or interpretations that may be relevant.

A theoretical framework that incorporates such a systemic perspective is the Ershad coaching framework for coaching in Islamic contexts (van Nieuwerburgh and Allaho 2017). At its centre lies the GROW-like alignment wheel, which encourages the coachee to explore their goals, options, realities and way forward in the context of their (religious) beliefs, the self, their life and the people in their life. Whilst designed for use within Islamic contexts, the framework can be suitable for other cultural contexts too.

In the following case study, we describe a coaching scenario from the Middle East and how some of the coaching tools described have been used. It crosses several cultural challenges, and we would like to encourage you to see beyond nationalities, religious or gender stereotypes.

> **Case Study 2**
>
> A Lebanese team leader, based in the Gulf Cooperation Council region, came to coaching because she struggled to reach her potential, as perceived by her managers, and get promoted. She worked in an international company with activities across the wider Middle East and team members from several Arab countries. Her initial coaching goal was to control her emotions better and improve her communication with superiors, especially about her achievements.
>
> The first session served to better understand the goals and specific challenges she faced. The picture that emerged was of a well-qualified, experienced professional who successfully interacts with clients and her team. She seemed to place great emphasis on empowering her team members to learn, shine and get recognition from "above".
>
> During the pandemic, she made a big effort to keep her team motivated and maintain performance. However, she felt that her superiors did not listen when she asked for more resources for her team or recognition of their achievements. As her frustration and mistrust increased, this turned into an "us vs them" mentality. She tried different ways to make the manager listen. Yet the more she tried, the more unresponsive the manager appeared to get. She hoped coaching might help address her high levels of frustration and find ways to get heard "above".
>
> We began the coaching sessions with her emotions, including finding names for the emotions she felt towards the various parties. This served to create emotional literacy. As an educational element, the coach provided clarification around what EQ is (not), specifically with an apparent coachee misconception that suppressing/controlling her emotions would be the solution. Mindfulness practice, something the coachee had been introduced to through corporate training, was integrated in the between-session activities to assist her emotional awareness development.
>
> As a next step, a CBC approach was added to move from mindfully recognising emotions in a situation to exploring her thoughts and beliefs in the moment, her behaviours and the consequences. This brought to light beliefs around social norms, values and acceptable behaviours, both with respect to national cultures, gender roles and managerial culture. When exploring her norms and actions from her manager's perspective, she was able to develop different perspectives on how her emotions and actions may be perceived or how the manager's interpretation of her role as a team leader may differ. This more granular perspective allowed for a level of cultural literacy and acceptance of difference between her and her manager as individuals (stage 4 of Bennett's model). In addition, she was able to recognise a common challenge of middle managers like her around the globe who find themselves sandwiched

between their team's needs "on the ground" and the strategic demands of senior managers "up there".

Moving towards adaptation (stage 5) included finding ways to adapt to the different cultures of her team and her manager. A conversation emerged around her protective, caring and nurturing (gender) role that came out towards her team and how to reconcile this with her more strategic, corporate leadership role in a way that allowed her to remain authentic. Practising mindfulness and EQ enabled her to manage hers and her manager's emotions better. Specifically, with her new emotional literacy, she was able to recognise and, if appropriate, express emotions more constructively.

6.6 Conclusion

With the increase in global, dispersed teams, intercultural coaching can help address many of the cultural challenges at all levels of an organisation. Moreover, coaching skills and the coaching process can equip individuals and teams with the capabilities for effective cultural interactions. Whilst more research is needed to better understand specific cultural coaching expectations and leverage the many diverse perspectives on coaching for a richer intercultural coaching experience for all, coaching with the development of intercultural sensitivity and cultural literacy in mind may lead to more harmonious and trusting working relationships.

Chapter Review Questions

1. Think of a time in your life when you needed to make an important decision. Maybe you had to decide which subject to study or whether to move abroad for study or work:

    – Was there someone who helped you find a way forward?
    – What did they do or say that really helped you?
    – How was their role similar or different to that of a coach?

2. In Chapter 5, you read a case study on leadership coaching. In this chapter we looked at coaching at all hierarchy levels:

    – How might coaching need to be different for people at different hierarchy levels of an organisation (e.g., coaching topics and goals)?
    – How might cultural context impact your answer?

3. Thinking about multicultural teams and the various coaching tools we introduced:

- Which type of workplace coaching might you use?
- Can you think of a coaching tool that may be especially useful with a multicultural team?

4. Think of a situation where you interacted with someone from a different culture to yours (please think beyond nationality here):

    - Did you approach the interaction from your own cultural perspective (ethnocentric) or did you consider both perspectives (ethnorelative)?
    - If you were to coach yourself, what would you do to move to the next stage of Bennett's model?
    - At which stage of Bennett's model may a coach need to be to integrate indigenous approaches, traditions or value systems in their coaching practice?

5. Coaching and CP research is crucial for successful intercultural coaching. Considering what you read in this chapter:

    - If you had to coach a cross-cultural researcher, what cultural skills may be particularly relevant for your coachee?
    - How will you consider the author's cultural perspective, next time you read a paper on coaching or CP?

Recommended Further Reading

- Abbott, G.N., and R. Salomaa. 2016. Cross-Cultural Coaching: An Emerging Practice. In *The Sage Handbook of Coaching*, ed. T. Bachkirova, G. Spence, and D. Drake, 453–469. Loas Angeles, CA: Sage.
- Al-Sadik-Lowinski, B., and R. Kattenbach. 2019. Female Career Coaching for a Multinational Company in China. In *Management Practices in Asia*, ed. C. Prange and R. Kattenbach, 239–252. Cham: Springer.
- Bennett, M.J. 2017. Developmental Model of Intercultural Sensitivity. In *International Encyclopedia of Intercultural Communication*, ed. Y.Y. Kim, 1–10. Hoboken, NJ: Wiley.
- Dodds, G., and D. Grajfoner. 2018. Executive Coaching and National Culture in the United Arab Emirates: An Interpretative Phenomenological Analysis. *International Coaching Psychology Review* 13 (1): 89–105.
- King, S., C. van Nieuwerburgh, L. Bolton, A. al Serkal, L. el Assaad, and M. Mattar. 2021. Exploring the Need for an Indigenous Coaching Psychology for the Middle East: A Panel Discussion at the International Psychology Conference Dubai (IPCD). *The Coaching Psychologist* 17 (1): 32–37.

References

Adair, J.G. 2006. Creating Indigenous Psychologies: Insights from Empirical Social Studies of the Science of Psychology. In *Indigenous and Cultural Psychology: Understanding People in Context*, ed. U. Kim, K.-S. Yang, and K.-K. Hwang, 467–487. New York: Springer.

Athanasopoulou, A., and S. Dopson. 2018. A Systematic Review of Executive Coaching Outcomes: Is It the Journey or the Destination That Matters the Most? *The Leadership Quarterly* 29 (1): 70–88. https://doi.org/10.1016/J.LEAQUA.2017.11.004.

Barrett, L.F., R. Adolphs, S. Marsella, A.M. Martinez, and S.D. Pollak. 2019. Emotional Expressions Reconsidered: Challenges to Inferring Emotion From Human Facial Movements. *Psychological Science in the Public Interest* 20 (1): 1–68. https://doi.org/10.1177/1529100619832930/FORMAT/EPUB.

Bennett, M.J. 2017. Developmental Model of Intercultural Sensitivity. In *International Encyclopedia of Intercultural Communication*, ed. Y. Young Kim and K.L. McKay-Semmler, 1–10. Medford, MA: Wiley. https://doi.org/10.1002/9781118783665.ieicc0182.

Dagley, G. 2006. Human Resources Professionals' Perceptions of Executive Coaching: Efficacy, Benefits and Return on Investment. *International Coaching Psychology Review* 1 (2): 34–45.

Dodds, G., and D. Grajfoner. 2018. Executive Coaching and National Culture in the United Arab Emirates: An Interpretative Phenomenological Analysis. *International Coaching Psychology Review* 13 (1): 89–105. Available at: http://search.ebscohost.com/login.aspx?direct=true&db=a9h&AN=128141453&site=ehost-live.

Gan, G.C., and C.W. Chong. 2015. Coaching Relationship in Executive Coaching: A Malaysian Study. *Journal of Management Development* 34 (4): 476–493. https://doi.org/10.1108/JMD-08-2013-0104/FULL/XML.

Geber, H., and M. Keane. 2013. Extending the Worldview of Coaching Research and Practice in Southern Africa: The Concept of Ubuntu. *International Journal of Evidence Based Coaching and Mentoring* 11 (2): 8–18.

Goleman, D. 1995. *Emotional Intelligence: Why It Can Matter More Than IQ*. New York: Bantam Books.

Grajfoner, D. 2020. Coaching and Coaching Psychology in the Workplace: Analytical Perspectives and Development in Theory and Practice. *KAIROS—Slovenian Journal of Psychotherapy* 14 (1/2): 11–27.

Grant, A.M. 2008. Past, Present and Future: The Evolution of Professional Coaching and Coaching Psychology. In *Handbook of Coaching Psychology: A Guide for Practitioners*, ed. S. Palmer and A. Whybrow, 23–39. London: Routledge.

Grant, A.M. 2012. An Integrated Model of Goal-Focused Coaching: An Evidence-Based Framework for Teaching and Practice. *International Coaching Psychology Review* 7 (September): 146–165.

Grant, A.M., L. Curtayne, and G. Burton. 2009. Executive Coaching Enhances Goal Attainment, Resilience and Workplace Well-Being: A Randomised Controlled Study. *The Journal of Positive Psychology* 4 (5): 396–407. https://doi.org/10.1080/17439760902992456.

Hay, J. 1999. *Transformational Mentoring: Creating Developmental Alliances for Changing Organizational Cultures*. Watford: Sherwood.

Kabat-Zinn, J. 2003. Mindfulness-Based Interventions in Context: Past, Present, and Future. *Clinical Psychology: Science and Practice* 10 (2): 144–156. https://doi.org/10.1093/CLIPSY.BPG016.

Kim, U., K.-S. Yang, and H. Kwang-Kuo. 2006. Contributions to Indigenous and Cultural Psychology: Understanding People in Context. In *Indigenous and Cultural Psychology: Understanding People in Context*, ed. U. Kim, K.-S. Yang, and H. Kwang-Kuo, 3–26. New York: Springer.

King, S., and C. van Nieuwerburgh. 2020. How Emirati Muslims Experience Coaching: An IPA Study. *Middle East Journal of Positive Psychology* 6: 73–96.

King, S., L. Lambert, P. Y. Ng, and P. Rosinski. 2021. Keeping with the Times: Coaching, Culture and Positive Psychology. In *Positive Psychology Coaching in the Workplace*, ed. W.-A. Smith, I.

Boniwell, and S. Green, 85–105. Cham: Springer. https://doi.org/10.1007/978-3-030-79952-6_5.
Law, H., S. Ireland, and Z. Hussain. 2007. Evaluation of the Coaching Competence Self-Review Online Tool Within an NHS Leadership Development Programme. *International Coaching Psychology Review* 1 (2): 56–67.
McCarthy, G., and J. Milner. 2013. Managerial Coaching: Challenges, Opportunities and Training. *Journal of Management Development* 32 (7): 768–779. https://doi.org/10.1108/JMD-11-2011-0113.
Palmer, S., and K. Szymanska. 2008. Cognitive Behavioural Coaching. In *Handbook of Coaching Psychology: A Guide for Practitioners*, ed. S. Palmer and A. Whybrow, 86–117. London: Routledge.
Palmer, S., and A. Whybrow. 2019. Handbook of Coaching Psychology: A Guide for Practitioners. In *Handbook of Coaching Psychology: A Guide for Practitioners*, 2nd ed., ed. S. Palmer and A. Whybrow. London: Routledge.
Passmore, J., and Y.-L. Lai. 2019. Coaching Psychology: Exploring Definitions and Research Contribution to Practice. *International Coaching Psychology Review* 14 (2): 69–83.
Passmore, J., and H. Law. 2009. Cross-Cultural and Diversity Coaching. In *Diversity in Coaching*, ed. J. Passmore, 304. London: Kogan Page.
Passmore, J., A.M. Grant, M.J. Cavanagh, and H. Parker. 2010. The State of Play in Coaching. *International Review of Industrial and Organizational Psychology* 25: 125–168.
Plaister-Ten, J. 2013. Raising Culturally-Derived Awareness and Building Culturally-Appropriate Responsibility: The Development of the Cross-Cultural Kaleidoscope. *International Journal of Evidence Based Coaching and Mentoring* 11 (2): 53–69.
Raina, M.K. 2002. Guru-Shishya Relationship in Indian Culture: The Possibility of a Creative Resilient Framework. *Psychology and Developing Societies* 14 (1): 167–198.
Rosinski, P. 2003. *Coaching Across Cultures: New Tools for Leveraging National, Corporate and Professional Differences*. London: Nicholas Brealey Publishing.
Rosinski, P. 2010. *Global Coaching: An Integrated Approach for Long-Lasting Results*. London: Nicholas Brealey Publishing.
Rosinski, P., and G. Abbot. 2010. Intercultural Coaching: Integrating Culture into Coaching. In *Excellence in Coaching: The Industry Guide*, ed. J. Passmore and Association for Coaching, 175–188. London: Kogan Page.
Rothman, A., and A. Coyle. 2018. Toward a Framework for Islamic Psychology and Psychotherapy: An Islamic Model of the Soul. *Journal of Religion and Health* 57 (5): 1731–1744. https://doi.org/10.1007/s10943-018-0651-x.
Salovey, P., and J.D. Mayer. 1990. Emotional Intelligence. *Imagination, Cognition and Personality* 9 (3): 185–211. https://doi.org/10.2190/DUGG-P24E-52WK-6CDG.
Shliakhovchuk, E. 2021. After Cultural Literacy: New Models of Intercultural Competency for Life and Work in a VUCA World. *Educational Review* 73 (2): 229–250. https://doi.org/10.1080/00131911.2019.1566211.
van Nieuwerburgh, C. 2016. Interculturally-Sensitive Coaching. In *The Sage Handbook of Coaching*, ed. T. Bachkirova, G. Spence, and D. Drake, 439–452. Los Angeles: Sage.
van Nieuwerburgh, C., and R. Allaho. 2017. *Coaching in Islamic Culture: The Principles and Practice of Ershad*. London: Karnac Books.
Whitmore, J. 1992. *Coaching for Performance: A Practical Guide to Growing Your Own Skills*. London: Nicholas Brealey Publishing.
Whitmore, J. 2017. *Coaching for Performance: The Principles and Practice of Coaching and Leadership*, 5th ed. London: Nicholas Brealey Publishing.
Whittington, J. 2012. *Systemic Coaching and Constellation: An Introduction to the Principles, Practices and Application*. London: Kogan Page.
Wilson, H.B. 1974. Cultural Literacy Laboratory. *McGill Journal of Education* 9 (1): 86–95.

Chapter 7
Uncertainty and Trust in International Business Communication

Yvonne McLaren-Hankin and Panagiota-Penny Karanasiou

> In this chapter, we discuss issues of uncertainty and trust in international business communication with reference to two specific contexts. Firstly, we look at the organisational context. We focus on crisis situations, specifically the crisis of trust in the world's banks and the role of social media in crisis communication. Secondly, we look at the workplace context, and specifically multilingual business negotiations. Here, uncertainty and lack of trust can stem from different perceptions and expectations held by participants, as well as the undetermined nature of the relationships between them.

7.1 Uncertainty, Crisis and Trust-Building in International Business Communication

Managing uncertainty is a major challenge in international business and one that often hinges on communication. Depending on the situation, actors (e.g. individuals, groups, organisations or businesses) might choose to manage uncertainty in international business through face-to-face negotiation, building (or rebuilding) of trust, communication via social media and / or openly acknowledging risks and uncertainties to stakeholders. This is not an exhaustive list of possibilities, however. In this chapter, we explore how and why uncertainty arises in different contexts and how communication is used to address uncertainty and bolster trust. Sections 7.2 and 7.3 look at organisational communication, i.e. communications between organisations

Y. McLaren-Hankin (✉)
Heriot-Watt University, Edinburgh, Scotland, UK
e-mail: Y.McLaren-Hankin@hw.ac.uk

P.-P. Karanasiou
University of Edinburgh, Edinburgh, Scotland, UK
e-mail: info@pkcommunicate.co.uk

and their stakeholders. Section 7.2 looks at the case of the ongoing crisis of trust in the global banking sector, which has its roots in the financial crisis of 2007/2008. Uncertainty surrounding the role of banks in the crisis and the manner in which they operated has led to a loss of trust in the banking and finance sectors, which organisations in those sectors have been forced to address. Section 7.3 examines the role of social media in creating and responding to uncertainty in contexts of organisational crisis. The rapid growth in the use of social media in recent years brings with it both challenges and benefits for organisations. Section 7.4 presents a final case study from a different context, that of face-to-face international business negotiations, specifically cross-cultural negotiations in which an interpreter is present. As we will see in Chapter 13, whilst interpreters play a major role in any multilingual and cross-cultural face-to-face communication, the very presence of an interpreter can bring with it further uncertainties stemming from client perceptions, expectations and experiences of using an interpreter. These frequently clash with the expectations that interpreters themselves have when working in those settings. In all of the cases we discuss, we explore the causes and implications of uncertainty in international business contexts and the communicative strategies adopted in response.

Crisis situations are particularly associated with uncertainty. There are a number of well-known examples of organisational crises. The Deepwater Horizon disaster in 2010 was triggered by an explosion on a BP oil rig in the Gulf of Mexico which killed 11 people and led to the largest marine oil spill in the history of the oil industry. The Volkswagen emissions scandal in 2015 involved car manufacturer Volkswagen having installed software in its diesel cars to "cheat" in emissions tests: the software could detect when the car was being tested and changed the car's performance so that it rated better in the tests than in reality. In 2009, India was rocked by the near-collapse of the electronics company Satyam Computer Services, as a result of corporate fraud carried out by the company chairman and co-founder. The scale of the fraud made it one of the largest such cases in India's corporate history (Padgett et al. 2013). One of the biggest scandals in recent years involved social media platform Facebook which, in 2018, was found to have sold data on tens of millions of its US users to research firm Cambridge Analytica without their consent; the data was subsequently used by Cambridge Analytica to target advertising at US voters and encourage them to vote for Donald Trump as US President. More recently still, Huawei, the Chinese multinational technology corporation and one of the world's largest smartphone suppliers, has been accused of using its 5G equipment to spy on western countries, stealing intellectual property and posing a threat to the national security of those countries.

Crises such as these are unpredictable events (although some might dispute this) that have the potential to have an extremely negative impact on the organisation, including its financial performance and its reputation. Uncertainty is a key characteristic of organisational crises. The threatening nature of a crisis means that the organisation has to take action in response, which usually involves some kind of communication to provide information to affected stakeholders. Stakeholders are any group affected by the behaviour of an organisation. They may be internal to the organisation (e.g. employees, shareholders) or external (e.g. media, regulatory authorities, customers, the general public). Crisis communication aims to provide information to stakeholders to reduce uncertainty and confusion, and allow for a mutual understanding of the situation; the organisation hopes this will prevent (further) uncertainty, chaos or even panic, prevent losses and ensure performance stability.

The consequences of any kind of organisational crisis potentially include reputational damage and a loss of confidence and trust in the organisation. Pelsmaekers, Jacobs and Rollo state that trust is "generally considered to be *relational*, i.e. pertaining to people's beliefs about and/or attitudes to others" (2014, 3, italics in original) and it is true that trust is often examined as a feature of interpersonal relationships, such as between participants in a meeting or between two people in the workplace. However, Jones and Sin provide a broader definition of trust, one that allows for the possibility of trust in a group or institution and therefore by extension in a company or other organisation which is our focus here: trust is "the belief that some person (or group or institution), if given control over one's affairs, or some aspect of those affairs, will act in one's best interests, furthering those interests in so far as they can and, at the very least, doing them no harm" (2013, 152). Indeed, some scholars (e.g. see Gillespie and Dietz 2009) have examined trust as a factor in organisational relationships, such as between a company and its stakeholders. Regardless of the type of relationship involved, our perception of whether someone or some company or organisation can be trusted is based on certain characteristics. In the model of trustworthiness developed by Mayer et al. (1995), which is perhaps the most frequently used model, there are three such characteristics, known as "dimensions" of trustworthiness. These are *ability*, *benevolence* and *integrity*. *Ability* is "that group of skills, competencies, and characteristics that enable a party to have influence within some specific domain" (1995, 717); it relates to *competence* or *expertise*. *Benevolence*, on the other hand, sometimes also termed *empathy*, involves consideration of others; it is "the extent to which a trustee is believed to want to do good *to the trustor*, aside from an egocentric profit motive" (Mayer et al., 1995, 718, italics in original). Finally, *integrity* covers responsibility and ethical behaviour, and involves "the trustor's perception that the trustee adheres to a set of principles that the trustor finds acceptable" (Mayer et al. 1995, p.719).

In the model, then, we (the trustor) base our perception of the trustworthiness of another individual or group or organisation (the trustee) on our assessment of the ability, empathy and integrity of that individual or group or organisation. However, the role of communication in this process differs, according to whom we are dealing with. In the case of an organisation, our knowledge and impressions of that organisation are, in most cases, formed on the basis of organisational (or media) communications. This is why organisational communications in situations of uncertainty, crisis and trust loss are so important. At such times, organisations usually seek to demonstrate "renewed trustworthiness" through "behaviours and verbal responses that *actively demonstrate* ability, benevolence, and integrity" (Gillespie and Dietz 2009, 134, italics in original); this might include expressions of regret, acknowledgement of responsibility or corporate apologies. In the case of individuals we know or whom we encounter personally, we base our perception of whether or not they can be trusted on the (direct) knowledge and experience we have of them. In situations of face-to-face communication, and particularly where participants come from different linguistic and cultural backgrounds, uncertainty and a lack of trust can arise due to language difficulties and a lack of cultural awareness. In such situations, interpreters can play a key role in mediating between participants to reduce any uncertainty and facilitate effective communication.

7.2 Rebuilding Trust in the Banking Sector

The global financial crisis began in 2007/2008 and scholars such as Earle (2009), De Cremer (2010) and Bourne and Edwards (2012) have highlighted that at the heart of the crisis lay a loss of public trust and confidence in the banking sector. High-profile scandals involving unethical and sometimes illegal behaviour, including mis-selling of financial products, money laundering and helping clients evade taxes, led customers to question the integrity of banks and their motives. De Cremer (2010) summed this up when he stated that customers believe that "banks routinely act more as agents interested in the products that they sell rather than in providing services promoting the interest of their clients" (2010, 79). As a result, the banking sector has been widely seen as unscrupulous, unreliable, uncaring and untrustworthy. In terms of the model of trustworthiness we discussed above (Mayer et al. 1995), it is the dimensions of ***empathy*** and ***integrity*** that have been most lacking. This applies not just to the banking sector as a whole, but also to individual banks: in the UK, in the 2010s, banks such as RBS, HSBC and Barclays were fined when it came to light that they had been engaging in a range of unethical practices such as mis-selling insurance policies and mortgages and conspiring to fix interest rates and foreign exchange rates.

Following the crisis, banks came to realise that they needed to restore their reputation and rebuild trust with their stakeholders. To do this, they needed a completely new organisational culture and set of values that their employees supported and upheld, and new policies and practices that complied with legal, moral and ethical principles. As we saw above, organisational communications play a pivotal role in this context; we focus therefore on how banks have tried to redress the perceptions of stakeholders through their external communications.

> **Case Study 1: Barclays Bank**
> Barclays is the second largest UK bank and has suffered from one of the most tarnished reputations in the British banking sector. It was one of the five most complained about banks in the UK (Dailly 2013) and suffered serious damage to its reputation as a result of its role in the LIBOR rate rigging scandal (LIBOR is the London Interbank Offered Rate, a rate banks charge each other to borrow money), and the mis-selling of Payment Protection Insurance (PPI).

This involved millions of customers being mis-sold insurance policies to pay off loans or mortgages if they died, became ill or lost their job.

In 2012, recognising that it had suffered a catastrophic loss of trust amongst stakeholders and society more generally, Barclays commissioned a review of its operations, to establish how it could overcome the uncertainty created by its behaviour and rebuild stakeholder and societal trust. The terms of reference of the review were to examine the bank's 'historical culture' (p1)—i.e. its 'values, principles and standards of operation'—and to make recommendations for change. The resulting **Salz Review** report, published in April 2013, called for a cultural shift in the bank, as well as greater openness and transparency; it made 34 recommendations in total, covering standards, values, recruitment and induction of staff, pay principles, and the role of the Board and senior leadership. One of the key responses from Barclays was the development of a project that aimed specifically to change the organisational culture and develop a new, sustainable set of values and behaviours for all employees. In terms of trust and trustworthiness, this clearly aimed at signalling ***integrity***.

Barclays disseminated information about its programme of change by various means. These included specially organised events such as the "Barclays Values Jam 2013", an online discussion forum lasting 68 hours and involving 50,000 employees across the world; and "Stakeholder Dialogue Days", events at which Barclays engaged in face-to-face dialogue with external stakeholders including representatives from NGOs, think tanks, corporate clients, academia, government organisations, investors, consumer groups and industry bodies, with the aim of discussing stakeholders' perceptions and expectations of Barclays and the challenges ahead. Barclays also used a range of printed and digital communications, including its annual report, its website and press releases (see McLaren-Hankin 2019), as well as specially commissioned documents, to disseminate information about changes to its culture and values, and the results of engagement with stakeholders on these matters. One such document was a new **Code of Conduct** published in 2013 and entitled 'The Barclays Way'. Codes of conduct are documents that lay out the values of an organisation and the conduct that is expected of employees. They stipulate what is acceptable and what is not acceptable in the organisation.

In the case of Barclays, it was especially important that one common code was implemented as there had previously been different codes of conduct for different divisions in the bank, and this had led to inconsistency in behaviours and practices. In addition, one of the problems with the way in which Barclays was previously run was that employees were afraid to speak up if they had concerns about the behaviour of others in the organisation. To address this, the new Code of Conduct explicitly encouraged employees to report anything they thought was not in line with the bank's values and it reassured them that they should not feel afraid to do so.

The Barclays Code of Conduct was clearly designed to provide a new, unified, consistent framework for employee behaviour that ensured that there was no uncertainty over what is right and what is wrong. It was intended to create certainty amongst employees about how they should behave and what action they should take if they were concerned about the behaviour of others. This is an example of change to what Gillespie and Owen (2013) call "bank culture". Such change requires "clear articulation of a set of trust-enhancing core values that connect with the bank's broader social purpose" followed by "ensuring that these values are not only espoused but also understood and enacted in the daily behaviours and decision making of all employees" (Gillespie and Owen, 2013, 10). A Code of Conduct also helps create certainty amongst other stakeholders and can contribute to trustworthiness, as it addresses issues of *benevolence* (in this case, consideration of employees and understanding of their concerns) and, above all, *integrity*. The Barclays Code of Conduct received a lot of press coverage, meaning that many stakeholder groups became aware of its existence. Other top banks in the UK also published new codes of conduct around the same time (e.g. RBS and Lloyds Banking Group, both in 2013), showing that banks recognised the need for cultural change if trust in the sector was to be restored.

7.3 Crisis Communications

Our attention now turns to organisational crisis communication with particular attention paid to the role of social media. Crisis communication has been given several definitions due to the different understandings of crisis. Some existing definitions (Fearn-Banks 1996; Barton 2001) contribute negative connotations to the word crisis and combine it with a possible threat, where others (Friedman 2002) connect crisis with possible opportunities. Crisis communication is "the collection, processing and dissemination of information required to address a crisis situation" (Coombs 2010, 20) and therefore it involves providing information that is needed urgently (e.g. by customers or the public). Organisations now routinely use social media for this purpose. Social media are particularly useful for organisations in crisis situations because they allow information to be disseminated quickly and to a large audience located anywhere in the world. This applies not only to organisational crises in the business world, but also to natural disasters, public health crises (the COVID pandemic is a good example of this) or terrorist attacks. All such events require timely and targeted communicative responses that are tailored to a range of audiences with diverse backgrounds.

However, social media are not just used by organisations in these situations; they are also used by stakeholders whose social media activities can fuel an organisational crisis, or even cause it in the first place. In other words, a crisis may originate online but it may also be triggered by events that occur offline but which, once reported on social media, "go viral". In either case, if organisations do not respond quickly enough, the crisis may rapidly spiral out of control. Research has shown that organisation-related social media usage increases during crises, and that the news of a crisis, including inaccurate or unverified information, is quickly shared online by users (van der Meer et al. 2017). Demand for information is particularly high during the initial stages of a crisis, when stakeholders may be forced to make sense of the situation by themselves and might have to base their understanding of the crisis on speculations, which can lead to a spread of inaccurate information (van der Meer et al. 2017; Eriksson 2018). As a result, some scholars argue that crises in the contemporary business environment have actually become more frequent and severe thanks to social media (e.g. see Gruber et al. 2015). If, on the other hand, organisations do respond quickly and provide the required information, this can reduce uncertainty, contain the crisis, restore trust in the organisation, and limit potential damage to the organisation.

Of all the social media available for communication between stakeholders and organisations, Twitter has become one of the most used. Twitter is an online social networking and microblogging service that was launched in 2006. It now has an average of 330 million monthly active users. Twitter allows users to post, read and respond to messages, and to "retweet" messages posted by others; in addition, by means of the "hashtag" facility, users can quickly search for messages on topics of interest to them and contribute to the discussion. As a result, Twitter can be viewed as a form of "electronic word of mouth" (Jansen et al. 2009). Perhaps more than any other medium, Twitter affords immediacy and directness: it is a source of real-time news by means of which information can travel faster than by any other medium. This means that organisations can use Twitter to respond swiftly to a potentially damaging situation, but also that users can very quickly engage in collective action, sometimes causing considerable damage to an organisation.

Gruber et al. (2015) discuss a case at a university in the US that demonstrates the power of Twitter in a crisis situation. Although the example is from the context of higher education, the events could have taken place in any type of organisation. In June 2012, the president of the University of Virginia was asked to resign by the university's board due to concerns about the lack of a university strategy. A so-called "firestorm" followed on social media during which stakeholders (including students, alumni, staff and the media) used Twitter to share news and information in real time, to express their views and to rally together in support of the president. Twitter was used as a forum for collective action: stakeholders came together to call for transparency and action on the part of the board. Such was the extent of the firestorm on social media that the board was forced to back down and reinstate the president. Gruber et al. (2015) conclude from their discussion of the incident that the situation at the university "produced a shroud of uncertainty, and the corresponding negative attention by both mainstream and social media outlets yielded a crisis-like environment" (2015, 169). The only way for the board of the University to resolve the uncertainty and to bring the crisis to an end was to reverse the decision that created the uncertainty in the first place.

This example shows how stakeholders can exploit the properties of social media such as Twitter to drive an organisational crisis and force the organisation in question to take action. These same properties can be harnessed by organisations themselves to respond in situations of uncertainty, as we see below.

> **Case Study 2: Toyota**
>
> In 2010, the Japanese car manufacturer Toyota was forced to recall millions of vehicles due to important safety-related defects. This crisis is an interesting one to look at because it involves a Japanese company that operates in markets on all four corners of the globe. When the crisis broke, the Japanese public were stunned by events: Toyota is a symbol of Japan around the world, it had built its reputation on quality and reliability, and it was a source of national pride. It was clear to all that public trust in the company was at stake.
>
> The crisis broke initially in the US where the vehicle recall was to take place. However, as a result of social media such as Facebook and Twitter, the news of the crisis quickly spread around the world, to Europe, China, and Japan. Groups even emerged on social media attacking Toyota. There was also much criticism of Toyota reported in the press (e.g. see Hemus 2010), based on allegations that the company had ignored the problem until it was forced to take action and that remedial action could have been taken much earlier. Toyota itself conceded that it needed to listen more carefully to customers and respond faster to complaints.
>
> However, in terms of its communicative response when the crisis struck, Toyota did act promptly and positively. Part of the action it took involved using social media. Toyota created a dedicated social media team whose role was to coordinate news from different parts of the company and to disseminate this news via platforms such as Facebook, Twitter and YouTube. The media and the company's website were full of messages providing information and reassurance, and Toyota's call centre worked hard to answer customer enquiries. In this respect Toyota responded well and the company even added new followers on Facebook during the crisis (Rajasekera 2013). Toyota realised the importance of social media at an early stage in the crisis and used these new media to its advantage.
>
> Furthermore, there was another memorable, intercultural dimension to this crisis and the company's response. Following criticism that he had failed to address customer concerns quickly enough at the start of the crisis, company president Akio Toyoda made a sincere personal apology and bowed in a press conference, taking responsibility for the crisis and for resolving it. This act was undoubtedly partly a result of the family history of the company and the organisational culture—Toyoda stated "I am the grandson of the founder, and all the Toyota vehicles bear my name. For me, when the cars are damaged, it is as though I am as well." (Clark 2010)—but it was also viewed as part of Japanese business culture in which leaders are viewed as personally responsible

> and personal apologies are expected (Rowe 2010). The act of apologising and bowing by Toyoda was an attempt to display his regret at what had happened and to assure the public that action would be taken to restore their trust in the company.

7.4 Uncertainty in the Workplace: The Case of Interpreted Business Negotiations

In this section, we shift our focus from uncertainty in organisational contexts to uncertainty in the workplace. More specifically, we look at multilingual business negotiations involving representatives of companies from different countries. Uncertainty in this context can stem from the presence of participants who have diverse linguistic and cultural backgrounds and who may not have an awareness or understanding of linguistic or cultural differences. This uncertainty can in turn affect trust and interpersonal relationships, and this can impact on the negotiation process.

Business meetings that are facilitated by a professional interpreter can present an extra set of opportunities and challenges. The perception of the interpreter's role in business negotiation meetings by interpreters themselves and clients alike is one of these challenges, since different perceptions of role can lead to unwanted results. An interpreter is an integral and a very important part of the communication process: interpreters are responsible for most of the communication between participants and thus have a very complex role to play (see Chapter 13).

In a study conducted by Karanasiou (2017) regarding the perception of the role of interpreters in business settings by businesspeople, results showed that participants were fused between what interpreters call the "visibility" or the "invisibility" doctrine. There are businesspeople who hire interpreters and expect them to relay only what the businessperson is saying in the given negotiation meeting. Others expect the interpreter to take up more roles, including becoming a trusted member of the client's negotiation team and thus negotiating to the best of their ability and knowledge, to protect the interests of the client's team. These two perceptions are quite contradictory and sometimes the line between them is fused. As a result, the mandate given by clients to interpreters can be quite blurred and can fluctuate between these two opposing doctrines.

Karanasiou's (2017) qualitative study of those businesspeople showed that clients want their interpreters to become their team members and negotiate *with* or even *for* them. Despite this openly enabling role that clients give to interpreters, clients also expect interpreters to be perceptive enough to understand their boundaries and the limits to this enabling condition. They expect them to be active team members with equal distribution of power who comprehend the dynamics and the boundaries of their position. Therefore, interpreters should not take over the negotiation process but rather protect and advise the client when appropriate. Clients reported that they need a trusted ally who, as a skilled linguist with a deep knowledge of the culture, will protect them and advise them on various issues, such as how to avoid culturally inappropriate behaviour. Since interpreters are both skilled linguists and cultural experts, they are aware of what is culturally acceptable and therefore, when a *faux pas* occurs, they should not replay it, but rather take action to protect the outcome of the negotiation. For an interpreted interaction to be successful, clients need to trust the interpreter to act in this way and to respond to any such uncertainty which arises.

Explaining feelings and emotions was another element that came up in Karanasiou's (2016; 2017) studies. Business meetings are largely based on feelings, emotions, power distribution, trust and group dynamics (Karanasiou 2017; McCall and Warrington 1984). Although interpreters are traditionally instructed during their training or by their professional associations not to interpret or explain anything that was not spoken in words, Karanasiou (2017) found that interpreters who act solely as language facilitators are considered as providing a machine-like service which is not needed by clients. An inactive interpreter can harm the negotiation process. If counterparts understood the same language and culture, they would have understood more than words alone can say. Therefore, interpreters that receive these unspoken messages are seen as hiding those extra and very crucial messages. This impacts on trust and interpersonal relationships and can create uncertainty in the interaction. According to the clients' perceptions, interpreters as skilled professionals should be able to understand more than words and so they should pass on these underlying meanings to the team members. Withholding information does not help the negotiation process, as a large part of a meeting lies with the interpersonal dynamics and relationships.

Interpreters in business negotiation settings can be an integral, dynamic and substantial part of a meeting, as they manage turn-taking, coordinate dynamics, and participate in a team, potentially affecting the whole outcome of the meeting. Businesspeople should not entrust their negotiations to untrained interpreters but should rather hire professionals who are skilled and trained to understand the boundaries of their complex role (see Chapter 13 on Translation and Interpreting in the intercultural business workplace). Moreover, businesspeople should inform interpreters, and negotiate with them, about ***how*** they want interpreters to practise their role before the meeting takes place. This should take into account the fact that interpreters are not there to carry out the meeting for their client only, but rather to facilitate communication for everyone, even if more than one interpreter is participating in the meeting, representing each negotiating party. In that way, there would be less uncertainty, interpreters would know what is expected, they would offer better services to businesses and conduct more fruitful and efficient negotiations together with their clients.

7.5 Contexts of Uncertainty: Drawing the Strands Together

We have covered a range of different contexts from the business world in which uncertainty is a characteristic feature. We have learnt that uncertainty may develop for a variety of reasons and that actors may adopt a range of communicative strategies in response, in order to manage uncertainty and, where possible, resolve the situation.

Firstly, we looked at the context of organisational communication, i.e. communication between organisations and their stakeholders. Uncertainty has been a major factor in the global banking sector over the last 15 years, stemming from the global financial crisis of 2007/2008, and it is clear that crisis, uncertainty and loss of trust go hand in hand. We saw that there has been a crisis of trust in banks, that stakeholders lost confidence in banks as a result of unethical behaviour by bankers and the failure by banks to admit that what they did was wrong. However, banks have responded through a range of actions and communications aimed at regaining the trust of their stakeholders. They have used conventional tools such as their websites to communicate messages of integrity ("we are ethical") and empathy ("we care"). In addition, UK banks like Barclays have published new codes of conduct that serve a particularly important purpose in this context. They set out clearly the values and behaviours expected of employees and, by doing this, they dispel any uncertainty amongst employees about what is right and what is wrong, and at the same time they reassure other stakeholder groups that the bank can be trusted to operate ethically. In our second example from the organisational context, we looked at organisational crisis communication. We saw how social media, particularly Twitter, are used by organisations as a crisis communications tool, so to *respond* to uncertainty and restore trust, but we also saw that they can be used by stakeholders to *create* uncertainty in the first place and trigger a crisis. Social media are particularly useful in such situations because of the speed of communication that they offer and also their geographical reach.

Secondly, we looked at the context of face-to-face business negotiations. We saw that uncertainties may arise amongst participants due to language and cultural differences which influence the way in which people behave, but also the expectations they have of others. If an interpreter is present, this can lead to additional uncertainties, especially in relation to the role of the interpreter, which may be perceived differently by the various participants (interpreters themselves, the clients, other businesspeople involved in the negotiation). Uncertainties and differences can impact on trust, and this can affect the dynamics of the negotiation and the outcome. A clear discussion of roles and expectations before the negotiation takes place can help resolve any potential uncertainties and threats to trust and ensure that communication takes place successfully.

Chapter Review Questions

1. How can trust be conceptualised? What are the key characteristics of trustworthiness according to Mayer et al. (1995)? [*Answer to be informed by Sect.* 7.1]
2. What is an organisational Code of Conduct? What purpose does it serve? And what role does it play in managing certainty and (re)building trust? [*Answer to be informed by Sect.* 7.2]
3. Why do social media now play a key role in organisational crises? In what ways can they create uncertainty? And how can they be used to reduce uncertainty? [*Answer to be informed by Sect.* 7.3]
4. What are the challenges of interpreted negotiation meetings? Think of a few examples. [*Answer to be informed by Sect.* 7.4]
5. What evidence is there of similarities or differences in terms of certainty and uncertainty and crisis management across (organisational) cultures? [*Answer to be informed by Sects.* 7.1–7.3].

Recommended Further Reading

- Gruber, D.A., R.E. Smerek, M.C. Thomas-Hunt, and E.H. James. 2015. "The Real-time Power of Twitter: Crisis Management and Leadership in an Age of Social Media." *Business Horizons* 58: 163–172.
- Karanasiou, P.P. 2016. "Public Service Interpreting and Business Negotiation Interpreting: Friends or Foes?" In *Challenges and Opportunities in Public Service Interpreting*, ed. T. Munyangeyo, G. Webb, and M. Rabadán, 191–211. London: Palgrave Macmillan.
- Mayer, R.C., J.H. Davis, and F.D. Schoorman. 1995. "An Integrative Model of Organisational Trust". *Academy of Management Review* 20(3): 709–734.
- McLaren-Hankin, Y. 2019. "Rebuilding Trust in the Banking Sector: Engaging with Readers in Corporate Press Releases." In *Engagement in Professional Genres: Deference and Disclosure*, ed. C. Sancho Guinda, 87–100. Philadelphia: John Benjamins.
- van der Meer, T.G.L.A., P. Verhoeven, H.W.J. Beentjes, and R. Vliegenthart. 2017. "Communication in Times of Crisis: The Stakeholder Relationship under Pressure." *Public Relations Review* 43: 426–440.

References

Barton, L. 2001. *Crisis in Organisations II*, 2nd ed., Cincinnati: College Divisions South Western.

Bourne, C., and L. Edwards. 2012. Producing Trust, Knowledge and Expertise in Financial Markets: The Global Hedge Fund Industry 'Re-presents' Itself. *Culture and Organisation* 18 (2): 107–122.

Clark, A. 2010. "Toyota boss Akio Toyoda apologies ahead of US grilling." *The Guardian*, 23 February. https://www.theguardian.com/business/2010/feb/23/toyota-president-toyoda-apologises-congress, last accessed 2 February 2023.

Coombs, T.W., and S.J. Holladay. 2010. *The Handbook of Crisis Communications*. Chichester: John Wiley & Son.

De Cremer, D. 2010. Rebuilding trust. *Business Strategy Review* Q2–2010: 79–80.

Dailly, M. 2013. "Rebuilding Trust in British Banking." British Bankers Association's Complaints Seminar, London, 22 October 2013. Retrieved from https://www.fs-cp.org.uk/sites/default/files/mike-dailly-speech-bba-complaints-seminar20131022.pdf, 11 June 2015.

Earle, T.C. 2009. Trust, Confidence, and the 2008 Global Financial Crisis. *Risk Analysis* 29 (6): 785–792.

Eriksson, M. 2018. Lessons for Crisis Communication on Social Media: A Systematic Review of what Research tells the Practice. *International Journal of Strategic Communication* 12 (5): 526–551.

Fearn-Banks, K. 1996. *Crisis Communication: A Casebook Approach*. Mahwah, NJ: Lawrence Erlbaum Associates.

Friedman, M.L. 2002. *Everyday Crisis Management*. First Decision Press.

Gillespie, N., and G. Dietz. 2009. Trust Repair after an Organisation-level Failure. *Academy of Management Review* 34: 127–145.

Gillespie, N. and G. Owen. 2013. Restoring Trust in the Financial Services Sector. A Report Published by the Industry and Parliament Trust. *Notes from the Policy Event Meeting 'Restoring Trust in the Financial Services Sector'*, October 2013. https://espace.library.uq.edu.au/view/UQ:313548/UQ313548_fulltext.pdf, last accessed 29 September 2023.

Gruber, D.A., R.E. Smerek, M.C. Thomas-Hunt, and E.H. James. 2015. The Real-time Power of Twitter: Crisis Management and Leadership in an Age of Social Media. *Business Horizons* 58: 163–172.

Hemus, J. 2010. "Accelerating Towards Crisis: A PR View of Toyota's Recall." *The Guardian*, 9 February 2010. https://www.theguardian.com/business/2010/feb/09/pr-view-toyota-reputation-management, last accessed 2 February 2023.

Jansen, B.J., M. Zhang, K. Sobel, and A. Chowdury. 2009. Twitter Power: Tweets as Electronic Word of Mouth. *Journal of the American Society for Information Science and Technology* 60 (11): 2169–2385.

Karanasiou, P.P. 2017. *Fulfilling the Interpreting Mandate in Business Negotiation Meetings. The Perspectives of Interpreters and Clients*. Unpublished PhD Thesis, Heriot-Watt University, Edinburgh.

Karanasiou, P.P. 2016. "Public Service Interpreting and Business Negotiation Interpreting: Friends or Foes?" In *Challenges and opportunities in public service interpreting*, ed. T. Munyangeyo, G. Webb, and M. Rabadán, 191–211. London: Palgrave Macmillan.

McCall, J.B., and M.B. Warrington. 1984. *Marketing by Agreement: A Cross-cultural Approach to Business Negotiations*. New York: John Wiley & Sons.

McLaren-Hankin, Y. 2019. Rebuilding Trust in the Banking Sector: Engaging with Readers in Corporate Press Releases. In *Engagement in Professional Genres: Deference and Disclosure*, ed. C. Sancho Guinda, 87–100. Philadelphia: John Benjamins.

Mayer, R.C., J.H. Davis, and J.H., and F.D. Schoorman. 1995. An Integrative Model of Organisational Trust. *Academy of Management Review* 20 (3): 709–734.

Padgett, D.R.G., S.S. Cheng, and V. Parekh. 2013. The Quest for Transparency and Accountability: Communicating Responsibly to Stakeholders in Crises. *Asian Social Science* 9 (9): 31–44.

Pelsmaekers, K., G. Jacobs, and C. Rollo. 2014. Trust and Discursive Interaction Inorganisational Settings. In *Trust and Discourse: Organisational Perspectives*, ed. K. Pelsmaekers, G. Jacobs, and C. Rollo, 1–10. Amsterdam: John Benjamins.

Rajasekera, J. 2013. Challenges to Toyota Caused by Recall Problems, Social Networks and Digitisation. *Asian Academy of Management Journal* 18 (1): 1–17.

Rowe, P. 2010. Public Apology Part of Business Culture in Japan. *San Diego Tribune*, 6 February. https://www.sandiegouniontribune.com/sdut-public-apology-part-business-culture-japan-2010feb06-story.html

Stevens, B. 2009. Corporate Ethical Codes as Strategic Documents: An Analysis of Success and Failure. *EJBO Electronic Journal of Business Ethics and Organisation Studies* 14 (2): 14–20.

van der Meer, T.G.L.A., P. Verhoeven, H.W.J. Beentjes, and R. Vliegenthart. 2017. Communication in Times of Crisis: The Stakeholder Relationship under Pressure. *Public Relations Review* 43: 426–440.

Part III
Economy

Chapter 8
Economy as Intercultural Challenge

Ullrich Kockel

> This chapter argues that, rather than a uniform global phenomenon, economy is culturally contingent, conditioned by historical, geographical, ecological, social and ideological factors. Contact between different cultural modes of economy can lead to friction making crises worse but may also hold potential to find creative solutions for contemporary problems. Following a summary of historical, geographical and conceptual frameworks that help the reader understand economy as culture, the chapter examines a key trope of mainstream economics, the universally rational actor. It then considers the 'informal' economy, showing how cultural embedding works, before introducing alternative models of economy, many with religious foundations.

8.1 Economy as Culture: Historical, Geographical and Conceptual Frameworks

This chapter argues that, rather than a uniform global phenomenon, economy is culturally contingent, conditioned by historical, geographical, ecological, social and ideological factors. Contact between different cultural modes of economy can lead to friction making crises worse but may also hold potential to find creative solutions for contemporary problems. Following a summary of historical, geographical and conceptual frameworks that help the reader understand economy as culture, the chapter examines a key trope of mainstream economics, the universally rational actor. It then considers the 'informal' economy, showing how cultural embedding works, before introducing alternative models of economy, many with religious foundations.

U. Kockel (✉)
University of the Highlands and Islands, Inverness, Scotland, UK
e-mail: Ullrich.Kockel@uhi.ac.uk

© The Author(s), under exclusive license to Springer Nature Switzerland AG 2023
K. Strani and K. Pfeiffer (eds.), *Intercultural Issues in the Workplace*,
https://doi.org/10.1007/978-3-031-42320-8_8

The link between culture and economy has been extensively debated for decades (see, e.g., Henry and Kossou 1985; Ray and Sayer 1999; Simonsen 2001; Castells 2010). Culture has come to be seen both as a resource for development and as giving shape to specific **modes of transaction** (Kockel 2002a, 2020b). However, despite a politically driven rhetoric of cultural diversity, in political practice, the neo-liberalist market economy is taken singularly as the universally valid model, providing the yardstick for successful development.

8.1.1 Endogenous, Moral and Institutional Economy

But there can also be a more radical aspect to the rhetoric of culture. A particular group, company or region may try to pursue a genuinely 'alternative' path, with emphasis on **endogenous** (=generated from within) rather than externally directed development. The cultural rhetoric may become an ethnic one; Ray (1998, 8–9) suggested that we see culture as local knowledge, 'ways of doing things and ways of understanding the world.' The link between culture and economy could then be conceived of as strategies for transforming this knowledge into local resources for development. In many cases, the re-valuation of local knowledge involved may well highlight what can be described as pre-industrial values and orientations (Kockel 2012).

The historian E. P. Thompson and others have pointed to the continued existence of such older ideas, and economist Fred Hirsch (1977) has argued that even neo-liberal market economies cannot exist without non-market elements. What Thompson (1971) called the **moral economy** is more than an accidental survival from a pre-industrial period. Rather, it is a vital condition of modern capitalism (Kramer 1986, 49). World-systems theory, developed by Immanuel Wallerstein and others since the late 1960s (Robertson and Lechner 1985) has tried to analyze this interdependence from a holistic global perspective. Many protagonists in this debate came from the **Global South** and were influenced by Liberation Theology, highlighting a connection between economics and religion (see Sect. 8.5 below).

The socio-cultural boundedness of economic processes has been highlighted by economists in the **institutionalist** tradition (Hirsch 1977; Adams 1980; Gruchy 1987), who emphasize the importance of 'institutions' in the anthropological sense of established modes of thinking and doing. They share the concern with socio-cultural boundedness with the **Historical School** of economics (Balabkins 1987; Röpke 1990; Plumpe 1999), which emphasizes the historical, geo-cultural and wider contextual conditions of economic activity; their best-known protagonist was **Max Weber** (see below). The anthropologist Gudeman (1986, 26) described what one might call **vernacular models** of the economy, that is, of the process as perceived by 'local' participants, with 'their life and history, their historical consciousness, their social construction ... part of what we call "development"'. Orthodox economics views such perceptions as 'constraints', 'causes for failure' or 'political and social blockages to technological change', while they are 'simply the conditions of and for "development"' (ibid.).

Adam Smith, credited as the founder of modern economics, still maintained 'a strong sense of the cultural matrix of economic phenomena' (Bekemans 1994, 263); successive generations of economists have progressively lost interest in this matrix. Bekemans (ibid., 261) argued that to study the relationship between culture and economy, we need to think of economics as a societal science, with values, history, institutions and 'socio-cultural realities' forming 'an integral part of its explanatory framework.' This is necessary if we are 'to comprehend actual economic developments and systems' (ibid., 262).

8.1.2 Economy and Cultural Tradition(s)

Stöhr's (1986, 66) definition of development as enhancement of 'human capabilities on the basis of their respective historical, societal and natural conditions' stressed regional identity and territorial political participation as significant factors. Highlighting power relationships, Gudeman (1986, 157) made a similar point when he suggested we need to rethink various common, taken-for-granted concepts, such as *imperialism* or *dependency*, 'in terms of who gets to model whom'. Regional identity becomes a key factor for development as a catalyst for both 'cooperation among diverse interest groups…and for the retention or recuperation of initiative and creative personalities' (Stöhr 1986, 71). Brugger (1986) argued that regional identity may be a cultural response to increasing globalization of the economy.

Viewed as a force to be utilized for development, cultural *traditions* have become an important feature of local economies, for example in the form of work patterns ill-suited to the factory routines of the Fordist production line model associated with '*branch plant*' (Sonn and Lee 2012) industrialization typical in developing countries. Reference to cultural tradition(s) also provides a means of temporarily silencing outside interests trying to induce change without being fully familiar with local circumstances. Although in these cases local people may be said to be themselves responsible for being stereotyped as 'backward', such reference to 'tradition' gives powerful protection against disruptive changes. Individual or collective interests at local level can thus win time to evaluate innovations, and perhaps develop their own responses to critical situations, by declaring virtually any current practice as 'traditional'.

8.1.3 Formalism vs Substantivism

Notions and actions that 'from the perspective of the dominant discourse' appear to be just 'irrational traditionalism' may in fact represent 'an alternative logic'

(Herzfeld 1997, 454). This tension between a globalizing, universalizing discourse and a more localizing one has been evident since the 1950s in one of the 'grand debates' in economic anthropology, between substantivists and formalists, those who see economy as culturally embedded and therefore context-specific, and those who see it as governed by universal rules akin to the rules of physics. Based largely on the work of Karl Polanyi (1944), **substantivism** advocates 'an ethnographically grounded rejection of formalist models that seek to disinter the economic from all other social forms of life' (Herzfeld 1997, 457–8); while *formalism* (Schneider 1974; Haskell 1996) adopts the claims of neo-liberal economics to universal validity. The subsequent debate on culture and economy has challenged not just economic models as representations of everyday life, but the positioning of economics as a science employing a superior worldview and underlying logic (e.g., Kockel 2002b; Boyle and Simms 2009; Jackson 2009). This ideological elevation of economics has been compared by some critics to the position of the Mediaeval Christian Church (see Sect. 8.5 below).

8.2 Rational 'Economic Man'

Mainstream economics claims to be a universal theory reflecting global truths, interests and values. But just as its core concept of ***comparative advantage*** (Maneschi 1998, 1) has been shown (e.g., Heierli 1986) as having been particularly opportune serving the purposes of the British Empire at the time it was formulated, Herzfeld (1997, 459; orig. emph.) reminds us 'that "global" interests are *always* particular interests … encoded and enacted as teleology'. A foundational concept in economics has been *homo oeconomicus*, 'rational' Economic Man (Schneider 1974), an individual actor driven by universally valid economic motives.

8.2.1 Individual and Society

Anthropologists have long pointed out that this concept of human nature, far from being universally valid, is culturally contingent. Even within Europe—let alone on a global scale—very different ideas about the individual exist. Tim Ingold contrasts the Latin idea of *persona* with the Finnish *henkilö*, the former referring literally to 'the speech of an actor … heard through the mask' (Ingold 1998, 8). Originally, 'person' referred to 'the mask, the social role, the part played in society' by the individual; the Finnish concept comes from *henki*, meaning 'a kind of inner essence or vital force, the breath of life that flies away when you die' (ibid.).

Schiffauer (1997, 35–49) analyzed different conceptualisations of the relationship between individual and society in American, British, French and German political culture, which he mapped along a continuum from the isolated to the deeply culturally embedded individual. Glasman (1996) described the transition from Communism to

Capitalism in Poland after 1989, when the country stood at a crossroads between a Central European model of culture and economy, rooted in the Catholic social ethic and the collectivist values of the Labour Movement on the one hand, and a transatlantic neo-liberalism built on an ascetic Protestant ethic (Weber 1930) and market individualism on the other hand.

8.2.2 The 'Free Market' as a Politico-Cultural Construct

In *The Great Transformation*, Polanyi (1994) argued that the so-called free market was not based on natural order, as Adam Smith had proposed. Prior to the industrial revolution in England, most cultures throughout the world used two different modes of transaction—***reciprocity*** and ***redistribution***. The modern *free market* originated in England in the form of highly contested legislation that was a major factor in the civil war of the 1600 s (Polanyi 1944). The legislation's primary features were enclosure of land to facilitate its free sale and purchase as a commodity, and the clearance from the land of peasants, forcing them to sell their labour to the manufacturing industries emerging at the time. This ***commodification*** of land and labour broke down barriers to trading, while the rising cash economy favoured the emerging international markets, providing a basis for the industrial revolution (Henderson 1996, 87). It also created population movements on a scale previously only seen as a result of war or natural disaster—but now migration became an integral part of how the economic system was supposed to work, creating one of the major contradictions political proponents of neo-liberalist market economy have to grapple with.

8.2.3 Self-interest and the Common Good

Ethnographic observations during fieldwork in Europe (e.g., Kockel 2002a) support the view that *homo oeconomicus* is by no means the self-centred individual portrayed in economic theory—quite apart from the fact that *homo oeconomicus* is more often a woman than a man. However, much of this fieldwork was carried out in regions where, although they may be English-speaking (for example Ireland), the cultural grammar is not an English one and, from an anthropological perspective at least, discrepancies are therefore to be expected. Economists may counter that, regardless of any cultural grammar, what appears as co-operative or community spirit is really nothing but egoism in disguise.

That may be so. But it is nowadays widely accepted even within economics that self-interest must incorporate responsibility for the environment, and for the society living in it (Attfield 1994, 241). There is growing recognition that 'quite trivial actions on the part of millions of consumers produce far-reaching aggregated effects' (ibid.). 'The consequences of our actions determine the horizon of our responsibility', and 'responsible action' must, by definition, take account of 'other systems in addition to our own' (Bossel 1987, 114). Frykman (1999) noted that the individual of contemporary social and cultural theory has been one who primarily interprets rather than acts, although some thinkers (e.g., Joas 1996) have tried to reframe that perspective, and some (e.g., Maffesoli 1996) have argued the individualistic model of economy may paradoxically have contributed to the creation of a mass society that spells the decline of the individual. Granovetter (1985) highlighted the embeddedness of economic action in social structures, and Beckert (2007), returning to Polanyi's work (see above), critically developed this perspective towards a new sociology. However, these attempts at rethinking the tension between individual and society in the market economy context have not resolved the fundamental problem underpinning the contradiction in pursuing both individual self-interest and the common good.

The moral philosopher Adam Smith wrote of an 'invisible hand' working to ensure that the competitive pursuit of individual self-interest would benefit the common good. However, Smith also argued that allocation of resources by markets would work efficiently only if power and information were distributed equally among actors, and the transactions caused no harm to others—what we nowadays call 'externalities'. The vision of a *homo oeconomicus* ruggedly pursuing individualistic goals is often labelled 'social-Darwinist', but recent re-visiting of Charles Darwin's *The Descent of Man* and *The Origin of Species* has revealed how his work was appropriated for an ideology glorifying competition and 'the survival of the fittest', a phrase coined actually not by Darwin, but by Herbert Spencer, who wrote for *The Economist*. Darwin, by contrast, held 'that humanity's survival was based on our genius for cooperating, bonding and even altruism' (Henderson 2014, 24). However, 'the power of this meme of the "invisible hand" lives on in laissez-faire economics at the Chicago School, in business schools, corporate boardrooms, on Wall Street and in the revolving door "technocrat" politicians installed in many countries by financial interests' (ibid., 25).

Ever since the Romantic movement of the early 1800s, visionaries right across the political spectrum have postulated a *neue Mensch* (= new humanity). Will this 'new humanity' finally emerge, or is it merely one of the abiding myths, part of our modern folklore, like *homo oeconomicus*?

Case Study 1: Market Rationality- The Cobra Effect

The term 'cobra effect' is used to describe a situation where and economic action that assumes market rationality "backfires" and creates the opposite of the intended effect. It goes back to an anecdotes set in India during British colonial rule, when the colonial government was concerned at the spread of venomous snakes. The authorities offered a reward for every dead cobra. At first, this strategy succeeded, and large numbers of dead snakes were handed in. However, people began breeding cobras as a source of income. The government, becoming aware of this, discontinued the scheme in an attempt to discourage further breeding, but the breeders reacted by setting free the now-worthless animals. This meant a further increase in wild cobra numbers—what had seemed a rational solution had actually made the problem worse (Siebert 2002).

A similar episode happened under French colonial rule in Hanoi, where the authorities launched a campaign to eradicate rats, offering a reward for each animal killed. To claim their payment, people had to present a rat's tail. Soon officials began to notice rats without tails. People would capture rats and cut off their tails before releasing so they could reproduce, creating more rats and thus increasing proceeds from rat-catching (Vann 2003).

For more on this, listen to Dubner, S. 11 October 2012. The Cobra Effect. *Freakonomics*, LCC. https://freakonomics.com/podcast/the-cobra-effect-2/ [retrieved 17 January 2022].

8.3 Informal Economy: Substantivism Embodied or Cultural Survival?

It has long been observed that throughout Europe an increasing number of jobs are carried out outside the formal economy (e.g., Aydalot 1984; Alessandrini and Dellago 1987). The term ***informal economy*** is used in this context as an analytical label for such activities within an economy that do not conform to established ***institutions*** of this larger economy, that is, those sets of rules and practices according to which a system is generally supposed to function.

An aspect of informal economy that illustrates much of what has been discussed in this chapter so far is the 'Whole House', a structure that, in the European context, has been described as a pre-industrial relic, a remnant of an earlier stage of cultural evolution, which is thus as foreign to 'us' as if it were found in another country. Outside of Europe, similar structures have been observed. In a study of the domestic economy in Colombia, Gudeman and Rivera (1990) distinguish between the 'corporation' (formal economy) and the 'house' (informal economy)—reflecting Polanyi's distinction of *formal* and *substantive* economy. The key purpose of the latter is to maintain economic autarky, while the former exists for the purposes of economic exchange. Both constellations are 'economically operating social groups in which cultures of livelihood are embodied' (Bird-David 1997, 472). Similar institutions are found elsewhere, however, including in industrial economies:

> Economies range from the capitalist extreme, where corporations are at the centre, and draw on houses in ever expanding margins across political and cultural domains, to the remote local extreme, where houses are at the centre, being impinged on by outside corporations, whose margins they came to be. (ibid.)

One might surmise that this reflects merely a linear evolutionary process in which the global periphery lags behind the global core in its socio-economic development.

Occupational pluralism is particularly important because it is so common. Together with non-commercialized transactions like LETS (Local Exchange and Trading Systems; see below), it is a key characteristic of informal economy in regions like the West of Ireland, where, rather than being relics of cultural survival, they have facilitated innovation and progress. Through their ready adoption of occupational pluralism, European immigrants to the West of Ireland, for example, partly discredited sustained attempts by development authorities, to extinguish traditional institutions by referencing 'European values'—especially to a work ethic that portrays wage dependent factory routine labour as an ideal. These migrants have thus helped preserve a system that allows them to spread risk. Within this system, they can pursue new ideas creating endogenous employment opportunities. This pattern of work organization has considerable innovative potential and seems to offer real opportunities, as Elsasser and Leibundgut (1984) suggested for the Swiss uplands. Urban locations in Europe have also developed straight from a pre- into a post-industrial structure (Kockel 2002a, ch.4), and there at least, the 'Whole House' may also still, or again, be a valid concept. On the other hand, instances where this institution seems to persist in Europe may indeed just be relics of an older socio-economic system. To help decide the matter, it would be useful to see more research on similar structures in these urban locations rather than on the rural periphery, where they are easily dismissed as relics without even a second look.

Case Study 2 Culturally Embedded Economy—The Individual and the 'Whole House'
The "Whole House" can be seen in operation in the system of occupational pluralism that has been widely observed in rural Europe, for example in the West of Ireland (Kockel 2002a). Figure 8.1 shows a typical combination of sources of income for an extended family—where "family" designates people living together, but who are not necessarily blood-relatives (see Weber-Kellermann 1974, 14) —involved in informal economy activities following a pattern called "occupational pluralism" or "pluriactivity".

8 Economy as Intercultural Challenge

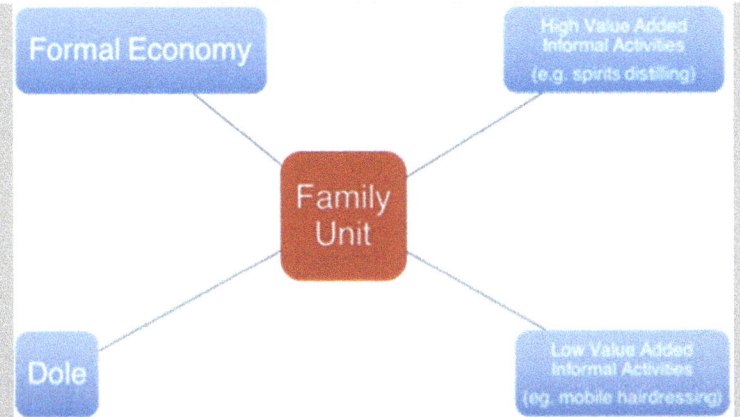

Fig. 8.1 Typical sources of "family" income earned by involvement in informal economy (after Kockel [1993])

While deceptively like the *gig economy* with its multi-jobbing precariat that has become so prevalent in post-industrial societies, the 'Whole House' offers a person communal support structures absent from the ideal model of the isolated individual (Fig. 8.2) that underpins the spread of the gig economy.

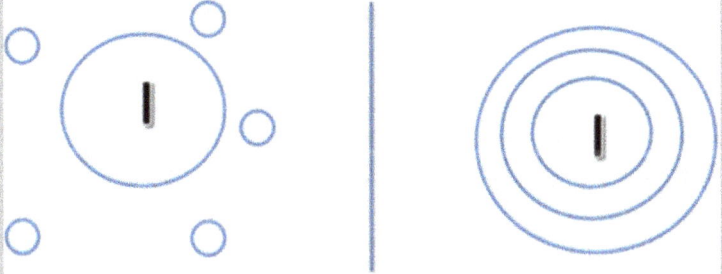

Fig. 8.2 Two contrasting concepts of the individual -isolated (left) and socio-culturally embedded (right)

8.4 Alternative Economics

Arguing from the perspective of an emerging ***development economics***, Weeks (1978, 27) saw orthodox economic concepts as a 'universally applicable … prescription for capitalist underdevelopment'. In the 1980s, challenges like this generated an initiative known as *The Other Economic Summit* (TOES).

8.4.1 From TOES to the SDGs

TOES brought together a very diverse group of thinkers and doers—alternative economists, Greens and community activists from various backgrounds around the world—seeking other ways of managing the economy. TOES also contested the right of the then G7 leaders to speak on behalf of the world. 'Beyond traditional economic textbook definitions of capital, efficient markets, rational actors and property rights, new definitions emerged, of social and human capital, ecological assets, amenity rights and recognition of the domains beyond markets, the commons' (Henderson 2014, 14).

One example of these leaders drawing on informal economy structures and practices was the Kenyan Wangari Maathai. In her book *Replenishing the Earth* (Maathai 2010), she argued that the key to empowerment and conservation lies not in market rationality but in traditional spiritual values—care for nature, gratitude and respect, and a commitment to the common good—which inspired the Green Belt Movement that she founded to reclaim community land from deforestation. While educated in the Christian faith, Maathai drew inspiration from many traditions, including the Jewish mandate *tikkun olam* (= repair the world) and the Japanese dictum *mottainai* (= don't waste).

However, developments like the Green Belt Movement often face resistance and structural violence not just through vertical hierarchies of power—be that state, corporate or financial—but through group violence that can rupture multi-ethnic societies. Another thinker associated with TOES, Frances Stuart, has researched this problematic. Using statistical evidence and in-depth studies of West Africa, Latin America and Southeast Asia, she examined what she called 'horizontal inequalities'—ethnic, religious or racial—as a source of conflict. These horizontal inequalities represent, at a more local level, what at the global level has been described as 'the clash of civilizations' (Huntington 1996); but while the global perspective is based on deductive reasoning and has been subject to considerable criticism, the more local perspective is based on strong evidence. Culturally conditioned horizontal inequalities can be a major obstacle to implementation of the United Nations' ***Sustainable Development Goals*** (SDGs), which are aimed at overcoming vertical inequalities.

8.4.2 Culture as a Resource

The idea of utilizing culture and identity as resources for economic development became popular in Europe at a time when globalization destroyed traditional industries, increasingly turning large parts of the 'developed world' into 'resource peripheries' (Tykkyläinen 1988). 'New World' wines flood the global market, following the idea of comparative advantage (see above), with little regard for the regional culture of the old wine-growing regions of Europe. Riesling produced in Australia may be an instance of 'glocalization' (Robertson 1992)—the context-dependent local form globalization takes—but viticulturist in Central Europe whose generations-old family business goes to the wall as a result might have a different view. Turning the vineyard into a heritage centre may seem an option, but how many wine museums can any region, any village, sustain?

In a study of alternative life-style networks in rural southwest England, Purdue et al. (1997) argued that such networks encourage ecological and cultural innovation, generating a new, culturally rooted sense of place and belonging. Local exchange trading systems, for example, may facilitate economic transactions where the 'invisible hand' fails in allocating resources as needed for local—rather than corporate—benefit. Such networks are components of a region's 'cultural innovation milieu' (O'Doherty et al. 1999). At the local and the small regional scale, for example in the Pays Cathare, around Galway Bay, or in the Cotswolds valleys near Stroud, they may even become significant agents in shaping the public domain (Kockel 2002a).

This also points to another major aspect of identity formation, largely overlooked in the debate on culture and economy, p. the significance of work for identity formation. This is not just a matter of whether someone does have a job or not, although the answer to that question clearly is important. Moser (1998) discussed 'the cultural meaning of work in post-industrial societies' and showed how work is about much more than holding a job, and how it entails a whole range of cultural traits and practices (see Chapters 2 and 3 of this volume). There is, among others, the phenomenon of 'occupational folklore', defined by Tristram Coffin in 1973 as the traditional artistic means of expression used by people who derive their identity, or at least a large part of it, more from the way they earn their livelihood than from their home region or their ethnic descent (Toelken 1986, 219). Here, identity in relation to a peer group is grounded not so much in social status, income, power or other elements that may be relevant to an individual but based on a high level of technical skills that must be recognized by other members of the group (ibid., 226).

8.5 Economics and Religion

The significance of religion and beliefs for an intercultural understanding of economy has been highlighted throughout this chapter. Being a major part of culture, this needs to be considered closely.

8.5.1 Christianity and Capitalism

The religious roots of modern economic ideas were identified most famously in Max Weber's work on *The Protestant Ethic and the Spirit of Capitalism* (1930), which traced the dominant ideas of how the economy works to the religious value system of ascetic Protestantism. Although his analysis remains controversial, it provides a basis for later research and reflections on economic ethics from different perspectives. For example, Rabbi Jonathan Sacks, in his 1998 IEA Hayek Memorial Lecture (Sacks 1999), reflected on the work of liberal market philosopher Friedrich Hayek through the lens of an economic morality based on Judaism. In his analysis of 'Germany's path towards the new economy and the American challenge', economic historian Werner Abelshauser (2005) links the success of the German post-World War II economic model to the ethos of the Historical School with its strong foundations in the Catholic social ethic and Lutheranism, a form of Protestant theology Max Weber had concluded does not correlate with the ethos of individualistic economics typical of the Calvinist Protestantism prevalent in Anglocentric cultures. More recently, Harvard theologian Harvey Cox (2016) controversially traced what he described as the 'deification' of the market—its elevation to the status of Divine authority, comparing economic dogma to that of the Mediaeval Church.

Liberation theology, which emerged as a primarily Roman Catholic movement in Latin America during the 1960s, was a key influence shaping the otherwise predominantly neo-Marxist 'world systems theory' of global socio-economic development. It emphasized a 'liberating praxis', giving emphasis to the social and economic needs of the world's poor and oppressed (Gutiérrez 1973). The movement's influence led to conflict with the Vatican, but the pontificate of Pope Francis has seen an increase in its acceptance, with recent encyclicals, most notably *Laudato Si'* (2015), endorsing its main themes, tying them to earlier encyclicals on the Catholic social ethic, most notably *Rerum novarum* (1891) and *Populorum progressio* (1967). However, liberation theology is not exclusively Catholic; it has been applied, for example, from an interreligious perspective infused with Protestant and indigenous ideas, in the context of Scottish land reform (McIntosh 2008).

8.5.2 Non-Christian Traditions and the Future Earth

Non-Christian spiritual traditions have become increasingly influential in shaping economic thinking. In his landmark book *Small is Beautiful,* Schumacher (1973) outlined a Buddhist economics based on the concept of 'right livelihood', which defines labour not as an input to, but an output of production, and thus valuable for its own sake. He also emphasized the need for 'intermediate' technology—labour-intensive production securing rural employment in particular—and the substitution of Western economists' dedication to 'market value' by a concept of 'use value' (see also Henderson 1996, 21). His thinking inspired many activists like Wangari Maathai (see above). Recent decades have seen a resurgence of Indigenous perspectives, especially in response to climate change, and this is likely to have an impact on economic thinking in years to come.

The rise of Islamic finance (see Chapter 9 of this volume) is just one example of challenges to the received Western model of economy emanating from Islam, which makes these challenges particularly interesting in the context of Huntington's (1996) hypothesis of an impending culture war between a historically dominant 'Judeo-Christian' and a 'Muslim' worldview. Huntington's theory—like some highly popular approaches to intercultural communication and conflict, such as Hofstede's (1984) 'cultural dimensions' theory—suffers from a rather 'shallow essentialist' (Kockel 2012) view of culture that, in its tendency to simplify and stereotype, runs counter to anthropological insights into cultural practice. However, more important in the present context than the finer points of theory is the re-examination of cultural notions of 'value' that different religious traditions share in their opposition to received 'Western' views of the economy.

> **Case Study 3: The Muslim Cola Challenge to 'Western' Values**
> In the early years of the twenty-first century, several brands of cola drinks emerged that were marketed under the banner of 'ethical' consumption, inspired by the teachings of Islam, which were referenced in the very brand name, *Mecca Cola*. The name refers to the spiritual centre of the Muslim world, to which each Muslim is obliged to make a pilgrimage at least once in his or her lifetime. *Mecca Cola*, which was launched in France, was inspired by *Zamzam Cola*, an Iranian-made drink named after a holy spring in Mecca. The emphasis was placed on the basis of the company's business ethos in the teachings of Islam, stressing especially their commitment to *zakāt*, charitable giving, which is one of the 'Five Pillars' of Islam. The commitment was therefore made to give a share of the company's profits to charitable causes. This made the product attractive for consumers looking for an ethical alternative to soft drinks produced by large capitalist multinationals.
>
> **Further Reading:**
> Justo, Rachida and Cristina Cruz. 2009. "Mecca-Cola: Message in a Bottle." *Journal of Research in Marketing and Entrepreneurship* 10(1): 40–56.
> http://www.cbsnews.com/news/the-muslim-cola-wars/ [accessed 13 September 2022].

8.6 Conclusion

Walter Weisskopf, in *Alienation and Economics* (1971), emphasized that notions of value are arbitrary and culture-bound, arguing that the US economy, for example, overvalues material compared to spiritual wealth, and competitive activities over co-operation. Hazel Henderson (1996, 138) relates an interesting conversation she had with a project director at the Japan Techno-Economics Society:

> He pointed out that from the quantities and configurations of material artifacts and technologies created by various cultures it was possible to infer a great deal about their value systems. He noted, for example, on one end of the scale the Balinese, who create exquisite music, dances, rituals, stories and clothes, but are rather uninterested in hardware. On the

other end of the scale are the Americans, who ... are even unable to enjoy leisure activities such as hiking without an incredible quantity of gear—let alone our uniquely energy- and materials-intensive hobbies, such as those involving snowmobiles, beach buggies and camping vehicles.

Already at the turn of the nineteenth to the twentieth century, Georg Simmel, in his *Philosophy of Money* (2001, 480–501), critically diagnosed the elevation of a culture of material things at the expense of a culture of the person—what he described as the 'material subjectivation of the spirit'. However, this transformation has not led to rational *homo oeconomicus* gaining ground in actual practice; their practices are strongly reminiscent of belief in magic rather than market rationality. And in this, they may not be alone. There is a long tradition of narrative research dealing with fairy tales and other oral traditions. It would be interesting to see what researchers in this field make of concepts and storylines in modern economics, and how these compare, cross-culturally, with other ways of telling the story of the economy.

Review Questions

1. To what extent do the examples of the "cobra effect" corroborate, or challenge, the concept of *homo oeconomicus* as rational actor? What other examples of the "cobra effect" can you think of, and to what extent do these examples illustrate culture-specific behaviour or universal principles?
2. How significant is the fact that both examples are set in Asia, and under colonial rule?
3. Considering Fig. 8.1, can you think of other examples of high or low value-added activities, and what makes them suitable for informal economy?
4. Considering Fig. 8.2, what can you see as the potential benefits and problems for the individual in each model?
5. The *zakāt* must be distributed in the community from which the revenue was taken. Consider how this works in practice with a company selling its products in the UK but supporting "world causes".

Recommended Further Reading

- Hann, C., and K. Hart. 2011. *Economic anthropology.* Cambridge: Polity.
- McIntosh, A. 2004. *Soil and Soul. People versus Corporate Power.* London: Aurum.
- Raworth, K. 2017. *Doughnut economics. Seven ways to think like a 21st century economist.* London: Random House.
- Sahlins, M. 1974 *Stone Age Economics.* London: Tavistock.
- Sen, A. 2001. *Development as Freedom.* Oxford: Oxford University Press.

References

Abelshauser, W. 2005. *The Dynamics of German Industry*. Oxford: Berghahn.
Adams, J., ed. 1980. *Institutional Economics*. Den Haag: Martinus Nijhoff.
Alessandrini, S. and B. Dellago. 1987. *The Unofficial Economy*. Aldershot: Gower.
Attfield, R. 1994 *Environmental Philosophy*. Aldershot: Avebury.
Aydalot, P. 1984. Questions for Regional Economy. *Tijdschrift Vor Economische En Sociale Geografie* 75: 4–13.
Balabkins, N. 1987. Line by Line: Schmoller's Grundriss: Its Meaning for the 1980s. *International Journal of Social Economics* 14 (1): 22–31.
Bassand, M., E. Brugger, J. Bryden, J. Friedmann, and B. Stuckey, eds. 1986. *Self-reliant Development in Europe*. Aldershot: Gower.
Beck, U. 1997. *The Reinvention of Politics*. Cambridge: Polity.
Beckert, J. 2007 *The Great Transformation of Embeddedness: Karl Polanyi and the New Economic Sociology*, MPIfG Discussion Paper 07/1. Köln: Max-Planck-Institut für Gesellschaftsforschung.
Bekemans, L. 1994. Economy and Culture in European Society—Methodological Considerations. *History of European Ideas* 19 (1–3): 261–268.
Bird-David, N. 1997. Economies: A Cultural-economic Perspective. *International Social Science Journal* 154: 463–475.
Bossel, H. 1987. Viability and Sustainability: Matching Development Goals to Resource Constraints. *Futures*, April: 114–128.
Boyle, D., and A. Simms, eds. 2009. *The New Economics*. London: Earthscan.
Brugger, E. 1986. Endogenous Development: A Concept between Utopia and Reality. In *Self-reliant Development in Europe,* ed. Bassand et al., 38–58. Aldershot: Gower.
Brunner, O. 1956. *Neue Wege der Sozialgeschichte*. Göttingen: Vandenhoeck & Ruprecht.
Castells, M. 2010. *The Rise of the Network Society*. 2nd ed. with a new pref. Oxford: Wiley-Blackwell.
Cox, H. 2016. *The Market as God*. Cambridge/MA: Harvard University Press.
Elsasser, H. and H. Leibundgut. 1984. *Erfahrungen mit der Mehrfachbeschäftigung im ländlichen Raum der Schweiz*. Paper read at a symposium on Occupational Pluralism and Development in Rural Areas, Gießen/Germany, September.
Frykman, J. 1999. Belonging in Europe: Modern Identities in Minds and Places. *Ethnologia Europaea* 29 (2): 13–24.
Glasman, M. 1996. *Unnecessary Suffering*. London: Verso.
Granovetter, M. 1985. Economic Action and Social Structure: The Problem of Embeddedness. *American Journal of Sociology* 91: 481–510.
Gruchy, A. 1987. *The Reconstruction of Economics*. New York: Greenwood.
Gudeman, S. 1986. *Economics as Culture*. London: Routledge and Kegan.
Gudeman, S., and A. Rivera. 1990. *Conversations in Columbia: The Domestic Economy in Life and Text*. Cambridge: Cambridge University Press.
Gutiérrez, G. 1973. *A Theology of Liberation*. Maryknoll/NY: Orbis.
Haskell, T. 1996. Persons as Uncaused Causes: John Stuart Mill, the Spirit of Capitalism, and the "Invention" of Formalism. In *The Culture of the Market*, ed. T. Haskell and R. Teichgraeber, 441–502. Cambridge: Cambridge University Press.
Heierli, U. 1986. Division of Labour and Appropriate Technology — from Adam Smith to E. F. Schumacher. In *Self-reliant Development in Europe*, ed. M. Bassand et al., 9–37. Aldershot: Gower.
Henderson, H. 1996. *Creating Alternative Futures*. West Hartford, CT: Kumarian.
Henderson, H. 2014. *Mapping the Global Transition to the Solar Age*. London: ICAEW and The Centre for Tomorrow's Company.
Henry, P., and B. Kossou. 1985. *La dimension culturelle du développement: Une étude conjointe CEE/UNESCO*. Paris: Les Nouvelles Éditions Africaines.

Herzfeld, M. 1997. Anthropological Perspectives: Disturbing the Structures of Power and Knowledge. *International Social Science Journal* 154: 453–462.
Hirsch, F. 1977. *The Social Limits to Growth*. London: Routledge and Kegan Paul.
Huntington, S. 1996. *The Clash of Civilizations and the Remaking of World Order*. New York: Simon & Schuster.
Ingold, T. 1998. Person, Village and Culture: Notes on the Translation of Three Key Concepts. *EAGLE Street: Newsletter of the Finnish Institute in London* 9, June, 8.
Jackson, T. 2009. *Prosperity without Growth*. London: Earthscan.
Jeggle, U., G. Korff, M. Scharfe, and B. Warneken, eds. 1986. *Volkskultur in der Moderne*. Reinbek: Rowohlt.
Joas, H. 1996. *The Creativity of Action*. Cambridge: Polity.
Justo, R., and C. Cruz. 2009. Mecca-Cola: Message in a Bottle. *Journal of Research in Marketing and Entrepreneurship* 10 (1): 40–56.
Kockel, U. 1993. *The Gentle Subversion: Informal Economy and Regional Economic Development in the West of Ireland*. Bremen: ESIS.
Kockel, U. 2002a. *Regional Culture and Economic Development*. Aldershot: Ashgate.
Kockel, U., ed. 2002b. *Culture and Economy*. Aldershot: Ashgate.
Kockel, U. 2012. 'Being From and Coming To: Outline of an Ethno-Ecological Framework. In *Radical Human Ecology*, ed. L. Williams, R. Roberts, and A. McIntosh, 57–71. Aldershot: Ashgate.
Kramer, D. 1986. Marktstruktur und Kulturprozeß. Überlegungen zum Verhältnis von Kultur und kapitalistischer Gesellschaft. In *Volkskultur in der Moderne,* ed. U. Jeggle, G. Korff, M. Scharfe, and B. Warneken, 37–53. Reinbek: Rowohlt.
Maathai, W. 2010. *Replenishing the Earth: Spiritual Values for Healing Ourselves and the World*. New York: Doubleday.
Maffesoli, M. 1996. *The Time of the Tribes*. London: Sage.
Maneschi, A. 1998. *Comparative Advantage in International Trade: A Historical Perspective*. Cheltenham: Elgar.
McIntosh, A. 2008. *Re-Kindling Community. Schumacher Briefing 15*. Cambridge: Green Books.
Moser, J. 1998. On the Cultural Meaning of Work in Post-industrial Societies. *Ethnologia Europaea* 28 (1): 55–66.
O'Doherty, R., J. Dürrschmidt, P. Jowers, and D.A. Purdue. 1999. Local Exchange and Trading Schemes: A Useful Strand of Community Economic Development? *Environment and Planning a: Economy and Space* 31 (9): 1639–1653.
Plumpe, W. 1999. Gustav von Schmoller und der Institutionalismus: Zur Bedeutung der Historischen Schule der Nationalökonomie für die moderne Wirtschaftsgeschichtsschreibung. *Geschichte Und Gesellschaft* 25 (2): 252–275.
Polanyi, K. 1944. *The Great Transformation*. New York: Farrar & Rinehart.
Purdue, D., J. Dürrschmidt, P. Jowers, and R. O'Doherty. 1997. DIY Culture and Extended Milieux: LETS, Veggie Boxes and Festivals. *Sociological Review* 45 (4): 645–646.
Ray, C. 1998. Culture, Intellectual Property and Territorial Rural Development. *Sociologia Ruralis* 38 (1): 3–20.
Ray, L., and A. Sayer, eds. 1999. *Culture and Economy after the Cultural Turn*. London: Sage.
Riehl, W. 1855. *Die Familie*. Stuttgart: Cotta.
Robertson, R. 1992. *Globalization*. London: Sage.
Robertson, R., and F. Lechner. 1985. Modernization, Globalization and the Problem of Culture in World-Systems Theory. *Theory, Culture & Society* 2 (3): 103–117.
Röpke, J. 1990. Evolution and innovation. In *The Evolution of Economic Systems*, ed. K. Dopfer and K. Raible, 111–120. Basingstoke: Macmillan.
Sacks, J. 1999. *Morals and Markets*. IEA Occasional Paper 108. London: Institute of Economic Affairs.
Schiffauer, W. 1997. *Fremde in der Stadt*. Frankfurt/M.: Suhrkamp.
Schneider, H. 1974. *Economic Man*. New York: Free Press.

Siebert, H. 2002. *Der Kobra-Effekt*. München: DVA.
Simmel, G. 2001. *Philosophie des Geldes*. Köln: Parkland.
Simonsen, K. 2001. Space, Culture and Economy—a Question of Practice. *Geografiska Annaler B* 83 (1): 41–52.
Sonn, J., and D. Lee. 2012. Revisiting the Branch Plant Syndrome: Review of Literature on Foreign Direct Investment and Regional Development in Western Advanced Economies. *International Journal of Urban Sciences* 16 (3): 243–259.
Stöhr, W. 1986. Changing External Conditions and a Paradigm Shift in Regional Development Strategies?. In *Self-reliant Development in Europe,* ed. M. Bassand, E. Brugger, J. Bryden, J. Friedmann, and B. Stuckey, 59–73. Aldershot: Gower.
Thompson, E.P. 1971. The Moral Economy of the English Crowd in the Eighteenth Century. *Past & Present* 50: 76–136.
Toelken, B. 1986. Industriekultur oder Folklore der Arbeitswelt: Beobachtungen in den USA. In *Volkskultur in der Moderne*, ed. U. Jeggle, G. Korff, M. Scharfe, and B. Warneken, 219–229. Reinbek: Rowohlt.
Tykkyläinen, M. 1988. Periphery Syndrome—a Reinterpretation of Regional Development Theory in a Resource Periphery. *Fennia* 166 (2): 295–411.
Vann, M. 2003. Of Rats, Rice, and Race: The Great Hanoi Rat Massacre, an Episode in French Colonial History. *French Colonial History* 4: 191–203.
Weber, M. 1930. *The Protestant Ethic and the Spirit of Capitalism* London: Allen & Unwin.
Weber-Kellermann, I. 1974. *Die deutsche Familie*. Frankfurt/Main: Suhrkamp.
Weisskopf, W. 1971. *Alienation and Economics*. New York: Dutton.

Chapter 9
Intercultural Issues in Finance

Lina Fadel, Ken Brown, and Abdulkader Mostafa

> An informed appreciation of cultural nuances and differences is central to global financial literacy and the establishment of trust, yet, it is often overlooked. With this in mind, the chapter focuses on three main themes. First, it discusses how financial centres are operating in a globalised world and associated challenges, with a focus on London and New York. Second, it looks at money and mobile payments, with a focus on the case of M-Pesa in Kenya. We conclude with a discussion of the cultural factors at work in the case of Islamic finance and the risk-averse Japanese financial system.

9.1 Introduction

Over the past twenty years, globalisation and the rise of technological advancement, travel opportunities and global training have resulted in major changes in finance and the labour markets. These influences have also manifested in an increasing homogeneity in financial practices and trainings across the world. Such homogeneous financial practices, however, are the result of Western influence and while seen across the world today, they have not been fully endorsed by certain cultural sensitivities in Africa, India, China and the Arab World. Despite the illusions of globalisation, complex intercultural challenges continue to shape finance and financial institutions

---

L. Fadel (✉) · K. Brown · A. Mostafa
Heriot-Watt University, Edinburgh, Scotland, UK
e-mail: lina.fadel@hw.ac.uk

K. Brown
e-mail: kenneth.brown@hw.ac.uk

A. Mostafa
e-mail: a.mostafa@hw.ac.uk

© The Author(s), under exclusive license to Springer Nature Switzerland AG 2023
K. Strani and K. Pfeiffer (eds.), *Intercultural Issues in the Workplace*,
https://doi.org/10.1007/978-3-031-42320-8_9

in our changing world. These challenges necessitate cultural literacy and make an understanding of culture and cultural specificities essential to overcoming obstacles to making sound financial decisions in intercultural contexts.

Discussion in the following sections will focus on culture, how it came to influence scientific disciplines such as economics and finance and manifests in financial situations and systems. The discussion then moves on to examining how the world becoming increasingly interconnected does not always translate into interconnected financial centres and unified financial decisions. Subsequently, the chapter provides an overview of how culture informs money-related practices, including money-transmission across cultures, and we present two case studies that demonstrate such financial practices and the underlying cultural factors. The chapter concludes with a discussion of how culture-specific needs and religious beliefs inform and shape financial systems and products, drawing on examples from the Muslim world and East Asia.

9.2 The Centrality of Culture in Finance

Recent studies show how culture continues to influence capital structures (Chui et al. 2002; El Ghoul et al. 2018), cash holdings (Ramirez and Tadesse 2009), to name a few. Evidently, scholars have come to accept the need for a realisation of the underlying cultural structures that characterise certain financial phenomena, especially when employing financial theory alone falls short of providing sufficient elucidation. In all, there was a 'cultural revolution' (Zingales 2015) entering the field of finance, supporting the view that the cultural/intercultural perspective of finance should not be taken as a rejection of its fundamental assumptions.

Attempts to integrate culture into economics have resulted in a new branch of economics, namely 'Cultural Economics: Z1', when the cultural revolution in finance was still in its infancy. Even as the term 'cultural finance' came to be widely recognised and used, thanks to early and impactful work such as Grinblatt and Keloharju's (2001) study of culture in finance, scholars were still questioning whether finance had a cultural dimension (Hens and Wang 2007) and whether 'national culture' was a meaningful concept (Minkov and Hofstede 2012) in the first place. Not only has there been an eruption of economic and financial work on culture in recent years, but also the term 'cultural finance' has become widely used to refer to 'a multidisciplinary research stream [that] has incorporated national culture to explain cross-country differences in various financial studies' (Breuer et al. 2014, 289).

In the following sections, we offer general guidelines to shepherd you through an understanding of how financial systems operate despite the forces of globalisation.

9.3 Finance in a Globalised World and the Globalisation of Finance

Globalisation is most typically defined along the lines of economic and industrial relationships and interconnected political entities (Kluver 2000). The relevance of globalisation to any account of finance and financial markets cannot be overstated, for globalisation is overwhelmingly affecting interrelationships around the world. Kluver and Fu (2004) argue that 'the transmission of cultural capital across cultures has a significant impact on the economic, political, and social development of nations'. The authors provide vivid examples to aid our understanding of how that transmission is being facilitated: whether expressed by the desire to receive and be influenced by ideas and values from abroad, the internationalisation of sports heroes like David Beckham and Rafael Nadal, or music—or even the Egyptian McDonald's serving their patrons McFalafel, it is clear that a 'global culture', or what Kluver and Fu (2004) also refer to as 'cultural globalisation', is emerging and may be here to stay.

Financial globalisation has no doubt come with its challenges. It has, however, mostly created opportunities for, and brought great benefits to, national economies, financial systems and capital markets and has generally been conducive to growth. Two decades ago, investors would have been restricted to borrowing from a domestic bank; however, thanks to the forces of globalisation, they now can shop around the world for better and cheaper loan deals. Resistance to the global, however, can still be seen in some financial contexts where religious and cultural values continue to shape financial practices. This, for example, can be seen in the rise of Islamic banking and finance, a financial model that addresses a culture-specific need to preserve the socio-religious values of Islam in financial transactions.

In financial terms, a better grasping of what globalisation denotes and connotes requires an understanding of the financial centres and the evolution of finance from the 'mainstream' unitarist Anglo-Saxon system to a pluralist financial system that recognises unique cultural requirements. A discussion of financial centres follows.

9.4 Financial Systems and Centres

Within the scope of finance, there are systems for a reason. Changes in the political economy, globalisation and socio-cultural differences are all valid ways to debunk the myth of the single global financial system. Indeed, we read—and hear—critiques of the ultimate universal model, in reference to the **Anglo-Saxon model**, and calls identifying the need for new models that delimit capital tyranny. This is clear in statements made by such world leaders as former French President Nicolas Sarkozy who, in the wake of the 2008 global financial meltdown, celebrated 'the return of the state', 'the end of the ideology of public powerlessness' and how the world 'had turned the page on the Anglo-Saxon model'. While the Anglo-Saxon financial system is seen as having failed and the need for more financial autonomy has become more pronounced all over the world in recent years, no consensus has yet been reached as to what a viable financial system should look like, nor has it been determined as to how certain financial problems are to be addressed.

The following section draws on how cultural differences inform a better understanding of financial practices, decisions and phenomena. We discuss three main themes—certainly not an exhaustive list; however, these should be sufficient to demonstrate the workings of culture within the field of finance. First, we discuss how financial centres are operating in a globalised world and associated challenges, with a focus on London and New York. We then move on to looking at money and mobile payments in the cases of M-Pesa in Kenya and cryptocurrency in Nigeria. We conclude with a discussion of the cultural factors at work in the case of Islamic finance and the risk-averse Japanese financial system.

9.4.1 The Case of London and New York

A financial centre like London can offer the whole range of financial products to businesses, traders and investors alike. There are a number of roles that financial centres like London can provide. Firstly, there is the pooling of savings: when institutions, like pension funds and insurance companies, collect savings and invest across markets, they are diversifying risk. Companies can access that pool of savings to raise capital for investment projects. This is a vast pool of savings, and it is being repeated across different markets. Secondly, we have the transfer across time and space: financing house purchases now and paying pensions later. Thirdly, there is the pooling of risk: here insurance companies offer protection.

Information costs: financial markets gather information about companies; analysts will assess their creditworthiness and work out what the value of the companies should be. This would be very difficult without the financial markets. Financial centres like London and New York have evolved over a long period of time; they have hundreds of years of history as financial centres. It is hard for a country to establish an international financial centre from scratch.

The London and New York cases cannot be replicated easily. Financial centres like Dubai, Shanghai and Moscow would all like to be major international financial centres, but at the current time, they are not a threat to London or New York. They do not have the full infrastructure. A key feature of an international financial centre is that it is run by international people. London and New York have been traditionally open to people from any location as long as they have the skills needed by that centre. Other centres are not so open to foreign nationals; they have weaker regulations, and English is not the first language. Now, if those are not the workings of globalisation, then what is? The following section looks at money in different cultural contexts.

9.5 Money: Transmission and Saving

Money is essential to the smooth working of an economy. Without money, we would have a system of barter, where goods and services would be traded for other goods and services, rather than for money. Today's story is different, and money is moving into a digital era. In parts of Africa, for example, where cash is not used that much, transfers take place via mobile money. Africa is a vast continent, with disparate populations outside the main cities where there is little financial infrastructure and many people do not have bank accounts or credit cards. In these areas in the past, bartering may have played a large role in facilitating trade.

Africa has been the world leader in adopting mobile payment systems. It is the continent that had the fastest take up of mobile money usage in the world. It has been easier to pay for goods and services over the phone in Africa than in many of the larger OECD economies. One of the reasons for the rapid take up of mobile payments in Africa was a lack of confidence in traditional financial institutions. It was quicker (and safer) to transfer small amounts of money using mobile networks (initially with M-Pesa in Kenya). Many parts of Africa did not have an extensive network of ATMs, so mobile money provided that service.

9.6 Mobile Payments

Most people would not have bank accounts and any savings would be effectively kept 'under the mattress', which was vulnerable to theft. The uptake of mobile payment systems has disrupted the way banking and finance have operated in the continent. The banking infrastructure was very limited, and the mobile payments system offered great convenience to users. There has been a vast and rapid cultural change which has also brought about faith in the mobile payment system; for example, if a person only had enough money for a bus fare home, they would rather use the money to buy mobile airtime and to call someone to send more money to them.

Mobile payment systems have had a less rapid take up in the richer OECD countries because there has been a long-established network of financial institutions at a local level and a system of regulations that has evolved over many decades, where protection of the customer is a key concern. Africa had very low penetration by financial institutions across the whole population of African countries, so not many people had access to well capitalised financial institutions. Africans seem to trust mobile operators more than they do financial institutions. This is different from the situation in Europe and other richer parts of the world where there is widespread trust in financial institutions such as pension funds, insurance companies and banks. It is not perfect and there have been mis-selling scandals involving banks in the UK, but there are strong and effective regulators acting in the consumers' interest. There is still widespread corruption and bribery in many African countries, however, which enhances the need for transparency and honesty.

The African nations that have been the keenest adopters of mobile payments have been those in the east of Africa: Kenya, Uganda and Tanzania. The main providers are M-Pesa and Airtel. M-Pesa is the Swahili word for money; the rapid development of online systems has other implications for Africa as well. In Europe and America, over the past decades, there has been massive investment in retail distribution, through shopping outlets and malls. In many African countries, the online shopping market reduces the need for an extensive retail network.

Mobile technology is changing the way business is conducted in Africa. In the richer countries, businesses have always been able to keep in touch with market prices for their goods. This was not the case in Africa. Farmers would go through middlemen, but now they know where the markets are and where the demand is, thanks to the dissemination of information over the mobile networks. Farmers are able to direct their crops to where the markets are. Mobile technology is changing the culture of business across continents, but it is Africa where it has had the biggest impact in changing existing financial cultures.

Case-Study 1: M-Pesa

M-Pesa was set up by Vodafone and Safaricom in 2007 in Kenya. At the time, individuals in Kenya were very poorly served in terms of financial services. There was not an extensive banking infrastructure and it was risky, expensive and slow to transfer money from one person to another. M-Pesa revolutionised personal finance firstly in Kenya and then in many other African countries. By 2021 it had 50 million monthly active users across Africa. A major driver of this growth was during the pandemic (2020/21), with transaction volumes increasing dramatically. The service enabling users to transfer funds remotely was essential during this period.

M-Pesa grew rapidly because the conditions at the time allowed it. Kenya had few banks outside the cities and it was risky to carry money or to trust people with money. The structure of the modern Kenyan family, characterized by intimacy, affection and strong ties, was another key factor that fueled a cultural need for M-Pesa transactions (Nyairo 2015). Mobile phone penetration had risen very quickly, with mobile networks essentially missing out the need to develop a fixed line telephone infrastructure. Once it was seen that M-Pesa offered many advantages; faster, cheaper, and guaranteed transfers of money, mobile phone users were quick to embrace the service. Businesses have been built on the back of M-Pesa which has allowed sections of the population to set up businesses that had been shut out before. The service has been a key factor in lifting hundreds of thousands of Kenyans out of poverty.

What M-Pesa does is increase financial inclusion (i.e., giving access to financial services). If people are excluded from financial services, it means it is difficult to transfer money to support family members or even receive wages. Before M-Pesa, nearly 50% of Kenyans were financially excluded. By 2021, 84% of Kenyans had access to formal financial services (and another

5% informally via shopkeepers and moneylenders). M-Pesa has led to greater financial resilience in Kenyan families. They are better able to stand up to economic shocks such as bad weather affecting crops, sudden illnesses, or through temporary layoffs at work. They are able to maintain spending through money transfers from other family members. This has allowed Kenyan families to fare better than other families in similar situations in other African countries.

Mobile banking allows remittances to be easily transferred from outside Africa. In 2018, remittances into Africa from family members outside Africa exceeded $48 billion. The mobile phone has allowed African countries to jump ahead in communications development by leapfrogging past fixed lines. Mobile banking offers the same opportunity to jump ahead in financial services. Traditional banking and rolling out branch networks is expensive and slow; mobile banking, as Kenya has shown, by contrast, offers a quick route to financial inclusion that benefits most of the population.

Kenya compares very favourably with countries with more traditional established financial services. In an index of financial inclusion from 2017, Kenya was ranked number 43 out of 143 countries. Kenya was ranked above Czech Republic (#45), China (#48), Russia (#52), Brazil, South Africa, and Turkey (#60, 61, & 62 respectively). Top of the list was Denmark, with the UK number 19 and the US number 28. Kenya is likely to have climbed higher on this list since 2017.

Consider:

1. What are the benefits of mobile banking to a developing country? What are the conditions necessary for it to succeed?

    The benefits of mobile banking would be a safer system of transferring money. It would be quicker, easier, more certain and could be trusted more. Previously, with the largely unbanked Kenyan state, people would have to take risks to transfer money and they could be robbed of the money if they tried to transfer in person. With a safe secure mobile network, with millions of transactions each day, Kenyans trust M-Pesa with their money.

    The conditions needed for an uptake of mobile banking would be, strong mobile phone penetration in the country and an established business to run the system. In Kenya, it was Vodafone that was running M-Pesa not the government. The people may not trust the government.

2. Which parts of society in developing countries are likely to particularly benefit from this service?

    Mobile banking allows everyone to participate, so the whole family can have mobile accounts and easily transfer money. Sons and daughters that go off to university will have access to money transfers from family members if they are struggling. Mobile banking has allowed many more women to set up in

business and control their finances. It gave women more financial independence in households headed by males.
3. What do you understand about financial inclusion? What is so problematic about financial exclusion?

   Financial inclusion means that people can access financial services, i.e. they can set up bank accounts and start saving money and use the financial system to pay for goods and services and send money to people. Being financially included would mean that an individual could build up a credit history and then be able to access credit to start a business.

   Financial exclusion can keep people trapped in poverty. Without financial inclusion, it would be difficult to get credit, and this would limit the life choices for individuals. An individual would find it difficult to set up a business and carry out normal commercial transactions. Expanding a small business while being financially excluded would be very difficult.
4. Describe how Kenyans conducted their financial activities before M-Pesa launched? What were the main problems?

   Transferring money would have been difficult, especially out of the large cities. There would be very little financial infrastructure in rural Kenya, so this would have been a risky, potentially dangerous task. The traditional money transfer companies like Western Union would charge large commissions to transfer money to banks in the large cities. The main problems were the risks involved, the time it took and the cost of transferring money and having a secure place to keep the cash.

9.7 Alternatives to Conventional Financial Systems

The above discussion demonstrated a changing financial world and alternatives to the conventional financial systems. While some might not be viable, others may provide a more reliable financial solution. Do these exist? And what do they offer? To address these questions, we explore the two cases of finance in the Islamic world and Japan.

9.7.1 Islamic Banking and Finance

Islamic finance provides a good example of how cultural and religious beliefs can influence both the national and global financial markets. Islamic Finance is based on the following key principles: (1) prohibition of interest on transactions; (2) transactions must be backed by real assets; (3) prohibition of engagement in transactions that entail excessive uncertainty or speculation (e.g. gambling); (4) prohibition of engagement in immoral and Islamic unacceptable activities (e.g. tobacco or alcohol production); (5) the returns must be based on risk sharing (Ayub 2009). The engagement in transactions that are not aligned with the Islamic principles and Sharia law (especially in the giving or receiving of interest) is considered by Islam as committing great sins whereby severe punishment is declared for those engaging in such transactions (Hanif 2014).

The first seed of Islamic finance was planted in a remote village in Egypt in 1963—a small Islamic bank experiment that ended in 1968. Islamic finance, or the closest version to what we have today, emerged in 1975 with the formation of the first modern commercial Islamic bank in the world in Dubai (DIB) (Ayub 2009). Prior to 1975, Muslims had no choice but to rely on the conventional financing services to meet their needs (a necessary evil!) (Hanif 2014). However, Islamic financing was initially more costly than the conventional option due to the limitation in the number of Islamic banks and the nature of the demand for Islamic banking products. The introduction of Islamic finance in Muslim countries unearthed a strong, cost-inelastic and growing demand from those Muslims that feared their Lord and were willing to pay higher costs in order to please Him. The industry today is yet to reach 100 million customers worldwide, according to EY's World Islamic Banking Competitiveness Report of 2016.

Worldwide, Islamic finance has already been integrated into the global financial system and there is strong evidence that it has spurred the development of the banking sector. The Islamic finance market has expanded rapidly at 10–12% annual growth rate over the past decade and the number of Islamic financial institutions worldwide has risen ever since its inception in 1975 to over 300 in more than 75 countries (El Qorchi 2005). They are concentrated in the Middle East and Southeast Asia (with Bahrain and Malaysia being the biggest hubs), but also appearing in Europe and the United States. There has also been a surge of interest in Islamic finance from non-Muslim countries such as the UK, Luxembourg, South Africa and Hong Kong.

This recent growth in global Islamic finance can be attributed to three main reasons. The first is the philosophical focus on equity-like sharing of risk and reward that attracted Muslim and non-Muslim market participants. The second is the growing oil sector in the gulf region with soaring demand for Islamic investment assets. The third is the strong demand from Muslim communities in non-Muslim countries. To a great extent, Islamic banking has so far been spared from the recent serious financial crisis and demonstrated a great deal of resilience due to the close link between profitability and productivity and prohibition of speculative activities (Gheeraert 2014). This sheds light on the Islamic model of finance as a more ethical method of financing and encouraged the World Bank Group to use Islamic finance in client countries to develop stable and resilient financial sectors, reduce poverty and improve access to finance. In Scotland, the Ethical Finance Hub (EFH) has been established in 2016 with a vision to creating a financial system where integration of environmental, social, governance and faith-based values become the norm and not the niche.

The intercultural integration in the global financial sector can be illustrated by the launch of the first Japanese overseas Islamic branch in 2015 in Dubai by the Bank of Tokyo-Mitsubishi UFJ. The Japanese bank looks for ways to tap the large pools of wealth and liquidity of the Islamic customer base. The Global Finance magazine has perceived the launch as the Japanese bank being learning to speak Arabic (see Chapter 8). In 2013, London city played host to the first World Islamic Forum outside the Muslim world. British Prime Minister David Cameron declared: "I don't just want London to be a great capital of Islamic finance in the Western world; I want London to stand alongside Dubai and Kuala Lumpur as one of the great capitals of Islamic Finance anywhere in the world". In 2014, The UK was the first non-Islamic country in the world to issue a sovereign sukuk (the Islamic equivalent to bonds) when it raised £200 million which was followed by the second offering of £500 million in March 2021. Islamic finance has gained a foothold outside the Islamic world; the UK is but one example. Whether Islamic Finance can maintain its growth momentum and offer a more resilient and viable 'alternative' to conventional financing is subject to extensive research. In the following section, we look at how Japan provides another example of how different cultural factors call for different financial models.

9.7.2 The Case of Japan

The risk-aversion culture in Japan shapes the Japanese financial market and investment decisions. The structure of the financial market in Japan is unique and differs substantially from other global financial markets. At the end of World War II, the Zaibatsu holding companies that controlled large clusters of firms were replaced by the Keirestu conglomerates system led by the largest banks that closely involved with their borrowers over the long run. The leader banks usually have major holdings of bonds and common stock of the borrowers, and it is also common for the banks to be seated in the companies' board of directors. This close relationship between firms and their leading bank led to an extreme high financial leverage of Japanese companies. It is common for the debt of a Japanese company to exceed shareholders' equity by a multiple of five or six times (Suzuki and Wright 1985).

On the investment side, the Japanese tend to be more risk-averse than their peers in other countries. The total value of venture capital completed transactions in Japan in 2015 stood at just $800 million as compared to $72 billion in the United States and $49 billion in China. Too few Japanese are starting new companies. According to a 2014 report from the Global Entrepreneurship Monitor, less than one in three adults in Japan considered starting a new company a smart career choice—the second-lowest proportion in the study. The report shows also that those that expressed their fear of failure accounted for 55% of potential Japanese entrepreneurs, the second-highest rate in the study (*The Japan Times online*, May 2015). During a visit to the United States in 2016, Prime Minister Shinzo Abe stated that risk-averse culture stifling Japanese innovation while 'risk-takers' are respected in the United States. This is something Japanese business people need, he added "something to think about in the future is, how can Japan drive an entrepreneurial spirit?" he added (*Business Standard online*, May 2015).

9.8 Conclusion

There is without a doubt an explicit turn to a cultural vision of nearly everything. Even disciplines, such as finance, which were once seen as purely 'mathematical' and too scientific to explain along cultural lines are today seen through a cultural lens. Evidently, cultural intelligence is key to understanding the impact that culture and cultural differences have on financial systems around the world. In this chapter, we have discussed how intercultural differences have become a reality in our multicultural cities, organisations and financial contexts. Despite increased economic interconnectedness across the world, culture remains a major determinant of financial practice and behaviour in some countries and cultural contexts where cultural values and beliefs supersede a global financial vision. Forces of culture continue to shape our world and financial decisions in numerous ways, and if we are we are to form a comprehensive understanding of financial phenomena around the world, cultural literacy would be an essential skill to learn and enhance.

Chapter Review Questions

1. Stock exchanges came into being in Europe much earlier than in other parts of the world and have developed into financial centres which attract an international workforce. Discuss the cultural reasons why the London and New York cases cannot be replicated easily.
2. The effects of globalisation on finance and financial systems have been felt around the world. Why then have some countries been more able to quickly integrate with the global economy than others? Can you think of any cultural issues that may have caused this disparity?
3. Why has Africa been such a leader in cutting-edge forms of payment system and what have been the cultural issues that have driven this process?
4. Explain why Islamic finance which belongs to a specific cultural group and has just emerged 40 years ago is currently seen by non-Muslim communities as providing an ethical and resilient financing option?
5. How has the Japanese risk-aversion culture shaped the financial sector in Japan and influenced the Japanese entrepreneurial spirit?

Recommended Further Reading

- Chui, A.C.W, X. Li, and W. Saffar. 2021. National Culture and the Choice Between Bank Debt and Public Debt. *Pacific-Basin Finance Journal* 70 (C).

- Gravina, A.F., and M. Lanzafame. 2021. Finance, Globalisation, Technology and Inequality: Do Nonlinearities Matter? *Economic Modelling* 96: 96–110. https://doi.org/10.1016/j.econmod.2020.12.026.
- Henchoz, C., T. Coste, and B. Wernli. 2019. Culture, Money Attitudes and Economic Outcomes. *Swiss Journal of Economics and Statistics* 155: 2. https://doi.org/10.1186/s41937-019-0028-4.
- Kanagaretnam, K., G.J. Lobo, C. Wang, and D. J. Whalen. 2015. Religiosity and Risk-Taking in International Banking. *Journal of Behavioral and Experimental Finance* 7: 42–59.
- Stulz, R.M., and R. Williamson. 2003. Culture, Openness and Finance. *Journal of Financial Economics* 70 (3): 313–349.

References

Ayub, M. 2009. *Understanding Islamic Finance*, vol. 462. Hoboken, NJ: Wiley.

Breuer, W., et al. 2014. Bank vs Bond Finance: A Cultural View of Corporate Debt Financing. In *Handbook of Research on Global Business Opportunities*, ed. B. Christiansen. New York: IGI Global.

Chui, A., A. Lloyd, and C. Kwok. 2002. The Determination of Capital Structure: Is National Culture a Missing Piece to the Puzzle? *Journal of International Business Studies* 33: 99–127. https://doi.org/10.1057/palgrave.jibs.8491007.

El Ghoul, S., O. Guedhami, C.C.Y. Kwok, and Y. Zheng. 2018. Zero-Leverage Puzzle: An International Comparison. *Review of Finance* 22 (3): 1063–1120.

El Qorchi, M. 2005. Islamic Finance Gears Up: Finance and Development. *International Monetary Fund* 42 (4).

Gheeraert, L. 2014. Does Islamic Finance Spur Banking Sector Development? *Journal of Economic Behavior & Organization* 103: 4–20.

Grinblatt, M., and M. Keloharju. 2001. How Distance, Language, and Culture Influence Stockholdings and Trades. *The Journal of Finance* 56 (3): 1053–1073.

Hanif, M. 2014. Differences and Similarities in Islamic and Conventional Banking. *International Journal of Business and Social Sciences* 2 (2). Available at SSRN: https://ssrn.com/abstract=1712184.

Hens, T., and M. Wang, ed. 2007. Does Finance Have a Cultural Dimension? In *B. Strebel-Aerni: International Finance*. Zurich: Schulthess.

Kluver, R. 2000. Globalization, Informatization and Intercultural Communication. *American Communication Journal* 3 (3).

Kluver, R., and W. Fu. 2004. The Cultural Globalization Index. *Journal of Foreign Policy* 10.

Minkov, M., and G. Hofstede. 2012. Is National Culture a Meaningful Concept? Cultural Values Delineate Homogeneous National Clusters of In-country Regions. *Cross-Cultural Research* 46 (2): 133–159.

Minkov, M., and G. Hofstede. 2014. Nations Versus Religions: Which Has a Stronger Effect on Societal Values? *Management International Review* 54 (6): 801–824.

Nyairo, J. 2015. *Kenya@50: Trends, Identities and the Politics of Belonging.* Contac Zones RB.

Ramirez, A., and S.A. Tadesse. 2009. Corporate Cash Holdings, Uncertainty Avoidance and the Multinationality of Firms. *International Business Review* 18 (4): 387–403.

Suzuki, S., and R.W. Wright. 1985. Financial Structure and Bankruptcy Risk in Japanese Companies. *Journal of International Business Studies* 16 (1): 97–110.

Zingales, L. 2015. The 'Cultural Revolution' in Finance. *Journal of Financial Economics* 117 (1): 1–4.

Chapter 10
Currency, Identity and Trust: Cryptocurrencies, Central Bank Digital Currencies and the Case for the Bahamian Sand Dollar

Dimitrios Syrrakos, Sophia Kuehnlenz, and Rory Shand

> The chapter focuses on the intercultural aspects of money and national currencies. It draws on the historical evolution of the use of money and assesses major developments since 1945. In doing so, the links between national money and identity are addressed through the issue of trust, both from an institutional and cultural perspective. Emphasis is also placed on the switch to international money, the advent of cryptocurrencies and the creation of Central Bank Digital Currencies. The latter is showcased via the Bahamian Sand Dollar and its implications for financial integration, national identity and work-based practices in the tourism industry.

10.1 Background to National Currencies

National money and nationhood were, and still are, inextricably linked. National currencies are legal tender and act as means of exchange and storing wealth within specific geographical boundaries thus providing the core facilitator of economic transactions. National currencies are also associated with institutions which have the sole ability to issue them, with their monopoly issuance status linked to the powers of

D. Syrrakos (✉)
Keele Business School, University of Keele, Keele, Newcastle, UK
e-mail: D.Syrrakos@keele.ac.uk

S. Kuehnlenz · R. Shand
Manchester Metropolitan University, Manchester, UK
e-mail: s.kuehnlenz@mmu.ac.uk

R. Shand
e-mail: r.shand@mmu.ac.uk

nation states. This was the case with early modern Spain during the fifteenth and early sixteenth centuries when the inflow of gold from American colonies facilitated the issuance of paper contracts of exchange and thus payment, in, the circulation of paper money in Europe (Vilches 2010). Failure to effectively coordinate the inflow of gold supplies to the Spanish economy led to many episodes of unsustainable inflation and ultimately financial collapse (Vilches 2010). The practice of issuing paper contracts, however, was adopted in Genova and further developed in Venice. Following suit, the Bank of England was created in 1694 to finance the war against France. This broke from past practices involving feudal nobleman supplying the Realm with gold (and men) as a means of cementing their allegiance to the Crown. The 'model' of financing military expenditure based on central banks was widely adopted thereafter.

The financing of military expenditure with the issuance of national currency had wider psychological implications as it strengthened the link between national money-currency and national identity during the nineteenth and the first half of the twentieth centuries. In the UK, the outbreak of WWI led to the collapse of the gold standard with the enactment of the Realm Act of 1916, which forbade the outflow of gold and suspended gold convertibility (Eichengreen 1990). The link between national money and national identity contributed to the development of a sense of collective purpose, tradition and destiny further nourishing national identity (Helleiner 1998). This was further entrenched by the circulation of standarised banknotes and coins within national boundaries, facilitated by the widespread use of printing machines (Helleiner 2003).

The use of 'national' currency, via common banknotes and coins, had profound implications beyond facilitating economic transactions. Whereas gold and gold coins, in particular Spanish, Dutch and English gold coins, were instantly accepted as they were fully backed by gold, other countries' national currencies were not as easily convertible. Converting currencies was further inhibited by different metrics systems adopted, for example between England and France. As such, the use of national currencies and banknotes eliminated all monetary barriers to *intra*-national trade, but the national currencies' fluctuating conversion rates became an impediment to international trade. A solution was provided by using an anchor currency such as the pound sterling for the most part of the nineteenth century and the US dollar since 1945 (Tew 1985).

The central banks' monopoly status over banknote issuance and the governmental control exercised on them effectively meant that economic policies were conducted with a view to stimulate the domestic economy. Any spill-over effects to other countries were largely ignored. Currency manipulation also led many countries into pursuing nationalistic economic policies in periods of hardship. This usually took the form of competitive devaluations, causing an increase in exports and thus mitigating any increases in unemployment rates. This, however, had a negative impact on other countries unemployment rates (Eichengreen 1992). In most cases, distinguishing between a national and a nationalistic economic policy is a challenging task, especially as they both assist in meeting national economic objectives. The use of national currencies though unequivocally accelerated the sense of national pride and unity. Gold was/is a universal commodity; national currencies are not. They are used for the purpose of enhancing countries' welfare. The widespread adoption of the US dollar, for example, contributed to the sense of unity and belonging in the United States during the eighteenth and nineteenth centuries. Its continuous depreciation since 1971 though has led to an erosion of the trust attached to it as a means of storing wealth and an equivalent deterioration in the Federal Reserve's credibility.

By adopting expansionary monetary policies national central banks and governments were able to fund government expenditure, in accordance with the political preferences of the government, to issue debt and to engage in international transactions with other nations that accept the currencies under perspective as a means of settling international payments and debt obligations. This has led to a consensus, according to which national currencies and exchange rate policy are employed to enhance the general welfare and to remedy socio-economic problems like poverty, inequality, high unemployment, etc.

The 1929 stock market crash, and the myriads of economic problems that followed in the 1930s, accelerated the belief that solutions confined within markets alone do not always lead to optimal economic outcomes and in some instances, especially when they involve severe recessions, government intervention could confer superior economic results (Keynes 1931). In this emergent economic thinking, persistently high unemployment rates were an externality of a market economy rather than an inescapable inevitability of economic activity. Exchange rate policy (and short-term capital controls) was a key economic tool for governments to tackle higher unemployment in the Western world from 1945 to the mid-1970s.

10.2 Exchange Rates and Trust

10.2.1 Exchange Rate Policy Since 1945 and the Gold-Dollar Standard

The advent of Keynesianism as official government policy in most Western economies from 1945 to mid-1970s carried significant implications in the economic practices of the period according to which fiscal and monetary policy were not always constrained by deficits and debts, especially during periods of harsh economic recessions. In these cases, aggressive government intervention via fiscal stimuli and expansionary monetary policies reduced the length of recessions and mitigated their impact on the countries' economic activity. These are the types of policies governments have resorted to during 2020–2021 in order to prevent a complete economic and financial collapse.

The period from 1945 to 1973 often referred to as the '*Golden Age of Capitalism*' was predominantly based on a specific variation of the Bretton Woods Agreement signed in 1944 (Walters 1991). Keynes, himself in favour of the use of capital restrictions, had proposed a globalised payments system. The US authorities, in their efforts to contain the expansion of communism, envisaged and realised a global payments system with the US dollar as its anchor currency. The system became widely used in the Western world and the fixed gold price of the US dollar elevated its status to the major reserve currency used for settling international payments and managing debt guarantees (Gomes 1993). The gold-dollar standard was effectively a quasi-fixed exchange rate regime due to the fixed gold price of the US dollar and the limited fluctuation bands of the rest of the currencies in the system.

The gold-dollar standard functioned relatively well up to the late 1960s. Funding social programmes and the Vietnam War and the quadrupling in oil prices in the early 1970s led the Nixon administration to break the fixed gold value of the US dollar. This had immense consequences not only for international monetary relations but also the trust attached to national currencies. The link to gold was severed while the dollar had successfully emerged as the major international reserve currency from 1945 to 1973. '*The \$US is our currency, but it is your problem*' assertion by the then US Treasury Secretary John Connelly reflected the acute problems that followed. These remain largely unresolved.

Keynesianism, by focusing on national economic policy, and by placing the emphasis on the need to meet domestic economic objectives such as lower unemployment, further strengthened the bond between national currencies and national identity and to a large extent national pride. Devaluations, when announced, were indeed perceived as a blow to national sovereignty and in many cases as national humiliation causing political instability. During this period, Keynesian economic policies were also combined with economic targets such as the 5-year growth plans in France and promoting national champions in industry. In this way, the period was a culmination of almost three centuries process that rendered national currencies, national identity and national pride almost indistinguishable.

10.2.2 Fixed Versus Flexible Exchange Rates

The collapse of the gold-dollar standard in 1973 led to two divergent tendencies in international monetary and currency relations, one in favour of flexible exchange rates and one in favour of fixed exchange rates. The Anglo-Saxon countries have since led the former and the European Union (EU) and China have led the latter, with all countries having to choose one form of currency arrangements over the other. The dilemma of fixed versus flexible exchange rates has dominated economic policymaking since 1973 with wider socio-economic implications. Flexible exchange rates provide monetary autonomy and adjustment of the currency values in line with domestic economic priorities (Friedman 1953; Friedman 1968; Sohmen 1961; Johnson 1972). Flexible exchange rates, however, are also pro-inflationary. On the other hand, fixed exchange rates provide stability and a favourable trade environment, but they are also more deflationary (Triffin 1982; Zis 1983; Kenen 1989; McKinnon 1996). The choice over the two regimes does not relate to currency values only but carries implications for the structures of the economies under perspective. Countries choosing flexible exchange rates tend to prioritise domestic demand and consumption

(United States, UK etc.) whereas countries opting for fixed exchange rates place more emphasis on international trade flows (Germany, China etc.). As a result, the currency regime reflects specific economic structures and economic policy options.

The most advanced type of fixed exchange rate regimes involves the adoption of a single currency, like the Eurozone, which consists of 19 EU member countries. Such a currency union further accelerates monetary and economic integration, but at the same time can potentially alienate large parts of EU citizens in all 19 member countries that have joined the Euro (Theodore 2019). This stems from the inherently unstable dynamics of the supranational nature of the single currency in one hand and the local economic challenges on the other (Theodore et al. 2017). While the Eurozone's monetary policy is designed in Frankfurt and executed for the entire Eurozone, the single monetary policy can hardly reconcile the local needs of the North Finish economy with the Portuguese South (Strobel 2005). Everything, however, is a matter of scale in economic policy. In this way, the EU's intercultural dimension of money (and value) developed during the previous three decades was severely undermined, if not threatened all together. The seemingly well-founded Eurozone came close to lose members countries and its institutional arrangements were placed under immense scrutiny (Negri et al. 2021). The Eurozone's existential threat has been overcome but at the cost of an emergent lack of trust among its member countries that still prevails.

Be it as it may, prior to the establishment of the Eurozone, the monetary policy adopted in Rome was hardly addressing evenly the economic needs of the Italian South and the Italian North. Put in an international context, the origins of California's recurrent economic impasses are not the same as Puerto Rico's, or South Dakota's, or North Carolina's, and New York's but all these states/regions are subjected to the Federal Reserve's monetary policy. Likewise, the inner-city problems in London are entirely different from the ones in rural Scotland but the Bank of England's monetary policy applies equally to both parts of the UK, while banks in Scotland have retained the right to print banknotes in circulation.

The common thread in all these examples is the relative ineffectiveness of monetary policy across different regions and countries and subsequently the way this impacts the publics' perception of a common identity attached to the use of the national currency (Arestis et al. 2005). This extends to national institutions that in turn enjoy the public's trust in setting and implementing economic policies. A sudden loss of trust, regardless of its origins and causes, reduces immensely the effectiveness of the policies implemented. Western monetary institutions were inflicted such a loss of trust during the Great Recession in 2007–2009 that have not regained since. Unprecedented electronic printing of money or Quantitative Easing (QE) during the pandemic lockdowns and the bailing out of large parts of national economies have caused a deterioration in the credibility attached to national currencies as means of storing wealth and thus correctly reflecting value. The acceleration of inflation has further undermined trust. Intercultural ties are also vital in determining the effectiveness of international institutions, with trust across different countries' institutions linked directly to them. The Dutch public for example fully trusts the European

Central Banks policymaking. This enhances the ECB's anti-inflationary policy across the entire Eurozone. On the other hand, this is less the case for the French public.

The break of the fixed gold value of the US dollar produced a boom-and-bust economic cycle, culminating in the Great Recession (Roubini 2006; Reinhart and Rogoff 2011). QE would have been impossible to undertake under the gold-dollar standard. Facilitated by the ultra-low interest rates prevailing since 2010 this has fuelled a credit boom with features resembling the 2005–2008 period. The use of credit as money and consequently the use of debt as money have accelerated a new global identity of debt. This identity has no national boundaries. China is a telling example in that it has emerged as one of the most indebted countries. The intergenerational shift in China from the highest saving rates in the world towards a high-spend economy is simply astounding. This worldwide decline in saving rates and the implications for bank deposit multipliers and investment have been difficult to plan for. QE was meant to be a short-term remedy, but the structural issues are long-due. As a result, taking on debt (be it individual-household level debt, private sector-firms level debt, industrial and corporate debt, and finally national and international debt) is the dominant socio-economic driving force, a characteristic of a global identity. The rise of this identity though has eroded traditional economic relations and norms evolved during the last 3 centuries akin to the erosion potentially caused by cryptocurrencies. This rise of a global identity has also produced a counter movement in favour of localism. As the dividing lines are no longer based on the distinction between centre/left-wing versus rightwing policies but on globalisation versus nativism (Krastev 2017), the new global identity is confronted by a resurgence of a new national identity. The fissures of Trumpism and Brexit to globalisation though, do not mean that the features of the new national identity are indeed crystallised or homogenous across different spectrums.

Despite this, the growing lack of trust to international monetary organisations has paved the way to new ways of finance that place decentralisation at the heart of their processes. It is perhaps ironic that the same process is now taking place in reverse. In other words, as globalisation was driven by financial liberalisation and deregulation from the late 1970s to 2010s without a well-defined set of rules, localism/nativism is asserting itself via a new way of finance that does not adhere to new underlying principles, at least for now. In the UK, this mistrust has been fostered by events prior to the pandemic like the financial crisis and scandals around MPs expenses and discussions of mistrust and the failure of government (Crewe and King 2013; Flinders 2012; Hay 2007). The gradual but continuous loss of trust surrounding international organisations such as the International Monetary Fund, World Bank and the World Trade Organisation as well as national institutions such as central banks since 2009 has led to the realisation of alternative means of payments and storing wealth based on cryptocurrencies.

10.3 Explaining Central Bank Digital Currencies

The Great Recession severely undermined public trust in centralised monetary institutions (De Filippi et al. 2020) and the banking system more generally. In the wake of the crisis, Bitcoin, as the first cryptocurrency was created to address the problem of having to rely on untrustworthy third parties to make and receive payments. In the current (traditional) banking system a trusted third party in the form of a bank ensures the legitimacy of financial transaction. Such trusted intermediaries not only ensure that the payer possessed enough funds to make each payment. These intermediaries also confirm that funds can only be spent once by the relevant account holder and hence ensure that double-spending cannot take place. As such, these intermediaries are vital in establishing trust and accountability within the banking system.

However, the creation of Distributed Ledger Technology (DLT) tied to Bitcoin and all the other cryptocurrencies enables financial transactions between parties without the need for a trusted third party (Nakamoto[1] 2008; Lewis 2018). The set-up of the (Bitcoin) network and the underlying technology itself have not only solved the double-spending problem that could occur without a third party. The fact that each transaction is verified by participants of the whole system while at the same time, all transactions that have ever taken place are visible and publicly available on the respective blockchain (also called ledger) has created trust in this alternative payment system.[2] Hence, with the underlying technology and the set-up of the cryptocurrency system, trusted financial intermediaries are no longer required in order to make and receive payments. The underlying technology and set-up of cryptocurrency ecosystems of course not only enables financial transfers without a third party. To entice participants of the respective system to verify transactions and agree on them (using computational puzzles), crypto-money (for example Bitcoin) is created and used as remuneration for the efforts of individual participants. And similar to the transfer of payments, no central authority or third party is needed to create these coins. Instead, coins are automatically generated according to a specific protocol underlying the respective system. This of course also means that these cryptocurrency systems allow complete decentralisation and by doing so break down the barriers of the traditional banking system, primarily accessibility to it. They have thus contributed to the emergence of a global platform, not necessarily aligned to traditional politics that combines financial innovation with decentralisation, accessibility and inclusivity. Blockchain technology can therefore be understood as a secure, privacy maintaining and efficient alternative to the current financial and banking system.

However, when considering alternative means of payments and money, mass adoption of cryptocurrencies has not taken place. If a currency aims at representing money and is hence to be used for regular payments, it must fulfil the functions of money

---

[1] Nakamoto is a pseudonym for an unknown person or a group of people.

[2] It should be noted that while all transactions are visible, actual identities are not. All that can be seen are wallet addresses (string of letters and numbers) indicating the ownership of the respective tokens. This of course means that anonymity can be maintained.

(unit of account, medium of exchange and store of value). While arguably cryptocurrencies can be seen as a unit of account and a medium of exchange, they are by no means a store of value. To meet this crucial function, the value of money (and hence the currency) has to remain stable over time. The huge volatility in price observable for traditional (first generation) cryptocurrencies such as Bitcoin or Ethereum is indicative of anything but a stable value over time. More recently and especially after the cryptocurrency price rallies in 2017/2018 stablecoins have emerged to address the issue of volatility while employing distributed ledger (blockchain) technology (European Parliament 2019; Daskalakis and Georgitseas 2020; Bank of England 2020; Group of Central Banks 2020). With fulfilling the three functions of money, stablecoins' ability to challenge central banks' monopoly when it comes to creating means of payments could potentially undermine the national and international financial system especially when considering stability. Hence, the use of a stable cash-like instrument outside the current monetary system seems to have spurred, at least initially, research conducted by central banks with regard to Central Bank Digital Currencies (CBDCs).

Additionally, and particularly within advanced economies, we have seen a trend towards so called cashless societies (Bank of England 2020). In fiat currency regimes the trust in central banks with regard to the preservation of the functions of money is crucial not only for the stability but also for the functionality of the system. In such systems, cash is not only a unit of account, medium of exchange and store of value, but it is also used to settle payments with immediate finality (Group of Central Banks 2020; Carstens 2021). Thus, money in the form of cash constitutes a public good contributing to the stability of the overall monetary system (Bank for International Settlements 2020). It should be stressed that, while CBDCs could potentially use blockchain technology, they are not cryptocurrencies. CBDCs will be, similar to cash today, centrally controlled and created by public institutions (central banks). CBDCs will be legal tender while overall monetary stability remains firmly at the core of the system. And due to the adherence to anti-money-laundering and combating the financing of terrorism laws (AML/CFT), complete anonymity will also not be a feature of CBDCs. CBDCs are being created to ensure the public has continued access to central bank money, to set the payment system up for an increasingly digital world all while the role of central banks at the centre of the financial system is to be retained.

Overall, the motivation to create a CBDC in the short to the medium term is greater for emerging and developing economies than it is for advanced ones (Boar and Wehrli 2021). The establishment of the Bahamian Sand Dollar[3] in October 2020 as the first 'live' CBDC is a case in point. Below, the example of the Bahamian Sand Dollar is employed to explore and explain the theoretical and practical set-up of domestic retail CBDCs[4] that are to be expected in the (near) future.

---

[3] https://www.sanddollar.bs/.

[4] While DLT may be employed for the wholesale market as well, the overall structure and set-up of a wholesale CBDC and its payment mechanisms would not change much since access to digital risk-free central bank money by financial institutions already exists. The establishment of a retail

Case Study: The Bahamian Sand Dollar

Financial inclusion was a main motivator for the creation of the Bahamian Sand Dollar. The explicit intended outcome of Project Sand Dollar which was followed by the nation-wide introduction of the CBDC continues to be the ability to offer unbanked, underbanked and financially excluded citizens access to not only risk-free central bank money but also to regulated payments and other financial services (Central Bank of the Bahamas 2019, 2022). Issues emerging from the geographical peculiarities of the Bahamas with regard to affordable, consistent and, during crises (natural and otherwise) immediate access to financial services can be solved with this new digital form of central bank money. At the same time, the aim has been to decrease service delivery costs while payments efficiency is expected to increase. It is also hoped that with the usage of the Sand Dollar, money laundering, counterfeiting and other illicit activities possible through cash-usage can be addressed.

The Bahamian Sand Dollar as a domestic retail CBDC represents the digital version of the Bahamian Dollar and is hence accepted legal tender (Central Bank of the Bahamas 2019, 2022). It offers, similar to cash, near instantaneous settlement of payments with finality. The Sand Dollar is created by the Central Bank of the Bahamas and is therefore a centralised and regulated unit of account and means of payment (Central Bank of the Bahamas 2022). And since only the Central Bank of the Bahamas can issue the Sand Dollar, the liability also lies with the central bank. As with all other CBDC proposals, the value of the Bahamian Sand Dollar is of course the same as the face value of the cash version of the currency. However, it must be noted that the level of anonymity of payments using cash is not replicated with this digital version of the currency (Central Bank of the Bahamas 2022).

The employed model for the retail CBDC is a hybrid one where the core ledger on which all individual holdings of the digital currency are maintained, is controlled by the central bank. The same is true for the creation and destruction of Sand Dollars which remains firmly with the central bank. For the future the central bank plans the establishment of a centralised KYC (know your customer) register to maintain identification and profile data for customers who do not have this information with respective financial institutions (Central Bank of the Bahamas 2022). This register will not only support compliance with AML/CFT standards, such a register could potentially also allow for helicopter drops in times of crisis. To create the core ledger, to modernise the country's digital payments system, to increase payment efficiency and to reduce transaction and service costs, the central bank has partnered with private (international) technology firms. Similarly, and in line with the hybrid model, all customer facing activities are handled by supervised financial institutions

---

CBDC would have far reaching consequences as this resembles a new form of money which requires a whole new infrastructure. Therefore the focus here is on the retail side.

(SFIs) which are given access to the payment infrastructure and core ledger (permissioned network). Such SFIs are allowed to offer overlay services such as the creation of wallets and the establishment of points of sale while being responsible for KYC checks. The enrolment into the Sand Dollar infrastructure (e.g. individuals or companies wanting to use the CBDC) is also handled by these supervised financial institutions, which most often are local financial institutions.

The retail Sand Dollar is both an account- and token-based system consisting of individual and business accounts. To maintain cash-like attributes of the CBDC, the central bank has opted for limits on the digital currency while, at the same time the CBDC is only available domestically. The individual account infrastructure consists of two tiers of individual wallets (Central Bank of the Bahamas 2022). A tier 1 wallet has a $500 holding limit, with a $1,500 monthly transaction limit. Government issued identification does not have to be produced if the customer opts for the tier 1 wallet. At the same time, this type of eWallet cannot be linked to a bank account. Tier 2 wallets do require authentication of the customer while, at the same time, the eWallet can be linked to a bank account. The limit on a tier 2 wallet is fixed at an $8,000 holding limit, with a $10,000 monthly transaction limit. To register for a business account, merchants must evidence their status as business producing a valid business licence and a VAT Certificate. Additionally, all business wallets must be tied to a bank account into which excess receipts can be transferred. Merchant wallets holding limits range from $8,000 to $1,000,000 while annual transactions are unlimited (Central Bank of the Bahamas 2022).

The Bahamian Sand Dollar facilitates domestic retail transactions, while addressing a variety of obstacles that hinder financial integration and efficiency. Despite the upper and lower thresholds in the sums allowed in CBDC holdings and transactions, the introduction of the Bahamian Sand Dollar can be judged as broadly successful. The CBDC has significantly reduced the need and the associated costs of transporting notes and coins across the islands, it has reduced the cost and speed of financial transactions all while enhancing efficiency in markets. The fact that the CBDC represents the digital version of the Bahamian Dollar has assisted in its reliability as a store of value and its functionality as a means of payment. The latter is further facilitated by the fact that payments can be made via mobile phones or payment cards accessible on all islands. Put together, all these factors have also strengthened the sense of belonging and identity in the 30 inhabited Bahamian islands. This success has incentivized other countries' central banks to conduct research and consider launching their own CBDCs, with China being the first major economy contemplating such move.

10.4 Conclusion and Further Developments

Profound changes have taken place during the last decade in the way finance is conducted and economic and monetary policies are applied. This is the case from an institutional as well as an individual perspective. Further, the changes are characterised by relentless speed. While the role of gold seems to have been reduced as a benchmark of value, this has also contributed to a decline in the role of anchor currencies, be it the Pound Sterling or the US dollar. No wonder the international monetary system is fragmented. Cryptocurrencies can lay claim they have resolved the core problem of the financial system namely the over-reliance on the banking sector by-passing banking facilities. While it remains to be seen whether this is the case, the experience of Central Bank Digital Currencies seems to successfully bridge the gap between the system based on traditional banking services and the complete departure from it based on cryptocurrencies. The Bahamian Sand Dollar's effectiveness and meeting of its objectives corroborates this assertion. The validity of the argument put forward by proponents of cryptocurrencies that they 'democratize' financial services by enhancing accessibility without the barriers of banking services is constrained by the lack of regulation. This regulatory framework is provided by Central Bank Digital Currencies.

The financial transactions and payroll services conducted in CBDCs pave the way for the adoption of the Bahamian Sand Dollar for international payments. This will have immense implications at the workplace if adopted for payments from all over the world. One expansion of their use could see most income generated from tourism in Small Island Developing States to be registered in CBDCs. This will cause a revolution in the tourism industries' working practices involving re-training of a big proportion of the workforce in the industry.

> **Chapter Review Questions**
>
> 1. Explain the role played by trust and intercultural aspects in monetary policy effectiveness.
> 2. Explain why flexible exchange rates are fostering intra-cultural aspects whereas fixed exchange rates are influenced by intercultural aspects.
> 3. Explain the main motives for the establishment of cryptocurrencies.
> 4. Explain the significance of the Bahamian Sand Dollar in strengthening the sense of national identity.
> 5. Explain why the adoption of the Bahamian Sand Dollar for international payments would revolutionise the tourism industry's work practices and the way firms in the tourism industry should respond to this.

Recommended Further Reading

- Auer, R., and R. Böhme. 2020. The Technology of Retail Central Bank Digital Currency. *BIS Quarterly Review*, March: 85–100.
- Central Bank of the Bahamas. 2022. *Digital Bahamian Dollar*. [Online]. Available from: https://www.sanddollar.bs/.
- Lewis, A. 2018. *Basics of Bitcoins and Blockchains: An Introduction to Cryptocurrencies and the Technology That Powers Them*. Coral Gables: Mango Publishing Group.
- Nakamoto, S. 2008. *Bitcoin: A Peer-to-Peer Electronic Cash System*. [Online]. Available from: https://nakamotoinstitute.org/bitcoin/.

References

Arestis, P., S. Basu, and S. Mallick. 2005. Financial Globalisation: The Need for a Single Currency and a Global Central Bank. *Journal of Post Keynesian Economics* 27 (3): 507–531.
Auer, R., and R. Böhme. 2020. The Technology of Retail Central Bank Digital Currency. *BIS Quarterly Review* (March): 85–100.
Bank of England. 2020. Central Bank Digital Currency Opportunities, Challenges and Design. Future of Money. Available from: https://www.bankofengland.co.uk/paper/2020/central-bank-digital-currency-opportunities-challenges-and-design-discussion-paper.
Bank for International Settlements. 2018. Central Bank Digital Currencies. [Online]. Available from: https://www.bis.org/cpmi/publ/d174.pdf
Bank for International Settlements. 2020. Central Banks and Payments in the Digital Era. In *BIS Annual Economic Report 2020* [Online], 67–96. Available from: https://www.bis.org/cpmi/publ/d154.pdf.
Boar, C., and A. Wehrli. 2021. Ready, Steady, Go?—Results of the Third BIS Survey on Central Bank Digital Currency. *BIS Papers* 14. Available from: https://www.bis.org/publ/bppdf/bispap114.htm.
Carstens, A. 2021. Central Bank Digital Currencies: Putting a Big Idea into Practice, 1–14. [Online]. Available from: https://www.bis.org/speeches/sp210331.htm.
Central Bank of the Bahamas. 2019. Project Sand Dollar: A Bahamas Payments System Modernisation Initiative. Available from: https://www.centralbankbahamas.com/publications/main-publications/project-sanddollar-a-bahamian-payments-system-modernization-initiative.
Central Bank of the Bahamas. 2022. *Digital Bahamian Dollar*. [Online]. Available from: https://www.sanddollar.bs/.
Crewe, I., and A. King. 2013. *The Blunders of Our Governments*. London: Oneworld.
Daskalakis, N., and P. Georgitseas. 2020. *An Introduction to Cryptocurrencies: The Crypto Market Ecosystem*. Abingdon: Routledge.
De Filippi, P., M. Mannan, and W. Reijers. 2020. Blockchain as a Confidence Machine: The Problem of Trust & Challenges of Governance. *Technology in Society* 62 (April): 101284. https://doi.org/10.1016/j.techsoc.2020.101284.
Eichengreen, B. 1990. *Elusive Stability. Essays in the History of International Finance 1919–39*. Cambridge: Cambridge University Press.

Eichengreen, B. 1992. *Golden Fetters: The Gold Standard and The Great Depression, 1919–1939.* Oxford: Oxford University Press.
European Parliament. 2019. *The Future of Money: Compilation of Papers. Study for the Committee on Economic and Monetary Affairs.* Luxembourg: Policy Department for Economic, Scientific and Quality of Life Policies. Available from: https://doi.org/10.1057/978-1-137-60231-2_31.
Flinders, M. 2012. *Defending Politics: Why Democracy Matters in the 21st Century.* Oxford: Oxford University Press.
Friedman, M. 1953. 'The Case for Flexible Exchange Rates' in *Essays in Positive Economics.* Chicago: University of Chicago Press.
Friedman, M. 1968. The Role of Monetary Policy. *The American Economic Review* 58: 1–17.
Gomes, L. 1993. *The International Adjustment Mechanism: From the Gold Standard to the EMS.* Basingstoke: St. Martin's Press.
Group of Central Banks. 2020. *Central Bank Digital Currencies: Foundational Principles and Core Features.* Available from: www.bis.org.
Hay, C. 2007. *Why We Hate Politics.* Cambridge: Polity Press.
Helleiner, E. 1998. National Currencies and National Identities. *American Behavioral Scientist* 41 (10): 1409–1436.
Helleiner, E. 2003. *The Making of National Money: Territorial Currencies in Historical Respective.* Ithaca: Cornell University Press.
Johnson, J. 1972. The Case for Flexible Exchange Rates, 1969. *Federal Reserve Bank of St Louis*: 12–24.
Kenen, P. 1989. *Exchange Rates and Policy Coordination.* Manchester: Manchester University Press.
Keynes, J.M. 1931. The Economic Consequences of Mr Churchill. In *Essays in Persuasion.* London: Macmillan.
Krastev, I. 2017. *After Europe.* Philadelphia: University of Pennsylvania Press.
Lewis, A. 2018. *Basics of Bitcoins and Blockchains: An Introduction to Cryptocurrencies and the Technology That Powers Them.* Coral Gables: Mango Publishing Group.
McKinnon, R.I. 1996. *The Rules of the Game: International Money and Exchange Rates.* Cambridge, MA: The MIT Press.
Nakamoto, S. 2008. *Bitcoin: A Peer-to-Peer Electronic Cash System.* Available from: https://nakamotoinstitute.org/bitcoin/.
Negri, F., F. Nicoli, and T. Kuhn. 2021. Common Currency, Common Identity? The Impact of the Euro Introduction on European Identity. *European Union Politics* 22 (1): 114–132.
Reinhart, C., and K.S. Rogoff. 2011. The Forgotten History of Domestic Deb. *The Economic Journal* 121 (552): 319–350.
Roubini, N. 2006. The BW 2 Regime: An Unstable Disequilibrium Bound to Ravel. *International Economics and Economic Policy* 3: 303–332.
Strobel, F. 2005. Leaving EMU: A Real Options Perspective. *Applied Economics* 37: 1449–1453.
Sohmen, E. 1961. *Flexible Exchange Rates.* Chicago: University of Chicago Press.
Theodore, J. 2019. *Survival of the European (Dis) Union: Responses to Populism, Nativism and Globalisation.* Basingstoke: Palgrave Macmillan.
Theodore, J., J. Theodore, and D. Syrrakos. 2017. *The European Union and the Eurozone Under Stress: Challenges and Solutions for Repairing Fault Lines in the European Project.* Palgrave Macmillan.
Tew, B. 1985. *The Evolution of the International Monetary System, 1944–1988,* 4th ed. London: Hutchinson.
Triffin, R. 1982. The World Monetary Scandal: Sources…and Cures. *Economic Notes*: 1–19.
Vilches, E. 2010. *New World Gold: Cultural Anxiety and Monetary Disorder in Early Modern Spain.* Chicago: The University of Chicago Press.
Walter, A. 1991. *World Power and World Money: The Role of Hegemonic and International Monetary Order.* Harvester Wheatsheaf.
Zis, G. 1983. Exchange Rate Flexibility and the International Liquidity 'Problem.' *Intereconomics* 18: 230–235. https://doi.org/10.1007/BF02928223.

Part IV
Language

Chapter 11
Global Englishes: Dialogue and Communication in the Workplace

Mairéad Nic Craith, Philip McDermott, and Nicola Bermingham

> This chapter considers the role of English as the language of business, exploring how in an increasingly globalised world, English is now central to workplace communication. After contextualising the growth of English, we consider the status of the language in different continental locations. We make a distinction between English as a Native Language (ENL), English as a Lingua Franca (ELF) and Business English as a Lingua Franca (BELF). In conclusion, we consider questions of ownership and appropriation in relation to the language itself, examining the implications of language choice in shaping how contemporary workplaces operate.

11.1 Introduction

You are probably reading this textbook because you are studying a course through the medium of English. Have you stopped to think about why this may be the case? Is it a 'natural' choice for us to conduct our academic business in English? Why do academics teach and publish primarily in English (Nic Craith 2016)? Why has English become the language of the business world? Where does the impetus come from? Why has English come to the fore out of the 7,139 languages that are spoken in

M. Nic Craith (✉)
Institute for Northern Studies, University of the Highlands and Islands, Inverness, Scotland, UK
e-mail: Mairead.NicCraith@uhi.ac.uk

P. McDermott
School of Applied Social and Policy Sciences, Ulster University, Belfast, Northern Ireland, UK
e-mail: p.mcdermott@ulster.ac.uk

N. Bermingham
Department of Languages, Cultures and Film, University of Liverpool, Liverpool, UK
e-mail: N.Bermingham@liverpool.ac.uk

the world today (Ethnologue 2022)? This chapter considers the drive towards English in the academic and business worlds and the implications of that language choice in shaping contemporary workplaces and how we operate today and in the future.

11.2 English as an International Language of Business

The development of English as an international language of business has its roots in two key periods of globalisation. The first was the consolidation of the British Empire, essentially an economic project, which required a standard language to both administer the empire and to facilitate trade to and from the colonies. Culturally, this period anchored perceptions that English was a language of economic progression for its speakers while local languages were often deemed as unfit for use within the capitalist understanding of progression. Ireland was one such example where English replaced Irish as the primary medium of communication by the early nineteenth century (McDermott 2011; Nic Craith 1993). The period of empire also established English as a dominant language in swathes of Africa, South Asia, Australasia and the Pacific, North America and the Caribbean. English is therefore an example of a pluricentric language (such as Spanish, Chinese, French, Hindi, Urdu, Serbo-Croatian, Malay-Indonesian, etc.) because of its Imperial past. Consequently, this process caused the decline of many regional and indigenous languages which were viewed as barriers to free market (Fig. 11.1).

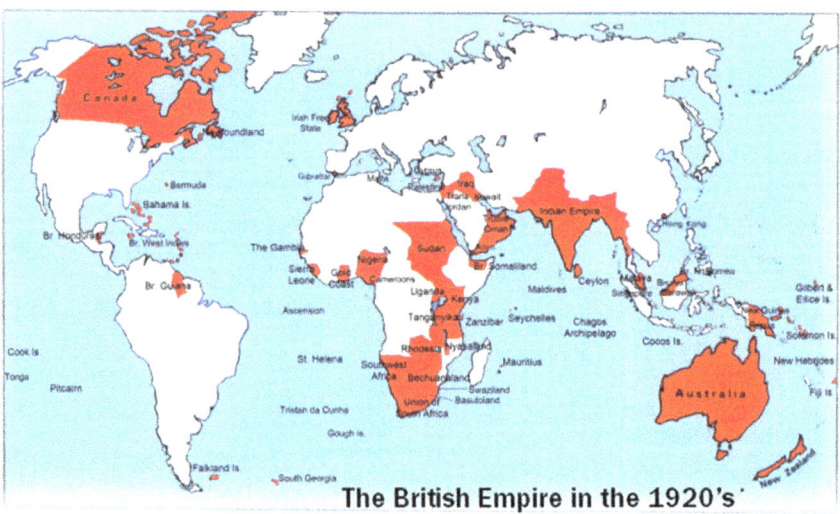

Fig. 11.1 Map of the British Empire (1920s) (*Source* https://commons.wikimedia.org/wiki/File:Map_of_the_British_Empire_(1920%27s).png)

A second key determinant in establishing English as a globally dominant language was the rise of the United States as a global power and the biggest champion of the free market economy. While the notion of prestige for English was initiated in the period of the British Empire, the rise of English in the US in the twentieth century consolidated this further. The use of English as a lingua franca in business is a process deeply embedded in politics and economics which is not without ramifications. Even in the contemporary world of business, the choice of transnational companies to utilise English at the expense of local languages can prove contentious (see Louhiala-Salminen et al. 2005).

The rise of English as a language of global economy has been contextualised by Kachru (1992, 3) who developed three distinct categorisations which help us to consider the use of English today (see Fig. 11.2). Although it is 30 years since Kachru developed the framework, it still has relevance.

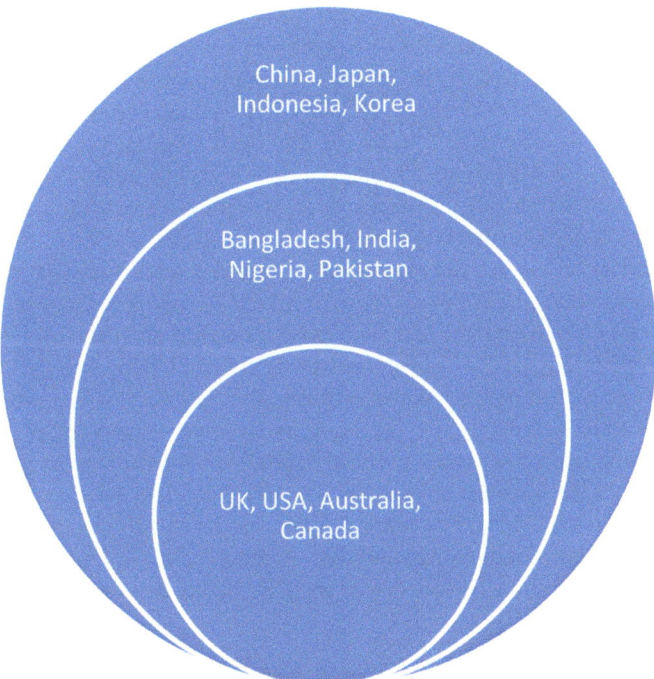

Fig. 11.2 Three Circles of World Englishes (*Inner Circle Countries*: countries that represent traditional bases of the English language. *Outer Circle Countries*: regions where English has become strongly embedded as a second institutional language. *Expanding Circle Countries*: places where the influence of English as a foreign language is gaining ground. *Source* Adapted from Kachru [1992, 356])

11.3 English or Englishes

The position of English spoken in inner, outer and expanding circle countries is not the same. For example, the position of English in the USA is not the same as that spoken in Malaysia (a point to which we shall return). In the following three text boxes, we briefly consider the position of English in three locations: Scotland (as an inner circle location), Malaysia (as an outer circle location) and Dubai (as an expanding circle country).

11.3.1 English and Scots

English is the dominant language in the UK—but some people in lowland Scotland speak a language called Scots. Scots is not the same as Scottish English—but it is a contested language (Nic Craith 2000). Sometimes it is argued that Scots is just 'bad' English or an English dialect, but this is too simple a perspective and ignores the role of politics and power in shaping exactly what a language is. There was a time when Scots and Scottish Gaelic were the dominant languages of Scotland. These linguistic traditions were divided along political and geographic lines. Gaelic was spoken mainly by Highlanders whereas Scots was prevalent among the Lowlanders in the south. Scots was the language spoken by King James VI of Scotland and I of England when the crowns of these two countries were united in 1603. When James went to court in London, he was 'mocked' for his poor English. The 1707 Act of Union between England and Scotland resulted in a dominant role for England and the English language was promoted in its standard form through institutions like education. Consequently, the use of Scots went into decline and the perception of Scots as a 'dialect of English' emerged, much to the annoyance of many Scots in recent years, Scots has gained political capital as a linguistic marker of identity, especially in the run up to the 2014 independence referendum (McDermott 2019). At the beginning of the twenty-first century, Scots was considered as one of Scotland's indigenous languages and has become slightly more visible in the public space and in the realm of education. This is due to some moderate language policy initiatives (Scottish Government 2015).

11.3.2 English in Dubai

The position of English is strongly emerging as a lingua franca in Dubai. In 2010, Mick Randall and Mohammad Amir Samimi noted that developing economies in the Gulf states rely heavily on expatriates. There are now more expatriates than locals in Dubai, which has had a strong impact on the amount of English spoken there. In 2009, it was estimated that there were about 100 languages spoken by the 200 nationalities and 150 ethnic groups in Dubai (*The National*, 22 March 2009). The residents primarily speak Arabic, Farsi, Urdu, Hindi and Malayalam. Pidgin versions of Arabic and Farsi are also spoken. Some practical tradespeople such as carpenters and electricians are more likely to speak Arabic. English, though, is increasingly coming to the fore in Dubai in the retail sector, and in the medical field. Randall and Samimi (2010, 44) point out that there: "can be few societies in the world where a second language is necessary to carry out basic shopping tasks, from buying food in supermarkets to clothes in shopping malls".

11.3.3 English in Malaysia

The politics of language are strongly at play in Malaysia and the language debate is a highly emotive issue. Competing groups disagree on the significance of English versus Malay. Malays and Chinese, for example, have resisted or promoted English or Bahasa Malaysia in different contexts and these views have been influenced by politics and globalisation. In Malaysia, both English and Malaysian were used as media of educational instruction since its independence in 1957. Starting in 2012, however, the Malaysian government stopped English as the medium of instruction in certain key subject areas. While this could be regarded as having a negative impact on English, Phan Le Haa et al. (2013) have interpreted it positively as a rejection of the over-reliance on English in education and the language sector. This Act, known as 'To Uphold Bahasa Malaysia and To Strengthen the English Language' (MBMMBI), is presented as a 'timely response' by the Malaysian government against globalisation. These three delineations effectively illustrate that imperialism in the nineteenth century, followed by a more recent wave of economic globalisation in the twentieth century, have solidified the perception that English is *the* global language. Moreover, each case indicates that knowledge of English comes with some form of cultural and social capital and is thus coterminous with individual and societal economic progression. However, such statements are overly simplistic and ignore the complexities of English use globally and the roles those other languages have in business contexts. As we have already noted, there is hardly a homogeneity in status for those who speak English. Varieties such as American or British English might be valued more than, say, Indian or African Englishes in business contexts. This is shaped by hierarchies of power in business contexts which mirror wider global views and historical colonial attitudes. Moreover, in Malaysia and many other contexts globally, we see a clear clash between globalisation but also the continuing prevalence of linguistic nationalism as a force (McDermott and McMonagle 2019; McDermott and Nic Craith 2019).

Indeed, the case described above also reflects the situation in inner circle countries such as the UK and the USA. Here, hierarchies exist between the 'standard' forms of the middle-classes versus 'non-standard' forms such as accented varieties of English spoken by immigrants or local and regional dialects. In such cases, sociolinguistic studies on recruitment by companies have shown high levels of discrimination based on the 'type' of English one speaks and how that variety correlates with social markers such as race or class (Cocchiara et al. 2016). Language, therefore, is a crucial marker within the social pyramid. As the use of the English language has expanded globally, hierarchies have not disappeared, and this proves that English is not in fact a pre-emptor to social mobility.

> **Case Study 1 English in Call Centres in India**
>
> In India, English had been the preserve of a small number of those in high castes up until the impact of globalisation extended the language's use to those of lower socio-cultural standing. Such shifts in the linguistic demography opened new opportunities for these 'new speakers' of English to be employed in the business outsourcing processes associated with globalisation. The Indian call centre has been one such product which brings the speaker of Indian English into direct communication with speakers of varieties of British and American English. However, the market use of English in this way in outer circle countries like India maintains both global and localised hierarchies with regard to English use, whereby existing elites continue to benefit most from having English-language proficiency (Bloomaert 2010). For example, the use of English by the call centre worker in India is considered a low-status form of English, or "low mobility" in Blommaert's (2010) terms, when contrasted with the "high-mobility", prestigious forms of English, which are characterised by normative accents and standard orthographies and are used by those of higher castes in professional areas such as academia, civil occupations or business management. This is often reflected in the treatment and pay of workers, which suggests that speaking English does not necessarily lead to actual equality of opportunity (May 2014, 383).

11.4 The British Council: Promoting Global English?

One organisation involved in the spread of English globally is the British Council. Founded in 1938, the body's first charter was drafted in 1940 with a mission to "create friendly knowledge and understanding between the people of the UK and other countries" (British Council 2017). This articulation, however, does not convey the importance that wider political and economic concerns of the 1930s had in the establishment of the institution. The Council was born in a period of huge economic uncertainty with the impact of the Great Depression still felt globally. Moreover, the political dynamics of the world were shifting with the wane of the British Empire and the rise of the United States. In Europe, polarised politics from fascism to communism were indicative of an uncertain world order just before the outbreak of World War II.

The work of the British Council, therefore, can be viewed as a cultural reaction against such instabilities, with language utilised as a tool to maintain and promote "the UK's international standing, prosperity and security" (British Council 2017). The perceived connection between economic prosperity and the use of the English language in global business has helped the British Council in its remit to promote knowledge of the English language abroad. As a result, while the organisation claims to be primarily a cultural and education body, its remit feeds into the global spread of English for business purposes and wider notions of soft power (see Graddol 1997; Nye 2008; Codó and McDaid 2019). As Phillipson notes, since the 1940s, the British Council has played "a key role in maintaining the position of English in post-colonial states, and in the post-communist world where globalisation was preached through the trinity of the market economy, human rights, and English" (2004, 49). If this is the case, then the spread of global languages cannot be detached from international relations and the Western ideal of capitalist economics.

At present, the British Council works in more than 100 countries. In 2019–2020, the organisation connected directly or indirectly with 791 million people. As well as teaching the English language, the Council's work also places heavy emphasis on British culture and ideals of freedom, democracy and equality. In this way, learning English is not only considered as acquiring a new form of communication but is intrinsically linked to wider cultural values. Most British Council teachers are from the UK and other Western countries and their engagements with people in other countries could be construed as introducing, by stealth, a value system via the practice of language learning (Nye 2008). Therefore, for some, the work of agencies like the British Council is viewed within the context of cultural imperialism. Such practice aims to transmit, through cultural means, the values of the Western world (in this case, Britain) to regions or countries that may have a quite a different view of culture, politics, social life and economy (Tomlinson 1999).

11.5 Global Languages: Numbers or Commerce?

It is unsurprising that debates on linguistic globalisation have focused on the growth of English as a global lingua franca. Such a position has been facilitated by the role of English in global business alongside the cultural power channelled via bodies like the British Council (see Phillipson 2003; Crystal 1997). However, in both historical and contemporary contexts, globalisation has also had a profound impact on the increased use of other languages as well. When we consider statistics relating to the most spoken global languages, English, French, Spanish and Portuguese feature prominently. This illustrates how the historical context of economy, trade and power manifested through European imperial pasts have a continued legacy on the linguistic realities of the world today.

While these languages have left an undeniable imprint, it is also clear that linguistic power is also considered in relation to commercial might. In some cases, a previously dominant force has subsided and, while the number of speakers remains high, or even increases, the perception of the language associated with that nation or civilisation also diminishes. As empires have waxed and waned, some languages have declined in importance only to re-emerge again. Portuguese as the language of one of the world's foremost imperial powers of the fifteenth and sixteenth centuries established its presence in South America as well as in parts of Africa and Asia. However, the decline of the Empire and its use in the developing world rendered Portuguese as a language less compatible with the world order of, say, nineteenth-century colonialism, dominated by French, English and to a lesser extent German. This was despite the fact that a large number of Portuguese speakers were evident across several continents in 1900. Portuguese at this time was arguably a 'global' language in numeric terms but was not necessarily viewed as a language of commercial 'prestige'. However, in the 1990s and 2000s, the rapid growth of the Brazilian economy rendered Portuguese again as a useful linguistic commodity, and interest in the language increased (see Roberto and Simões 2014). Despite recent downward trends, the Brazilian economy is still in the top ten largest economies by GDP in the world, indicating that the Portuguese language may continue to be an important business commodity globally and regionally within the Americas.

In addition to Portugal and Brazil, Portuguese, as a transcontinental language, is the official language of Angola, Cabo Verde, Guinea-Bissau, Mozambique and São Tomé and Príncipe, and has co-official status in East Timor, Equatorial Guinea and Macau. In contexts such as Cape Verde, European Portuguese continues to be the prestige variety that is used in most formal settings (Bermingham et al. 2021). In Mozambique and Angola, however, as these countries' economies gain strength internationally, local endonormative standards of Portuguese are being developed (Gorski Severo 2016). This calls into question the suitability of having just two official standards of Portuguese given the linguistic variation across Portuguese-speaking nations (Müller de Oliveira 2013) and demonstrates how economic developments and linguistic prestige are closely linked.

Alterations to a language's status are, therefore, often due to changing political and economic circumstances. For example, despite China's status as the most populous country on earth for centuries, Chinese languages have only garnered the status of 'global' languages in recent decades. The economic reforms from the 1980s, which led to huge growth in the Chinese economy, rendered Mandarin, Cantonese, and others as 'useful' to businesses from outside China wishing to capitalise on this more open stance. While Mandarin is still largely spoken by native speakers, the number of learners is also growing (Chen and Chung 2011, 315). Much, therefore, depends on changing political and economic circumstances.

Statistics from Ethnologue (2022) illustrate the ranking order of languages spoken in the world, combining both native speakers and learners of each language. The figures also provide a striking illustration of how numerous factors might add weight to a language's claim to be 'global'. English, for instance, ranks highly for the number of native (L1) speakers, for the number of second language speakers (L2) and in a combined total of both L1 and L2 speakers. This is undeniably driven by economic developments globally. Mandarin Chinese is the largest language in the world when counting only first language (native) speakers. This is due to the significant population of China, but the figures are also blurred by the grouping of thirteen "Chinese" languages which share a writing system and literature. A key difference between English and Mandarin is the location of speakers: Mandarin is concentrated, while English is spread out. Since the size of Mandarin is primarily due to numbers of native speakers, it is hardly surprising that the language is largely concentrated in countries in Asia. In contrast, the range of non-native speakers in English means that it is spoken in a greater range of countries and particularly in Africa (Ethnologue 2022).

Other languages such as Malay have high numbers of both L1 and L2 speakers (Mansor et al. 2018). While Malay may not be characterised as a 'global' language per se, it has become a lingua franca in South-East Asia. For example, knowing the lingua franca in Indonesia or Malaysia is an important means through which native speakers of other lesser-used languages can contribute to their regional economy. Therefore, it would be questionable for us to say that Malay is a global language of business in the way English is. What is notable here, however, is that the conditions for Malay, with such high numbers of speakers in a growing economic region, mean that there may very well be an increase in the number of international L2 speakers if the region's current economic development continues. This again mirrors Graddol's assertions that socio-economic change may very well shape which languages we view as truly 'fit for purpose' in a global business sense.

11.6 English as a Business Lingua Franca

Given the process of globalisation that we have outlined above as well as the influence of bodies such as the British Council, English has undeniably come to be the leading language of international business. English is now central to communication in multinational workplace contexts and part of daily communication for business professionals across the globe, as business structures have started to change in response to rapid globalisation. The growing importance of the Internet in contemporary societies has also had an impact on the ways in which people communicate. The intersection of growing online communication, and increasing business collaboration across country borders has led to a situation where organisations have had to become equipped to engage in international interactions (Kankaanranta and Louhiala-Salminen 2013).

As an illustrative example of the cross-border dynamics of an international company and the impact this can have on its communicative needs, Kankaanranta and Louhiala-Salminen (2013) outline the potential following case: A company based in Finland merges with a German company, and this newly merged business decides to place part of their operations in Portugal and the other in India. The accounting section of this corporation might then have responsibility for communication across all of these locations. This is just one such example where contemporary businesses need to manage communication across various linguistic contexts. In response to such complex business dynamics, most organisations have chosen English as the language for their business communication. However, as Kankaanranta and Louhiala-Salminen

(2013) argue, the language that has come to be used in such global corporations is not English—in the sense of English spoken by native speakers—but English as a Lingua Franca (ELF) a variety which encompasses native and non-native varieties of English. In keeping with this last point, academics studying ELF emphasise that speakers of ELF should not aim to mirror the speech of native speakers of English. Instead, they focus on the need to develop overall competence in rhetorical strategies, listening skills and accommodation skills (Nickerson 2005). Knowing how to communicate effectively is a core aspect of participating in the business world. Business professionals "need to know what, why, how, and when to communicate when they are sharing knowledge and building networks" (Kankaanranta and Louhiala-Salminen 2013, 26). This type of linguistic knowhow goes beyond the native/non-native paradigm that has dominated linguistic debates for many years.

To explain the distinction in varieties of English, terms such as ENL (English as a Native Language) have been used to contrast with ELF (English as a Lingua Franca). The concept of BELF (English as Business Lingua Franca) stems from discussions on the use of ELF in business settings and is used to define a language that does not belong to one group, but is a shared language whose core characteristic is its applicability in business situations (Ehrenreich 2010; Louhiala-Salminen et al. 2005. The study of BELF has now come to be a pivotal point of focus in academic studies on international business communication (Ehrenreich 2010).

BELF is a shared language, used primarily to facilitate communication in international businesses. It is a resource that is necessary for large multinational corporations to carry out daily activities. The language can be categorised as a 'global' language in that it is not a priori conceptualised as being 'English' as spoken in the United Kingdom or the United States. It has instead been described as a language that is "highly situation-specific", characterised by its dynamism and its hybridity and transculturality (Baker and Ishikawa 2021). It is idiosyncratic in nature, and encompasses a range of different varieties (Kankaanranta and Louhiala-Salminen 2013) (Table 11.1).

Table 11.1 Comparison between ELF and BELF approaches

Criterion	ELF	BELF
Successful interactions	NS-like language skills	Business communication skills
Speaker aims to	Emulate NS discourse	Get the job done
NNSs are viewed as	Learners	Full communicators
Problems	Poor language skills	Poor business communication skills
'Culture'	National cultures of NSs	Business community cultures

Based on Kankaanranta and Louhiala-Salminen (2013, 29)

Case Study 2 The Use of English in the Professional World in Hong Kong
Since the early 1980s Hong Kong has shifted from labour-intensive manufacturing industries to knowledge services. This shift occurred at the same time as Hong Kong's transition from being a British Colony to the Chinese SAR.[1] Evans (2010) evidences clear tensions in the use of English versus Cantonese in Hong Kong. While the latter is commonly used in oral communication in the civil service, English is primarily used for written communication. Overall, there has been a gradual decline in the institutional role of English in the region. This decline has been accompanied by major changes in the education sector. Soon after the handover in 1997, English-medium second-level schools were obliged to switch to Chinese as the medium of instruction. Putonghua (Mandarin) was made compulsory as a language subject. The switch to Chinese as a medium of instruction is hardly surprising but raises interesting questions. If the role of English in education is significantly reduced, does that lead to a fall in the standards of English and how does that impact on business in the region (Choi and Adamson 2020)?

This case illustrates two clear conflicting trends. While globalisation encourages even greater use of English, economic reintegration within China has placed emphasis on greater use of Cantonese. Indeed, these issues have generated tensions within Hong Kong itself. Evans' findings indicated that English continues as the written medium of communication while Cantonese is the medium of oral communication—especially in informal situations. While there is a widespread perception of falling standards in English, there are also indications that the status of English has risen. Significantly, from a business perspective, the results indicate that the need to use all the skills in English (reading, writing, speaking and listening) in the professional sector increases with rank and experience.

The fact that written English remains central in the workplace is driven by several factors, internal and external. The fact that Hong Kong was a British colony for more than 150 years has undoubtedly strengthened the position of English. Internally, English remains significant in government administration, in the legal system, in third-level education and in professional training. Externally, Hong Kong is influenced by the strong role that English plays in business internationally and the region's integration over time into the global economy is part of this process. Although aware of the limitations of his findings, Evans' study reaffirms the central continuing significance of English (as well as Cantonese) in the professional and business worlds in Hong Kong.

---

[1] The Joint Declaration was signed in 1984 and the final transfer of sovereignty took place in 1997.

11.7 Ownership of English?

In a global context, English has a high-level status, but one may well ask, who owns English anymore? Does it belong to what Kachru (1992) described as inner circle countries (such as the UK and the USA) or can ownership of the language also be claimed by outer circle countries (such as India) or even expanding circle countries (such as China)? According to Lull (2000), de-territorialisation is a process whereby the relationship between cultural representations (including language) is disconnected from their original territory. In the case of English, we believe that the "obvious" connection between the English language and the UK has been severed (Nic Craith 2006).

Many nation-states that have adopted English as their second language are asserting that it is 'their language, through which they can express their own values and identities, create their own intellectual property and export goods and services to other countries' (Graddol 1997, 2). This applies not just to the world of economics and business but also to the world of art and creativity. Salman Rushdie, for example, has argued that the debate about the appropriateness of English in post-British India is irrelevant for the younger generation (Crystal 1997, 136). Although the older generation may have concerns about the suitability of English in an independent India, the younger generation has made it their own. The children of independent India do not see English as tainted by the process of colonisation. Instead, they claim ownership of English and "Indianize" it. They use it as an Indian language, (Crystal 1997). More recently, the Bengal-Scottish poet Bashabi Fraser has described her initial embarrassment at writing in English rather than in Bengali. For many years, she kept her writing in English to herself, but this has now changed. She recognises that her use of English is quite distinctive. "In speaking her own language, Fraser is expressing her own distinctive identity, which is neither oppositional nor destabilizing. Instead, she is inhabiting the system and changing it from within" (Nic Craith 2020, 175).

New speakers of English are not simply absorbing the language in a passive manner. Instead, they are actively shaping it and making it their own. In consequence, there are new forms of English emerging and these new varieties have been given names from 'Englog', the variety of English spoken in the Philippines, to 'Japlish', the variety spoken by Japanese to 'Hinglish', which is a mix of Hindi and English. In post-apartheid South Africa, many black people have taken on a new version of English which is peppered with indigenous words. Their use of English is an expression of freedom from Afrikaans which has been regarded as a language of oppression (May 2007).

In some sense, English no longer reflects the status of its speakers in the UK or even in the US. One could not claim that the English spoken by the Irish, the Australians of Japanese descent or Afro-Americans, for example, really belongs to the Anglo-Saxons (Nic Craith 2002). There is no longer one English spoken the world over. Indeed Crystal (2000) predicted that the world would become tri-English. This is one in which people speak a local variety of English at home, a more national variety at work or school and an international variety when dealing with business internationally. Two decades later, Crystal's work continues to provide a useful framework of English language use in a continually globalising world. All languages are work in progress and many circumstances (political, economic and cultural) determine their expansion or decline. The globalisation of English is unprecedented in the history of languages. What that means for the future of Englishes in the workplace and beyond, we can only barely begin to imagine.

Chapter Review Questions

1. What are the factors that have determined the rise of English globally? How have these global factors impacted on the rise of English in your region? Are there any factors in your area that have influenced the use of English?
2. When you communicate in English among your fellow-students, how standard is the English that you use? Are there any expressions or words that you use in your locality that would not be understood by those from somewhere else?
3. English has rapidly become a world language. Do you think it will continue to grow at such speed? How much English is used in social media in your country?
4. Studies on Business English as a Lingua Franca (BELF) have found that it can be perceived as a 'neutral' option in multilingual business settings. This is because it is not the mother tongue of any of its users, and therefore can act as an empowering communicative resource by removing tensions over who 'owns' the language. To what extent do you think this argument can be supported?
5. Do you think employing a language such as BELF in the workplace helps foster feelings of togetherness among employees, or is it indicative of the dominance of English over other languages? What does it mean for linguistic and cultural diversity in contemporary societies?

Recommended Further Reading

- Alharbi, N. 2018. English as a Lingua Franca in the Gulf Cooperation Council States. In *The Routledge Handbook of English as a Lingua Franca*, ed. J. Jenkins, W. Baker, and M. Dewey, 126–137. Abingdon: Routledge.
- Choi, T.H., and B. Adamson. 2020. China's Belt and Road Initiative: Opportunities and Linguistic Challenges for Hong Kong. In *Multilingualism and Politics*, ed. K. Strani, 261–284. Basingstoke: Palgrave Macmillan.
- Ehrenreich, S. 2009. English as a Lingua Franca in Multinational Corporations—Exploring Business Communities of Practice. In *English as a Lingua*

Franca: Studies and Findings, ed. A. Mauranen and E. Ranta, 126–151. Newcastle upon Tyne: Cambridge Scholars.
- McDermott, P. 2019. From Ridicule to Legitimacy? Contested Languages and Devolved Language Planning. *Current Issues in Language Planning* 20 (2): 121–139.
- Mullin, J., C.P. Haviland, and A. Zenger. 2014. Import/Export Work? Using Cross-Cultural Theories to Rethink Englishes, Identities, and Genres in Writing Centers. In *Reworking English in Rhetoric and Composition: Global Interrogations, Local Interventions*, ed. B. Horner and K. Kopelson, 150–165. Carbondale, IL: Southern Illinois University Press.

References

Baker, W., and T. Ishikawa. 2021. *Transcultural Communication Through Global Englishes: An Advanced Textbook for Students*. London: Routledge.

Bermingham, N., R. DePalma, and L. Oca. 2021. De Jure But Not de facto: Pluricentric Portuguese in Post-Colonial Cabo Verde. *Sociolinguistica* 5 (1): 91–111.

Blommaert, J. 2010. *The Sociolinguistics of Globalization*. New York: Cambridge University Press.

British Council. 2017. *Langauges for the Future: The Foreign Languages the United Kingdom Needs to Become a Truly Global Nation*. https://www.britishcouncil.org/sites/default/files/languages_for_the_future_2017.pdf (accessed 29 September 2023).

Chen, C.Y., and W.L. Chung. 2011. Research on the Learning Effects of Multimedia Assisted Instruction on Mandarin Vocabulary for Vietnamese Students: A Preliminary Study Involving e-Learning System. *Educational Research and Reviews* 6 (17): 919.

Choi, T.-H., and B. Adamson. 2020. Toward an Effective Transition to Adopting English as the Medium of Instruction: A Case from Hong Kong. In *EMI: Multidisciplinary Perspectives from Chinese-Speaking Regions* ed. L I.W. Su, H. Cheung, J.R.W. Wu. Routledge. (accessed 29 September 2023).

Cocchiara, F.K., M.P. Bell, and W.J. Casper. 2016. Sounding 'Different': The Role of Sociolinguistic Cues in Evaluating Job Candidates. *Human Resource Management* 55 (3): 463–477.

Codó, E., and J. McDaid. 2019. English Language Assistants in the 21st Century: Nation-State Soft Power in the Experience Economy. *Language, Culture and Society* 1 (2): 219–243.

Crystal, D. 1997. *English as a Global Language*. Cambridge: University Press.

Crystal, D. 2000. The Future of English as a World Language. *Concord*, January: 4–7

Ehrenreich, S. 2010. English as a Business Lingua Franca in a German Multinational Corporation: Meeting the Challenge. *International Journal of Business Communication* 47 (4): 408–431.

Ethnologue. 2022. https://www.ethnologue.com/guides/ethnologue200. (acessed May 2022).

Evans, S. 2010. Business as Usual: The Use of English in the Professional World in Hong Kong. *English for Specific Purposes* 29 (3): 153–167.

Gorski Severo, C. 2016. Lusofonia, colonialismo e globalização [Lusophony, Colonialism, and Globalisation]. *Fórum Linguístico* 13 (3): 1321–1333.

Graddol, D. 1997. *The Future of English? A Guide to Forecasting the Popularity of the English Language in the 21st Century*. London: The British Council.

Kachru, B. 1992. *The Other Tongue: English Across Cultures*. University of Illinois Press.

Kankaanranta, A., and L. Louhiala-Salminen. 2013. What Language Does Global Business Speak? The Concept and Development of BELF. *Ibérica* 26: 204–209.

Le Haa, Phan, J. Kho, and B. Chng. 2013. 2013. Nation Building, English as an International Language, Medium of Instruction, and Language Debate: Malaysia and Possible Ways Forward. *Journal of International and Comparative Education* 2 (2): 58–71.

Louhiala-Salminen, L., M. Charles, and A. Kankaanranta. 2005. English as a Lingua Franca in Nordic Corporate Mergers: Two Case Companies. *English for Specific Purposes* 24 (4): 401–421.

Lull, J. 2000. *Media, Communication, Culture: A Global Approach*. Cambridge: Polity Press.

Mansor, N.R., S.N. Azmy, and S.Z. Yusoff. 2018. Malay as the Language of Advanced Knowledge: Scientific Review in National Academia Scholarship. *International Journal of Asian Social Science* 8 (9): 694–705.

May, J.J. 2007. Language: The Gatekeeper of Humanity. Implications of South Africa's Language in Education Policies. *Online Yearbook of Urban Learning, Teaching, and Research*: 34–45.

May, S. 2014. Contesting Public Monolingualism and Diglossia: Rethinking Political Theory and Language Policy for a Multilingual World. *Language Policy* 13 (4): 371–393. https://doi.org/10.1007/s10993-014-9327-x

McDermott, P. 2011. 'Irish Isn't Spoken Here?' Language Policy and Planning in Ireland. *English Today* 27 (02): 25–31.

McDermott, P. 2019. From Ridicule to Legitimacy? Contested Languages and Devolved Language Planning. *Current Issues in Language Planning* 20 (2): 121–139.

McDermott, P., and S. McMonagle. 2019. Language and a Continent in Flux: Twenty-First Century Tensions of Inclusion and Exclusion. *Anthropological Journal of European Cultures* 28 (2): 66–71.

McDermott, P., and M. Nic Craith. 2019. Linguistic Recognition in Deeply Divided Societies: Antagonism or Reconciliation? In *The Palgrave Handbook of Minority Languages and Communities*, ed. G. Hogan-Brun and B. O'Rourke, 159–180. Basingstoke: Palgrave.

Müller de Oliveira, Gilvan. 2013. Um Atlântico ampliado: o português nas políticas linguísticas do século XXI [An Expanded Atlantic: Portuguese in the Linguistic Policies of the 21st Century]. In *O Português No Século XXI-Cenário Geopolítico e Sociolin- guístico*. ed. da Moita Lopes and Luis Paulo, 53–73. São Paulo: Parábola Editorial.

Nickerson, C. 2005. English as a Lingua Franca in International Business Contexts. *English for Specific Purposes* 24 (4): 367–380.

Nic Craith, M. 1993. *Malartú Teanga: An Ghaeilge i gCorcaigh sa Naoú hAois Déag*. Bremen: ESIS.

Nic Craith, M. 2000. Contested Identity and the Quest for Legitimacy. *Journal of Multilingual and Multicultural Development* 21 (5): 399–413.

Nic Craith, M. 2002. *Plural Identities, Singular Narratives: The Case of Northern Ireland*. New York: Berghahn.

Nic Craith, M. 2006. *Europe and the Politics of Language, Citizens, Migrants and Outsiders*. Basingstoke: Palgrave.

Nic Craith, M. 2016. The Anglicization of Anthropology: Opportunities and Challenges. In *The Anthropologist as Writer*, ed. H. Wulff, 73–90. New York: Berghahn.

Nic Craith, M. 2020. From Bengal to Scotland: Hybridity, Borders and National Narrative. In *A Literary Anthropology of Migration, and Belonging*, ed. C. Fagerlid and M.A. Tisdel, 157–180. Cham: Palgrave Macmillan.

Nye, Joseph S. 2008. Public Diplomacy and Soft Power. *The Annals of the American Academy of Political and Social Science* 616: 94–109.

Phillipson, R. 2003. *English Only Europe? Challenging Language Policy*. London: Routledge.

Phillipson, R. 2004. English as Threat or Resource in Continental Europe. In *Globalisation and the Future of German*, ed. A. Gardt and B. Hueppauf, 47–64. Berlin: De Gruyter.

Randall, M., and M. Amir Samimi. 2010. The Status of English in Dubai: A Transition from Arabic to English as a Lingua Franca. *English Today* 26 (1): 43–50.

Scottish Government. 2015. Scots Language Policy. https://www.gov.scot/publications/scots-lan guage-policy-english/.

Simões, A.R.M. 2014. Portuguese. In *Manual of Language Acquisition*, ed. C. Fäcke, 412–432. Berlin: De Gruyter.
Tomlinson, J. 1999. *Globalization and Culture*. Chicago: University of Chicago Press.

Chapter 12
Multilingualism in the Workplace

Bernadette O'Rourke and Sara C. Brennan

> As the world becomes increasingly globalised, contemporary workplaces often become sites of linguistic diversity. Multilingualism can be both an asset and a challenge to be managed. After introducing key concepts (multilingualism, new speakers, and lingua franca), the chapter examines how language came to play a critical role in contemporary workplaces, how multilingual individuals can leverage their language skills into professional and personal mobility, and how modern enterprises seek to manage their increasingly multilingual workforces. A focus on the role of multilingualism in market development and customer service will be followed by an in-depth look at new speakers in contemporary workplaces.

12.1 Introduction

Increased mobility and technological advances mean that workplaces and workers in the contemporary economy are more and more globalised. As supply chains have spread around the world, corporations have established contacts or offices in other (sometimes several) countries, and people have moved internationally for professional or personal reasons. Employees of even the smallest, most local enterprises are likely to encounter people from different linguistic backgrounds on a regular or even daily basis (as colleagues, as bosses, as clients, as business or trading partners, etc.), either face-to-face or through the use of communications technologies.

B. O'Rourke (✉)
University of Glasgow, Glasgow, Scotland, UK
e-mail: Bernadette.ORourke@glasgow.ac.uk

S. C. Brennan
Université Toulouse Capitole, Toulouse, France
e-mail: sara.brennan@ut-capitole.fr

© The Author(s), under exclusive license to Springer Nature Switzerland AG 2023
K. Strani and K. Pfeiffer (eds.), *Intercultural Issues in the Workplace*,
https://doi.org/10.1007/978-3-031-42320-8_12

The likely presence of several languages in the normal interactions of any given business in the globalised economy makes *multilingualism* a central feature of the contemporary workplace (Blackledge and Creese 2010). As defined by the European Commission, multilingualism refers to 'the ability of societies, institutions, groups and individuals to engage, on a regular basis, with more than one language in their day-to-day lives' (EC 2007, 6). A multilingual individual is therefore 'anyone who can communicate in more than one language, be it active (through speaking and writing) or passive (through listening and reading)' (Wei 2008, 4). Multilingualism also includes bilingualism, which refers to the ability to communicate in two languages.

In the context of the workplace, there are several options for managing the multilingualism of employees so as to best facilitate communication among individuals with diverse linguistic backgrounds:

> When companies go international [...] they basically have three linguistic options... They may bring in language professionals, i.e. translators and interpreters, to facilitate communication between staff with different linguistic backgrounds. Alternatively, they may rely on some staff members, usually staff members based in the subsidiary, to accommodate speakers of the majority partners' language, in which case communication will be between native speakers and non-native speakers. A third option is the choice of a lingua franca [...]. All these options may co- exist within one single company and oftentimes do. (Piller 2009, 321)

As Chapter 13 focuses on interpreting and translation in the workplace, this chapter will explore the other two main options available for navigating multilingualism at work: the accommodation to the majority language by non-native speakers, whom we shall define as *new speakers*; and the selection of a *lingua franca* for workplace communication.

New speakers of a given language are understood here as individuals who do not learn the language through family transmission in the home or through exposure to its use within their local community, as is usually the case for native speakers of that language. Instead, they acquire it through the education system or as adult learners, often by taking night classes or by using language learning software (O'Rourke et al. 2015). So, new speakers are individuals who actively use a language that is different from their native language or mother tongue in social life, often including in the workplace.

Case Study 1

A Korean employee who transferred from Kia's headquarters in Seoul, in which Korean was the language of the workplace, to their office outside Madrid in Spain, for example, can be defined as a new speaker of Spanish, having learned the language through school or as an adult language learner, and would communicate with native Spanish speakers in the office through that language. The management of multilingualism in that workplace would thus take place through the use of the local majority language (here, Spanish) by new speakers (who would be native speakers of Korean, English, Dutch, or

> any other language). Can you think of any other examples? Do you know any known speakers? Are you a new speaker yourself?
>
> In some cases though, such international companies might choose to adopt one language for communication in the workplace and across all their outposts, whether they be in Korea or Spain or anywhere else. In this case, the enterprise would select a lingua franca, which can refer to 'any lingual medium of communication between people of different mother tongues, for whom it is a second language' (Samarin 1987, 371). In this case, employees for example in the Kia offices in both Seoul and Madrid would use English as their medium of communication, regardless of where the employees were from or what their native language is.

12.2 Language(s) in the Workplace: From Local Problem to Global Opportunities

While communication and multilingualism play an increasingly important role in the contemporary globalised economy, this has not always been the case. During the era of industrial manufacturing, the use of language by workers on the factory floor was often viewed as detrimental to their productivity and efficiency, as talking was seen to demonstrate a lack of focus on their work. Taylorism, a late nineteenth-century theory of management developed by F.W. Taylor (1856–1915), sought to maximise the efficiency of industrial production by breaking the process down into standardised tasks that could be performed repeatedly and as quickly as possible by any trained worker (Urciuoli and LaDousa 2013; Boutet 2001). From a Taylorist perspective, communication between workers was seen as a time-wasting distraction that prevented employees from concentrating on their tasks; as such, communication was to be avoided and was thus often closely regulated, and even sometimes forbidden apart from explicitly work-related interaction (Boutet 2001, 20).

The globalisation of the economy has fundamentally altered this dynamic. The term *globalisation* can be used to refer to the increased circulation of people, products, money, and ideas around the world, which has been facilitated by technological advances in transportation, media, and information and communication technologies, and which has profoundly impacted international relations, cultural practices, and social organisation (Blommaert 2010, 13). The impact of globalisation can be seen in almost every aspect of life: on any given day we can stream TV shows from the United States of America, buy cars from Japan, bump into tourists from Estonia on the street, go to school with classmates from Nigeria, take a low-cost flight to Iceland, or pick up an Indian takeaway on the way home from a night out.

Another globalised site is the workplace. Multinational corporations (MNCs) have spread around the globe, and local small and medium-sized enterprises (SMEs) are often bought by international investors. Sites of production can now be situated thousands of miles from their parent companies or from the ultimate sites of distribution, and the materials of production might be sourced from around the world. For example, technological advances have enabled call centre operators in the city of Johannesburgh in South Africa to respond to customer service calls from the state of South Carolina in the United States. Beyond the enterprises and their products and services, the employees of the contemporary workforce are also increasingly globalised: whereas many individuals are (or must be) mobile and ready to move around the world for work, others are relatively immobile and yet globally connected through communication technologies. Therefore, workplaces have come to be characterised by increasing linguistic and cultural diversity, as more people from varied places and backgrounds interact in person or via technology.

In direct opposition to Taylor's earlier philosophy, these globalisation processes have rendered language and communication central to the contemporary workplace. Facilitated by technological advances, multilingual communication has become an essential element of managing transnational networks and supply chains that cross linguistic and cultural boundaries. Thanks to video-conferencing and computer-mediated technologies (e.g. email, instant messaging, chat, VOIP), written correspondence, meetings, and negotiations can all take place at a (great) distance in more or less real time (Gunnarsson 2013, 162–163). This means that multilingual and multicultural communication has become a regular, if not daily, element of work in the globalised workplace. In order to adapt to expanding and constantly shifting global markets, as well as the increased emphasis on technology and multitasking, the workforce of the industrial era has thus effectively become a 'wordforce' (Heller 2010) that produces communication rather than goods.

While such widespread multilingualism has long been a dimension of the workplace outside Western Europe, North America, and Australia, international migration has for the past several decades contributed to the increasing diversification of the previously mainly monolingual workplaces in these countries as well (Hewitt 2012, 269). The increasing linguistic diversification of the workplace has generated new concerns for the efficiency and safety of enterprises with employees from a range of linguistic backgrounds (Roberts 2007; Alcorso 2002): How can meetings be conducted when many of an enterprise's employees do not share the same native language? How can new markets be reached and new business partnerships be negotiated across linguistic boundaries? How can emergency procedures be made clear to a linguistically diverse workforce (or indeed wordforce)? The management of multilingualism and linguistic diversity has become a key concern for (transnational or otherwise) enterprises in the globalised economy.

The global context in which many cultures interact presents challenges and opportunities. What cultural conflicts can you anticipate? How might one promote dialogue between cultures? Two common approaches to addressing the issues—the accommodation of new speakers to the majority language, and the selection of a lingua franca—will be discussed in Sect. 12.4. In the meantime, Sect. 12.3 will take a closer look at the relationship between the increased multilingualism and the heightened mobility of the globalised economy.

12.3 Multilingual Skills and Mobility

As resource extraction and industrial manufacturing have been relocated to parts of the world in which labour is less expensive (e.g. China), the knowledge-, information-, and service-economies have boomed, leading to a greater emphasis on language and communication skills as essential for both office jobs and manual labour work. With increasing emphasis on the information and service industries, productivity in many spaces of the contemporary economy has come to be measured 'not by the number of pieces produced, but by the number of phone calls taken, words translated, products or services sold, or successful interactions with tourists', rendering language and communication as skills central to efficiency and thus profits (Duchêne and Heller 2012, 326). Moreover, given the central importance of managing communication across linguistically diverse networks (of producers, distributors, and consumers) and within linguistically diverse workplaces, multilingualism is very often valued as a critical work skill in the globalised economy, as it enhances the flexibility of an employee and cost-efficiency of the workforce.

A customer service representative bilingual in Russian and French can help clients who speak either language, while a project manager fluent in Urdu and Italian can help a Pakistani company negotiate with an Italian one, all potentially without the need to hire an interpreter or translator.

In light of the value placed on communication skills and particularly on multilingualism, language and mobility intersect in a variety of ways in the workplaces of the contemporary globalised economy. Many people learn new languages to increase their personal and professional mobility in a variety of senses, in order to: find employment in other regions or countries; open up access to new markets and sites of production or distribution; facilitate partnerships or mergers with other enterprises; enhance their appeal to multi- or transnational corporations; generally indicate their willingness to 'move between jobs, branches, and countries' as flexible potential employees on global markets that prize flexibility (Gunnarsson 2013, 179). The cognitive benefits of multilingualism have also become widely accepted in recent years, with the ability to communicate in more than one language seen as linked to enhanced intellectual development. Furthermore, multilingualism is often now considered as a marker of open-mindedness, sensitivity to cross-cultural differences, and tolerance (Jaffe 2007). Such attributes are often seen as important for the mobile employees of the contemporary economy, who tend to regularly work across geographic as well as cultural boundaries.

Even for workers who remain geographically immobile and continue working in their home country, multilingualism can still represent an important skill for their daily work activities. Mergers with or buy-outs by other companies can introduce linguistic diversity into physically immobile workplaces by embedding them within transnational networks. So even if a workplace is immobile, the clientele that it serves or market that it targets may not be. Given the massive increase in mobility worldwide, the customers, clients, or patients that professionals and other works interact with and serve are often speakers of other languages. The mobility of the client base is particularly evident in industries such as tourism, in which mobility is an essential characteristic of the target customers. Tourism companies indeed often seek out multilingual workers to better cater to certain segments of tourists.

> **Case Study 2**
> As many Spanish tourists visit Edinburgh, for example, tour companies often hire Spanish-speaking guides to provide tours in the native language of these prospective customers. If you've been to any of the main tourist attractions in Edinburgh, can you recall the range of languages on offer for guided tours?
>
> Beyond facilitating international mergers and enhancing the tourist experience of Edinburgh Castle, workers' multilingual skills can also be seen as critical for the provision of healthcare or social services to an increasingly linguistically diverse population, as these professionals 'need to interact *with* and provide services *to* individuals with whom they do not share the same [first language] or even any common language' (Angouri 2014, 3–4).
>
> As these examples indicate, multilingualism has come to be seen as a valuable skill for a wide range of employees of the globalised economy: customer service representatives, doctors, and project managers alike are all often called upon to mobilise diverse linguistic repertoires to successfully carry out their jobs and achieve professional and personal mobility in the multilingual workplace.

12.4 Multilingual Workers, Lingua Franca, and New Speakers

As Sect. 12.3 discussed above, the multilingualism of the contemporary workforce and of individual employees can generate substantial benefits for the enterprises of the globalised economy. Multilingual individuals are able to draw on their linguistic repertoires to manage both strategic and social communication in the work environment, 'mak[ing] use of multilingual resources and/or interactional activities to build rapport with co-workers or clients and to achieve their communicative goals while doing their work' (Hua 2014, 236). However, many enterprises seek to manage linguistic diversity in multilingual workplaces by establishing a lingua franca. The decisions to adopt a lingua franca in many contexts depend on how well speakers of different languages can understand each other in the workplace.

Case Study 3

Employees who speak such closely related, mutually intelligible languages as Norwegian and Swedish, for example, could continue using their first languages in the workplace because these languages are so similar. In order to host a meeting with representatives from an Italian company, however, these speakers would likely switch to using English as a lingua franca, as speakers of Scandinavian and Romance languages cannot easily understand each other's mother tongues.

As pointed to by this example from Scandinavia, English is often chosen as the lingua franca of inter- and transnational workplaces and networks, given its positioning as the world language *par excellence* and its reputation as the language of commerce (Gunnarsson 2013). Whether English or any other language is chosen, official or unofficial language policies are often instituted in multilingual workplaces to position the selected language as the lingua franca in order to facilitate communication. In this situation, many (if not most or even all) of the employees of an enterprise may end up using a language other than their native one for workplace communication. Depending on the dynamics of the enterprise, a policy of using the chosen lingua franca may extend to all the employees of an organisation, or only to certain echelons of workers:

> Although bilingual and multilingual individuals have been and still are found in companies and organisations all over the world, many large organisations uphold an idea of linguistic unity. For practical and ideological reasons, large organisations often choose one official, corporate language. This language is used as a lingua franca in meetings and written communication, and it also functions as a symbolic expression of organisational unity. In many cases, the official/corporate language penetrates the whole organisation, which means that all employees are assumed to master this language. In other cases, the official language is an elite language used at top-level meetings and for external, international contacts, while other languages are used in the daily interaction at work […]. (Gunnarsson 2013, 164)

While often seen as a practical or unifying option for managing linguistic diversity in the workplace, the selection of a lingua franca is not without complications. For example, as the choice of a lingua franca applies both to spoken and written communication, issues can arise in terms of transparency and accountability when some or all of the employees of an enterprise are using a language other than their native one (Angouri 2014, 2). Drafting a new corporate policy handbook, for instance, may prove challenging when all the contributors are faced with writing a formal, jargon-heavy, and potentially legally binding document in a language that is not their mother tongue.

Working with another student who is learning the same language as you, imagine that you work for the same company and are in a business meeting where that language is the lingua franca. Try to write a brief formal statement setting out the corporate values of that company in your lingua franca. Is this statement as clear and precise as it would be in your native language? Were there any concepts or words that were challenging to express in the lingua franca?

As mentioned above, however, not every enterprise seeks to establish one language as the lingua franca for (some or all of) its employees, regardless of linguistic background. In other cases, the native language of the majority of the employees—often the local language of the area in which the enterprise is based—becomes the expected medium of communication in the workplace. Even though potentially all the employees of a given enterprise might function as new speakers in the workplace in the case of a lingua franca policy, this latter policy of accommodation would generate a dynamic of new speakers using the more dominant language of the enterprise's native speakers. As will be discussed later on in section X, the dynamic of a workplace in which employees are expected to speak the language of the majority of the enterprise introduces a wide range of both opportunities and challenges for new speakers of that language, as linguistic skills in some cases can be used as a measure of entrepreneurial capability or managerial success.

12.5 Multilingualism, Niche Markets, and Customer Service in a Globalised World

In an increasingly globalised economy expanding in all directions across a linguistically diverse world, multilingualism often plays a vital role in both the development of new (niche) markets and the provision of customer service. The strategies adopted by entrepreneurs in their efforts to access new markets have made clear the importance of being able to operate multilingually. Based on their study of the strategies mobilised by small business owner/managers in the north-western UK attempting to enter the Chinese market, for instance, Daryanto et al. (2013, 651) argue that multilingual websites play a critical role in the process of expanding into new markets: by creating versions of their website in the language of the foreign markets they seek to access, enterprises can localise their products or services and thus better appeal to customers in these countries. As the entrepreneurs themselves may not speak any Chinese languages, for example, the growth of their business into China would then likely depend on web development and customer services provided by multilingual enterprises able to accommodate the multilingualism of this new client base.

One industry on which such companies looking to expand into new, multilingual markets might rely is that of call centres, which have been identified as one of the most characteristic sites of economic activity in the globalised economy for the centrality of language to their operations. Within such a workplace, in which the ability to efficiently communicate with as many customers as possible is paramount, multilingual employees can play a particularly important role in efforts to respond to or make contact with linguistically diverse populations. In their study of bilingual call centres at the border between the United States and Mexico, for example, Alarcón and Heyman (2013) interviewed an operator who was bilingual in Spanish and English about how he was expected to flexibly manage cold calling people who might speak either language:

> What they did with me... was that they gave me a list of numbers. And I said OK. Here you have 200 numbers. You are going to work from 3 PM to 9 PM. You do questionnaires. I had my telephone, activated it with the headset in place, entered the number, waited for them to answer, and then I began my script. I had two screens. The E for English and the S for Spanish. And it had my script. I could not deviate at all. If the client responded with "Bueno" [standard Spanish telephone greeting], "Haló" [English borrowing, greeting in Spanish], then the S script. If the client speaks in English... Then in English. ... I had to give an immediate response, English or Spanish. If I spoke in English and it seemed that they did not understand, I would make a swift change to Spanish [...]. (Alarcón and Heyman 2013, 15)

The multilingual skills of the call centre operator, and his related ability to quickly and accurately judge the language of an unseen, unknown person at the other end of the phone, were thus crucial for the call centre's ability to successfully manage client relations in a bilingual area along an international border. Call centres in India, meanwhile, provide a vivid example of how not only the diversity of languages in the globalised workplace is managed, but also of how the diversity of accents is managed as well. English is a lingua franca of multilingual India and one of the country's two official languages: while English is the first language of thousands of Indians, there are tens of millions of Indians who are new speakers of English. In part due to the large number of English speakers there, India has become a global hub for the call centre industry. Indian English, however, is not always valued in the call centre workplace, particularly, for example, when customer service is being provided to American callers for American corporations. Many Indian call centres thus prefer to hire Indian employees who master an American or a British English accent. The 2005 documentary film *Nalini by Day, Nancy by Night* indeed offers a privileged glimpse of how individuals seeking to work in call centres attend course after course to try to perfect their American accents, while those individuals who are hired call themselves by American names during work hours.

12.6 The Opportunities and Challenges of Being a New Speaker in the Workplace

As anyone who has learned another language knows, the language learning process is just that: a process. The foundations of a language can sometimes be learned relatively quickly: greetings, essential vocabulary, and basic sentence structure might not always take very long to learn in a classroom, but then what about all the rest? It can take months, years, perhaps even decades to learn how to use a new language across a range of social settings, with varying degrees of formality and with widely diverse vocabularies and topics of conversation. The dynamic of becoming and being a new speaker of a language can thus also be seen as a process marked by many questions, decisions, opportunities, and challenges: what language(s) do future new speakers choose to learn, and why? At what point do these speakers attempt to use their new language socially? What form of the language (standard, colloquial, etc.) do the new speakers try to use? How do native speakers of a given language respond to new speakers' efforts to speak it? Do such interactions encourage the new speaker to keep learning and speaking the language, or do they add worries or fears? How do new speakers learn the different vocabularies associated with different social spheres, ranging from a local bar to an executive boardroom? As this last question hints, the experience of new speakers as workers in the multilingual workplace provides a perfect example of the process of becoming, being, and being accepted as a new speaker of a given language. Multilingual workers are indeed an area of specific interest for the New Speakers Network (http://www.nspk.org.uk/), and a report prepared by the Network's working group focused on workers explored issues pertaining to new speakers in the globalised workplace (Duchêne et al. 2013). Drawing on the research of Network members, this report detailed several key phases in the process of becoming and being a new speaker in the workplace: (1) becoming a new speaker for and at work; (2) entering work as a new speaker; and (3) being a new speaker at work. We'll take a brief look at each of these phases to see how new speakers navigate workplaces in which they attempt to speak their new language.

As mentioned above, many new speakers have learned their new languages in order to enhance their professional mobility. Some may learn a certain language so that they have a better chance of moving to another country and finding a job there: an Estonian worker hoping to work in Japan, for instance, might learn Japanese so that she is a better candidate for a job there. Other new speakers, meanwhile, might have learned another language to improve their employment chances at home: an American hoping to build a career in finance, for example, might learn Mandarin in order to appeal to American firms looking to make deals in China. While such new speakers began learning other languages in preparation for entering the job market, the process of becoming a new speaker can also begin in the workplace after an individual already has a job; for example a deaf academic who typically uses American Sign Language who relocates from the United States to work at Heriot-Watt University would have to become a new speaker (or signer) of British Sign Language in order to function in that workplace. If a company is planning on crossing linguistic boundaries to enter a new market, for instance, they might ask some of their existing employees to learn the language of that market; in other cases, enterprises that hire workers from other linguistic backgrounds or merge with foreign companies might provide language courses to help new employees become new speakers of the local language. The globalised, multilingual workplace thus generates numerous starting points for the process of becoming a new speaker. Can you think of any other industries, sectors, corporations, professions, etc. in which learning a certain language might be particularly valuable?

Learning a new language and becoming a new speaker to find employment, however, does not always guarantee easy or straightforward entry into the workplace. In some cases, being a new speaker of a language can be seen as a positive asset by an enterprise's recruiters: as German cars are often associated abroad with the stereotype of high-quality German engineering, a German car company might prefer to hire German new speakers of Spanish (rather than native Spanish speakers) when expanding into South America in order to maintain the connection between 'German-ness' and a reputation for automotive engineering. In other cases, however, new speakers might be disadvantaged or even excluded when applying for other jobs, as their language competence is seen as inferior to that of a native speaker. In many non-Anglophone countries, for example, new speakers of English (regardless of their competence) are often excluded from English language teaching positions, for which employers prefer to hire native English speakers from Australia, the United Kingdom, or the United States. Becoming a new speaker in the hopes of improving employment prospects thus does not always guarantee entry into the workplace.

Once a new speaker is successfully chosen for a job in a workplace in which her new language is the medium of communication, she must navigate the process of carrying out her professional responsibilities in that new language. As mentioned earlier in this section, language learning is a long, uneven process, so new speakers may face a range of challenges in the workplace: while their oral command of the language may be very strong, quickly writing emails and reports to meet deadlines might be more difficult, making certain work tasks more stressful. The many assumptions or prejudices associated with language use may impact on the work opportunities made available to new speakers. For example, new speakers may not be selected to lead team presentations or pitches to clients because their speech is not deemed to sound 'native' enough; this closing off of access to leadership roles could then impact on their eligibility for promotion. While learning a new language may help new speakers to prepare for and enter the workplace, the process of being a new speaker does not stop at recruitment: these multilingual individuals then face the multifaceted challenges of both adjusting to operating professionally in a new language and proving or defending their linguistic legitimacy and professional capacity to colleagues who might judge their non-native language use.

Chapter Review Questions

1. What is multilingualism? Would you consider yourself to be multilingual? Describe a (hypothetical) situation in which a lingua franca is chosen—how does it work? What language is everyone expected to speak? Can you think of a few people you know who are new speakers? How did they acquire their 'new' language?
2. How has the role of language in the workplace changed since the industrial era? What developments helped bring about these changes?
3. What language(s) do you see as most closely with mobility? Are they more closely associated with professional mobility (i.e. with getting a job, a promotion, or a raise), with personal mobility (i.e. with working and living in another country, with having a job that involves international travel), or both?

4. Think about local business (shop, restaurant, office, etc.) that you know—can you think of the ways that the daily commercial life of this business might involve multiple languages or cross-linguistic boundaries? How is the dynamic of choosing a lingua franca for a multilingual workplace different from having new speakers accommodate speakers of the local majority language?
5. Imagine the world in 50 years—do you see any certain language(s) serving as the lingua franca of global business? How can becoming a new speaker of a given language help (potential) employees in the globalised multilingual workplace? What challenges do they face?

Recommended Further Reading

- Cenoz, J., D. Durk Gorter, and S. May. 2017. *Language Awareness and Multilingualism*. Cham: Springer.
- Feely, A.J., and A. Harzing. 2002. Language Management in Multinational Companies. *Cross Cultural Management: An International Journal* 10 (2): 37–52.
- Lüdi, G., K. Hochle Meier, and P. Yanaprasart, eds. 2016. *Managing Plurilingual and Intercultural Practices in the Workplace: The Case of Multilingual Switzerland*. Amsterdam: John Benjamins.
- Lorente, B.P. 2012. The Making of Workers of the World: Language and the Labor Brokerage State. In *Language in Late Capitalism: Pride and Profit*, ed. A. Duchêne and M. Heller, 183–206. London and New York: Routledge.
- Meyer, B., and B. Apfelbaum, eds. 2010. *Multilingualism at Work: From Policies to Practices in Public, Medical and Business settings*. Amsterdam and Philadelphia: John Benjamins Publishing.

References

Alarcón, A., and J.M. Heyman. 2013. Bilingual Call Centers at the US-Mexico Border: Location and Linguistic Markers of Exploitability. *Language in Society* 42 (01): 1–21.
Alcorso, C. 2002. Improving Occupational Health and Safety Information to Immigrant Workers in NSW. Working Paper No. 78, ACIRRT. Sydney: University of Sydney.
Angouri, J. 2014. Multilingualism in the Workplace: Language Practices in Multilingual Contexts. *Multilingua—Journal of Cross-Cultural and Interlanguage Communication* 33 (1–2): 1–9.
Blackledge, A., and A. Creese. 2010. *Multilingualism: A Critical Perspective*. London: Continuum.

Blommaert, J. 2010. *The Sociolinguistics of Globalization*. Cambridge and New York: Cambridge University Press.

Boutet, J. 2001. La part langagière du travail: bilan et évolution. *Langage et Société* 4 (98): 17.

Daryanto, A., H. Khan, H. Matlay, and R. Chakrabarti. 2013. Adoption of Country-Specific Business Websites: The Case of UK Small Businesses Entering the Chinese Market. *Journal of Small Business and Enterprise Development* 20 (3): 650–660.

Duchêne, A., and M. Heller. 2012. Language Policy in the Workplace. In *The Cambridge Handbook of Language Policy*, ed. B. Spolsky, 323–334. Cambridge: Cambridge University Press.

Duchêne, A., M. Moyer, and C. Roberts, eds., 2013. *Language, Migration and Social Inequalities: A Critical Sociolinguistic Perspective on Institutions and Work (Vol. 2)*. Multilingual Matters.

European Commission. 2007. Commission of the European Communities. Final Report. High Level Group on Multilingualism. Available at: https://op.europa.eu/en/publication-detail/-/publication/b0a1339f-f181-4de5-abd3-130180f177c7. Accessed 1 December 2022.

Gunnarsson, B.-L. 2013. Multilingualism in the Workplace. *Annual Review of Applied Linguistics* 33: 162–189.

Heller, M. 2010. Language as Resource in the Globalized New Economy. In *The Handbook of Language and Globalization*, ed. N. Coupland, 349–365. Malden, MA and Oxford: Wiley-Blackwell.

Hewitt, R. 2012. Multilingualism in the Workplace. In *The Routledge Handbook of Multilingualism*, ed. M. Martin-Jones, A. Blackledge, and A. Creese, 267–280. London: Routledge.

Hua, Z. 2014. *Exploring Intercultural Communication: Language in Action*. Oxford and New York: Routledge.

Jaffe, A. 2007. Minority Language Movements. In *Bilingualism: A Social Approach*, ed. M. Heller, 50–70. Basingstoke and New York: Palgrave Macmillan.

O'Rourke, B., J. Pujolar, and F. Ramallo. 2015. New Speakers of Minority Languages: The Challenging Opportunity—Foreword. *International Journal of the Sociology of Language* 231: 1–20.

Piller, I. 2009. Intercultural communication. In *The Handbook of Business Discourse*, ed. F. Bargiela-Chiappini, 317–329. Edinburgh: Edinburgh University Press.

Roberts, C. 2007. Multilingualism in the Workplace. In *Handbook of Multilingualism and Multilingual Communication*, ed. P. Auer and L. Wie, 405–422. Berlin: Walter de Gruyter.

Samarin, W. 1987. Lingua franca. In *Sociolinguistics: An International Handbook of the Science of Language and Society/Soziolinguistik: Ein internationales Handbuch zur Wissenschaft von Sprache und Gesellschaft*, ed. U. Ammon, N. Dittmar, and K. Mattheier, 371–374. Berlin: Walter de Gruyter.

Urciuoli, B., and C. LaDousa. 2013. Language Management/Labor. *Annual Review of Anthropology* 42: 175–190.

Wei, L. 2008. Research Perspectives on Bilingualism and Multilingualism. In *The Blackwell Guide to Research Methods in Bilingualism and Multilingualism*, ed. L. Wei and M.G. Moyer, 3–17. Malden, Oxford and Victoria: Blackwell Publishing.

Chapter 13
Translation and Interpretation in Cross-Cultural Business Workplace Practices

Min-Hsiu Liao, Pedro Jesús Castillo Ortiz, Jemina Napier, and Kester Newill

> International business is conducted in multilingual environments, necessitating a variety of translating and interpreting (T&I) activities. It is crucial that companies planning to successfully expand into a different linguistic community consider the relationship between language and culture because the costs of making mistakes can be high. We have all heard anecdotes about how poorly translated brand names or company slogans have caused unintended offence or hilarity in the target market. In this chapter, we are going to learn about what T&I is, different types of T&I activities, and how they play a significant role in the business context.

M.-H. Liao (✉) · J. Napier
Department of Languages and Intercultural Studies, Heriot-Watt University, Edinburgh, Scotland, UK
e-mail: m.liao@hw.ac.uk

J. Napier
e-mail: J.Napier@hw.ac.uk

P. J. Castillo Ortiz
University of Granada, Granada, Spain
e-mail: pedrocastillo@ugr.es

K. Newill
University of Stirling, Stirling, Scotland, UK
e-mail: kester.newill@stir.ac.uk

© The Author(s), under exclusive license to Springer Nature Switzerland AG 2023
K. Strani and K. Pfeiffer (eds.), *Intercultural Issues in the Workplace*,
https://doi.org/10.1007/978-3-031-42320-8_13

13.1 Key Concepts in Translation and Interpretation

When a company expands into international markets, it becomes crucial for that company to consider how to engage with different linguistic communities. T&I are essential activities that enable the company to sell its products abroad, attend trade exhibitions abroad, collaborate with partnerships abroad or deal with customers' complaints. While it is true that English is regarded as the lingua franca in many global business contexts, it is unrealistic to expect that all stakeholders, at all stages of business activities, are capable of communicating in English. Therefore, if you work in a business context, it is very likely that you will experience T&I services of one kind or another at some point during your working life. You may be responsible for arranging this service in order to enable interlingual communication—for example, before a visit from your business partner. If you can speak more than one language, there is a good chance that you will be asked to perform **ad-hoc translating or interpreting tasks**—for instance, to deal with a customer complaint in a different language. In many more cases, you will be a T&I service-user—for example, as a participant in a sales negotiation. This chapter outlines the most important things you need to know about T&I, as a potential commissioner, user and performer of translation and interpreting in the business context.

In daily language, the term **translation** and **interpretation** (or its active form, translating and interpreting) may be used in a more general or metaphorical way to refer to almost any process between one layer of meaning and another. T&I academics sometimes use translation as a general term to cover both translation and interpretation. However, using these terms more precisely will help you to order the right service that you need. Different national and international organizations all provide their definitions on translation and interpretation, such as International Association of Conference Interpreters (AIIC) and Chartered Institute of Linguistics (CIOL). Below is the distinction between the two modes explained by the United Nations (n.d.): "Translation at the United Nations refers to the translation of the written word, that is, the translation of written texts from one language to another. The translation of the spoken word, whether simultaneously or consecutively, is referred to as 'interpretation'". This explanation stresses that modes—one as written and the other as spoken, as the distinctive features between translation and interpretation.

The definition provided by other organizations, such as UK National Occupational Standards of Interpreting (2006, 11) and the Victorian Government in Australia (n.d.), further includes the transference from signed language into another signed or spoken language. Sign languages refer to languages used by deaf or hard-of-hearing people that are separate from spoken/written languages and have evolved in deaf communities.

Companies that require T&I services on a daily basis may have dedicated **staff** or in-house translators/interpreters as part of a team that deals with interlingual communication. Alternatively, freelance translators/interpreters can be hired to assist with translating and interpreting when the occasional need arises. We also mentioned **ad-hoc translating or interpreting tasks** above—that is, asking untrained person to translate or interpret. These practices are common in the business context because it saves the companies time and cost to hire a professional. However, the expertise required to perform translating and interpreting tasks are often underestimated, and the company can run the risk of spending even more time and money to recover the damage caused by non-professional translator and interpreter.

T&I activities can be categorized in different ways, depending on the purpose and context of the activities. Examples include translation of corporate literature or commercial documents, medical interpreting, court interpreting, etc. Table 13.1 shows a model presented by Janssens et al. (2004), with a specific focus on business context T&I practices in international companies. In this table, T&I activities are presented in a spectrum of "perspectives", from that requiring least human intervention, i.e. the mechanical perspective, to those requiring most human intervention, involving the consideration of cultural differences and power negotiation.

Table 13.1 illustrates the complexities involved in the production of T&I. It is common, though misleading, to assume that to translate only requires one "to change words into a different language", as defined in the Cambridge online dictionary. Within a business context, Janssens et al. (2004) have identified different functions of T&I activities and different roles that a translator can play.

From a mechanical perspective, translation is almost invisible, and the aim is to pursue accuracy and consistency (Janssens et al. 2004, 419). From a cultural perspective, translators and interpreters are expected to pre-empt cultural difficulties and make changes accordingly (421). From a political perspective, the primary concerns of the translators and interpreters are not necessarily the linguistic or the cultural differences, but the power dimension: *who* is involved in using this T&I

Table 13.1 Translation strategies in the business context

	Mechanical perspective	Cultural perspective	Political perspective
Assumptions	Universal language and homogeneous culture	Languages are key to the creation of cultures	Competition due to status and power relationships of languages and cultures
Role of translators	Transmitters of the original message	Mediators between different cultural meaning systems	Negotiators between competing value systems and codes of ethics
Expected outcome	Production of translated texts which are as close to the source text as possible	Production of translated texts which consider culturally specific needs	Production of translated texts which reflect the influence of exchange among the different stakeholders
Examples	Multilingual terminology management in a global company	Translation of an advertisement into a different language	Interpretation in a meeting of business negotiation

Adapted based on Janssens et al. (2004, 428)

and what *their aims of communication* are (424). At various stages and in various forms of business communication, we can place T&I activities along this spectrum of human intervention.

In this respect, the sections that follow are organized approximately from interactions with the most interventions (business interpreting) to interactions with the least human intervention (computer-aided translation).

13.2 Business Interpreting

When is interpreting required in a cross-cultural business setting nowadays? Table 13.2 gives you some examples of business settings where interpreters may be required. The table is divided into external and internal business contexts. These include situations where spoken (or signed) exchanges take place and, when different languages are used in the exchange, interpreters may be required.

Once we have developed an idea of the situations where interpreters may be required in business settings, the next question is, how are these interlinguistic exchanges managed, and how do interpreters "technically" manage the interaction?

13.2.1 Modes of interpreting

There are, in essence, three modes of interpreting:

Dialogue interpreting (or liaison interpreting): the interpreter mediates between two parties (or sometimes more) in face-to-face interaction. The interpreters switch between two (or more) languages and interpret back and forth between all parties. Dialogue interpreting is used more often in meetings or negotiations where privacy is key, or in situations when participants are interacting at short intervals.

Table 13.2 Examples of business contexts potentially requiring interpreters

External: with people outside the company	Internal: between people in the same company
– Import/export settings – International sales deals meetings (preliminary, deal signing, follow-ups) – Foreign investment: exploratory visits, meetings with national, regional and local regulatory bodies – Business synergies and company mergers – Trade fairs and international exhibitions – Business conferences and events – Purchase of services – Tourism: guided tours	– Control visits (health and safety, quality assurance, human resources…) – Team briefing sessions – Development of new line products and services – Staff training – Setting up franchises – Internal business meetings

Dialogue interpreting tends to take place in offices, meeting rooms or company facilities.

Consecutive interpreting: the interpreter waits for the speaker to finish a chunk of speech and then relays it in a different language, often with the aid of note-taking. Consecutive interpreting is mostly used in long speeches, such as presentations and speeches on product development, marketing strategies and the like.

Simultaneous interpreting: the interpreter renders the speech while the speaker is speaking at the same time, with a time lag of a few seconds. The interpreter usually sits in a soundproof interpreting booth, listens to the speaker through a headset and speaks to a microphone. Where technical equipment is not available, or only one or few delegates require interpreting, the interpreter may sit close to the listeners and speak quietly into their ear, which is known as whisper interpreting or *chuchotage*. Simultaneous interpreting is the most common mode in place in business conferences, usually held in conference centres and hotel conference rooms which allow for the installation of built-in or temporary simultaneous interpreting equipment. Sign language interpreters typically work in all contexts in simultaneous mode due to the fact that one of the languages is silent, so there is no interference between two languages being spoken at the same time.

These three modes are often used with the physical presence of all parties, including the interpreter, in the same location. However, with technological advancement, new interpreting modes have become possible. For example, videoconferencing makes it possible to use the method of **remote interpreting,** i.e. the interpreter is physically located in a different place from some or all parties involved and communicates via telephone, video or other technologies. In his study of media interpreting, Castillo (2015, 290) explains that in radio interviews conducted between a studio-based host and an out-of-studio guest, it is possible for interpreters to be located either with the host or with the interviewee.

The mode of interpreting is usually determined or agreed upon according to several factors, such as:

- the physical setting (an office, a meeting room, a restaurant, a conference and exhibition centre)
- the clients' experience in working with interpreters
- the clients' budget
- the interpreter's advice, if given the opportunity to assess the possibilities for the creation of best interactional space.

13.2.2 Ethics and client expectations

Now we turn to ethics and clients' expectations when hiring interpreters. Privacy, confidentiality and high economic stakes are often the overarching aspects that frame business meetings. When an interpreter is added to the "communicative equation", ethical aspects must be considered, both by interpreters and companies (those which hire interpreters and those who depend on this service hired by others). Concepts of neutrality and allegiance usually surface in the course of interpreter-mediated events. The literature is vast in the field of ethics of interpreting (cf. Ozolins 2015). There are also many different professional codes of ethics, whose origins are to be found in public service interpreting such as police, court and healthcare interpreting. While in the cases of social service interpreting interpreters are generally expected to be "neutral"—although not without contest of whether neutrality is really achievable or even desirable—it is even more problematic to expect business interpreters to be neutral since they are often hired by one party of the interaction. It is inevitable that a strong ethic of power, hierarchy and team loyalty are imposed on business interpreters (Ozolins 2015, 327).

It is clear that interpreters working in business settings face challenges which surpass interlinguistic transfer and touch upon issues where ethical decisions must be made. These ethical questions arise in situations of conflict of interests, strategic politeness, sharing of private information, request for allegiance and loyalty and even bribing. As Karanasiou puts it, "most of the time, the interpreter in business negotiations settings is given no choice but to become part of a team" (2016, 199). Some scholars have argued that instead of expecting interpreters to be neutral or impartial, perhaps **trust** (Tipton 2010) and **cooperation** (Pym 2000) are more useful concepts to frame the interpreter's position in business settings. The example below highlights the need for interpreters to consider ethics when working in a business context.

> **An example of the interpreter's need to consider ethics**
>
> During an interpreted meeting between programme managers of Isuzu and General Motors Truck Group (GMTG), the Isuzu programme manager went over the agenda and asked if there were any questions.
>
> The GMTG program manager said, "We would like to spend time with the vehicles today or tomorrow and drive the vehicle if possible—maybe during lunch."
>
> [Isuzu]: "This is a late request." (smiling)
>
> [GMTG]: "We have concerns and we need to let our manager see what the vehicle is like. Also, we could give an update on where we are relative to Contract Signing, which is a milestone in our product development process."
>
> [Isuzu]: "When?"
>
> [GMTG]: "Maybe at the end of the Planning section?"
>
> At this point, the interpreter turned to me and said, "We have been into the meeting for six minutes and there have already been two surprises. The Japanese aren't very good with surprises."
>
> Adapted from Ferraro and Briody (2017, 159)

This example, along with what has been discussed in this section on business interpreting, demonstrates the expected outcome of "political perspective" in Table 13.1: "production of translated texts which reflect the influence of exchange among the different stakeholders". The interpreters' decision-making is more affected by who they work with, what the relationships among the participants are, rather than the linguistic or cultural features reflected in the speeches or conversations.

13.3 Business Translation

In this section, we discuss translation activities in the business context, which require high cultural awareness. The genre that has likely received most attention in translation studies in business contexts is promotional texts, such as advertisements, brochures and websites. Tourism marketing has become a focus of attention of translation scholars because they particularly present challenges in cross-cultural communication.

Hogg et al. (2014) carried out a case study based on ten major museum websites in the UK and in China. They argue that being culturally sensitive to the target readers is key to enhancing international tourists' experiences. Translation in tourist destinations does not only provide information, such as guiding directions, explaining the sites or the exhibited objects, but is also important in welcoming visitors and reducing the gap between the visitors' cultural expectations and a foreign culture. The study examines the English translation of visitors' information on the websites of Chinese museums and finds that although the quality of the language is not flawed, the way the texts "talk" to the visitors is very different from the way an English museum would usually talk to their visitors. The excerpts below give you an idea of what these differences are.

> **Case study 2: Museum websites**
> **An example in English: Website of the National Museum of Scotland**
> Cloakroom
> Our cloakroom facility is located in the Entrance Hall, on Level 0. There is a charge of £1.50 per item for this service.
> We will only accept bags, cases or rucksacks if they weigh less than 15kg.
> Please note that due to limited space we can only accept buggies if they are folded.
> Photography policy
> We are happy for you to take photographs, including flash photography, in the galleries, but photography is not permitted in special exhibitions or unless otherwise stated.
> **A translated English example: Website of Beijing Capital Museum**
> - Leave large bags at the checkroom and take your valuables with you.
> - Video cameras are not allowed in exhibition halls. Don't use flash or tripod when taking photos.

The Chinese information is provided in the format of regulations, and the language is more detached and authoritative, i.e. stating what visitors can and cannot do. By contrast, the English information is more interactive, including the use of pronouns *we* and *our*, and highlights what is offered to the visitors. The fundamental differences of the textual features may be explained by the different values placed on museums as social institutions in different societies. In this case study, Hogg et al. (2014, 162) point out that, in China, museums are more commonly perceived as cultural education centres, whereas in UK, museums are common tourist destinations for the purpose of entertainment.

Besides museums, particular types of products or services can all be perceived differently in different cultures, and therefore need to be promoted or communicated to the target readers with different linguistic approaches. Malamatidou's (2018) study compares tourism websites in Greek and in English and found that in both language versions, adjectives are crucial in influencing how visitors may feel about a tourist site. For example, the adjective *beautiful* in "Afternoon in the beautiful city of Bath" (342) guides the readers to imagine the outlook of the city. Besides evaluative and emotive adjectives such as *lovely, best* and *amazing,* other adjectives commonly used in tourism website describe colour, brightness or size of a place.

Cross-cultural awareness in a range of written business communication types has also been discussed, such as sales letters, sales invitations and business emails (e.g. Chakorn 2006; Connor et al. 1995; Ho 2021; Lorenzo-Dus and Bou-Franch 2013; Zhu 2000; and also an overview in Olohan 2010).

From the perspective of an employee, self-promotion material, including CVs, job application letters and personal websites are not exempt from translation challenges. Regarding cultural differences in job application letters, Torresi (2010, 43) explains that, for instance, while it is important in American English for cover letters to contain explicit self-assertive and enthusiastic statements, in Italy a more neutral description of what is included in the CV is more common. Al-Ali (2004) points out that in Arabic job application letters, a unique feature is that applicants tend to glorify the institution of the prospect employer. Below is an example of the Arabic job application letters.

An example of an Arabic job application letter (Al-Ali, 2004, 22–23)
In the name of Allah the most Merciful and the most Gracious.
Professor Doctor, President of (XX) University,
Peace, Mercy and Blessing of Allah be upon you, and then:
I have read the advertisement in (XX) newspaper issued on the 2nd of January 2001, regarding the teaching assistant positions at (X University).
Since I am very interested in securing a job in an honourable institution like your university where I can participate and serve my country, I hereby submit my application for the position of 'teaching assistant' in the Department of Arabic Language, Faculty of Arts.

> And I am very pleased to tell you that I graduated with the degree of Bachelor of Arts in Arabic from (XX) University in 2000 with the grade of 'excellent', (attached are the required credentials).
> I am also glad to inform you that while I was studying at the university, I worked for several private and evening schools where I gained valuable experience.
> I am quite sure that you will spare no effort to inform me, in due time, of your decision regarding my application.
> With best wishes and respect, and may Allah reward you.

To approach these types of texts, the translator needs to be able to point out to their customers the different norms between the source text and target text cultures, and perhaps advise the customers to provide more culturally appropriate texts. This ability can be theorized by the term *generic competence*: "the ability to respond to recurrent and novel rhetorical situations by constructing, interpreting, using and often exploiting generic conventions embedded in specific disciplinary cultures and practices to achieve professional ends" (Bhatia 2004, 144). This means that a translator needs to have the ability to first identify how a text is usually produced in a particular format (including linguistic and non-linguistic conventions), in a professional context in a particular culture, and then decide what conventions need to be observed in order to achieve the same communicative purpose in the same professional discipline in the target culture. The generic competence is more than the language ability, i.e. to be able to understand or use a language accurately and is important to the "cultural perspective" in Table 13.1.

13.4 Computer-Aided Translation

Compared with culturally sensitive translation, machine-perspective translation is usually faster and less costly. This method is operated under the assumption that all language versions of texts are *the same* and can be managed as a uniform text. Although a cultural-sensitive approach makes sense, it may be unrealistic sometimes. For example, if a text is going to be translated into several languages at the same time, it may be too costly to consider individual cultural differences. In an interview with employers working in multinational companies, Harzing et al. (2011) report that despite evaluating poorly on the quality of automatic translation, many people have used machine translation from time to time to communicate with a business partner or a colleague who speak a different language. Instead of completely relying on the machine, what is more common is **computer-aided translation (CAT)**, i.e. a translation process in which translators use computer software to manage, edit and store translations.

The operation CAT tools are often embodied within a wider industrial context of managing digital translation activities as a commercial and industrial product. A standardized process often discussed in translation studies is known as **GILT**: **globalisation, internationalisation, localisation and translation** (Jiménez-Crespo 2013, 24). Globalization occurs when a company has made the decision to expand globally, and therefore recognizes the need of translation. Actions taken at this stage may include contact professional translation companies and identify business partners abroad. Internationalization occurs when the product is prepared for translation. This may involve the removal of any culturally specific items or any other features that may present challenges when translating into different languages. This step is essential in that it reduces the time and resources in the translation process. An example is when the Starbucks removed text from its logo to avoid the costs of translating the logo into different languages for different markets.

The final steps are localization and translation. Localization and translation may be performed at the same time. In an industrial setting, localization usually refers to the process of dealing with technical dimensions of a product, such as the user interface or the functionality of the website. Translation deals with linguistic material. So, we can see that in this mechanical perspective, the translation of language actually comes at the last stage of the project management, and by this time, it is assumed that the source text can be translated into all language versions without cultural differences presented much of a challenge. This model also demonstrates that translation activities are complicated processes that do not involve only linguists but also other professionals such as software developer, marketing and advertising professionals.

Some specific computer-aided tools that may be used during the translation process may include, for example, **terminology management**—extracting terms from written texts, storing and organizing the terms, identifying key terms from the source text and suggesting or automatically inserting the translation from the term base. In this way, the project managers can easily check how a translator has complied with the standardized translated terms and ensure consistency across all translated versions. **Translation memory** allows translators to operate under standardized work processes and automatically saves all the translations into the database. On subsequent projects, if a similar segment or sentence comes up, the tool will automatically suggest or insert the translations into texts. This function increases the ease and efficiency of quality control of translated projects.

In a way, we can say that the machine-perspective translation, although showing consideration to cultural differences (e.g. the internationalization step in the GILT process), prioritizes the consistency of the translation, and the cost-effectiveness of the project.

13.5 Sign Language Interpreting and Translation

Sign language interpreters and translators do the same job as interpreters and translators with spoken and written languages, but they work with deaf people who use a signed language (see Chapter 16 on deaf people in the workplace).

Sign language interpreters and translators are trained language professionals and will interpret/translate in both language directions from a signed to a spoken language and vice versa, or between a signed and written language, or between two signed languages. The processes for regulation, training, qualification and accreditation vary from country to country, but the most important thing is to make sure that any sign language interpreter/translator that is employed in business contexts should be suitably qualified in their respective country. Any qualified sign language interpreter/translator will be expected to adhere to professional codes of conduct and follow ethical guidelines.

Depending on the country, the requirements for providing sign language interpreting (SLI) services will vary according to whether there are any legislative provisions, and if funding is available through the Government. Here we provide various examples. In the UK where deaf people use British Sign Language (BSL), BSL was initially recognized as a legitimate language by the UK Government in 2003, but it was not legally recognized as a language until 2015 when the Scottish Government enacted the BSL (Scotland) Act. It has since been legally recognized by the UK Government in the BSL Act 2022. But the rights of deaf people to access SLI in the UK is mandated through the Equality Act (2010) and the UK and Scottish Governments, and the Welsh and Northern Irish assemblies, have funding in place to cover the costs of SLI in healthcare, legal, educational and employment settings through different dedicated schemes. In the United States, deaf people use American Sign Language (ASL), which is the 4th most commonly learned second language in colleges. Despite this, ASL is not officially recognized by the US Government in any legislation. But the Americans with Disabilities Act mandates access provision for deaf people either through captioning or ASL interpreting, and companies are expected to make accommodations for, and cover the costs of, any access needs for deaf employees or service users. In Malaysia, deaf people advocate the use of Bahasa Isyarat Malaysia (Malaysian Sign Language), but the Malaysian Ministry of Education recognizes a signed code system, which more closely corresponds to spoken Malay. There is some Government funding for SLI service provision. Alternatively, in the United Arab Emirates, deaf people use various forms of Arabic Sign Language, but there has not yet been any official recognition and there are minimal provisions. There is an active deaf community in UAE though who are lobbying for improved services for deaf people.[1] Australian Sign Language (Auslan) was first officially recognized as a legitimate language by the Australian Government in 1987 in a white paper on the languages of Australia (Lo Bianco 1987). SLI provision is managed on a federal level through the National Disability Insurance Scheme,

---

[1] See http://www.thenational.ae/uae/health/well-provide-every-opportunity-for-deaf-people-sheikh-nahyan-vows.

where deaf people apply for funds to secure SLI services in various aspects of their lives, including work and social contact. Healthcare interpreting is funded through a nationally funded dedicated service, and educational interpreting is funded on a state-by-state basis. There is currently no official recognition of Chinese Sign Language by the Chinese Government although the deaf community suggests that there are in fact many dialects. The only formal SLI provision is for TV news broadcasts, but there is no funded provision of SLIs for deaf people at work or in any other context.

In terms of intercultural management, it is important to recognize that interactions can occur with deaf people across several different service, workplace, employment or management contexts. For example, deaf people are customers seeking to purchase services. Let's take the example of banking services. A deaf customer seeking to open a bank account or take out a mortgage will need to have a sign language interpreter provided at the point of contact in a branch. Alternatively, in some countries, there are video relay interpreting (VRS) services that have been established. In VRS, a sign language interpreter is based in a call centre and a deaf person can make calls to service providers using a video phone and the interpreter relays the call to someone else through the telephone (Brunson 2011). As an example, in the UK, a company called SignVideo has contracts with several banks to provide VRS for their customers and has various other contracts with councils and other organizations to make their services accessible through BSL interpreters.[2] In some countries, work has focused on developing processes of machine sign language translation to recognize sign language and translate into the spoken or written form, or vice versa at points of service provision; for example in airports in Dubai,[3] in and post offices in the UK (Wray et al. 2004).

Deaf people work in a range of workplaces and may need interpreters in order to participate in team meetings or training events, or just to interact with work colleagues (Dickinson 2017). As discussed in Chapter 16, deaf people are increasingly found in professional positions, such as lawyers (Kurlander 2008) or chief executive officers (Oatman 2008). Deaf people working in professional roles are more likely to use designated interpreters, where they have a small pool of interpreters who work with them on a regular basis every day at work. Managers and employers may need to take the needs of deaf employees, colleagues and customers into account, so the provision of SLIs is one way that this can be done. It is particularly important to consider how SLIs are used in job interviews to ensure that deaf people are given the best opportunity to showcase their skills and knowledge. An unprepared interpreter can misrepresent a deaf person,[4] so ensuring that an interpreter is familiar with the role and any specific terminology will mean that they can effectively interpret the interview.[5]

---

[2] See www.signvideo.co.uk.

[3] See http://www.bbc.co.uk/news/av/business-25849295/sign-language-translator-and-other-dubai-inventions.

[4] https://www.youtube.com/watch?v=eC5LuNvAx4s.

[5] https://www.youtube.com/watch?v=FgoXsJDpddg.

In 2022, there are estimated to be 41 countries that have legally recognized their national sign language. As such, Government agencies, charities and companies are urged to make their services and information available in the local signed language. For example, deaf translators can be employed to produce translations of website content into a signed language (see e.g. Lloyds Bank's BSL website translations in collaboration with company Signly https://www.lloydsbankinggroup.com/media/press-releases/2019/lloyds-bank/lloyds-bank-launches-pioneering-british-sign-language-online-translation-tool.html).

13.6 Conducting Business Through T&I

In this chapter, we have introduced some key features of translating and interpreting activities and highlighted cases in business contexts. To conclude, below is a checklist for using T&I services in a business context.

- Identify the need of T&I and budget the cost appropriately! Disasters happen when you assume that your business partners (or you) have the language ability to translate or interpret in business contexts, or that they would hire translators or interpreters without confirmation in advance.
- Identify language requirements—always check. Do not assume that a person from a certain country necessarily speaks a certain language—the language profile can be complicated in multilingual or immigrant societies, such as South Africa or India.
- Do not assume that deaf people are comfortable writing notes, because they need to keep eye contact with the interpreter to follow the discussion.
- Have you used the terminology correctly—translating or interpreting, consecutive or simultaneous interpreting, for example? Failing to do so can result in booking a service that is different from what you need.
- Have you checked who will provide (and pay for) the appropriate equipment needed, e.g. simultaneous interpreting booth, computer-aided translation software—the company, the translator/interpreter or the agency?
- Have you given the translator/interpreter enough time and information to prepare wherever possible, e.g. the PPT presentation of the speaker, the partners' or speakers' names, a product-specific terminology bank, and the intended target users from the market research?
- In cases where the content is sensitive, such as those involving patents, exclusive trade deals and multi-million-dollar operations, have you prepared confidentiality agreements to be signed by the translators/interpreters?
- Do you have a clear aim of what you want to achieve through this T&I service? For example, do you want the advertisement in a different language version tailored for the local culture to best attract consumers, or should all language versions render the same message? A clear aim helps translators/interpreters to design their linguistic (and extra-linguistic) strategies.

- During the process of translation/interpreting, remember that the translator/ interpreter may continue to seek clarifications in order to help them complete the job. To avoid placing undue levels of stress on the interpreter, try to avoid speedy delivery, unclear pronunciation, jokes, references to a specific culture that may not be understood by others or speaking in long chunks.
- Providing users' feedback to the translator/interpreter always helps them reflect on their performance and improve next time!

Chapter Review Questions

1. Create a scenario that would fit each of the perspectives in the model of Lambert and Steyaert (2004).
2. As a cross-cultural communication consultant, advise how the letter in Box 13.3 can be tailored for a job application in the UK.
3. You are working for a management team in a national museum in your country. In order to attract more international visitors, the museum has decided to provide different language versions of websites. Produce a list of instructions for the translator agent regarding your requirement and any specifications.
4. What can companies hiring a translator/interpreter do to help them carry out the tasks more efficiently and confidently?
5. Below are some strategies that have been proposed for companies to achieve success in global business. Discuss the strengths and weaknesses of these strategies.

   - Emphasize the use of English as a lingua franca and ask partners or potential clients to use English in their communications.
   - Prepare in advance for linguistic expertise (translator/interpreter) and budget in T&I services according to the objectives of the company and potential partners and/or customers.
   - Always have in-house translators and/or interpreters of as many languages as possible to cover most global markets in the world.

Recommended further reading

- Ho, M. 2021. Luxury Values Perceptions in Chinese and English: Deviation from National Cultures. *Journal of International Consumer Marketing*. https://doi.org/10.1080/08961530.2021.1950094.
- Jiménez-Crespo, M. (2013). Translation and Web Localization. London: Routledge.

- Janssens, M., J. Lambert, and C. Steyaert. 2004. Developing Language Strategies for International Companies: The Contribution of Translation Studies. *Journal of World Business* 39 (4): 414–430.
- Karanasiou, P. 2016. Public Service Interpreting and Business Negotiation Interpreting: Friends or Foes? In *Challenges and Opportunities in Public Service Interpreting*, ed. T. Munyangeyo, G. Webb, and M. Rabadán-Gómez, 191–211. London: Palgrave Macmillan.
- Napier, J. 2015. Comparing Spoken and Signed Language Interpreting. In *Routledge Handbook of Interpreting Studies*, ed. H. Mikkelson and R. Jourdenais. 129–143. New York: Routledge.

References

Al-Ali, M.N. 2004. How to Get Yourself on the Door of a Job: A Cross-Cultural Contrastive Study of Arabic and English Job Application Letters. *Journal of Multilingual and Multicultural Development* 25 (1): 1–23.

Bhatia, V. 2004. *Worlds of Written Discourse: A Genre-Based View*. London: Bloomsbury.

Brunson, J. L. 2011. *Video Relay Service Interpreters: Intricacies of Sign Language Access*. Washington, D.C.: Gallaudet University Press.

Castillo, P. 2015. Interpreting for the Mass Media. In *Routledge Handbook of Interpreting*, ed. H. Mikkelson and R. Jourdenais, 280–301. New York: Routledge.

Chakorn, O. 2006. Persuasive and Politeness Strategies in Cross-Cultural Letters of Request in the Thai Business Context. *Journal of Asian Pacific Communication* 16 (1): 103–146.

CILT The National Centre for Languages. 2006. National Occupational Standards in Interpreting, viewed 9 June 2022, https://dpsionline.co.uk/wp-content/uploads/2019/03/National-Occupational-Standards-Interpreting-2006.pdf.

Connor, U., K.W. Davis, and T. De Rycker. 1995. Correctness and Clarity in Applying for Overseas Jobs: A Cross-Cultural Analysis of US and Flemish Applications. *Text & Talk* 15 (4): 457–476.

Ferraro, G., and F. Briody. 2017. *The Cultural Dimension of Global Business*, 8th ed. London: Routledge.

Harzing, A., K. Köster, and U. Magner. 2011. Babel in Business: The Language Barrier and Its Solutions in the HQ-Subsidiary Relationship. *Journal of World Business* 46: 279–287.

Ho, M. 2021. Luxury Values Perceptions in Chinese and English: Deviation from National Cultures. *Journal of International Consumer Marketing*. https://doi.org/10.1080/08961530.2021.1950094.

Hogg, G., M. Liao, and K. O'Gorman. 2014. Reading Between the Lines: Multidimensional Translation in Tourism Consumption. *Tourism Management* 42: 157–164.

Lo Bianco, J. 1987. *National Policy on Languages*. Canberra: Australian Government Publishing Service.

Lorenzo-Dus, N., and P. Bou-Franch. 2013. A Cross-Cultural Investigation of Email Communication in Peninsular Spanish and British English: The Role of (In) Formality and (In) Directness. *Pragmatics and Society* 4 (1): 1–25.

Jiménez-Crespo, M. 2013. *Translation and Web Localization*. London: Routledge.

Malamatidou, S. 2018. A Pretty Village is a Welcome Sight A Contrastive Study of the Promotion of Physical Space in Official Tourism Websites. *Translation Spaces* 7 (2): 304–333.

Olohan, M. 2010. Commercial Translation. In *Handbook of Translation Studies (Volume 1)*, ed. Y. Gambier and L. Van Doorslaer, 41–44. Amsterdam: John Benjamins.

Ozolins, U. 2015. Ethics and the Role of the Interpreter. In *The Routledge Handbook of Interpreting*, ed. H. Mikkelson and R. Joudenais, 319–336. London: Routledge.

Pym, A. 2000. On Cooperation. In *Intercultural Faultlines: Research Models in Translation Studies I: Textual and Cognitive Aspects*, ed. M. Olohan, 181–192. Manchester: St Jerome.

Tipton, R. 2010. On Trust: Relationships of Trust in Interpreter-Mediated Social Work Encounters. In *Text and Context: Essays on Translation and Interpreting in Honour of Ian Mason*, B. Mona, O. Maeve, and M. Calzada Perez, 88–208. Manchester: St. Jerome.

United Nations. (n.d.). *Translation*. Department of General Assembly and Conference Management, viewed 9 June 2022, https://www.un.org/dgacm/content/translation.

Torresi, I. 2010. *Translating Promotional and Advertising Texts*. Manchester: St. Jerome.

Victorian Government, Australia. (n.d.). *Understanding Language Services*, viewed 9 June 2022, https://www.vic.gov.au/guidelines-using-interpreting-services/understanding-language-services.

Wray, A., S. Cox, M. Lincoln, and J. Tryggvason. 2004. A Formulaic Approach to Translation at the Post Office: Reading the Signs. *Language & Communication* 24: 59–75.

Zhu, Y. 2000. Structural Moves Reflected in English and Chinese Sales Letters. *Discourse Studies* 2 (4): 473–496.

Part V
Diversity

Chapter 14
Dignity and Diversity in the Workplace

Jane G. Bell, Katerina Strani, and Jafar Ahmad

> In a rapidly changing, globalised world, the employer of a multinational workplace needs to understand, manage and be able to maximise the benefits of a diverse workplace. The concepts of dignity and diversity in the workplace are critically analysed and discussion of key aspects of employee diversity follows, together with relevant case studies. The implications for employers are discussed throughout. Employment law in relation to workplace discrimination is examined, together with some international comparisons. The considerable benefits of an effectively managed, diverse workforce are highlighted, in relation to productivity, competitiveness and employee well-being. The chapter concludes with recommendations for employers.

14.1 Introduction

Contemporary markets and workplaces are increasing globalised and heterogeneous due to demographic transformations, economic and socio-political developments. People no longer live and work in an insular marketplace, but are part of a "worldwide economy, with competition coming from nearly every continent" (Mazur 2012, 5). **Dignity** and **diversity** are of crucial importance in this context. Failure to acknowledge this can lead to loss of productivity and increased staff turnover, or even loss of life (See Case Study 1). Recent advances such as adoption by the EU of Gender

---

J. G. Bell (✉) · K. Strani
Heriot-Watt University, Edinburgh, Scotland, UK
e-mail: Jane.G.Bell@hw.ac.uk

K. Strani
e-mail: A.Strani@hw.ac.uk

J. Ahmad
Global Affairs Canada, Ottawa, ON, Canada

© The Author(s), under exclusive license to Springer Nature Switzerland AG 2023
K. Strani and K. Pfeiffer (eds.), *Intercultural Issues in the Workplace*,
https://doi.org/10.1007/978-3-031-42320-8_14

Mainstreaming and the Social Model of Disability have prompted important changes in approaches to diversity management. However, in international workplaces, cross-cultural variation in concepts of diversity and of dignity presents challenges. These concepts are closely linked to cultural values, which in turn inform employment laws and practices. Hence, the contemporary international professional needs to be aware of considerable cross-cultural variation in employment practices, laws and values.

We focus firstly on the dimensions of race, ethnicity, religion, age and social class. Secondly, we examine gender and its **intersectionality** with the often-forgotten dimensions of disability, impairment and neurodiversity. Diversity management is then discussed, and examples of employment law are provided with reference to Europe and the Middle East, followed by management recommendations.

14.2 Defining Dignity and Diversity in the Workplace

14.2.1 Diversity

Generally speaking, diversity refers to the variety of people in a society, an organisation or any other group, with respect to race, gender, religion, age, social status, ability and other dimensions. Cox (1994, 6) describes diversity as the *representation* of people with distinctly different group affiliations. It is this aspect of representation that is crucial to diversity in the workplace—not just in terms of numerical composition, but, more importantly, inclusive behaviour of the members of the organisation.

Dimensions of diversity can be divided into two main categories:

Primary dimensions of diversity, or *bio-demographic diversity* (Horwitz and Horwitz 2007): race, ethnicity, age, sex and physical ability. These dimensions are the most distinctive. They exert primary influence on our identities and have the most impact on groups in the workplace and society. Sexual orientation also comes under this category, although it may not necessarily be a distinctive characteristic of an individual.

Secondary dimensions of diversity, or *task-relevant diversity* (Horwitz and Horwitz 2007): religion, education, language, family status, as well as communication style, experience etc. These dimensions refer to acquired attributes that are less visible and may have less influence on personal identity.

Some of these categories and dimensions may overlap. For example, in a predominantly white society, a black woman's identity includes two primary dimensions of diversity, an Asian disabled woman's identity includes three; and if these women are Muslim, or single parents, then their identities become more diverse and more complex. This combination of minority identities, which influence someone's experiences in society and in the workplace, points to intersectionality. Originally coined by Crenshaw in 1989, intersectionality refers to "the critical insight that race, class, gender, sexuality, ethnicity, nation, ability, and age operate not as unitary, mutually exclusive entities, but rather as reciprocally constructing phenomena" (Hill-Collins 2015, 1).

An additional dimension is gender identity, which may not correspond to sex at birth and can change over time. Gender is becoming an increasingly prominent, often visible marker of identity. **Gender** and **sex** are often used interchangeably but it is useful to distinguish between the two. The WHO (2021a) defines sex as "the different biological and physiological characteristics of females, males and intersex persons, such as chromosomes, hormones and reproductive organs", and gender as the "socially constructed" characteristics which "[vary] from society to society and can change over time".

Importantly, the concept (and term) diversity has been criticised as Eurocentric and West-centric (Piller 2014; Hall and Livingston 2003). It has also been criticised for categorising people in narrowly defined groups, which ignore the realities and complexities of real individuals in a workplace environment. Indeed, the term diversity management originates from the US, and the concept of diversity usually implies that:

a. there is one dominant group, usually white, male, able-bodied, around which the rest revolves.
b. this dominant group forms the majority of executives, senior management and sometimes the entire workforce, whilst other groups are much smaller in size, their number depending on the business's mission statement or targets. Whilst this may be the case in many companies today, the assumption that this should be the norm should be challenged.

Local context greatly affects the approach to diversity and diversity management in any country. Mazur (2012, 5) argues that diversity is in fact subjective and constructed, based on perceptions of the dominant group. She proposes the definition of diversity which will be adopted here: "the collective, all-encompassing mix of human differences and similarities along any given dimension" (ibid., 7).

14.2.2 Dignity

Article 1 of the Universal Declaration of Human Rights states: "all human beings are born free and equal in dignity and rights". The importance of working with dignity is emphasised by scholars as a fundamental employment right. In this context, workplace dignity is defined as "the self-recognized and other-recognized worth acquired from engaging in work activity" (Lucas 2017, 1). Working with dignity means that individuals can fulfil their potential by being valued, respected and given autonomy and personal space to express their identity. If dignity is undermined in the workplace, individuals become alienated, and their well-being is threatened. Concepts of human dignity vary cross-culturally (see Table 14.1).

Caveat: Table 14.1 offers a rather crude and essentialist distinction between "Asian" and "Western" cultures, which we neither endorse nor encourage. But what

Table 14.1 'Summary comparison of Asian versus Western understandings of dignity' (Lucas et al. 2012, 3)

	Asian	Western
Kim and Cohen (2010)	Earned, judged by others	Inherent, defended by the self
Lee (2008)	Relationally based, focus on duties	Individually based, focus on rights
Brennan and Lo (2007)	Meritocratic, degrees of difference	Democratic, equal
Consequence	Contingent, fragile, familial responsibility	Automatic, unassailable, individual status

Lucas, K., D. Kang, and Z. Li. 2012. Workplace Dignity in a Total Institution: Examining the Experiences of Foxconn's Migrant Workforce. *Journal of Business Ethics* 114 (1), 91–106

we want to illustrate is the cross-cultural differences in dignity in the workplace, which are neither fixed nor universal. Still, loss of dignity not only has a psychological impact on individuals, but also affects their relationships with co-workers, teamwork, productivity and performance. Given cultural differences and varying perceptions of dignity, ensuring and safeguarding workplace dignity is particularly challenging in the contemporary diverse working environment.

Case study 1
Foxconn's migrant workforce in a total institution[1] (2010)
In 2010, the working conditions of electronics manufacturing company Foxconn's migrant Chinese employees came to light, following a cluster of suicides at its Shenzen campus and at other sites, as well as a fire in a different factory that killed four employees. This sparked international outcry, and led to researchers Kristen Lucas, Dongjing Kang and Zhou Li conducting a case study which was published in the Journal of Business Ethics in 2013. Their study revealed working conditions at Foxconn were described as 'a life without dignity'. Workers lived on an all-encompassing compound where they had worked, eaten and slept in a prison-like existence and a highly controlled environment in all facets of workers' lives. Excessive overwork was common and demanded of workers at any time because they lived within the walls of the organisation. Employee movement was restricted, talking or laughing was severely punished, and this prevented worker relationships, or any team spirit being established. These imposed huge indignities on its workers according

---

[1] Canadian sociologist Erving Goffman coined the term "total institution" in his 1957 paper "On the Characteristics of Total Institutions". Total institutions, designed to establish uniformity and structure by minimising differences, can be broadly defined as places where people live and/or work together in a rigidly structured environment, cut off from the wider community. Examples include nursing homes, prisons, boarding schools, monasteries, army barracks, ships or orphanages.

> to the researchers and undermined their self-respect and self-worth to such an extent that, within a few short months, 14 young migrant workers jumped to their deaths from buildings on the Foxconn campus.
>
> In this case, workers' dignity was further undermined for cultural reasons. As Lucas, Kang and Li note, in Asian contexts, dignity is determined by evaluations made by others, and individual's worth is defined primarily by social worth, or what others think of them. This is based on Confucian teachings, where dignity is hierarchical and meritocratic. In Western contexts, dignity is something you are born with and is largely based on self-worth.
>
> The researchers encouraged Foxconn and its business partners to define and assess worker dignity so as to protect employees' sense of self-worth. Other changes, such as giving employees control over choice of roommates or encouraging off-site activities when they are not working would be steps in the right direction.
>
> Taken from Lucas et al. (2012).

14.3 Dimensions of Diversity in the Workplace: Race and Ethnicity

14.3.1 Race

To understand race in the workplace in the context of dignity and diversity, we must start from a critical view of the concept of race. An overwhelming body of literature confirms the fact that the concept of race is a social construct (e.g. Smedley 1999; Gunaratnam 2013; Aspinall 2009). In 1998, the American Anthropological Association released a statement on race, arguing that "physical variations in the human species have no meaning except the social ones that humans put on them" (AAA Statement on race, https://www.americananthro.org/ConnectWithAAA/Content.aspx?ItemNumber=2583).

We could define race, then, as a socially constructed classification of people into distinct groups on the basis of physical traits such as skin colour or other aspects of physical appearance. The social construct of race is particularly inadequate to describe the vast number of people of complex heritage who have multi-dimensional identities and senses of belonging. But whilst race may not exist biologically, it exists as a socially constructed category and, more importantly, as a defining feature of people's identity. This can be a source of pride and belonging, however, it is also used as justification for exclusion and oppression.

Racism is the belief that certain races are naturally or biologically inferior to a dominant race. In the workplace, this can be expressed as an assumption that certain groups are only good at manual work, others are particularly good at problem-solving and others (usually the dominant ones) are born leaders. Such racist prejudice serves only to strengthen hierarchies of domination and prevents people from reaching their full potential. These attitudes foster *institutional racism* and lack of opportunity for minorities. Creating a workplace hierarchy based on race, social class, skin colour or status in general creates deep-rooted divisions, hinders effective teamwork, is counterproductive, unfair, unjust and—in many countries—illegal.

> **Case Study 2**
> **Deloitte case study on multicultural teams**
> Researchers at Deloitte Australia, part of the International professional services network Deloitte, conducted a case study *when*? to examine work in multicultural teams, focusing on a newly established team working on a 3-month project on assignment in New South Wales in Australia. At the end of the assignment, the researchers interviewed team members from Australia, Japan, the United States and Germany, the manager, who was from Spain, and the client, who was from Australia. All team members had lived and worked in their country of origin. Team members were asked whether they thought culture was relevant to interactions within the team; whether cultural diversity enhanced their work experience; whether it was culture or personality that influenced workplace employee traits; and what they learned about working in a culturally diverse team.
> The study led to 4 key insights:
> 1. Responses varied regarding the role of culture v. the role of personality in teamwork. The Australian client, for example, did not think cultural background was relevant to the way the team interacted, while the Spanish team leader and Australian team members did. German team members saw a combination of culture and personality having a role in team interaction but argued that workplace employee traits are more closely aligned to personality than cultural background.
> 2. The working experience was enhanced by the cultural diversity. This contributed to their personal growth, formed friendships, but also challenged them to "think outside of my normal mode of analysis".
> 3. Cultural diversity can indirectly encourage project members to rethink their usual working habits and expectations, behave with fewer assumptions about the "right" way to address an issue and promote linguistic clarity. The quality of communication can in fact be "enhanced by linguistic diversity", because people needed to check clarity and understanding throughout. Language miscommunication also contributed to team bonding, and linguistic diversity was overall described as a positive experience for the team and its performance in delivering tasks.

> 4. The dominance of cultural diversity amongst team members reduces the bias to interact with people who have common characteristics and create a unique bond.
>
> The findings confirmed the business case for diversity, and specifically that "the diversity of the project team contributed positively to both task performance and process outcomes (i.e. overall team cohesiveness)". What's more, they showed that "the expectation of cultural differences caused team members to become more conscious of their own behaviours and to become more flexible and adaptive." Cultural diversity also "provided a unique point of connectivity and enjoyment."
>
> *Source* https://www2.deloitte.com/au/en/pages/human-capital/articles/working-multicultural-teams.html

14.3.1.1 Ethnicity

The terms "ethnicity" or "ethnic group" are sometimes used in lieu of race, but this leads to a simplistic conflation of the very different concepts of race and ethnicity, which ignores the history, oppression and power dynamics that are attached to the concept of race. Whilst race is often viewed as a fixed component of identity, ethnicity, like culture, is best viewed as a process. It includes cultural traits such as tradition, customs, religion, learned behaviour and a sense of national or any other group pride and belonging. Ethnicity, therefore, refers to a "sense of kinship, group solidarity and common culture", which is thought to influence world events culturally and politically (Hutchinson and Smith 1996, vii). Examples of someone's ethnicity are Pakistani (as opposed to Asian), Senegalese (as opposed to black), Korean, Malaysian or Emirati. Prejudices and stereotypes based on race can also be based on ethnicity, leading to institutionalised ethnic discrimination and unfair treatment of ethnic minorities.

14.4 Dimensions of Diversity in the Workplace: Religion, Age and Social Class

14.4.1 Religion

Within the context of religion, religious identity is expressed by one's adherence to a particular set of beliefs and values. In some cases, displaying religious symbols is necessary to fulfil certain religious obligations. Examples include Muslim women wearing a hijab or Sikh men wearing a turban. Religious identity constitutes an integral aspect of a person's overall social identity and religious views influence both personal and professional behaviour. Recognising and respecting different religious identities contributes to a healthy, prosperous workplace. However, religious identities can also exacerbate perceived differences amongst co-workers, particularly when organisational policies may contradict religious views and practices—for example, dress code, holidays or inflexible working hours. Given the increase in diversity in the workplace in parallel with an increase in religious awareness for some groups, challenges related to expressing religious identity are increasing.

However, research shows that insensitivity towards religious identities persists in some contexts, affecting the relationships amongst employees and/or between them and their employer in ways which could ultimately hinder their performance. For example, Weinberger's (2015) US study found that despite alcohol consumption being prohibited for observant Muslims, an employee who participated "in the intra-office gift swap" was given "a bottle of wine purchased specifically for her, which, as a Muslim, she will not drink" (388). Regarding the challenges associated with display of religious symbols in the workplace, one example is that of a British Airways employee who was refused permission to wear a crucifix visible to customers, prompting escalation of the case to the European Court of Human Rights (Eweida and others v. the UK 2013).[2]

The most serious challenges associated with religious prejudice are those directed against a particular religious identity. Since the events of 9/11, many Muslim employees in Western countries have faced discrimination, and they have dealt with it either by emphasising their religious identity, or by hiding it completely (Zaheer 2007). Whilst revealing membership or aligning with marginalised religious identity groups in the workplace entails risk, there are also potential gains associated with making the identity recognised, understood, and valued.

14.4.2 Age and Social Class

In addition to religion, age and social class can contribute to highlighting differences amongst co-workers. Discrimination based on age or social class is counterproductive, given the unique talents and experience that each employee brings to the workplace. Manifestations of age discrimination can be subtle or blatant; typical examples include refusing to hire or promote older or younger workers, curtailing their employee benefits, limiting training opportunities or limiting job responsibilities and duties. Even though there are circumstances where an individual's age may affect job performance (in manual work, for example), bias against "older" employees should be taken seriously because it can contribute to a culture of exclusion in the workplace. Equally, younger employees may also experience discrimination because of negative attitudes and stereotypes about youth and experience.

---

[2] Case of Eweida and Others v. the United Kingdom, 2013, European Court of Human Rights, https://hudoc.echr.coe.int/eng#{%22itemid%22:[%22001-115881%22]}.

Prejudice related to **social class** is another potential source of discrimination. Social class is defined as a dimension of the self that is rooted in objective material resources (via income, education and occupational prestige) and corresponding subjective perceptions of rank vis-a-vis others (Côté 2011, 1). Class-based discrimination can influence the workplace in a variety of ways, including the hiring process. Research on workplace regulation of regional accents highlights that "non-standard or urban dialects" can affect employability since "a prestigious and higher social class accent of English associated with being upper class and 'educated'" (Eustace 2012, 336). And research on social class bias suggests that most managers tend to favour middle-class applicants (Liu et al. 2007).

14.5 Sex and Gender Inequality

Sex and gender inequality are bad for business: think tank the McKinsey Global Institute estimates that reducing it could result in an increase of $12 trillion to global growth by 2025 (Woetzel et al. 2015, 25). However, women, particularly mothers, continue to be paid less than men in most countries, including Europe and the US. The UK gender pay gap continues to be significant, 15.4% amongst all employees in 2021 (ONS 2021). Women are often over-represented in part-time work and in low-paid jobs such as the service industry. In the UK, some progress can be seen at executive level, but overall progress remains slow.

Women often face limited opportunities for advancement and unequal treatment compared to men, due to biased performance attributions by their employers. Such attitudes can lead to **"glass door"** and **"glass ceiling"** discrimination. The glass door refers to an invisible barrier that prohibits *access* to certain jobs, for example, women in STEM. The glass ceiling describes the invisible barrier that prohibits *promotion* to positions of leadership and responsibility, for example, a lack of women or minorities in CEO positions.

One method of addressing gender discrimination in the workplace is greater transparency about pay structures; since 2018, the UK government has required all large companies to publish gender pay data. Other methods include encouraging firms to set targets for change, reviewing performance and promotion criteria to eliminate bias and reviewing flexible work practices to enable women and men to combine work and family. For example, hundreds of companies have committed to **Women's Empowerment Principles** (WEPs 2021, https://www.weps.org/).

In recent years, anti-discrimination measures have moved from treatment of women as a special group to **"gender mainstreaming"**, a globally recognised strategy which Rees (2005, 560) defines as "the promotion of gender equality through its systematic integration into all systems and structures, into all policies, processes and procedures, into the organisation and its culture, into ways of seeing and doing". Its adoption "comprises one of the entry conditions for admission to the European Union" (Rees 2005, 555).

Finally, implementation of these measures and reducing discrimination requires increased awareness of gendered policies. "**Gender awareness**" can be defined as "a person's readiness to recognize how gender differences and privilege are deeply embedded in the assumptions, expectations, practices and manifestations of organizations and society" (Van den Brink 2015, 485). However, gender-related cultural practices, assumptions and inequalities tend to be routine and ingrained in societies. Gender roles tend to be learned from an early age and considered "natural"—hence unquestioned. Employees may also have trans, non-binary and gender-fluid identities. All employees are entitled to dignity in the workplace, which may include use of preferred personal pronouns, for example "they/their" in the case of a non-binary employee. Intentional use of pronouns other than those specified by an individual is known as **misgendering**.

14.6 Disability and Impairment

"Human beings exist in a *continuum of competence* spanning a wide range of abilities and interests" (Smith 2013, 28). Approximately a fifth of the UK population has a lasting impairment of some sort, most acquired in later life, and this proportion is relatively constant over time, suggesting that the proportion may be similar in other countries. In this context, a key distinction must be made between **equality** and **equity**: the former entails giving all employees the same treatment, whilst the latter involves recognition of differing needs to reduce barriers to participation, hence giving each employee the treatment they need instead of giving everyone the same treatment.

Terminology related to disability reflects the philosophical approach adopted. The **medical model of disability** focuses on the individual, with the aim to treat or cure the disability (Oliver 1996). In contrast, the **social model of disability** distinguishes between **impairment**, the physical or psychological limitations of the individual, and **disability**, the loss or limitation of opportunities to take part in normal life due to societal factors such as exclusion or stigmatisation.

This distinction is particularly relevant to groups who do not consider themselves to be disabled but are labelled by others as such. For example, many Deaf people do not consider themselves disabled, but instead belonging to a linguistic and cultural minority. In the past, many countries and institutions banned the use of sign language, depriving Deaf people of access to workplaces and services (Kaupinen and Jokinen 2014, 131). Chapter 16 on Deaf people in the Workplace discusses contemporary trends and challenges in depth.

Furthermore, according to the World Health Organization, mental disorders are the leading cause of disability in many Western countries, "costing some 3% of GDP" (WHO 2021b). Neither mental health issues nor health conditions such as diabetes, chronic pain and gynaecological conditions are always obvious to others (see Sang et al. 2021). Given the impact on productivity, morale, workplace dignity and staff turnover, is in the interests of employers to support employees by making relevant adjustments (see 15.6.2 below).

14.6.1 Neurodiversity

The term neurodiversity refers to the concept of human beings comprising a variety of neurological types; the majority are referred to as "neurotypical" (CIPD 2018). **Neurodivergence**, a term which describes differences in brain function, is not an illness and cannot be "cured". Examples include Autism, Dyslexia and Dyspraxia. Many neurodivergent employees are diagnosed later in life, and some may not divulge their diagnosis for fear of stigmatisation.

Whilst most literature focuses on neurodivergent deficits such as reading difficulties, people with dyslexia can have above-average visual abilities and three-dimensional spatial reasoning (Eide and Eide 2011). Many neurodivergent individuals are of above-average intelligence and employers including Microsoft and Google increasingly value diversity of thought in the workplace; for example, JP Morgan found that autistic workers were "50 percent more productive" (CIPD 2018, 3). Furthermore, Attention Deficit Disorder is said to be prevalent amongst entrepreneurs; whilst "ADHDers" may suffer from hyperactivity, they can also be "at ease with uncertainty" (CIPD 2018, 6). In summary, employers can maximise the benefits of diversity and enable employees to reach their fullest potential by identifying employees' individual strengths and weaknesses.

14.7 Employer's Perspective: Diversity Management

Why does diversity need to be "managed"? Firstly, employers need to ensure that there are no cases of interpersonal or institutional racism or discrimination based on any of the dimensions examined above. Secondly, diversity management is key to reducing bias and ensuring dignity for every worker. Thirdly, employers should avoid the ethnocentric/West-centric trap of reducing diversity management to **tokenism**: keeping the dominant group intact whilst only nominally fulfilling diversity requirements by ticking boxes.

Diversity management should instead focus on removing barriers to access and enabling creativity to maximise every worker's potential and improve performance, productivity and innovation. Examples include paid or unpaid maternity/paternity leave; disability support; workplace adjustments to accommodate mental or physical impairments or neurodiversity; sick leave; flexible working hours and diversity training.

14.7.1 Reasonable Adjustments

Under UK and EU law, employers must make **reasonable adjustments** to reduce workplace disadvantages related to the disability of an employee or job applicant (ACAS, n.d.). For example, to enable neurodivergent employees to reach their fullest potential, employers must identify an individual's strengths and weaknesses. Regarding physical impairments, inexpensive adjustments can include building access ramps or making computer modifications. Many employees benefit from **adjustment latitude**: the ability to reduce or alter work effort when feeling ill or vulnerable. In this way, employer flexibility "can help prevent impairments turning into incapacity" (Baumberg 2015, 189).

Diversity policies and training require investment. However, there is a clear **business case for diversity**, because diversity gives an organisation a competitive advantage through:

- Increased productivity: employees who feel respected and valued have dignity, harmonious relationships and work more effectively. Morale is high, creativity fostered and decision-making improved (see Lucas 2007; Horwitz and Horwitz 2017).
- Reduced absenteeism and turnover rates: when parents and carers are unconstrained by pregnancy, childcare and fixed work schedules, but instead given flexible working options, on-site childcare facilities and maternity/paternity leave.
- Retention of business and increasing marketing capabilities through knowledge of diverse clientele in global markets.
- Creating the largest possible talent pool for recruitment, attracting and retaining the best talent.
- Problem-solving and system flexibility.
- Becoming an employer of choice (key to an organisation's reputation as a fair employer).
- Resource acquisition through increased creativity.

14.7.2 Workplace Discrimination and Employment Law

Despite the advantages of a diverse workforce, equality and equity (two different concepts) are not always enshrined in a country's employment law.

Workplace discrimination, which may occur in diverse working environments, stems from prejudice and employment stereotypes. **Stereotypes** are the most common form of bias and constitute a very limited view of the average characteristics of an imagined group. They focus on *simplified distinctive features*, which ultimately results in *undifferentiated judgements* about people, cultures, races, genders and social categories (O'Sullivan et al. 1994, 222). Stereotypes can also be positive, but equally harmful because they are still homogenising the target groups and are based on reductionist premises. In discussing this, Strani et al. (2016) argue that positive stereotypes are justified by "feel good feelings" (154) and purported good intentions.

Moreover, when stereotypes remain unchallenged, they become part of "commonsense discourse" (O'Sullivan et al. 1994, 223), where the stereotype is presented as obvious and indisputable. Leung et al. (2005) highlight two types of attribution error that managers can make: *universal attributions*, which assume that all employees "share the same orientations" and *cultural attributions*, which assume that all employees of the same nationality, region, religion etc. will behave according to the corresponding stereotype. Both of these attribution errors are dangerous.

In some cases, prejudices are so deeply ingrained that they become unconscious and unintentional. Self-awareness regarding biases and prejudices is fundamental to workplace relationships. There are many tools that measure unconscious bias towards age, race, gender or disability, such as the Harvard Implicit Association Test (https://implicit.harvard.edu/implicit/takeatest.html). Multinational companies are beginning to invest money in diversity and unconscious bias training to combat inequality and discrimination.

In principle, discrimination can be based on any dimension of diversity or group membership characteristic, including skin colour, religion, age, gender, disability, language or ethnicity. However, laws relating to equality vary significantly around the world. For example, UK Law (Equality Act 2010) defines nine protected characteristics as grounds of workplace discrimination. These characteristics are of equal importance:

1. age
2. disability
3. gender reassignment
4. marriage and civil partnership
5. pregnancy and maternity
6. race
7. religion or belief
8. sex
9. sexual orientation

Similarly, under US federal employment discrimination law, employers cannot discriminate against employees on the basis of: race, sex, pregnancy, religion, disability, national origin, age, military service, bankruptcy or debts, genetic information and citizenship status.

In some Middle Eastern countries, a different process is in place. In Saudi Arabia, the constitution does not guarantee equality on the basis of sex, race or ethnicity. Instead, the state protects human rights with respect to Islamic Sharia (see Mor Barak 2017). In this context, it is important to note that homosexuality is illegal in certain African, Asian and Middle Eastern countries. Moreover, whilst religious freedom is protected in some parts of the world, expressing atheist beliefs is punishable by death in 11 countries (Humanists International 2021, 15).

In the UAE, the government initiative of *Emiratisation* aims to increase representation of Emiratis in a private sector dominated by expatriates. For instance, there are recruitment agencies, head-hunters and support agencies for Emiratis only. Emiratisation includes investment in improved high-school and university education for Emiratis to enable them to compete with expatriates in the UAE private sector. These policies are overseen by the Ministry of Human Resources and Emiratisation. Similar government initiatives, such as Saudisation, Qatarisation and Omanisation exist in neighbouring countries.

14.8 Conclusion

In summary, whilst concepts of dignity and diversity vary significantly across cultures, a well-managed, diverse workforce gives an organisation access to the widest possible range of talent and the benefits of diversity of thought. Workplace discrimination is hugely detrimental to people's dignity and ultimately detrimental to business. Research shows that when employees do not feel valued, their performance will suffer (Horwitz and Horwitz 2007; Lucas 2017). Failure to preserve the dignity of employees may cost organisations in terms of low employee motivation and productivity, and high rates of absenteeism and staff turnover.

Key aspects of diversity management are flexibility, training, a strengths-based approach to allocation of responsibilities and willingness to make adjustments. Organisations also need to identify practices and assumptions which contribute to and maintain inequality. A growing number of companies are motivated to manage diversity more effectively, as research shows the economic benefits. However, in many countries more fundamental cultural change is required before barriers to workplace dignity such as stigmatisation of disability and women's disproportionate responsibility for the care of children and other family members can be reduced.

Chapter Review Questions

1. Based on your reading and your own experience, define dignity in a diverse organisation.
2. Why should intersectionality be considered when managing a diverse workplace?
3. Explain why "reasonable adjustments" and a strengths-based management approach are key aspects of diversity management.
4. Define Emiratisation and explain the motivation behind it and similar initiatives.
5. Visit the Women's Empowerment Principles website: https://www.weps.org/ Which Principles are most important, in your view? Have enough major companies committed to them to make a difference?

Recommended Further Reading

- Boeri, T., E. Patacchini, and G. Peri, eds. 2015. *Unexplored Dimensions of Discrimination.* Oxford: Oxford University Press.
- Deloitte: Best Diversity and Inclusion Global Case Studies and Best Practices. https://www2.deloitte.com/au/en/pages/human-capital/articles/diversity-inclusion-design.html.
- Derven, M. 2014. Diversity and Inclusion by Design: Best Practices from Six Global Companies. *Industrial and Commercial Training* 48 (2): 84–91.
- Grosfoguel, R., L. Oso, and A. Christou. 2015. 'Racism', Intersectionality and Migration Studies: Framing Some Theoretical Reflections. *Identities* 22 (6): 635–652. https://doi.org/10.1080/1070289X.2014.950974.
- Parker, P., and D. Grimes. 2009. Race and Management Communication. *The Handbook of Business Discourse*, ed. B. Chappini, 292–304. Edinburgh: Edinburgh University Press.

References

ACAS. (n.d). *Reasonable Adjustments.* https://www.acas.org.uk/reasonable-adjustments

Baumberg, B. 2015. From Impairment to Incapacity—Educational Inequalities in Disabled People's Ability to Work. *Social Policy and Administration* 49 (2): 182–198.

CIPD. 2018. *Neurodiversity at Work.* Uptimize. https://www.cipd.co.uk/Images/neurodiversity-at-work_2018_tcm18-37852.pdf

Côté, S. 2011. How Social Class Shapes Thoughts and Actions in Organizations. *Research in Organizational Behaviour* 31: 43–71.

Cox, T. 1994. *Cultural Diversity in Organizations: Theory, Research and Practice.* San Francisco, CA: Berrett-Koehler Publishers.

Eide, B.L., and F.F. Eide. 2011. *The Dyslexic Advantage: Unlocking the Hidden Potential of the Dyslexic Brain.* London: Hay House.

Eustace, E. 2012. Speaking Allowed? Workplace Regulation of Regional Dialect. *Work, Employment and Society* 26 (2): 331–348. https://doi.org/10.1177/0950017011432912.

Hall, R.E., and J. Livingston. 2003. Psychological Colonization: The Eurocentrism of Sociology vis-à-vis Race. *Current Sociology* 51 (6): 637–648. https://doi.org/10.1177/00113921030516006.

Hill-Collins, P. 2015. Intersectionality's Definitional Dilemmas. *Annual Review of Sociology* 41: 1–20.

Horwitz, S.K., and I.B. Horwitz. 2007. The Effects of Team Diversity on Team Outcomes: A Meta-analytic Review of Team Demography. *Journal of Management* 33 (6): 987–1015.

Humanists International. 2021. *The Freedom of Thought Report, 2021.* https://fot.humanists.international/download-the-report/

Hutchison, J., and A.D. Smith, eds. 1996. *Oxford Readers: Ethnicity.* Oxford: Oxford University Press.

Kaupinen, L., and M. Jokinen. 2014. Including Deaf Culture and Linguistic Rights. In *Human Rights and Disability Advocacy*, ed. M. Sabatello and M. Schulze, 130–145. Pennsylvania: Pennsylvania University Press.

Leung, K., et al. 2005. Culture and International Business: Recent Advances and Their Implications for Future Research. *Journal of International Business Studies* 35 (4): 357–378.

Liu, W.M., T. Pickett Jr., and A.E. Ivey. 2007. White Middle-Class Privilege: Social Class Bias and Implications for Training and Practice. *Journal of Multicultural Counseling and Development* 35: 194–206. https://doi.org/10.1002/j.2161-1912.2007.tb00060.x.

Lucas, K. 2017. Workplace Dignity. In *The International Encyclopedia of Organizational Communication*, ed. C.R. Scott, 1–13. Chichester: Wiley.

Lucas, K., D. Kang, and Z. Li. 2012. Workplace Dignity in a Total Institution: Examining the Experiences of Foxconn's Migrant Workforce. *Journal of Business Ethics* 114 (1), 91–106. https://doi.org/10.1007/s10551-012-1328-0

Mazur, B. 2012. Cultural Diversity in Organisational Theory and Practice. *Journal of Intercultural Management* 2 (2): 5–15.

Office for National Statistics. 2021. *Gender Pay Gap in the UK: 2021*. Available from https://www.ons.gov.uk/employmentandlabourmarket/peopleinwork/earningsandworkinghours/bulletins/genderpaygapintheuk/2021

Oliver, M. 1996. *Understanding Disability: From Theory to Practice*. Basingstoke: Palgrave Macmillan.

O'Sullivan, T., et al. 1994. *Key Concepts in Communication and Cultural Studies*. London: Routledge.

Piller, I. 2014. Superdiversity: Another Eurocentric Idea? *Language on the Move*. https://www.languageonthemove.com/superdiversity-another-eurocentric-idea/.

Rees, T. 2005. Reflections on the Uneven Development of Gender Mainstreaming in Europe. *International Feminist Journal of Politics* 7 (4): 555–574.

Sang, K., J. Remnant, T. Calvard, and K. Myhill. 2021. Blood Work: Managing Menstruation, Menopause and Gynaecological Health Conditions in the Workplace. *International Journal of Environmental Research and Public Health* 18 (4): 1951. https://doi.org/10.3390/ijerph18041951.

Shaw, S. 2006. Governed by the Rules? The Female Voice in Parliamentary Debates. In *Speaking Out*, ed. J. Baxter, 81–102. Basingstoke: Palgrave.

Smith, K. 2013. *Digital Outcasts: Moving Technology Forward Without Leaving People Behind*. Waltham, MA: Morgan Kaufman.

Strani, K., M. Fountana, S. Sokoli, and E. Monteoliva. 2016. Attitudes to Race in the Media: Evidence from Greece and the UK. *Rivista VOCI* XIII: 148–170.

The Equality Act 2010. UK Government Legislation. http://www.legislation.gov.uk/ukpga/2010/15/section/6.

Van den Brink, M. 2015. The Politics of Knowledge: The Responses to Feminist Research from Academic Leaders. *Equality, Diversity and Inclusion: An International Journal* 34 (6): 483–495.

Weinberger, M.F. 2015. Dominant Consumption Rituals and Intragroup Boundary Work: How Non-celebrants Manage Conflicting Relational and Identity Goals. *Journal of Consumer Research* 42 (3): 378–400.

WHO. 2021a. Gender and Health. https://www.who.int/health-topics/gender#tab=tab_1.

WHO. 2021b. Mental Health. https://www.euro.who.int/en/health-topics/noncommunicable-diseases/mental-health/mental-health.

Woetzel, J., et al. 2015. *The Power of Parity: How Advancing Womens Equality Can Add $12 Trillion to Global Growth*. McKinsey Global Institute.

Women's Empowerment Principles. 2021. https://www.weps.org/.

Zaheer, B. 2007. Accommodating Minority Religions Under Title VII: How Muslims Make the Case for a New Interpretation of Section *701 (J)*. *University of Illinois Law Review* 2007 (1): 497–532.

Chapter 15
Performing Gender in the Workplace

Maryam Sholevar and Kerstin Pfeiffer

> Despite an increase in the number of women in the labour market, gender inequalities and gender segregation persist. This chapter explores how gender is practised and performed in the workplace. It first outlines the key concepts of gender, performance, and culture before discussing dominant cultural stereotypes on how we "do" gender in the workplace. Two case studies on women in computing and female entrepreneurs illustrate how people negotiate, (re)produce, and challenge gendered cultures. You will thus gain insights into how workplaces and organisational culture(s) are shaped by socially accepted gender roles and can, in turn, reinforce and contest these.

15.1 Introduction

The concepts of sex and gender in the workplace emerged as a research area since the 1960s (Benschop 2006), when the subordinate position of women in male-dominated institutions and cultural practices was subjected to sustained critique. Although the experiences of transgender and non-binary people in the workplace are increasingly being explored (Connell 2010; Dray et al. 2020), the focus remains mostly on the binary between men and women, and their unequal position in the labour market (Benschop 2006). Particular attention is given to gender stereotypes and their influence on women's advancement (Heilman and Caleo 2018; Heilman 2012), as well as to organisational culture (Cleveland et al. 2000; Poggio 2000).

M. Sholevar (✉)
Edinburgh Business School, Heriot-Watt University, Edinburgh, Scotland, UK
e-mail: M.Sholevar@hw.ac.uk

K. Pfeiffer
Heriot-Watt University, Edinburgh, Scotland, UK
e-mail: K.Pfeiffer@hw.ac.uk

© The Author(s), under exclusive license to Springer Nature Switzerland AG 2023
K. Strani and K. Pfeiffer (eds.), *Intercultural Issues in the Workplace*,
https://doi.org/10.1007/978-3-031-42320-8_15

Women make up around 50% of the global workforce, but their experience of the workplace and outcomes differ from those of men: they tend to get paid less and face obstacles to career progression to name but two of the persistent and well-documented inequalities. These are both symptoms of horizontal and vertical asymmetries which see, for example, the division of men and women into different professions (horizontal asymmetry) and an underrepresentation of women in business and political leadership (vertical asymmetry). The recent COVID-19 pandemic exacerbated the existing gender disparities. Female participation in the labour market declined because many women are employed in sectors that were disproportionately impacted by the pandemic (e.g. the hospitality and services sectors), and because they took on a greater share of unpaid care work at home during lockdowns (Barua 2022).

This chapter focuses on the question what underpins the gendered inequalities we can observe in workplaces around the globe. It begins with an exploration of the central concept of culture, and its relation to gender and to performance, and the way in which gender shapes how people experience and engage with workplaces. Then, the practical impacts of assumptions about men and women in work environments are discussed.

15.2 Key Concepts: Culture, Gender, and Performance

Our sense of what is normal or acceptable in a workplace, our expectations of and assumptions about how men and women should behave in workplaces is defined by culture. Therefore, culture is the first key concept we will explore here. Secondly, we will explore gender as an organising principle for society and for organisations (which have often been likened to societies) that gives cultural meaning to being male or female. Based on the understanding that gender is inscribed in daily practices, that it is learned and performed depending on cultural norms of masculinity and femininity, we will then discuss the concept of performance and its relevance for how we think about ourselves and how we interact with others in the workplace.

15.2.1 Culture

Culture is a concept which is notoriously difficult to define due to the multiplicity of interpretations of the term, from intellectual and creative products such as a novel, a film, an opera, or a sculpture to integrated systems of beliefs, values, customs, and practices that people acquire by virtue of being part of society (see also Chapter 1). The English word "culture" has its etymological origins in the French and Latin words for "cultivation"; it this thus associated with helping something to be nurtured, to thrive, to grow. Our popular notions of culture as something that you develop rather than acquire all at once like a car or a bout of the flu, or of culture as a way of life reflect this idea of nurturing. Yet no matter how exactly we define culture, it is always a crucial aspect of what it means to be human; it permeates all human activity and is thus part of the fabric of every society; it shapes "the way we do things", as well as our understanding of why that should be so. Therefore, culture affects our behaviour and how we interpret behaviour of others.

In organisations or workplaces, culture manifests at different levels: as things, ideas, and behaviour patterns, impacting on organisational culture that is the values, expectations, and practices that inform the actions of employees. These expectations tend to be different for men and women based on notions of "natural" differences between them (Poggio 2000) and they play out for example in interactions.

15.2.2 *Gender*

Gender is a key marker of identity. Yet the terms sex and gender tend to cause conceptual confusion in everyday usage and, to a certain degree, in research. Initially, the distinction between sex and gender was made to distinguish between the biological categories of men and women (sex) and the socio-cultural meanings of differences between the sexes (gender) and the notions of masculinity and femininity. Our current understanding of sex is more nuanced; sex emerges from the interaction between biological and socio-cultural factors but retaining the distinction between sex and gender can be useful when thinking about workplaces because it allows us to focus on the meanings of perceived differences between men and women, and on power relationships (Benschop 2006; Cleveland et al. 2000).

The term gender is now usually used to refer to cultural roles which assign meaning, expectations, behaviours, resources, and identities differently to men and women. *Gender norms* (specifically gender binaries) rely on the perceived fixity between sex and gender, that is the notion that someone who is male presents and behaves (or should present and behave) in ways which are considered masculine, whilst and someone who is female should look and act in ways considered feminine.

However, gender roles and norms are socially constructed and culturally constituted, that is they are learned in childhood rather than inherited. Consequently, the behaviours, responsibilities, and rights associated with gender categories (masculine; feminine) and norms do not only differ across cultures, but they are also subject to change over time. The pink-blue divide provides a good example. Take a look at greeting cards or the children's section of a department store almost anywhere in the global north. Clothes, toys, and cards for small girls tend to be pink, those for boys blue. This association between colour and gender is relatively recent. When pink and blue first started to emerge as colours for small children in the nineteenth century, pink was reserved for boys because of its links to red and the associations of power and war. Blue, a colour usually linked to the Virgin Mary, was considered more feminine. It was only in the second half of the twentieth century that pink started to be marketed almost exclusively as a colour appropriate for women (Paoletti 2012).

According to the philosopher Judith Butler, gender is not something that we *are*, but something that we *do*. It is performed and performative:

> It's one thing to say that gender is performed and that is a little different from saying gender is performative. When we say gender is performed, we usually mean that we've taken on a role or we're acting in some way and that our acting or our role playing is crucial to the gender that we are and the gender that we present to the world. To say that gender is performative is a little different because for something to be performative means that it produces a series of effects. We act and walk and speak and talk in ways that consolidate an impression of being a man or being a woman. (Butler 2011)

Thus, gender is a repeated performance that is based on and reinforced by societal norms and that is itself performative, that is it creates the idea of gender itself, as well as the illusion of two distinct, "natural" sexes. So, according to Butler, the categories of men and women are created because we *act* like men and women, not because we *are* men or women. We have to work on our gender and getting it "wrong" can have negative consequences. Of course, this holds particularly true in countries where social policy and legislation directly impact on gender in public spaces by assigning different rights and responsibilities to men and women—for example, in Iran, where the legal system is determined by religious beliefs. Sex-based rights are enshrined in society, and these tend to disadvantage women. Before we look at doing gender, especially in the workplace, let's pause to think about performance in more detail.

15.2.3 *Performance*

Performance is a term with many definitions, yet we each have a sense of what we understand as a performance (Pfeiffer and McKerrell 2019). Consider what you may think of as examples: a concert, a play, a football match, a company's annual result. What most of these have in common is that all happen in a particular place (location) and involve someone doing something (performer) in front of someone else or several others (audience). Moreover, there is normally something to show or do (product or skill).

However, performance is also a part of everyday life. Think about how you interact with a lecturer as opposed to the way you behave around your parents or with someone at a first date. All three sets of people probably see different sides of you, even if you do not consciously try to change your behaviour. The sociologist Erving Goffman uses the language and imagery of the theatre to explore the nuances and significance of social interactions. According to Goffman, each of these situations above can be understood as a different stage of your life on which you perform a different role. "[A]ll the activity of an individual which occurs during a period marked by his *(sic)* continuous presence before a set of observers and which has some influence on the observers", can be considered a performance according to Goffman (1990 [1959], 32). In everyday social interaction, like in the theatre, there is a "front stage" area where the individual or actor performs. This usually involves a particular setting, a scenery, or location, props, and an audience. The performer knows that she or he is being watched by an audience and that the audience has expectations for the role they should play, what should happen in this situation, and how they themselves should behave. This knowledge informs the performer's behaviour. Therefore, everyday performances are always exercises in impression management according to Goffman. Whether they are conscious or intentional or not, everyday performances convey information about the performer's identity, and the audience constantly attribute meaning to them. In other words, everyday performances give meaning to performers, to others, and to social situations.

Let's look at an example to illustrate what Goffman's notion of the presentation or performance of self in everyday life can mean in practice. Consider a typical university situation: a lecture that you attend. The lecture takes place in a lecture hall with tiered seating, a front desk, and two large projection screens—the props that come with this setting, in which the person at the front performs the role of "lecturer". A lecture hall setting also usually involves a particular audience: students. As with many other scenarios, there is a social script (Goffman refers to this as the personal front of the performer) that suggests how actors should behave and interact in this situation. For example, there are expectations about the appearance and manner of someone who performs the role of lecturer. Such expectations are culturally continent but, in most cases, you would probably expect the lecturer to be dressed in clothes that befit a workplace setting, to stand up, to speak loudly and clearly, and to interact with their students at least sometimes. If they appear dressed in their pyjamas, lie across the desk, mumble their way through their lecture, and do not answer student questions, you might doubt their competence and ability to perform the role of lecturer even if they are an internationally recognised expert in their field. There are two reasons for this. Firstly, the casual, informal personal front (appearance and manner) of the actor, and the setting are incongruent in this case. This confuses the audience about the role that the actor plays in front of them. Secondly, there is a mismatch between the expectations attached to the role of lecturer and the execution in this scenario. Consequently, their performance is likely to be judged as a failure.

Performance is important for how we construct our social, cultural and personal identities, and the performance and performativity of gender are a key element in this process because gender is crucial to how we think about and interact with others: it shapes our impressions of and assumptions about other people and impacts on how we think about ourselves, our identity, as well as how we present ourselves to others. If we think of gender as a social practice, we can investigate how gender is "done" within particular environments such as workplaces.

15.3 "Doing Gender" in the Workplace

Over the past decades, social sciences and humanities scholars have focused on the impact of gender dynamics on social relations, particularly with regard to the marginalisation of women. Martin (2003), for example, conceives of gender as an institution, which allows her to focus on practices that normalise men's power over women in the workplace. In this next section, we will examine some of these practices.

15.3.1 Gendered Practice and Practising Gender at Work

In the past fifty years, the share of women in workforce participation has increased tremendously. However, the World Economic Forum's latest Global Gender Gap Report (2022) illustrates that whilst progress has been made towards gender equality, considerable "gender gaps" remain, particularly with regard to political empowerment of women and their economic participation and opportunities. The report estimates that, at the current rate of progress, it would take 132 years to reach gender parity (World Economic Forum 2022). Where does the gender gap come from?

The recent COVID-19 pandemic had a detrimental impact on women's economic opportunities, education, health, and political leadership. However, persistent gender stereotypes which lead to gender bias in the workplace (Heilman 2012) also play a role. **Gender stereotypes** can be both descriptive and prescriptive in nature. Descriptive components involve beliefs about how people of different genders normally act and what they are like; prescriptive elements involve beliefs about how they *should* act, thus creating expectations with regard to approved and disapproved behaviour. Whilst it might simply surprise us when someone does not act how we think most men or women act, we often react with anger and moral outrage if someone violates prescriptive gender stereotypes. For example, women are often stereotypically seen as empathetic, nurturing, and as avoiding impressions of dominance, whilst men are stereotypically seen as decisive, goal-oriented, and as avoiding impressions of weakness. These stereotypes impact on expectations of leadership styles, for example, and lead to **gender bias**. A successful woman in a leadership position who asserts her agency and authority can meet with disapproval and obstacles in her career progression, especially so if she is a working mother (Risman 2018) because she does not conform to the normative standards of feminine behaviour promoted by descriptive and prescriptive gender stereotypes. Yet even playing by the rules, as it were, that is knowing and adhering to femininity stereotypes in the workplace, does not guarantee that women are successful, respected, or regarded as equal, as Martin (2003) points out. However, gender stereotypes can not only harm women but also men, as the fact that **occupational gender segregation** exists illustrates. Male nursery teachers, for example, account for a relatively small number of nursery staff overall, because working with small children is traditionally considered a female occupation. The caring element involved in this is often considered a feminine attribute and has led to men being considered out of place in nurseries and finding it difficult to work in this sector. Organisations and workplaces can thus reproduce gender distinctions where jobs are "gender typed" (Benschop 2006; Poggio 2000).

Case Study 1: Was Computer Science Gendered?

After the Second World War, the number of women working in computer-related jobs increased significantly; around 50% of the programmers were female. Elsie Shutt, the founder of Computations, Incorporated (CompInc.), and Grace Hopper, the creator of the first compiler, were among those pioneers. Nevertheless, in 1984, everything changed, and women stopped pursuing it. By 2010, the percentage of female graduates with a degree in computer science and information science was cut in half and reached 17.5 percent (National Center for Education Statistics).

What was the reason behind this phenomenon? NPR's Planet Money team (2014) dug into this case to find the answer. It appeared that the first generation of personal computers, like the Commodore 64 or the TRS-80, targeted male users, and due to this type of advertising, men tended to have computers. The cultural impact of this assumption that men should have computers intensified with movies, books, and articles that men are better with computers than women.

Fisher and Margolis (2002) tracked nearly 100 graduates of the computer-science school at Carnegie Mellon University to find out why the proportion of female students was below 10%. Their findings showed that male students had a substantial experience with computers and were treated differently compared to female students. Girls at home and school always received the same message that computers are for boys.

NPR's Planet Money team could not answer why advertising agencies in the 80 s spread the assumption that computers are for men. Nevertheless, this case illustrated that creating new gender stereotypes and constraining women could be done quickly and explicitly.

An oversight of the evolution of computer science/engineering can shed light on this emerging gender gap. In the early days of computer science, computers were gigantic machines which were extensively operated by humans. It would be tedious work for data entry and verification. In a sense, it was a clerical task for which women were (and still are) considered better choices. This is the reason that most employees of clandestine code-breaking projects of World War II in the UK were women. There are, of course, some leading female scientists in the emerging field of computer science, but they were basically mathematicians since the early days of computer science were mostly about mathematics. However, as computers became industrialised, the emerging field of computer engineering overshadowed fundamental computer science. During the rapidly growing demand for higher education since the 1970s, most computer-related programmes were classified as engineering. Although masculinity has no impact in the domain of computer engineering, as it is generally assumed in other engineering fields, such as civil engineering, the stereotype was extended to computer engineering to become a male-dominated field in higher education and, subsequently, in the job market.

In the workplace, we often engage in practices that are normatively, culturally, or empirically associated with a particular gender, e.g. when we wear make-up or avoid an argument in a meeting. Many gendered practices are, as Martin (2003) points out, unreflexive because they are "learned and enacted in childhood and in every major site of social behavior over the life course" (352). In other words, they are practices that are culturally available to "do gender". The concept of doing gender goes back to West and Zimmerman (1987) who consider doing gender as "a complex of socially guided perceptual, interactional, and micropolitical activities that cast particular pursuits as expressions of masculine and feminine natures" (125). In West and Zimmerman's (1987) original conceptualisation, doing gender means enacting masculinity or femininity in light of the sex category to which an individual is perceived to belong, where sex is understood as the biological classification that distinguishes between two groups of human beings: male and female.

Research on gender in organisations and workplaces offers an understanding of how gender is enacted through doing and undoing gender. For Martin (2003), this includes gendering practices which are embedded in organisational practices and the actual practicing of gender that is constituted through social interaction. In recent years, the term has changed into doing genders since multiple types of masculinity and femininity should be considered when trying to understand gender (Risman, 2018). We should also note here that doing and undoing gender(s) can be conceptualised differently. On the one hand, doing gender can be considered to involve enacting gender in line with normative expectations. Undoing gender, then, involves acting in non-normative ways (Kelan 2010). In contrast, for Deutsch (2007), doing gender creates gender difference, and with it gender inequality, whilst undoing gender reduces gender difference and promotes equality. Deutsch's approach serves as a reminder that the concept of doing gender can explain elements of the different experiences that cisgender men and women, non-binary and transgender people have at work because doing and undoing gender involves power structures and hierarchies, which perpetuate gender inequalities.

15.3.2 Gender Identities and Gender Equality in the Workplace

Modern psychology considers masculinity and femininity not as opposite poles but as two different personality dimensions (Risman, 2018). Assumptions about men and women, masculinity and femininity are reflected in the structure, processes, and practices of organisations (Benschop 2006). This starts with the perception of some workplaces as gendered, for example nurseries and day care centres (feminine) and the military (masculine). Some jobs also carrying gendered connotations, e.g. when a female professor is mistaken for a secretary or a male nurse for a doctor. And it includes social interaction processes that shape workplace cultures (Martin 2003; Holmes 2006; Poggio 2000). Many of these have traditionally favoured what are considered masculine behaviours and values such as competition, strength, rationality, assertiveness, emotional restraint, and dominance. People who have already been socialised towards these gendered behaviours and values are therefore more frequently rewarded in the workplace, whilst those who do not conform to these (women, gender non-conforming employees, men who choose to take extended parental leave, for example) may find themselves at a disadvantage.

Gender and individual gender identity plays a significant role in the workplace, but traditional gender roles and stereotypes that cast men as assertive, competitive, and dominant and women as nurturing, cooperative, and submissive have become increasingly challenged and questioned in recent years. With the rise of the feminist and LGBTQIA+ rights movements, individuals are beginning to reject these societal expectations and are more openly expressing their gender identities (Dray et al. 2020).

Gender identity refers to a person's own sense of their own gender, which may be varied from the sex they were assigned at birth and the gender traits attributed by others (Castañeda and Pfeffer, 2018, 119–130). Gender identity differs from gender expression, and the latter refers to the way an individual communicates their gender identity to others through their appearance, behaviour, and language. Furthermore, gender expression is one of the ways to perform gender identity in the workplace. Others include mannerisms and communication styles (Holmes 2006), name and pronouns.

Performing gender identity in the workplace can significantly impact an individual's mental and emotional well-being. For some individuals, the pressure to conform to traditional gender norms or the fear of discrimination or harassment can lead to feelings of anxiety, depression, and stress. When individuals are able to express their gender identity freely and safely at work, it can have a positive impact on their mental and emotional well-being. It can lead to a sense of belonging and acceptance, which can improve their overall well-being.

The workplace has therefore historically been a significant contributor to reproducing and creating gender inequalities in society, but it can also play a crucial role in driving positive change (Kalev and Deutsch 2018, 257–269). Kalev and Deutsch (2018) assert that the industrial revolution was the main driver of the gendered division of labour at work. They continue that workplace segregation can lead to many inequalities for women, including limited formal opportunities and advancement, lack of access to training, negative impact on informal resources like social networks, and reinforcement of negative stereotypes about women's abilities and aspirations. In fact, gender bias can often influence hiring, promotion, and pay decisions within workplaces.

The underrepresentation of women and minoritised groups in leadership positions due to the **glass ceiling** which hinders their promotion prospects in male-dominated work environments (see also Chapter 14.5 Sex and Gender Inequality) can lead to increased pressure and isolation for women in other positions and stereotyped roles. In workplaces with a low number of women in senior roles, gender stereotypes tend to be more prevalent and problematic (Ely 1995). As Kunze and Miller (2017) have shown, female leadership brings a variety of benefits to workplaces, including closing the gender gap in promotions, because having female leaders provides other female employees with a role model in a leadership position who can advise them on their careers and advancement.

In recent years, much has been done to promote gender equality and gender parity in the workplace, from gender equality policies to gender quotas and targeted gender diversity (see also Sect. 14.5). Measures to promote equality within organisations are more effective when managers are involved as leaders of change rather than being responsible for the existing inequalities. Recruiting women and minorities for managerial positions, mentoring programs, and diversity taskforces, which can increase the proportion of women in powerful positions, could be a practical solution to enhance women's gender identity at work (Kalev and Deutsch, 2018, 257–269).

15.4 Gender Gap Hotspots

Whether there are genuine differences between men and women in the workforce rather than structurally produced gender differences is a controversial topic of debate. Whilst some reject the idea of any potential difference, some categorise some jobs requiring attributes associated with masculinity or femineity. The latter justifies the gender dominance in some jobs, such as the higher numbers of male workers in jobs requiring heavy manual labour or female workers those requiring multi-tasking. It should be noted that any difference between male and female characteristics is a mere tendency rather than an absolute division. Although there are massive gender gaps in such jobs (CareerSmart 2022; Poggio 2000), the gender gap is not the problem per se; the lack of opportunity for candidates of the opposite gender, however, is. The TV series *The Delivery Man*, for example, illustrates the difficulties a male midwife faces to gain social acceptance in a traditionally female-dominated field. However, in practice, male candidates had the historical advantage of getting engaged in female-dominated jobs. Whilst this gender gap is essentially important, in most debates, it is a distraction from the critically imperative gender gap where no gender-specific characteristics are required.

The gender gap typically comes from misconceptions about gender rather than intentional discrimination against women. For instance, it was genuinely believed in the Victorian era that the female brain could not handle study because women lack reason (Malane 2005). Although such views are less prominent now, the resulting gender gap lingers: those who present as masculine tend to have better outcomes and experiences in the workplace than those who are not, especially if they embody hegemonic masculinity. It is therefore perhaps unsurprising, that women in male-dominated work environments have sometimes felt the need to embrace aspects of masculinity to overcome prejudice and discrimination because of gender stereotypes that influence expectations of women at work including their tasks, authority, behaviour, and occupation. Female politicians such as Angela Merkel or Theresa

May tended to have less feminine haircuts as their power grew (Cochrane 2016); Margaret Thatcher even sought to deepen her voice to become more acceptable as a female leader. Engaging overtly in stereotypically masculine behaviour, however, can lead to disapproval and stigmatisation (Heilman et al. 2004; Dozier 2017).

> **Case Study 2: Are Entrepreneurial Women More Successful Than Men?**
> Having ICT skills and knowledge can help women's economic empowerment and entrepreneurship in today's age. Digital environments can offer women more opportunities for economic activities, e-commerce, efficiency, and productivity. The fourth industrial revolution can also open new possibilities for women using ICTs.
>
> According to American Express (2019), the 2019 State of Women-Owned Business Report, over the past five years (2014–2019), the number of women-owned businesses in the US has grown at a faster rate than all businesses as a whole. Specifically, the number of women-owned businesses increased by 21%, while the number of all businesses increased by only 9%. Similarly, employment by women-owned businesses rose by 8%, while for all businesses, it increased by only 1.8%. In terms of revenue growth, women-owned businesses and all businesses saw a similar increase, at 21% and 20%, respectively. Furthermore, the growth rate for women-owned firms has been significantly higher than that of all businesses. From 2014 to 2019, the number of women-owned firms increased at an average annual rate of 3.9%, while the number of all businesses increased at an average annual rate of 1.7%. This trend continues in the most recent year, with the number of women-owned firms growing at a rate of 5%, compared to 2.3% for all firms.
>
> A research project was conducted to explore the best practices of successful women entrepreneurs in the ICT sector and prepare women for the digital economy in the fourth industrial revolution (APWING 2018). Cross-case analyses of 21 successful female entrepreneurs from 21 APEC (Asia–Pacific Economic Cooperation) Economies revealed several success factors, including government ICT policies, government initiatives for women entrepreneurship, support from entrepreneur networks and ecosystem, active use of ICTs, customer-centred approach, and passion for entrepreneurship. Challenges faced by the women entrepreneurs included limited access to finance, gender discrimination, lack of mentors and coaching networks, lack of skills and experiences, and fear of failure. The study recommended building a gender-responsive entrepreneurial ecosystem, increasing mentoring and networking opportunities, funding opportunities, providing ICT and entrepreneurship training for women, and promoting women's welfare.
>
> The women entrepreneurs offered advice, including seeking mentoring and networking opportunities, taking risks and learning from failures, forming a solid team, and not letting gender biases overwhelm them.

15.5 Conclusion

In this chapter, we saw that gender is present and performed at three levels in the workplace. At the individual level, it reflects our culturally contingent notions of masculinity and femininity or the characteristics and behaviours we have come to associate with men and women. At the interpersonal level, gender shapes our interactions with others. Identical behaviour in men and women is often interpreted differently, and reactions to this behaviour can either reinforce or discourage it. However, gender also reflects a system of power relations and of classification at the social or structural level, which influences people's access to resources, e.g. through classifying some work as "men's work" or "women's work" (Cleveland et al. 2000) based on prevailing cultural norms. Consequently, gender inequality in the workplace is a complex phenomenon that can exist in organisational structures, processes, and practices, leading to a pronounced gender gap in terms of political empowerment, as well as economic participation and opportunities. "Undoing gender" and moving beyond gender in the sense of challenging the existing gender system with its rigid binary between male and female, masculine and feminine may reduce gender difference and thus close the gender gap.

> **Chapter Review Questions**
>
> 1. In how far is the performance of gender culturally contingent?
> 2. What is the difference between descriptive and prescriptive gender stereotypes, and how do they contribute to gender bias in the workplace?
> 3. How are gender practices constructed in the workplace, and how do they contribute to gender inequality?
> 4. What is the difference between "sex" and "gender"? Explain how understanding these terms is important in comprehending gender identity.
> 5. How does performing gender identity in the workplace impact an individual's mental and emotional well-being? Provide examples of how individuals can perform gender identity in the workplace and the potential consequences of not being able to express one's gender identity freely and safely.

> **Recommended Further Reading**
>
> - Best, D.L., and A. R. Puzio. 2019. Gender and Culture. In *The Handbook of Culture and Psychology*, ed. D. Matsumoto and H.C. Hwang, 2nd ed., 235–291. Oxford: Oxford University Press.

- Cleveland, J.N., M. Stockdale, K. R. Murphy, and B. A. Gutek. 2000. *Women and Men on Organizations: Sex and Gender Issues at Work*. Mahwah, NJ: Lawrence Erlbaum Associates.
- Faulkner, W. 2009. Doing Gender in Engineering Workplace Cultures. I. Observations from the Field. *Engineering Studies* 1 (1): 3–18.
- Kumra, S., R. Simpson and R.J. Burke, eds. 2014. *The Oxford Handbook of Gender in Organisations*. Oxford: Oxford University Press.
- Pološki Vokić, N., A. Obadić, and D. Sinčić Ćorić. 2019. *Gender Equality in the Workplace: Macro and Micro Perspectives on the Status of Highly Educated Women*. Cham: Palgrave Pivot.

References

American Express. 2019. The State of Women-Owned Business Report: Summary of Key Trends (Online). Available at: https://ventureneer.com/wp-content/uploads/2019/10/Final-2019-state-of-women-owned-businesses-report.pdf.

Asia Pacific Women's Information Network Center (APWINC). 2018. Case Studies of Successful Women Entrepreneurs in the ICT Industry in 21 APEC Economies (Online). Available at: https://www.apec.org/Publications/2018/12/Case-Studies-of-Successful-Women-Entrepreneurs-in-the-ICT-Industry-in-21-APEC-Economies.

Barua, A. 2022. Gender equality, dealt a blow by COVID-19, still has much ground to cover. Deloitte Insights. Available at https://www2.deloitte.com/xe/en/insights/economy/impact-of-covid-on-women.html

Benschop, Y. 2006. Of small steps and the longing for giant leaps. Research on the Intersection of Sex and Gender within Workplaces and Organizations. In *Handbook of Workplace Diversity*, ed. A. M. Teoksessa Konrad, P. Prasad & J. K. Pringle (toim.), 273–298. Lontoo: Sage.

Butler, J. 2011. *Bodies that matter: On the discursive limits of sex*. Taylor & Francis.

CareerSmart. 2022. Which Jobs Do Men and Women Do? Occupational Breakdown by Gender (Online). Available at: https://careersmart.org.uk/occupations/equality/which-jobs-do-men-and-women-do-occupational-breakdown-gender.

Castañeda, N., and C. Pfeffer. 2018. Gender Identities. In *Handbook of the Sociology of Gender*, ed. B.J. Risman, C.M. Froyum, and W.J. Scarborough, 119–130. Cham: Spinger.

Cleveland, J.N., M. Stockdale, K.R. Murphy, and B.A. Gutek. 2000. *Women and Men on Organizations: Sex and Gender Issues at Work*. Mahwah, NJ: Lawrence Erlbaum Associates.

Cochrane, L. 2016. The Power of the Political Bob. *Guardian*, 26 July. Available at: https://www.theguardian.com/fashion/2016/jul/26/pob-power-haircut-women-theresa-may-political-bob.

Connell, C. 2010. Doing, Undoing, or Redoing Gender? Learning from the Workplace Experience of Transpeople. *Gender and Society* 24 (1): 31–55.

Deutsch, F. M. 2007. Undoing gender. *Gender & Society* 21 (1): 106–127.

Dozier, R. 2017. Female Masculinity at Work: Managing Stigma on the Job. *Psychology of Women Quarterly* 4 (2): 197–209.

Dray, K.K., V.R.E. Smith, T.P. Kostecki, I.E. Sabat, and C.R. Thomson. 2020. Moving Beyond the Gender Binary: Examining Workplace Perceptions of Nonbinary and Transgender Employees. *Gender, Work and Organizations* 27 (6): 1181–1191.

Ely, R.J. 1995. The Power in Demography: Women's Social Constructions of Gender Identity at Work. *Academy of Management Journal* 38 (3): 589–634.

Fisher, A., and J. Margolis. 2002. Unlocking the Clubhouse: The Carnegie Mellon Experience. *ACM SIGCSE Bulletin* 34 (2): 79–83.
Goffman, E. (1990 [1959]) *The Presentation of Self in Everyday Life*. London: Penguin.
Heilman, Madeline E. 2012. Gender Stereotypes and Workplace Bias. *Research in Organizational Behaviour* 32: 113–135.
Heilman, M.E., and S. Caleo. 2018. Gender Discrimination in the Workplace. In *The Oxford Handbook of Workplace Discrimination*, ed. A.J. Colella and E.B. King, 73–88. Oxford: Oxford University Press.
Heilman, M.E., A.S. Wallen, D. Fuchs, and M.M. Tamkins. 2004. Penalties for Success: Reactions to Women Who Succeed at Male Gender-Typed Tasks. *Journal of Applied Psychology* 89: 416–427. https://doi.org/10.1037/0021-9010.89.3.416.
Holmes, J. 2006. Sharing a laugh: Pragmatic aspects of humor and gender in the workplace. *Journal of Pragmatics* 38(1): 26–50.
Kalev, A., and G. Deutsch. 2018. Gender Inequality and Workplace Organisations: Understanding Reproduction and Change. In *Handbook of the Sociology of Gender*, ed. B. J. Risman, C.M. Froyum and W.J. Scarborough, 257–269. Cham: Spinger.
Kelan, E.K. 2010. Gender Logic and (Un)doing Gender at Work. *Gender, Work & Organisation* 17 (2): 174–194.
Kunze, A., and Miller, A. R. 2017. Women helping women? Evidence from private sector data on workplace hierarchies. *Review of Economics and Statistics* 99 (5): 769–775.
Malane, R. 2005. *Sex in Mind: The Gendered Brain in Nineteenth-Century Literature and Mental Sciences*. Oxford: Peter Lang.
Martin, P.Y. 2003. 'Said and Done' Versus 'Saying and Doing' Gendering Practices, Practicing Gender at Work. *Gender & Society* 17 (3): 342–366.
National Centre for Statistics. Degrees in Computer and Information Sciences Conferred by Degree-Granting Institutions, by Level of Degree and Sex of Student: 1970–1971 Through 2010–2011. Available at: https://nces.ed.gov/programs/digest/d12/tables/dt12_349.asp.
Orme, G. 2021. Women Leaders Have Shone During The Pandemic: Men, Take Note. *Forbes*, 4 August. Available at: https://www.forbes.com/sites/gregorme/2021/08/04/women-leaders-have-shone-during-the-pandemicambitious-men-should-take-note/?sh=7d6fe62451c6.
Paoletti, Jo. B. 2012. *Pink and Blue: Telling the Boys from the Girls in America*. Bloomington: Indiana University Press.
Pfeiffer, K., and S. McKerrell. 2019. On Performance. In *Heritage and Festivals in Europe: Performing Identities*, ed. U. Kockel, C. Clopot, B. Tjarve, and M. Nic Craith, 18–28. London: Routledge.
Planet Money. 2014. Episode 576: When Women Stopped Coding [Podcast], 17 October. Available at: https://www.npr.org/sections/money/2014/10/17/356944145/episode-576-when-women-stopped-coding.
Poggio, B. 2000. Between Bytes and Bricks: Gender Cultures in Work Contexts. *Economic and Industrial Democracy* 21: 381–402.
Risman, B. J. 2018. Gender as a Social Structure. In *Handbook of the Sociology of Gender*, ed. B.J. Risman, C.M. Froyum, and W.J. Scarborough, 19–43. Cham: Spinger.
West, C., and D.H. Zimmerman. 1987. Doing Gender. *Gender & Society* 1 (2): 125–151.
World Economic Forum. (2022). Global Gender Gap Report 2022: Insight Report. July 2022. Available at: https://www3.weforum.org/docs/WEF_GGGR_2022.pdf

Chapter 16
Deaf People in the Workplace

Mette Sommer Lindsay, Audrey Cameron, and Jemina Napier

> Deaf people are part of the globalised workforce. Increasing focus on equality, diversity and inclusivity in workplaces requires consideration of deaf people's access to, and opportunities in, employment. Various accommodations can be made in the workplace, but with legal recognition of sign languages in many countries, and increasing media visibility, it is important to acknowledge the skills that deaf people bring to workplaces. In this chapter, we will learn about deaf people and sign languages, the challenges that deaf people can face at work (with a focus on the UK), and the skills and strategies they use to navigate workplaces.

16.1 Introduction

Deaf people are an important part of diverse, globalised workplaces. Hearing people who do not use sign language may find themselves working alongside or hiring deaf people. Our focus is on deaf people who use sign language and might often work with interpreters in work contexts. We examine legislative frameworks that exist to ensure that deaf people can access and maintain employment and gain promotion,

---

M. Sommer Lindsay (✉) · J. Napier
Department of Languages and Intercultural Studies, Heriot-Watt University, Edinburgh, Scotland, UK
e-mail: M.Sommer_Lindsay@hw.ac.uk

J. Napier
e-mail: J.Napier@hw.ac.uk

A. Cameron
Moray House School of Education and Sport, Institute for Education, Teaching & Leadership, University of Edinburgh, Edinburgh, Scotland, UK
e-mail: Audrey.M.Cameron@ed.ac.uk

drawing on findings from various projects that have focused on deaf people at work. We consider employers' responsibilities in providing workplace accommodations and finish with recommendations for employers.

16.2 Deaf People

According to the World Health Organization, more than 1.5 billion people (nearly 20% of the global population) have experience of "hearing loss". Deaf and hard-of-hearing people will have varying degrees of how much they can hear: some learn to speak, lip-read or listen using assistive devices such as hearing aids or cochlear implants; others learn sign language and network/socialise with other signing deaf people; and some will use all the above.

Some deaf people attend specialist deaf schools, and others attend local "mainstream" schools, and in addition to assistive devices such as hearing loops in the classroom, they may also have some kind of teaching assistance in class. When leaving school and moving on to further or higher education or entering the workplace, deaf people may ask for accommodations depending on their level of hearing and their preferences. Examples of such accommodations include vibrating pager or flashing light fire alarms or doorbells; loop systems for meeting rooms; positioning of desks so they do not have their back to the door and can see people enter the room, etc. Our focus in this chapter is on signing deaf people regardless the degree of their hearing loss.

The World Federation of the Deaf (WFD), which represents deaf membership organisations from 133 different countries, estimates that there are 70 million deaf people whose first or preferred language is a sign language. Deaf people may have learned sign language from a young age as their first language and have attended a deaf school or may have attended a mainstream school (either a deaf unit attached to a local school or as one deaf student in the classroom), with communication support in the classroom from interpreters or teachers who specialise in working with deaf children. Deaf people may also have learned to sign later in life and choose to use sign language as their primary language for everyday communication. Many deaf people use sign language(s), write and read, and some signing deaf people also use speech. So deaf people are often bilingual, and some are multilingual in several sign languages as well as several spoken/written languages.

In addition to using a sign language, deaf people have learned to be adept at using different communication strategies with people who can hear but cannot sign to navigate everyday life. For example, mouthing, gesturing, pointing, writing notes, writing in the air and using phone apps (Kusters 2017). These strategies may be effective for basic interactions, and deaf people in the UK can book sign language interpreters at work for more complex interactions (see Chapter 13 on Translation & Interpreting).

16.2.1 Are Sign Languages Different in Every Country?

Sign languages are bona fide languages that are different in grammatical structure from spoken languages; they are different in every country and the status of sign languages varies between countries (Napier and Leeson 2016). *Ethnologue* (www.ethnologue.com) lists more than 7,000 living languages; 148 are listed as "sign languages." The WFD suggests that there are over 200 different sign languages but only 71 have recognition through government policy, legislation or constitution (as of November 2022[1]). In countries where the national sign language is recognised by the government, typically this means that sign language interpreter (SLI) services must be provided to give deaf people access to public services, education and employment (see Chapter 13 on Translation & Interpreting). There are also international instruments, such as the United Nations Convention on the Rights of People with Disabilities, which stipulate that deaf people should have access to sign language and professional SLI services as a human right.

16.2.2 Are Deaf People Disabled?

Understanding what it means to be disabled is complex. As we saw in Chapter 14 on Dignity and Diversity in the Workplace, the social-relational model of disability regards that people are disabled by a society that is designed for able-bodied people who can walk, talk, see, hear and are not neurodivergent, rather than any "impairment" that they may have. Because society is built on the values of being able to speak and hear, referred to in Deaf Studies literature as "audism" (Bauman 2004), deaf people are disabled by society in most contexts. They experience barriers due to language, communication and cultural systems rather than physical barriers (e.g. access to buildings) (De Meulder and Murray 2017; Foster and McLeod 2003, 2004; Luft 2000; Shakespeare and Watson 2002). It has long been established that deaf people who use sign languages constitute a linguistic and cultural minority group alongside other indigenous and minority language groups based on their shared experience of using sign language rather than just being deaf (Lane et al. 1996). However, legislation and financial support mechanisms for workplace accommodations for disabled people include deaf people.

16.3 Deaf People at Work

In the workplace, disability is related to various kinds of discrimination and prejudice depending on the type of work context (Sang et al. 2021). Therefore, we need to unpack when and how deaf people are disabled at work and what strategies they

---

[1] See https://wfdeaf.org/news/the-legal-recognition-of-national-sign-languages/ for updates.

employ to navigate in workplace contexts. Increasing numbers of deaf people are entering employment after completing further and higher education qualifications (Barnes et al. 2007). More deaf people are in post-graduation employment (Sheikh et al. 2021), working in a range of professional contexts (Hauser et al. 2008; De Meulder 2017). However, previous survey-based research has identified that despite having educational qualifications and being highly skilled, deaf people:

- are proportionately less employed than hearing people and therefore are actively looking for work to a greater extent (Garberoglio et al. 2017, 2019);
- are significantly more likely to be underemployed or unemployed than their hearing peers, despite similar levels of qualification (Sheikh et al. 2021; Winn 2007);
- experience a lack of access to career guidance, so rely on family and friends for support and lack of choice in the types of work offered (Coogan and O'Leary 2018);
- tend to work in concentrated sectors that are more accessible for deaf people (Rydberg et al. 2011);
- do not generally have their accommodation needs met at work, so they experience inequalities (Punch et al. 2007; Punch 2016);
- are not aware of what funding they can access to get support at work (e.g. for interpreters) (Cameron 2013);
- have insufficient or no funding for the provision of interpreters in the workplace and find it difficult to book interpreters for job interviews (Napier et al. 2020);
- who disclose other disabilities (such as being deafblind) are most likely to experience pay inequality and underemployment (Cmar et al. 2018; Garberoglio et al. 2019);
- do not disclose that they are deaf on job applications for fear of experiencing discrimination (O'Connell 2021; Sheikh et al. 2021)
- experience anxiety and are fearful of losing their job due to communication difficulties and lack of alternatives in employment (Grote et al. 2021).

Deaf people are more likely to work in non-deaf related workplaces with hearing colleagues and hearing managers who do not sign (**hearing workplaces**). To understand how deaf people experience working in hearing workplaces, we present studies on deaf people's lived experiences at work. First, we present an overview of the barriers reported by deaf people and how these affect them, followed by the strategies that deaf people have developed in navigating the workplace. One such strategy is *entrepreneurship*, so we also consider experiences from deaf business owners who are employers. Finally, we touch on employers' perspectives on the benefits of having deaf employees, lessons learned and advice to consider for hearing people who may become a colleague, supervisor, line manager or employer of a deaf signer in the workplace.

16.3.1 Deaf People's Perceptions About Barriers in the Workplace

Workplace barriers for deaf people often relate to broader societal perceptions that impact how a prospective deaf job applicant or a deaf worker is perceived at work. Barriers are also primarily related to language issues, namely that deaf people use sign language and other hearing people in their workplace typically do not. Bristol and Dickinson (2015) note that even when SLIs are booked in the workplace, deaf people can experience feelings of social exclusion. Interpreters tend to only be booked for formal work meetings and not necessarily for social talk during breaks. This often leads to them experiencing a "glass ceiling" in terms of their progression at work (Atkins 2019; Bristoll 2009). Watson (2016) found amongst the 10 deaf participants in his study, some of them believed that being assertive was necessary to get their needs met.

In the pan-European DESIGNS project that focused on deaf people's experiences in employment,[2] Napier et al. (2020) conducted one-on-one interviews and focus groups with 39 deaf people in the UK, 13 in Ireland and 11 in Germany. They found several major gaps in the knowledge and experiences of deaf people at work that were consistent across the three countries. These primarily concentrated on understanding organisational/ work culture and included: how to apply for jobs; how to conduct themselves in job interviews; how to organise SLIs for work (as in educational institutions they are typically arranged by the institution); dealing with paperwork to access funding for accommodations. The deaf participants also noted difficulties with career progression due to a lack of confidence to apply for promotion and feeling isolated in hearing workplaces. These studies have predominantly focused on deaf people's experiences in hearing workplaces.

A focus group conducted with 7 UK-based deaf self-employed people as part of the DESIGNS project found that what led them to set up their own business is that they regularly experienced barriers in hearing workplaces (Sommer Lindsay 2018). One frequent barrier was the audism they experienced when applying for jobs, as seen in the following example (pseudonym used to protect identity).

> *When I returned to UK, I tried to apply for jobs, but I never got a job. I got many phone calls, and when I had a person who could help me making the phone calls, they found out that I was deaf, and asked a lot about my deafness, not about what I wrote in my applications. They always told me they would contact me later... After two years I gave up and got the idea to become self-employed as personal trainer.* (Karen)

This kind of audism was also reported by deaf people when they were in a job, what could be considered as "micro-aggressions" but what Robert calls "small oppressions" in the following example.

---

[2] See http://designsproject.eu.

> There have been many small oppressions in small ways. Like for example in the office, if the hearing employees were busy they were not disrupted but me, the other hearing colleagues would interrupt me frequently. There was a different attitude toward me as a deaf person, they respected the others and let them focus on their work, while they didn't respect me.
> (Robert)

Despite trying to overcome barriers by setting up their own businesses, deaf business owners can still encounter challenges, for example in accessing the informal networking that is often needed to secure contracts (Sommer Lindsay 2020).

Interestingly, even when accommodations are made and SLIs are present regularly in the workplace, this does not mean that barriers are automatically no longer present. The dynamics of having an interpreter present can impact on relationships with work colleagues. Case Study 1, by Richard Weinbaum who is deaf and works as an airplane design engineer, illustrates this.

Case Study 1: Richard Weinbaum

"Where I work, interpreters struggle because they don't know the jargon. If you fingerspell something they won't get it and they're having to ask. To give you an example, I worked over in America for 4 years and I was in the audience for a meeting and the word 'Elevator' comes up and the interpreter uses the sign for 'lift'. I burst out laughing and everyone was looking at me and I had to apologise for my laughter. The interpreter signed 'lift' for 'elevator' and of course planes don't have lifts! The elevators are on the wings and they didn't know that, but they needed that knowledge. Eventually, you just have to let it go and develop a mindset that will help you find your own way through all of this."

Source: DESIGNS project.

16.3.2 Deaf People's Strategies at Work

Following the above examples of different kinds of barriers experienced by deaf people at work, we now turn to deaf people's strategies to counter audism, demonstrate resilience and overcome such barriers.

As mentioned above, one such strategy is to set up their own business; a tendency in the UK, Europe and North America (Atkins 2019; Napier et al. 2020). In her study in Denmark, Sommer Lindsay (2022) conducted interviews with nine deaf Danish business owners and found various "push and pull" factors that contributed to their decision to set up a business, e.g. declining opportunities in deaf workplaces (push) to not getting enough challenges in a deaf-specific organisation and aspirations to develop their professional skills (pull). Although they experienced challenges, the deaf Danish business owners felt they were able to capitalise on being deaf in some ways as it gave them a unique selling point (USP). Many of them also navigated hearing norms by using humour, for example saying that the interpreter was their "ears".

Other strategies include hiding their deafness in situations where they do not face the hearing person, for example on their website or conducting business over the telephone using an interpreter but not revealing that they are deaf until they meet in person (Atkins 2019; Sommer Lindsay 2022). This is a strategy that deaf people use because they expect that hearing people will almost inevitably react upon discovering that they are deaf and, by disclosing their deafness in a job application, they fear that they may limit their chances of being invited to interview (O'Connell 2021).

As part of a larger study concerning experiences of working with interpreters in workplace contexts, Napier et al. (2019) interviewed three deaf people who could also use speech. They found that depending on the context and the skills of, or their familiarity with, the interpreters in a meeting, the deaf professionals used speech and lip-reading as a strategy to be "heard" in meetings because they felt the interpreters could not always accurately represent what they were saying or how they were saying it. This strategy is obviously only available to deaf people who can (or choose to) use their voice.

One of the clear strategies that has emerged through various studies of deaf people at work is the importance of working with interpreters closely to maintain business interactions (Sommer Lindsay 2022), and to maintain relationships at work and ensure that the deaf professionals' expertise is conveyed and represented well, for example in meetings or presentations (Young et al. 2019). Strategies for effectively working with interpreters are illustrated in Case Study 2 by Toby Burton, who is deaf and works as a chief financial controller.

Case Study 2: Toby Burton

"Working in business means every day is jam-packed with meetings, dealing with issues that crop up, presentations to attend, organisational matters etc. which means you absolutely have to have the right strategy for working with interpreters. Over the course of my career to date, I've not just employed one strategy - during those 20 years, I had to adapt my approach in response to the needs of the different jobs I've done, and the different companies and teams I've worked in.

I focused on building a good pool, a network of interpreters that I came to know well - 4 or 5 of them and they've been the ones on whom I've concentrated my attention on. That's not to say I haven't brought new people into the team, but I've kept the number of interpreters relatively small. That way I've been able to build a relationship with each of them and that's important. It meant when they are interpreting my signing into spoken English, they were able to match perfectly the tone and content of what I'm saying. I always book them well in advance because I need interpreting cover to enable me to conduct everyday business and sequences of meetings.

Without access to interpreters, it would have been impossible for me to have made the progress I have in my career. You absolutely have to work with interpreters; equally important is that this relationship runs smoothly. When I think back that was especially important at the start of my career because my hearing colleagues were feeling unsettled and weren't sure how to relate to me as a deaf person. So it was vital that when the interpreter came in, they were able to convey what I was saying with

> the right tone and demonstrate my ability to function in that working environment and participate fully in what was going on - that was incredibly important...
>
> During that early part of your career, I'd also say you have to work with skilled interpreters, in a way that's less of an issue for me now because the interpreters I work with know me well, but when I was starting out it's very important that when people were listening to the interpretation of me from the interpreter, and it doesn't matter if that interpreter is a man or a woman, that they heard me, 'Toby' talking to them - that's how you make the breakthrough and that enables you to get on with things."
>
> Source: DESIGNS project.

Both Richard (Case Study 1) and Toby (Case Study 2) also mentioned the fact that the advent of technologies has generated more options for accessible information and communication, such as speech-to-text apps, autogenerated captions, videophone technology for remote interpreting services, etc. There are also other documented examples of strategies used by deaf people to navigate workplaces that go beyond sign language interpreting and language/communication.

Self-employed deaf people in the UK whose services do not target deaf people specifically develop strategies to attract hearing customers (Sommer Lindsay 2018), for example by offering free sign language lessons; or they focus on being friendly and engaging, as shared by one participant in the example below.

I never use sign language interpreters, I always communicate directly with customers. Sometimes they are surprised when they see I am deaf, but I try to be friendly and welcoming and communicate directly with them. That way, they will never leave the stall. So, it seems to work, and often they buy something – maybe because I am deaf. I do not want to have an interpreter with me, I want hearing people to meet me halfway. I do like that we try to find ways to communicate, like with paper, through the phone or computer. (Lily)

As you can see, Lily also referred to the use of technology as a strategy. Like Lily, many participants stated that they do not use SLIs, either because they had never used them, or it is too complicated to book them, because it is harder to access government funding for interpreting support if you are self-employed; or the opportunities to book interpreters for only brief conversations are not realistic. Many of the deaf entrepreneurs did not employ other people and worked on their own, which made it easier for them to manage things. Alternatively, deaf people may opt to work in deaf organisations, such as charities that provide services directly to deaf communities in sign language.

16.3.3 Deaf People in Deaf Workplaces

There are many reasons that deaf people may prefer to work in organisations that provide dedicated services to deaf communities (**deaf workplaces**) and tend to employ several deaf people (although they are still situated in hearing-dominated structures and are often led by hearing people). Watson (2016) found that deaf people who worked in deaf workplaces commented on the following:

- accommodations were already in place and readily available when they joined the organisation; communication was easy and accessible in sign language with colleagues and supervisors;
- they received regular feedback and positive recognition from their supervisors who were easily accessible and encouraged their professional growth;
- they were able to share knowledge and experience with all work colleagues;
- they did note, however, that because they could socialise more easily at work, this affected their completion of work tasks;

Deaf employers or managers will often try to hire other deaf people because it makes the everyday lives of both the managers and the employees much easier and more comfortable. Deaf employees have a vested interest to have a deaf-owned business perform better, and they feel a sense of responsibility for giving deaf people jobs because they know that deaf people struggle in the broader labour marke.

However, after studying the experiences of deaf adults working in Ireland, O'Connell (2021) discovered that deaf people who work in deaf workplaces can still encounter barriers. Even in these workplaces, the hiring employers or senior managers are often hearing themselves. These services are funded by the governments that have representatives and interview boards that tend to predominantly involve hearing people and processes are based on hearing norms and expectations. As such, deaf people's chances of getting a job and being promoted within the organisation are still disadvantaged.

Thus far, this chapter has focused on the perceptions and experiences of deaf people in hearing and deaf workplaces, and as self-employed business owners. Before wrapping up, it is worthwhile giving attention to the perspectives of hearing employers on working with/hiring deaf people.

16.4 Hearing Employer Perspectives on Working with Deaf People

After studying the experiences of deaf employees working in coffee shops in India, Friedner (2013) found that employers feel that there can be added value for corporations that hire deaf people, for example because the limited opportunities to talk on the job in sign language with other non-signing colleagues deaf employees are perceived as hard working, plus customers perceive a positive social justice agenda for the business, so people return. This is perceived as creating an added economic benefit for the business. But she also found that whilst they are appreciated by colleagues and managers, deaf people are not offered career opportunities or more senior roles.

Additionally, Napier et al. (2020) conducted interviews with 30 different employers across a range of organisations in the UK ($n = 17$), Ireland ($n = 5$) and Germany ($n = 8$) as part of the DESIGNS project, and identified five key themes:

1. *Employment opportunities*: Deaf people have more access to employment opportunities if an employer has worked with deaf people before, or has friends who are deaf people and/or have family members who are deaf. What adversely impacts employment opportunities of deaf people most is employers not having any knowledge or experience of dealing with deaf people, and therefore having no awareness of how to work with or recruit them. Employers recognised that where there are deaf people working in their organisations, they mostly have jobs at operational levels. Progression and career development are key challenges, not only for deaf people but also for employers looking to develop their deaf staff.
2. *Advantages and disadvantages of employing deaf people*: Employers recognised the benefits of employing deaf people whom they regard as flexible, having spent every day adapting the way they interact with the society as best as they can thereby demonstrating their sense of determination. Staff working with a deaf person found that they learned alternative ways of communicating, turn-taking skills, direct communication and non-verbal communication skills. They also reported that deaf people are typically more loyal than their hearing colleagues, and that this contributes to the stability of the workforce. One of the barriers to employing deaf people identified by employers was the additional costs of paying for sign language interpreters and adaptations not covered by government funding.
3. *Equality, diversity and inclusion (EDI) policies*: A key factor that impacts employers' attitudes on employing deaf people is that many make assumptions about deaf people as disabled and their abilities. Whilst they may have robust EDI policies, including consideration of disabilities, there is typically no specific policy related to deaf people in organisations. Sign language interpreting services are seen as costly, for example (as not all countries have Access to Work funds like the UK). But having deaf employees can enhance the "USP" of a company. Larger organisations are better placed to apply EDI policies and can offer bespoke training programmes for people with disabilities, including deaf employees.
4. *Dynamics in the workplace*: Even in deaf workplaces, deaf and hearing staff still struggle with integration. Hearing staff do not always remember to be inclusive—this is compounded when staff have no or under-developed sign language skills. One hearing employer emphasised the importance of creating the right culture and having managers set the right tone, especially in relation to the use of sign language in the workplace. A number of other hearing employers recognised that their deaf employees often felt isolated and tried to foster a workplace where hearing employees are actively encouraged to include deaf colleagues in informal as well as formal discussions.

5. *Accommodations for deaf employees*: For employers in hearing workplaces, the challenges in relation to integration extend to access to information and workplace training, in addition to ensuring interpreters are booked. They also acknowledged that deaf people may need more time to assimilate new job tasks or work with new colleagues. Therefore, employers need to consider alternative ways of delivering job training (for example, signed videos) and appreciate the limitations of having things written down. One employer, in particular, recognised that e-learning is not suitable for all deaf people and that a more collective dialogic approach is more successful.

16.5 Advice for Future Employers, Managers, Supervisors and Colleagues

To ensure an inclusive organisational culture for deaf people in predominantly hearing workplaces, we draw once more on comments from deaf Chief Financial Controller Toby Burton (see Case Study 1). Based on his own experiences throughout his career he offers the following words of wisdom for employers:

> Drawing on my many years of experience, I think the first thing that employers need to think about when they first encounter a deaf employee is to put aside any concerns or anxieties and think about whatever hearing people can do; deaf people can do and treat everyone the same, not somehow differently. The only thing employers need to remember is that historically deaf people have had to face many obstacles. If they're to be successful, the focus needs to be on working out how to remove barriers from the workplace. In my experience, the best way to do that is to approach the most senior person in the organisation, the CEO or someone at the management level and get their backing to remove these barriers… The other thing is delivering deaf awareness/communication awareness training so that hearing colleagues can make the necessary adjustments, for example, not looking at the interpreter when they need to be looking at me – again, these things make it easier for deaf people to fit in and there are several things like that which are about removing barriers, all of which make deaf people's integration into the workplace easier… What's important is that colleagues treat deaf people not as an obstacle or as different from hearing people in terms of opportunities at work and career progression because if you let them, deaf people can rise in their chosen careers in the same way.
>
> Source: DESIGNS project case study, Toby Burton, Chief Financial Controller https://www.youtube.com/watch?v=c1gDyZI3ndw

---

Chapter Review Questions

1. What can a hearing employer do when a deaf employee is hired in the workplace?
2. How can you as colleague to a deaf person ensure a good work environment? (Think about examples that go beyond booking an interpreter).

3. What kind of positive benefits would a work organisation get by having deaf employees or employers?
4. How can you as colleague or manager encourage deaf colleagues to get more experience/qualifications/skills during the period that the deaf person is employed at the workplace?
5. What kind of challenges still exist within deaf workplaces?

Recommended Further Reading

- Bauman, H.D.L., ed. 2008. *Open Your Eyes: Deaf Studies Talking*. Minneapolis: University of Minnesota Press.
- Lane, H., B. Hoffmeister, and B. Bahan. 1996. *A Journey into the Deaf World*. Washington, DC: Dawn Sign Press.
- Listman, J., and K. Kurz. 2020. Lived Experience: Deaf Professionals' Stories of Resilience and Risks. *Journal of Deaf Studies & Deaf Education* 25 (2): 239–249.
- Napier, J., A. Cameron, L. Leeson, C. Rathmann, C. Peters, H. Sheikh, J.B. Conama, and R. Moiselle. 2020. *Employment for Deaf People in Europe: Research Findings from the DESIGNS Project*. Monograph no. 5, Centre for Deaf Studies Monograph Series. Dublin: Trinity College Dublin.
- Padden, C. and T. Humphries. 2005. *Inside Deaf Culture*. Cambridge, MA: Harvard University Press.

References

Atkins, W.S. 2019. A Study into the Lived Experiences of Deaf Entrepreneurs: Considerations for the Professional. *JADARA* 46 (2). Available at: https://repository.wcsu.edu/jadara/vol46/iss2/5.

Bauman, H.D.L. 2004. Audism: Exploring the Metaphysics of Oppression. *Journal of Deaf Studies & Deaf Education* 9 (2): 239–246.

Barnes, L., F. Harrington, J. Williams, and M. Atherton, eds. 2007. *Deaf Students in Higher Education: Current Research and Practice*. Coleford: Douglas McLean.

Bristoll, S., and J. Dickinson. 2015. Small Talk, Big Results. *Newsli* 92: 6–13.

Bristoll, S. 2009. But We Booked an Interpreter! The Glass Ceiling and Deaf People: Do Interpreting Practices Contribute?" In *Signed Language Interpreting: Preparation, Practice and Performance*, ed. L. Leeson, S. Wurm, and M. Vermeerbergen, 117–140. Manchester: St. Jerome.

Cameron, A. 2013. Employment Research Project 2012–13. Report Submitted to the Scottish Council on Deafness. Unpublished Research Report: Scottish Council on Deafness.

Cmar, J.L., M.C. McDonnall, and K.M. Markoski. 2018. In-School Predictors of Postschool Employment for Youth Who Are Deaf-Blind. *Career Development and Transition for Exceptional Individuals* 41 (4): 223–233.

Coogan, A., and J. O'Leary. (2018). *Deaf Women of Ireland (1922–1994)*. CDS/SLSCS Monograph No. 4. Dublin: Centre for Deaf Studies, Trinity College Dublin. Available at: http://www.tara.tcd.ie/handle/2262/86028.

De Meulder, M. 2017. The Emergence of a Deaf Academic Professional Class During the British Deaf Resurgence. In *Innovation in Deaf Studies: The Role of Deaf Scholars*, ed. A. Kusters, M. De Meulder, and D. O'Brien, 101–128. New York: Oxford University Press.

De Meulder, M., and J. Murray. 2017. Buttering their Bread on Both Sides? *Abstract Language Problems and Language Planning* 41 (2): 136–158 https://doi.org/10.1075/lplp.41.2.04dem

Friedner, M. 2013. Producing 'Silent Brewmasters': Deaf Workers and Added Value in India's Coffee Cafés. *Anthropology of Work Review* 34 (1). https://doi.org/10.1111/awr.12005.

Foster, S.B. 2019. Employment Experiences of Deaf College Graduates: An Interview Study. *JADARA* 21 (1). Available at: https://repository.wcsu.edu/jadara/vol21/iss1/5.

Foster, F.R., and J. McLeod. 2003. Deaf People at Work: Assessment of Communication Between Deaf and Hearing Persons in Work Settings. *International Journal of Audiology* 42: S128–S139.

Foster, F.R., and J. McLeod. 2004. The Role of Mentoring Relationships in the Career Development of Successful Deaf Persons. *Journal of Deaf Studies and Deaf Education* 9 (4): 442–458.

Garberoglio, C.L., S. Cawthon, and M. Bond. 2017. Deaf People and Employment in the United States 2016. National Deaf Center on Postsecondary Outcomes. Research Report. Available at: www.nationaldeafcenter.org.

Garberoglio, C.L., J. L. Palmer, S. Cawthon, and A. Sales. 2019. Deaf People and Employment in the United States. National Deaf Center on Postsecondary Outcomes. Research Report. Available at: https://repositories.lib.utexas.edu/bitstream/handle/2152/83052/Deaf%20People%20and%20Employment%20in%20the%20United%20States%202019.pdf?sequence=2&isAllowed=y.

Grote, H., F. Izagaren, and E. Jackson. 2021. The Experience of D/deaf Healthcare Professionals During the Coronavirus Pandemic. *Occupational Medicine* 71 (4–5): 196–203.

Hauser, P., K. L. Finch, and A. B. Hauser. 2008. *Deaf Professionals and Designated Interpreters: A New Paradigm*. Washington, DC: Gallaudet University Press.

Kusters, A. 2017. Deaf and Hearing People' Multimodal and Translingual Practices. *Applied Linguistics Review*. https://doi.org/10.1515/applirev-2017-0086.

Lane, H., B. Hoffmeister, and B. Bahan. 1996. *A Journey into the Deaf World*. Washington, DC: Dawn Sign Press.

Luft, P. 2000. Communication Barriers for Deaf Employees: Needs Assessment and Problem-Solving Strategies. *Work* 14 (1): 51–55.

Napier, J., A. Cameron, L. Leeson, C. Rathmann, C. Peters, H. Sheikh, J. B. Conama, and R. Moiselle. 2020. *Employment for Deaf people in Europe: Research Findings from the DESIGNS Project*. Monograph no. 5, Centre for Deaf Studies Monograph Series. Dublin: Trinity College Dublin.

Napier, J., and L. Leeson. 2016. *Sign Language in Action*. London: Palgrave Macmillan.

Napier, J., A. Young, R. Oram, and R. Skinner. 2019. 'When I Speak People Look at Me': British Deaf People's Use of Bimodal Translanguaging Strategies and the Representation of Identities. *Journal of Translation and Translanguaging in Multilingual Contexts* 5 (2): 95–120. https://doi.org/10.1075/ttmc.00027.nap.

O'Connell, N. 2021. 'Opportunity Blocked': Deaf People, Employment and the Sociology of Audism. *Humanity & Society* 46 (2): 336–358.

Punch, R. 2016. Employment and Adults Who Are Deaf or Hard of Hearing: Current Status and Experiences of Barriers, Accommodations, and Stress in the Workplace. *American Annals of the Deaf* 161 (3): 384–397.

Punch, R., M. Hyde, and D. Power. 2007. Career and Workplace Experiences of Australian University Graduates Who Are Deaf or Hard of Hearing. *Journal of Deaf Studies and Deaf Education* 12 (4): 504–517.

Richards, J., and K. Sang. 2019. The Intersection of Disability and In-work Poverty in an Advanced Industrial Nation: The Lived Experience of Multiple Disadvantage in a Post-financial Crisis UK. *Economic and Industrial Democracy* 40 (3): 636–659.

Robinson, O. 2017. Moving Towards Disability Justice. *Disability Studies Quarterly* 37 (3). Available at: https://dsq-sds.org/article/view/5970. Accessed 21 March 2019.

Rydberg, E., L. Coniavitis Gellerstedt, and B. Danermark. 2011. Deaf People's Employment and Workplaces—Similarities and Differences in Comparison with a Reference Population Scandinavian. *Journal of Disability Research* 13 (4): 327–345. https://doi.org/10.1080/15017419.2010.507375

Sang, K., T. Calvard, and J. Remnant. 2021. Disability and Academic Careers: Using the Social Relational Model to Reveal the Role of Human Resource Management Practices in Creating Disability. *Work, Employment & Society*. https://doi.org/10.1177/0950017021993737.

Shakespeare, T., and N. Watson. 2002. The Social Model of Disability: An Outdated Ideology? *Research in Social Science and Disability* 2: 9–28.

Sheikh, H., J. Napier, A. Cameron, L. Leeson, C. Rathmann, C. Peters, J.B. Conama, and R. Moiselle. 2021. Supporting Access to Employment for Deaf People Through Research-Informed Training Resources: The DESIGNS Project. In *UNCRPD Implementation in Europe—A Deaf Perspective: Article 9: Access to Information and Communication*, ed. G. De Clerck, 179–193. Brussels: European Union of the Deaf.

Sommer Lindsay, M. 2018. Deaf-led Businesses from a Sociological Perspective: An Emerging Workplace for Deaf People. Unpublished Major Review Report. Heriot-Watt University.

Sommer Lindsay, M. 2020. Deaf People's Coping Strategies in an Everyday Employment Context. *Deaf Studies Digital Journal* 5. https://doi.org/10.3998/dsdj.15499139.0005.011.

Sommer Lindsay, M. 2022. Deaf Business Owners' Experiences of, and Strategies in, Navigating an Audist Normative Structured Labour Market in Denmark. Unpublished doctoral Dissertation, Heriot-Watt University.

Watson, M. 2016. Exploring the Experiences of Deaf Employees Working in Deaf and Hearing Workplaces: A Phenomenological Study. Unpublished Doctoral Dissertation, Capella University.

Williams, J., and S. Mavin. 2012. Disability as Constructed Difference: A Literature Review and Research Agenda for Management and Organization Studies: Disability as Constructed Difference. *International Journal of Management Reviews* 14 (2): 159–179.

Winn, S. 2007. Employment Outcomes for People in Australia Who Are Congenitally Deaf: Has Anything Changed? *American Annals of the Deaf* 152 (4): 382–390.

Young, A., J. Napier, and R. Oram. 2019. The Translated Deaf Self, Ontological (In)security and Deaf Culture. *The Translator* 25 (4): 349–368.

Part VI
Cross-Cultural Scenarios

Chapter 17
Cross-Cultural Scenarios

Katerina Strani and **Steven Glasgow**

> This volume discussed aspects of international (and intercultural) workplaces relating to communication, leadership and trust. This chapter brings everything together and takes stock of the challenges and opportunities inherent in intercultural workplaces through cross-cultural scenarios. We discuss seven scenarios. The first two scenarios focus on leadership, virtual teams, ethnocentrism, Islamic finance, and gender in the workplace. Scenarios #3 and #4 focus on cross-cultural negotiation, intercultural issues in finance and translation and interpreting. Scenarios #5 and #6 focus on trust, dignity and diversity and intercultural perceptions of work, leisure and time and Scenario #7 discusses organisational culture and deaf people in the workplace.

17.1 Introduction

In this volume, we discussed various aspects of international (and intercultural) workplaces under the main headings of communication, leadership and trust. This chapter brings everything together and takes stock of the challenges and opportunities inherent in intercultural workplaces through cross-cultural scenarios. The pedagogical value of cross-cultural scenarios, sometimes also called 'critical incidents', has been demonstrated across training contexts and fields (Starr-Glass 2011; Sit et al. 2017). It allows learners and trainees to consolidate their knowledge and develop

---

K. Strani (✉)
Department of Languages and Intercultural Studies, Heriot-Watt University, Edinburgh, Scotland, UK
e-mail: A.Strani@hw.ac.uk

S. Glasgow
Edinburgh Business School, Heriot-Watt University, Dubai, UAE
e-mail: S.Glasgow@hw.ac.uk

strategies to see beyond differences and not treat cultural diversity as a barrier, but use it to their and their team's advantage. We discuss seven scenarios that focus on key themes. The first two scenarios focus on leadership, virtual teams, ethnocentrism and gender in the workplace. Scenarios #3 and #4 focus on cross-cultural negotiation, and translation and interpreting. Scenarios #5 and #6 focus on trust, dignity and diversity and intercultural perceptions of work, leisure and time, and Scenario #7 discusses organisational culture and deaf people in the workplace.

17.2 Scenarios #1 and #2: Leadership

17.2.1 *John and a Global Virtual Team*

John is a UK manager who has been tasked to lead a team on a new and exciting project, starting in September. Team members are located in Australia, Malaysia and the UAE (Abu Dhabi).

The team is quite diverse, with colleagues from India, Germany, the US and Poland. John is preparing thoroughly to lead this new team. He consults the relevant cultural guides for expats and notes down the characteristics of each culture, trying to anticipate the cultural issues that may arise in managing this team. John reads on online blogs and expat guides that Polish and German employees don't like small talk, as opposed to Americans, and that employees from India are used to hierarchies and transactional, top-down leadership styles.

On the basis of this information, he is planning his first online meeting with them in August, and he is going to set the rules early on, give everyone precise instructions and monitor the project's development closely. He has already set out the targets and deadlines and plans on sticking to them strictly to ensure consistency.

Do you think John's approach will be successful? What advice would you give John for his August meeting, and in preparing to manage the new team?

Discussion

John is faced with the challenge of leading a global team located in different continents, but also composed of colleagues who come from different countries and may have been through an acculturation process already, with everything that this entails (e.g. acculturative stress). It is also likely that these local multicultural teams in Australia, Malaysia and Abu Dhabi are already operating on the basis of negotiated cultures (cf. Clausen 2007). We do not know whether these teams in Australia, Malaysia and Abu Dhabi have worked together before, or even if these colleagues have met each other.

John clearly cares about this project and wants the team to succeed. It is good that he acknowledges the potential of cross-cultural differences in this global team and that he is trying to anticipate and deal with them early on. Despite John's best intentions, however, his approach may not be successful for the following reasons.

First, John is looking at culture as a static and fixed trait, which at the same time can be adapted to suit the needs of the project. He makes too many assumptions without having even met his new colleagues. For example, he assumes that colleagues' 'national culture' stereotypes or generalised characteristics will apply to this team, not taking into account that these colleagues from India, Germany, the US and Poland are working within a negotiated culture already and that they would have already gone through a process of acculturation in their jobs in Australia, Malaysia and Abu Dhabi. For example, it may be true that business cultures in India may be more hierarchical, however if these colleagues are working in the Australian branch, they may well have adapted to horizontal management structures, a shorter power distance and a transformational leadership style.

Second, John does not seem to have considered organisational culture—cultural guides for 'expats' rarely do, as they tend to be stereotypical and ethnocentric. Organisational culture is of paramount importance in multinational companies, and it is what keeps the company's identity and brand consistent. Colleagues' behaviours and attitudes towards meetings, tasks and the workplace in general are undoubtedly influenced by organisational culture, which more often than not forms part of their negotiated culture.

Third, by adopting and planning to enforce strict rules and deadlines and monitor them closely without first discussing this with the team, John adopts a transactional approach to leadership where he assigns tasks and expects them to be delivered. There is much more to project management than this mechanical approach. It would have been better for John to meet the colleagues first and build rapport with them so that he becomes part of the team; indeed, being part of the team is crucial for a leader, otherwise nobody will choose to follow them. Adopting a transformational style of leadership, where John discusses the project aims first and involves the team in deciding how to complete tasks and achieve goals will give him far better results and a more successful team overall. Respect for each other's cultures and working styles is key in ensuring that everyone feels valued. This style of transformational leadership will also help colleagues grow, take initiative and adopt innovative solutions.

Finally, John needs to take time zone differences between the UK, Australia, Malaysia and Abu Dhabi into account when scheduling the first online meeting. There is no convenient time for everyone, and he may well choose to have an online platform of discussion where communication takes place both asynchronously and synchronously if and where possible. John doesn't seem to have considered this at all. It would also be advisable to research local customs and holiday observances to make sure that his planned meeting(s) in August will be feasible. For a project starting in September, a first meeting in August is perhaps too late.

For key concepts, including organisational culture, see Chapter 2.
For cross-cultural communication in global virtual workplaces, see Chapter 3.
For leadership across cultures, see Chapter 5.

17.2.2 Susan in Saudi Arabia

Susan is a senior executive in a large multinational company based in the US. She has been part of an international US-based project team for more than 20 years and has travelled extensively. Susan is a high achiever and a good leader who always performs well. She is strict, efficient and takes great pride in her job. One day her boss announced to her that she was being seconded to the company's offices in Saudi Arabia to lead the local team, as she was the only person with the relevant experience for that particular assignment. Susan was very excited, as she had never been to Saudi Arabia before and was looking forward to leading a new team in a new country. The project was crucial and the deadlines tight.

However, things did not develop as smoothly as she had hoped. Susan led a small team of men who were all very experienced in their field, however they were not showing any signs of initiative and they never challenged Susan's suggestions, which led to inconclusive decisions. They also avoided looking at her directly or shaking her hand. Susan called a meeting and tried to address the team's lack of engagement, but again nobody responded, and they seemed offended. The project was coming to an end and there was no development. Susan also applied for a bank loan to meet some urgent costs for the project and was surprised to see that the bank asked for a share of the project's profits. Susan was worried that if the project was not going to be successful, then the bank would penalise them.

What went wrong in this scenario, and what would you advise Susan?

Discussion

Susan does not seem to have done any research in the country's customs and practices before travelling there to work. Perhaps due to her experience and the fact that she has travelled widely, her company in the US did not provide her with any training on her assignment. This was a major oversight and perhaps the main source of the problems in this scenario.

Firstly, the wider cultural context in terms of gender and leadership needs to be taken into account in this scenario. It is widely known that the teachings of Islam, Saudi Arabia's official religion, underpin social values, behaviour and customs in all aspects of life, including the workplace. As a result, gender segregation in the workplace and in all aspects of public life is common (Al-Ahmadi 2011). Physical contact and eye contact between genders are forbidden, and working in a mixed-gender environment is therefore a major difficulty for women in Saudi Arabia (Andrews 2013). This explains Susan's colleagues' reluctance to look at her directly or shake her hand.

Furthermore, it is worth considering that only 3.2% of managers in Saudi Arabia are women (Almathami et al. 2022). And according to one Saudi female academic, "the most crucial issue facing women leaders is the establishment of their credibility as agents of change" (see Thompson 2015). This could explain Saudi colleagues' reluctance to engage with a female leader, even though she was brought from abroad. Hierarchies are also strictly respected in Saudi Arabia, and therefore it is considered disrespectful to challenge authority (ibid.). This could explain why colleagues never challenged Susan's suggestions, which she falsely interpreted as them not showing initiative. By calling a meeting to confront them about 'not engaging' with her, Susan was effectively offending them by suggesting that their cultural norms and practices of not having physical contact between genders or not challenging authority were wrong. Colleagues undoubtedly felt offended and could not see how to engage with their new boss in these circumstances.

Finally, Susan was evidently unfamiliar with the basic tenets of Islamic Finance, which is based on equity participation and forbids charging interest (Hanif 2014). If Susan had been given the right training before she was sent off to her expatriate assignment in Saudi Arabia, she would have learned that under the principles of Islamic Finance, it is forbidden to charge interest on loans. Instead, banks have an equity participation system where they share company profits (ibid.). Where there are no profits to share, the bank would lose as well. There was no cause of concern for Susan, therefore, and there was no risk to taking a bank loan under these circumstances. Familiarisation with the local cultural economic context is paramount, however, and this constituted another weakness on Susan's behalf.

Overall, Susan's lack of training and preparation for this assignment is partly to blame for this scenario, and this was largely the responsibility of Susan's company and manager. However, Susan could have been proactive in researching the local culture in terms of norms and practices that govern business, employee relations and everyday life. Susan's ethnocentrism and lack of willingness to adapt was ultimately the source of the team's failure. Susan did not demonstrate willingness to understand Saudi colleagues' culture and instead saw them as inferior and ineffective, and tried to adapt them to *her* way of working. This is ethnocentrism *par excellence* and it is hugely detrimental to team work and performance. In addition to preparation and training, Susan could have attempted to partner with a member of the team and share leadership. The local (Saudi) colleague would have then acted as a mediator, building rapport and trust between Susan and the team while respecting work hierarchies and local customs relating to haptics and oculesics (Hall 1980; Gabbott and Hogg 2001). Cultural adaptation to such a degree would be necessary in this scenario and it would earn trust and respect for Susan and her adaptive approach to leadership.

For leadership across cultures, see Chapter 5.
For cross-cultural communication in global virtual workplaces, see Chapter 3.
For performing gender in the workplace, see Chapter 15.
For key concepts, including ethnocentrism, see Chapter 2.
For Islamic Finance, see Chapter 9.

17.3 Scenarios #3 and #4: Communication

17.3.1 *Wei in the US*

Wei is Chinese and works for a large company in Guangzhou. The company is in the process of negotiating a business deal with a potential partner in the US. The final stages of the negotiation and signing of the deal would take place in the US company's headquarters in Denver, Colorado. Wei speaks English fluently, which is why his boss decided to send him on the trip.

Wei arrived for the meeting tired after a very long flight. The American colleagues were very friendly but keen to start the meeting, as they were operating on a strict schedule and agenda. Wei had brought gifts for the team and made sure he handed each gift to each colleague individually with both hands. He was surprised to see that the US colleagues did not have a gift for him. They introduced themselves with a handshake and went in the boardroom. During the negotiations, Wei listened attentively to the proposals put forward by Ben who was leading the US team, but did not make any comments. Ben was explaining their position over and over again and Wei would nod but say nothing. They stopped for lunch and Wei noticed that the US team discussed other work matters.

In the end, Ben was frustrated at Wei's prolonged silences and lack of engagement and Wei was put off by the fact that Ben didn't seem to care about him, but only about the deal. The partnership did not materialise. What went wrong?

Discussion

In this scenario, there is lack of cross-cultural knowledge and intercultural competence on both parties. Wei speaks English fluently but is perhaps not familiar with US cultural norms and business practices which favour strict deadlines, business lunches and direct communication and negotiation styles. Ben is focused on the task at hand, and his team has clearly not researched Chinese customs or business practices. Had he done this, he would have known that in Chinese business settings, gift-giving is not only customary but also an important aspect of building a good business relationship. Ben and his team should have had a small gift for Wei upon his arrival too. That said, in the US, giving a gift to a negotiation partner may be perceived as bribery (D'Souza 2003), and some companies can have very strict rules on spending funds on gifts, which may explain why Ben did not have a gift for Wei. It may be worth raising this point with the company's finance team due to the cultural significance of gift-giving in China, and other East Asian countries. Where there is an *exchange* of small gifts, this could be considered customary and not bribery, and the gifts could be later donated or kept in the company.

More importantly, Chinese rules of conduct in all aspects of life are governed by Confucianism, which is more concerned with balance, respect and harmony in human relationships rather than profit (Witzel 2016). This explains why Chinese negotiators do not tend to rush into formal contract discussions, but take considerable time to build up trust with their negotiation partners (Zhu et al. 2007). In this case, Ben took

Wei straight into the boardroom to start the negotiation process, which did not sit well with Wei. Trust is fundamental in Chinese business relationships, and negotiations can collapse if a personal relationship is not built first (ibid.). Even during lunch, Ben and his team continued to discuss work matters and did not make an effort at all to build a relationship with Wei. It was evident that they were more interested in the transaction, which is against the spirit of Confucianism governing Chinese philosophy and business practices. If we consider this case from the perspective of intercultural perspectives of leisure and work, we also see that the US practice of a working lunch is not compatible with the balance and harmony in human relationships that is embedded in Confucianism. Put simply, lunch would not be considered a part of work but an opportunity to build the personal relationship that is so crucial for establishing trust.

Inevitably, cross-cultural differences in communication were also evident during the meeting. Wei's silence and observation demonstrates an attitude of respect and attentiveness rather than lack of engagement, as Ben wrongfully assumes. According to Lin and Miller (2003, 288), "members of high-context cultures (e.g. Chinese) are not likely to express their opinion openly and explicitly, whereas members of low-context cultures (e.g. American) appreciate openness and directness with little attention to hidden contexts". High-context communication takes into account the physical, situational, cultural, political and other contexts, and therefore people rely less on verbal communication and more on the context to convey meaning. Low-context communication focuses only on the "coded, explicit, transmitted part of the message" (Hall 1976, 79). Wei's silence is therefore completely misinterpreted by Ben in this case, and his insistence of inviting Wei to speak and repeating the US team's negotiating position only makes matters worse. But Wei hasn't done his homework either. Had he been aware of these business and communication practices in the US, he would have perhaps not been offended by Ben's behaviour and he could have reminded him of what is customary in China so that the relationship could be salvaged, or so that they could arrange another meeting in the future.

Overall, building a relationship prior, during and after the negotiation, taking into account customs and traditions of gift-giving and a balance between work and life, and being mindful of differences in communication practices, especially regarding negotiations, would have greatly helped both Ben and Wei conduct their business negotiation.

For cross-cultural business communication, see Chapter 3.
For key concepts, including high- and low-context communication, see Chapter 2.
For intercultural perspectives of work, leisure and time, see Chapter 4.

17.3.2 Delphine in Japan

A luxury fashion retailer in France wants to negotiate a new business deal in Japan. They start the conversation by email in English, but they quickly realise that they'd rather speak their own languages, as the lingua franca brings disadvantages to them and there are frequent misunderstandings. They agree for the French delegation to fly to Tokyo and negotiate with the help of interpreters. The French manager, Delphine, calls for a meeting and she is informed by the Finance team that hiring a professional French < > Japanese interpreter for three days together with flights, accommodation, expenses and their fee would cost EUR 4,000 in total. Gabriel, one of the French employees, completed a Japanese elective course during his final year at university, and offers to interpret during the negotiation. Delphine agrees to use Gabriel as the interpreter to lower the cost and they fly to Tokyo.

When they meet the Japanese delegation, Delphine gives her hand to the Japanese manager, Mr. Nakamura, for a handshake. Mr. Nakamura bows instead and gives Delphine his business card with both hands. Delphine takes it and gives it to Gabriel. Mr. Nakamura looks offended. During the negotiation process, Gabriel is unfamiliar with some of the business terminology and has to ask for clarifications constantly. Mr. Nakamura's interpreter has to step in and clarify important information. Gabriel is confused and feels out of his depth. Delphine points to some charts and graphs that show the company's performance, hoping to save the deal, but Mr. Nakamura ignores it. Delphine is also frustrated because Mr. Nakamura is mostly silent, and it is not clear to her whether he is interested in the deal at all. Delphine was also surprised to see a representative of a leading bank sitting at the meeting, who was observing and not participating at all. Neither Delphine nor Gabriel knew what the bank representative was doing and whether they should be included in the negotiations or not, and this confusion was evident in the meeting. Mr. Nakamura is not impressed with the French delegation and their lack of respect and does not sign the deal. His team also noted that the proposal seemed to be too risky and they did not want to engage in a deal that involved that level of risk.

What went wrong in this scenario? What advice would you give Delphine for future cross-cultural and multilingual negotiations?

Discussion

The main problem in this scenario is using an unqualified ad hoc interpreter who was unfamiliar with both the cultural and the business context of Japan to interpret an important business deal. Ad hoc interpreters are sometimes used in companies to cut costs and save resources (see Piller, 2009). In this case, however, Delphine chooses a colleague who does not even have the required language skills, let alone the professional interpreting or intercultural business skills needed for the task. Unfortunately, it is not uncommon for monolingual people to assume that basic knowledge of a language would be enough for an interpreting task that requires such specialism. Hogg et al. (2014) point out "no matter how accurate a translation may be, if the norms of the target community have been ignored, it is a poor translation". It is clear that Gabriel is unfamiliar not only with business terminology but also with cultural norms and practices in Japan, such as, for example, the exchange of business cards or bowing as a form of greeting instead of shaking hands (Okoro 2012, 135). When receiving someone's business card in Japan, one must take it with both hands, read it and then place it carefully in a safe place, such as their briefcase. Delphine did not study the card but gave it to Gabriel, which is highly offensive, as she showed a lack of respect and as if she didn't care about Mr. Nakamura and his credentials.

In terms of who was present in the meeting, it would have been customary to start with introductions, and spend time letting delegates present themselves. This almost ceremonial aspect of meetings is important in Japan (see Okoro 2012). If Delphine had hired a professional to interpret and facilitate the negotiation, instead of Gabriel who only learned some Japanese at school, she would have known that there is a very close relationship between companies and their leading bank in Japan. It is common for banks to be seated in companies' board of directors since they have a high financial leverage of Japanese companies (Suzuki and Wright 1985). Therefore, it is normal and expected for a bank representative to be sitting at the negotiation table.

Additionally, Japan's (and other East Asian countries') style of business etiquette is based on high-context communication where the message is mostly carried in the cultural, hierarchical, situational contexts, as well as non-verbal and paraverbal cues (including silence). As Okoro (2012, 137) states, "[W]hen a Japanese businessperson speaks, they expect the person to interpret what they mean by their knowledge of the cultural values that lie behind the words". The role of silence was also misinterpreted (see previous case study on Wei in the US). Gabriel was unaware of all this, in addition to his language and business terminology struggles. Mr. Nakamura's professional interpreter had to step in as a result, which was embarrassing for Delphine's team and made her lose face in front of her Japanese counterparts.

Losing face is extremely damaging in Japanese culture, and indeed in many East Asian cultures (Oetzel and Ting-Toomey 2003), and this was most probably the main reason why the negotiation fell through. Not hiring a professional interpreter for the task and using an in-house colleague with sub-par language and cultural expertise in Japanese was extremely offensive and made Delphine look as if she didn't consider the meeting—and the partnership—important. Trust was broken and the relationship, which is crucial in business partnerships in Japan, was ultimately damaged. Investing in a professional business interpreter who is aware of the cultural context and can navigate cross-cultural negotiations in Japan would have been the best strategy for Delphine. Delphine should have also received relevant training on Japanese cultural and business etiquette to avoid the mistakes of not producing a business card, not knowing what to do with Mr. Nakamura's business card, offering her hand instead of bowing, etc. She would have also been briefed on the cultural aspects of finance in Japan and in particular the risk-averse culture, which is evident in the negotiation when Mr. Nakamura rejects the terms of the agreement because they are deemed too risky.

Overall, in multilingual business negotiations, the language barrier is only the tip of the iceberg, and it is the lack (or disregard) of cultural awareness that makes or breaks successful communication in the end.

> *For translation and interpreting in cross-cultural business practices, see Chapter 13.*
> *For key concepts, including high- and low-context communication, see Chapter 2.*
> *For cross-cultural business communication, see Chapter 3.*
> *For intercultural issues in Finance, and the case of Japan, see Chapter 9.*

17.4 Scenarios #5 and #6: Trust

17.4.1 Samira in Malaysia

Recepee Co. is a trading company in Malaysia with more than 100 employees. The recent staff survey of Recepee Co. shows that 50% of employees are dissatisfied at work, and 30% of them intend to leave the company in near future. One of the company's largest projects is seriously behind schedule as a result. Samira is recruited as a project manager to resolve the situation.

Samira calls the first team meeting and notices that the team is diverse in terms of gender, age, ethnicity and religion. She emphasises that despite people's difference in cultural backgrounds, they must all work together to deliver the project. She sets ground rules by setting hard deadlines and micromanaging people to make sure that they understand tasks and deliver them on time. Two team members inform her that one of the deadlines falls within a Hindu festival that is celebrated in their community and they cannot deliver the tasks on that week. Samira dismisses this and says that the company cannot accommodate individual requests and will only respect national holidays. Another team member complains that she cannot work with her male colleague because he constantly undermines her and asks her to do all the menial tasks, keeping the important tasks for himself. When asked about it, he says that, as a young woman, his colleague cannot possibly have the experience to take on important tasks, and it's best if she sticks to simple tasks for this important project. A third team member complains that she is always asked to write the minutes of meetings, but she has already declared that she is dyslexic (HR are aware of this). Samira reprimands the team for making excuses and urges everyone to pull themselves together to deliver the task, or there would be penalties.

The team disengage from the project, ignore Samira's requests for meetings and updates, and two of them quit. In trying to replace the colleagues who have left the project, Samira misses every single deadline, and the project fails. What went wrong, and what would you advise Samira?

Discussion

Samira's leadership style is entirely inappropriate for this specific team and task. She is going beyond a transactional to an authoritarian leadership style and also chooses to micromanage people so that the project is completed on time. Micromanagement is rarely a successful strategy, as it undermines a person's autonomy and initiative and disregards their work practices or needs. This is the wrong approach, especially in a company where staff satisfaction is low and turnover is high. More importantly, Samira makes a series of mistakes that seriously undermine the dignity of her colleagues in this diverse team.

First, she dismisses the fact that two employees cannot work at a certain time because of a religious festival. This constitutes religious discrimination in the workplace, because it restricts religious practices or religious holidays (Fox 2000) and employees are treated unfairly as a result. Respecting religion in the workplace is an integral aspect of appreciating diversity. Second, a female colleague reports sexist and ageist behaviour, which Samira again dismisses. Third, a dyslexic colleague is asked to take minutes at meetings, which is discriminatory against the employee. Dyslexia is a recognised disability which involves reasonable adjustments at work. The employee could raise a complaint against Samira or even sue the company, since HR are already aware of her dyslexia. There is legislation in many countries that protects employees from all these types of discrimination, but even if legislation is not in place, such working practices are unethical and undermine employee dignity. It has long been proven that discrimination leads to higher stress levels and feelings of injustice (Dipboye and Colella 2005). And when employees' dignity is undermined, they lose motivation, it curbs their creativity, and this results in lower production and poorer results. In this context, it is important to note that dignity in Western understandings tends to be considered as something we are all born with and are entitled to, but in many Asian cultures, including the ones in this scenario, dignity is ascribed by others and often those who are superior to us. Employees felt that their dignity was undermined; it is not surprising, therefore, that they become disengaged and two of them quit.

Samira doesn't seem to realise that leadership and management is more about people and less about tasks. Projects cannot be completed successfully if the team is demoralised, demotivated, discriminated against and if their dignity is undermined. Ultimately, she did not try to gain people's trust, and her team did not commit to the project or the tasks as a result. If Samira had invested more in people and less in tasks, she would have succeeded. The fact that the company suffered from high turnover and low staff satisfaction already should have been a warning sign. Specifically, Samira could have given the Hindu colleagues the time off to celebrate their religious festival but asked them to complete certain tasks beforehand. She could have then redistributed some tasks to make sure that the team would manage with these employees off for some days. All projects need to have some leeway built in for eventualities such as sickness or prolonged absence anyway. She could have investigated the sexism and ageism allegations with the male colleague in question, and made sure that the female colleague was assigned the work she was originally meant to do. If required she could then have arranged for the male colleague to receive appropriate training on equality and discrimination in the workplace. And lastly, she could have simply allocated the writing of the minutes to someone else, and not the dyslexic colleague. It could even be a rotating task so that a different colleague is tasked with minute-taking each time.

For dignity and diversity in the workplace, see Chapter 14.
For leadership across cultures, see Chapter 5.

17.4.2 Emily in Dubai

Emily is an experienced luxury retail manager, a role which requires building and maintaining a base of highly wealthy clients. After an attractive financial offer from a rival company, Emily took a new position at a store in Dubai, moving there from the UK. Three months into the role, despite enjoying the work, she has struggled to adjust from a predominantly European clientele to Middle Eastern.

First, she found clients often did not turn up on time for meetings that were scheduled, sometimes arriving 2 or 3 hours after the designated time without any reason given. This was unusual for Emily who liked to keep a tight schedule. Emily also perceived clients to not respect her work boundaries as much in Dubai than in the UK, with many asking for her personal number and contacting her any time, day and night, regardless of her working hours. At times clients would also contact her to talk about their own personal lives, which Emily found too personal and not fitting with her work. There was also an instance when a client was upset that Emily had not sent her a personal message after a recent purchase. If Emily had done this in the UK, she believed she would have seemed pushy and intrusive.

Emily is enjoying her new challenge in Dubai but has yet to adapt her approach for the Middle Eastern market. What are the causes of Emily's problems? How could she better adapt her approach?

Discussion
Emily began a new job in Dubai without researching the working culture in the UAE and specifically the luxury retail industry. Had she done so, she would have been able to identify and anticipate the problems she faced. The main source of these problems is a stark difference in perspectives of work, leisure and time. Emily is setting clear boundaries between work and her personal time, which she sees as distinct. These boundaries are typical of Emily's working culture, and any change to those boundaries is undesirable to say the least (see Nippert-Eng 2008). Emily therefore regards phone calls relating to work from clients in what she considers 'after-hours' to be intrusive and disruptive. But the luxury retail industry culture in the UAE regarding this, where the customer is paying not just for a product but also

for a service, is different. In the UK, the expectation would also be to have follow-up check-ins to check customer satisfaction, but not outside working hours, which is a strict concept, and not to the extent that the Dubai client is expecting.

The cultural difference in perspectives of work and leisure and the ensuing problem with setting boundaries is coupled with a cultural difference in perspectives of time. Emily's clients are often very late (2 to 3 hours) and do not acknowledge it, which suggests that they do not see anything wrong with it. Anthropologist Edward Hall discussed these fundamental differences in people's temporal understandings, which were deeply ingrained in each culture and were connected to their overall behaviours and attitudes (see Edward Hall's *The Silent Language* 1959). Researchers have built on Hall's work and studied how certain cultures tended to view deadlines and business appointment times more flexibly when compared to others (White et al. 2011). This is clearly the case here, where Emily's time-orientation is strict and she is working according to "clock time" (Fulmer et al. 2014), while her clients are operating on "event time", which is subjective and situational (ibid.). This is coupled with the luxury retail industry's expectations for paying for a service that includes perks such as tolerance to being late or demands for flexible work.

What is interesting in this respect is that, according to some research, Islamic cultures are generally high on past-orientation and low on future-orientation, and therefore patience is highly valued (Alon and Brett 2007). This means that if Emily appears impatient and raises the delays or the expectations that impact her work-life balance, then this would not be welcomed by her clients. In this case, Emily needs to learn more about the culture of the luxury retail industry in the UAE and be prepared to make changes to her attitude, while setting expectations for her clients from the start. For example, she could block off a longer time slot for meeting clients anticipating that they are likely to be late, rather than expecting them to be 'on time' according to her understanding. In this way, she can use the 2- or 3-hour buffer time to complete other tasks without having to wait. Regarding the calls 'after-hours', Emily could again specify a rough time where she would not be available rather than being strict or agree to respond only by text at certain times. Having a separate work phone would also help separate work from personal life and she would not have to share her personal mobile number. The follow-up calls after a purchase can be scheduled at times that suits Emily. Fulmer et al. (2014) note how cross-cultural differences in time-orientation influence how people anticipate changes, so it is important that discussions with clients on these arrangements take place at the start. Clients would appreciate Emily's time and effort in establishing the relationship from the outset and Emily's approach will adapt to the realities of her new job without threatening the relationship with the clients.

For intercultural perspectives of work, leisure and time, see Chapter 4.
For key concepts, see Chapter 2.

17.5 Scenario #7: Organisational Culture, and Deaf People in the Workplace: Uwe in Greece

Uwe is a Business graduate from Germany who found a graduate job at a German company branch in Greece. Uwe is well aware of Hofstede's Dimensions from university, and he used the country comparison tool to compare the way people do business in Germany and Greece. According to Hofstede's country comparison, Uwe found that Germany was higher in Individualism and Long-Term Orientation than Greece, and much lower in Power Distance and Uncertainty Avoidance.

For these reasons, Uwe made sure that he did not challenge leadership and tried to respect hierarchies as much as he could. He made sure that all information about projects was laid out and available to colleagues and tried to minimise all risks in project development. One of the colleagues, Alex, was deaf, and Uwe made sure that there was always an interpreter "for Alex" during meetings. Uwe always consulted the interpreter about key decisions and asked her to assess Alex's understanding of the meetings so that he could adjust his approach if needs be. Uwe made sure to always chat to the interpreter during breaks and tried to build rapport with her as he wanted to make sure Alex felt included and participated equally in the team.

Despite his best efforts, however, his manager, Maria, said to Uwe that he did not fit in with the team very well. Alex raised a complaint against Uwe because they felt completely alienated and marginalised at work, not being able to chat with colleagues during breaks or follow-up on discussions. Alex said that Uwe always addressed the interpreter and not them directly and did not seem interested in Alex's views at all. Maria also observed that Uwe's approach was not consistent with the company culture, which did not place emphasis on titles and hierarchies, encouraged critical discussion during meetings, as well as being comfortable and creative with risk.

What did Uwe do wrong? What would you advise him to do to remedy the situation?

Discussion

Similarly, to the case study with John above, it seems that Uwe is looking at culture as a static and fixed trait and makes assumptions based on generic models without meeting the people first and without taking into consideration organisational culture at all. And this is a case where it was organisational culture that governed working relations and practices rather than expected behaviours based on stereotypes or generalised findings. Specifically:

Uwe did not challenge leadership and tried to respect hierarchies, because this is what the cross-cultural model he consulted stipulated. But he made the mistake of not observing practices first (see Clausen 2007). The company culture, as his manager Maria pointed out, was horizontal and did not place emphasis on titles and hierarchies. While it was very good that Uwe was organised and gave detailed project information to colleagues, the effort to minimise risk because he saw that Greece scored highly in Uncertainty Avoidance than Germany in Hofstede's country comparison tool was not the right approach. The manager pointed out that this was against the company culture that embraced risk and creativity in problem-solving.

The most important mistake that had the worst impact on Uwe's performance and led to reprimand from his boss was the way he behaved to his deaf colleague. Uwe was not aware of how to work with interpreters or with deaf people in the workplace. His intentions were undoubtedly good, and he wanted to be inclusive, but without the necessary training or onboarding he adopted the wrong approach. First, the assumption that the interpreter is there for the deaf person is false, but unfortunately a common one (see Napier et al. 2019). The interpreter is there to facilitate communication for all parties; hearing people need the interpreter as much as deaf people. Second, Uwe assumed that the deaf colleague has neither 'voice' nor agency. Uwe only communicated with the interpreter about the content of the meetings and to check Alex's understanding, instead of asking Alex about their needs or checking their understanding with them, but rather with the interpreter. During breaks, instead of trying to build rapport with his colleague Alex, Uwe again tried to build rapport with the interpreter. This led to Alex feeling excluded, which is in line with Bristoll's (2009) research findings about deaf people in the workplace.

To remedy the situation, Uwe must first point out to Maria that he did not receive any onboarding to familiarise himself with the company culture and to receive training on working with deaf people through interpreters. Second, he could request interpreters to be booked for the breaks and social talk too, not just for formal meetings, so that Alex feels more included in the team. Third, he should approach Alex and ask them (not the interpreter) about their needs, whether there are any challenges or barriers to understanding during meetings or during breaks. A conversation with Alex through the interpreter, rather than with the interpreter, on meeting Alex's needs and challenges in the workplace will constitute a very good step towards fixing the situation. Lastly, Uwe needs to change his formal and conservative, risk-averse approach to adapt to the company culture of horizontal hierarchies and risk-taking.

For deaf people in the workplace, see Chapter 16.
For dignity and diversity in the workplace, see Chapter 14.
For translation and interpreting in cross-cultural business practices, see Chapter 13.
For key concepts, including organisational culture, see Chapter 2.

References

Al-Ahmadi, H. 2011. Challenges Facing Women Leaders in Saudi Arabia. *Human Resource Development International* 14 (2): 149–166. https://doi.org/10.1080/13678868.2011.558311.

Almathami, R., C. Khoo-Lattimore, and E.C. Ling Yang. 2022. Exploring the Challenges for Women Working in the Event and Festival Sector in the Kingdom of Saudi Arabia. *Tourism Recreation Research* 47 (1): 47–61. https://doi.org/10.1080/02508281.2020.1821329.

Alon, I., and J.M. Brett. 2007. Perceptions of Time and Their Impact on Negotiations in THE Arabic-Speaking Islamic World. *Negotiation Journal* 23 (1): 55–73.

Andrews, S. 2013. Gender Communication in the Workplace. http://www.cedma-europe.org/new sletter%20articles/TrainingOutsourcing/Gender%20Communication%20in%20the%20Work place%20(Jun%2013).pdf.

Bristoll, S. 2009. But We Booked an Interpreter! The Glass Ceiling and Deaf People: Do Interpreting Practices Contribute?" In *Signed Language Interpreting: Preparation, Practice and Performance*, ed. L. Leeson, S. Wurm and M. Vermeerbergen, 117–140. Manchester: St. Jerome.

Clausen, L. 2007. Corporate Communication Challenges: A 'Negotiated' Culture Perspective. *International Journal of Cross-Cultural Management* 7 (3): 317–332. https://doi.org/10.1177/147059 5807083376.

D'Souza, C. 2003. An Inference of Gift-Giving Within Asian Business Culture. *Asia Pacific Journal of Marketing and Logistics* 15 (1/2): 27–38.

Dipboye, R.L., and A. Colella. 2005. The Dilemmas of Workplace Discrimination. In *Discrimination at Work the Psychological and Organizational Bases*, ed. R.L. Dipboye, and A. Colella, 425–462. Mahwah: Lawrence Erlbaum.

Fox, J. 2000. The Effects of Religious Discrimination on Ethno-Religious Protest and Rebellion. *Journal of Conflict Studies* 20 (2): 16–43.

Fulmer, A.C., B. Crosby, and M.J. Gelfand. 2014. Cross-Cultural Perspectives on Time. In *Time and Work*, vol. 2, ed. A. J. Shipp and Y. Fried. London: Routledge. https://doi.org/10.4324/978 1315798370.

Gabbott, M., and G. Hogg. 2001. The Role of Non-verbal Communication in Service Encounters: A Conceptual Framework. *Journal of Marketing Management* 17 (1): 5–26. https://doi.org/10. 1362/0267257012571401.

Hall, E.T. 1976. *Beyond Culture*. New York: Doubleday.

Hall, E.T. 1980. *The Silent Language*. New York: Praeger.

Hanif, M. 2014. Differences and Similarities in Islamic and Conventional Banking. *International Journal of Business and Social Sciences* 2 (2). Available at SSRN: https://ssrn.com/abstract= 1712184.

Hogg, G., M. Liao, and K. O'Gorman. 2014. Reading Between the Lines: Multidimensional Translation in Tourism Consumption. *Tourism Management* 42: 157–164.

Lin, X., and S.J. Miller. 2003. Negotiation Approaches: Direct and Indirect Effect of National Culture. *International Marketing Review* 20: 286–303.

Napier, J., A. Young, R. Oram, and R. Skinner. 2019. 'When I Speak People Look at Me': British Deaf People's Use of Bimodal Translanguaging Strategies and the Representation of Identities. *Journal of Translation and Translanguaging in Multilingual Contexts* 5 (2): 95–120. https://doi. org/10.1075/ttmc.00027.nap.

Nippert-Eng, C.E. 2008. *Home and Work. Negotiating Boundaries Through Everyday Life*. University of Chicago Press.

Oetzel, J.G., and S. Ting-Toomey. 2003. Face Concerns in Interpersonal Conflict: A Cross-Cultural Empirical Test of the Face Negotiation Theory. *Communication Research* 30: 599–624.

Okoro, E. 2012. Cross-Cultural Etiquette and Communication in Global Business: Toward a Strategic Framework for Managing Corporate Expansion. *International Journal of Business and Management* 7 (16): 130–138. https://doi.org/10.5539/ijbm.v7n16p130.

Piller, I. 2009. Intercultural Communication, in Bargiela-Chiap Pini. In *The Handbook of Business Discourse*, ed. F. Bargiela-Chiappini, 317–330. Edinburgh: Edinburgh University Press.

Sit, A., A.S. Mak, and J.T. Neill. 2017. Does Cross-Cultural Training in Tertiary Education Enhance Cross-Cultural Adjustment? A Systematic Review. *International Journal of Intercultural Relations* 57: 1–18. https://doi.org/10.1016/j.ijintrel.2017.01.001.

Starr-Glass, D. 2011. Between Stereotype and Authenticity: Using Action Research in a Cross-Cultural Management Course. *Journal of International Education in Business* 4 (2): 112–124.

Suzuki, S., and R.W. Wright. 1985. Financial Structure and Bankruptcy Risk in Japanese Companies. *Journal of International Business Studies* 16 (1): 97–110.

Thompson, M.C. 2015. Saudi Women Leaders: Challenges and Opportunities. *Journal of Arabian Studies* 5 (1): 15–36. https://doi.org/10.1080/21534764.2015.1050880.

Witzel, M. 2016. *Doing Business in China*. 4th ed. London: Routledge. https://doi.org/10.4324/9781315671666.

White, L.T., R. Valk, and A. Dialmy. 2011. What Is the Meaning of 'on Time'? The Sociocultural Nature of Punctuality. *Journal of Cross-Cultural Psychology* 42 (3): 482–493.

Zhu, Y., B. McKenna, and Z. Sun. 2007. Negotiating with Chinese: Success of Initial Meetings Is the Key. *Cross Cultural Management: An International Journal* 14 (4): 354–364. https://doi.org/10.1108/13527600710830368.

Glossary

Ability is one of the dimensions of trustworthiness in the model developed by Mayer, Davis and Schoorman (1995). It is also sometimes known as *competence* or *expertise* and refers to the skills or competencies that an individual or an organisation has.

Accommodations: adaptations that can be made to the workplace to ensure that people can do their job (e.g. screen readers for blind people, interpreters for deaf people, etc.)

Acculturation refers to the process of learning a new culture (usually the dominant culture) through immersion and adopting its values and practices. Acculturation is not a one-way process, but an interactive one, which is why it may lead to change in both cultures through continuous contact. Communication is central to this process.

Ad-hoc translator/interpreter: people who provide translation or interpretation without having a qualification or receiving training in relevant backgrounds.

Adjustment latitude: the opportunities people have to reduce or in other ways change their work-effort when ill. Such opportunities can be to choose among work tasks or work at a slower pace (Johansson and Lundberg 2004).

Anchor currency: a dominant currency for financial services and economic transactions facilitating the development of multilateral trade relations and thus contributing to increasing volumes of trade.

Anglo-Saxon Model (the): refers to an economic model of capitalism that is primarily practised in the English-speaking world such as, for example, the United States, UK and Canada.

Assimilation is the process where each cultural group is being absorbed into the dominant culture. This is also called *subtractive multiculturalism* (Triandis 1994, 241) because individuals are forced to abandon some of their own cultural principles in favour of the dominant cultural identity. Assimilation refers to the "melting pot" model in migration studies since the result resembles a fusion of various cultures

© The Editor(s) (if applicable) and The Author(s), under exclusive licence to Springer Nature Switzerland AG 2023
K. Strani and K. Pfeiffer (eds.), *Intercultural Issues in the Workplace*,
https://doi.org/10.1007/978-3-031-42320-8

molten into one, where individual cultures are not distinguishable, but the one culture that has absorbed all others is.

Audism, related to the concept of ableism, means that deaf people are discriminated against because they cannot hear, for example, by not being offered a job which requires the use of the telephone even when adaptative technologies or video-telephone relay interpreting services are available (Bauman 2004).

BELF: English as Business Lingua Franca. The acronym BELF was originally intended to stand for "Business English as Lingua Franca." However, this was later changed to "English as Business Lingua Franca" to place greater emphasis on the domain of use (business) than on the variety of English.

Belonging: a process and a result that binds communities, societies, groups and teams. Belonging is both self-determined and ascribed. It is self-determined in that people may feel a 'sense of belonging' to a place or a community and ascribed when external agents (the state, society, the workplace, the boss) determine who belongs and who doesn't, actively excluding those who don't. A sense of belonging is vital in the workplace and has been described as a route to resilience (Hickman and Mai 2015). *"To belong is to feel natural and unthreatened in a group. It is to understand and be understandable to other members of that group; to be able to recognize and be recognized within. In this sense, belonging is both a status, something held, and a practice, the ability to navigate the symbols, ideas and institutions of a group"* (Chin 2019, 721)

Benevolence is one of the dimensions of trustworthiness in the model developed by Mayer, Davis and Schoorman (1995). It is also sometimes known as **empathy** and involves consideration of others and goodwill towards others.

Blockchain is a type of Distributed ledger technology (DLT). Digital ledger on which all transactions are recorded and information is secured via cryptography. Copy of a blockchain is stored and updated on all devices linked to the network and can be accessed by anyone participating in the network. Consists of blocks containing information (e.g. transactions) that are linked together to form the blockchain. Nearly impossible to forge as each block (value) depends on the previous block (value). Can be public (permissionless, decentralised) and restricted (permissioned, centralised).

Branch plant: factory in one country belonging to a company with headquarters in another country. A national economy based mainly on branch plants is highly vulnerable.

Business case for diversity: workplace diversity gives an organisation a competitive advantage through:

- Increased productivity: employees who feel respected and valued have dignity, harmonious relationships and work more effectively. Morale is high, creativity fostered and decision-making improved (Lucas 2007; Horwitz and Horwitz 2017).
- Reduced absenteeism and turnover rates: when parents and carers are unconstrained by pregnancy, childcare and fixed work schedules, but instead given flexible working options, on-site childcare facilities and maternity/paternity leave.

- Retention of business and increasing marketing capabilities through knowledge of diverse clientele in global markets.
- Creating the largest possible talent pool for recruitment, attracting and retaining the best talent
- Problem-solving and system flexibility.
- Becoming an employer of choice (key to an organisation's reputation as a fair employer).
- Resource acquisition through increased creativity.

Central Bank Digital Currencies (CBDCs): created by central banks and specifically from a retail perspective an advanced and digital representation of cash. Can be accessed by the general public and must be the liability of the central bank to be considered a CBDC.

Coaching: a facilitation approach to unlocking a person's potential to maximise their own performance.

Coaching Psychology: a facilitation approach to enhancing well-being and performance in personal life and work domains underpinned by models of coaching grounded in established learning theories and psychological approaches.

Cognitive Behavioural Psychology: thinking processes that both influence and are influenced by emotional and behavioural responses.

Cognitive Behavioural Therapy (CBT): a scientific and empirical form of intervention aims to modify cognitive, emotional and behavioural process to test whether modification has positive effects.

Commodification: transformation process changing the value of anything solely in terms of an object of trade

Communication is the way we make ourselves understood within and across the groups to which we belong. It is also way that people make meaning in the world. Communication is contingent upon many layers and contexts, and any notion of communication as a linear and unidirectional process of a sender sending a message which is received by a receiver cannot apply to the realities of human communication.

Comparative advantage gains from trade accruing from differences in production cost enabling one economic agent to produce cheaper than another, making it profitable to trade.

Computer-aided translation (CAT): a translation process in which translators use computer software to manage, edit, and store translations.

Consecutive interpreting: a type of interpreting in which the interpreters wait for the speakers to finish their speech, or pause between their speech, before delivering the speech into another language.

Cryptocurrency is a highly volatile financial instrument employing blockchain technology to make and receive payments. Private coins (or currency) are generally mined within such networks to encourage block creation and hence the approval of transaction within the network.

Culture is a collective concept and refers to systems of meaning-making that are created over time through social interactions (see Hall 1996). Culture is the accumulated shared meanings and knowledge that are embedded in everyday life, social practices and norms.

Cultural Intelligence (CQ) describes the capability of one's self to recognise, adapt, function and work effectively in various intercultural contexts.

Cultural literacy: a critical understanding of a person's own culture as well as an ability to work well with people who are culturally different.

Cultural 'norms' are "sets of rules, standards and expectations that both generate and regulate social interaction and communication" (O'Sullivan 1994, 158). Norms are morally constraining and binding and are best viewed as the *dos and don'ts* of a social situation or an institution.

Cultural values or cultural value preferences are perceptions of what is right and wrong, what is fair and just and/or worthwhile in relation to their society, its institutions, and its members' way of life. Values give meaning to our actions, but they can be temporary and fluid (Mackie and Strani 2013).

Deaf workplaces: workplaces where many deaf people work, typically in organisations that provide dedicated services to deaf communities (e.g. charities) although they are still situated in hearing dominated structures and are often led by hearing people.

Dependency (theory): economic theory with focus on the disadvantages arising from a country's dependence on another for development; usually applied to (former) colonies.

Development economics: a set of economic theories addressing the specific issues by less developed countries or regions.

Dialogue interpreting (or liaison interpreting): a type of interpreting in which the interpreter mediates between two parties (or sometimes more) speaking different languages in face-to-face or online interaction.

Dignity: workplace dignity is defined as "the self-recognized and other-recognized worth acquired from engaging in work activity" (Lucas 2017, 1). Working with dignity means that individuals can fulfil their potential by being valued, respected, and given autonomy and personal space to express their identity. If dignity is undermined in the workplace, individuals become alienated, and their well-being is threatened.

Disability: loss or limitation of opportunities to take part in normal life due to societal factors such as exclusion or stigmatisation. The World Health Organisation states that "[d]isability results from the interaction between individuals with a health condition, such as cerebral palsy, Down syndrome and depression, with personal and environmental factors including negative attitudes, inaccessible transportation and public buildings, and limited social support" https://www.who.int/health-topics/disability#tab=tab_1.

Discrimination: the unfair or prejudicial treatment of people or groups on the grounds of certain characteristics, e.g. race, gender, age, disability.

Distributed ledger technology (DLT): blockchain technology that allows for transactions to be settled without trusted intermediaries. This is achieved via a consensus mechanism (e.g. Proof Of Work). Different to centralised networks, information is stored as (frequently updated) copies on all participating nodes (computers, mobile phones, etc.) in the system. DLT is in its infancy but it is expected that such a technology will not only be used to make payments but to generally store all kinds of other data in the future.

Diversity: a range of people, and points of view, with a variety of characteristics and from different social and ethnic backgrounds, and of different genders, sexuality, etc. "The collective, all-encompassing mix of human differences and similarities along any given dimension" (Mazur 2010, 7). Diversity is subjective and constructed, based on perceptions of the dominant group.

ELF: English as a Lingua Franca

Emotional intelligence (EI/EQ): an individual's ability to identify, assimilate, understand and manage emotions of oneself and others appropriately and effectively.

Empathy: see entry for **benevolence.**

Endogenous (development): growing from within. In economic contexts: growth drawing on local resources rather than external (foreign) investment and imports

ENL: English as a Native Language

Equality (in the workplace) broadly refers to equal opportunities, equal pay, and equal treatment overall.

Equity (in the workplace): recognition of differing needs to reduce barriers to participation, hence giving each employee the treatment that they need instead of giving everyone the same treatment.

Essentialism (cultural): a view that culture, identity and other related concepts are connected to 'blood and soil' understandings of belonging. Cultural essentialism reduces the notion of culture to a fixed set of knowledge, values, beliefs and attitudes which determines collective behaviours and attitudes (see Byram 1997).

Ethnicity: "sense of kinship, group solidarity and common culture", which is thought to influence world events culturally and politically (Hutchinson and Smith 1996, vii). Examples of someone's ethnicity are Pakistani (as opposed to Asian), Senegalese (as opposed to black), Korean, Malaysian, or Emirati. While race is often viewed as a fixed component of identity, ethnicity, like culture, is best viewed as a process. It includes cultural traits such as tradition, customs, religion, learned behaviour and a sense of national or any other group pride and belonging.

Ethnocentrism: the evaluation of other cultures based on preconceptions originating from the standards and norms of one's own culture; often leading to stereotyping, discrimination and/or bias.

Exchange rate policy: the policy aiming to influence the value of the domestic currency (to increase it or decrease it), in order to meet domestic economic policy objectives (e.g. lower inflation or lower unemployment).

Executive coaching: a formal one-on-one intervention with the aim to help senior executives develop purposeful and meaningful positive change in their leadership behaviours, enhancing efficiency and performance, and support their personal development.

Externality: this relates to market-based economic outcomes that are not optimal, that is free markets that do not produce the best possible results. Environmental externality is the most common. Under Keynesianism, excessively high unemployment is also a free-market externality that can only be resolved via government intervention.

Face: the concept of face originated in Chinese culture and is hugely important across Asia. It refers to someone's public image and social status achieved through success, which is seen as a reflection of someone's moral character. Face is generally associated with respect, honour, status, reputation, credibility, competence, family/network connections, loyalty and trust (Oetzel et al. 2001, 237). The concept of face is now used across cultures to describe the concern for our own public dignity and that of others.

A **firestorm** describes an instance where a large number of negative messages are posted on social media about an individual or a group (e.g. an organisation or a business).

Fixed exchange rates: fixed exchange rates do not allow for the value of national currencies to fluctuate freely based on supply and demand for these, as their values are fixed at rates pre-determined by the monetary authorities that issues them. Priority is placed on meeting the external constraint as a means of providing macroeconomic stability.

Flexible exchange rates: flexible or floating exchange rates allow for the value of national currencies to fluctuate freely in currency markets, as there is no specific exchange rate target. Priority is placed on meeting internal economic objectives.

Follower: a person who follows another; in leadership psychology a follower is someone in a subordinate role being managed by the leader.

Formalism (in economics and anthropology): closely linked to neoclassical economics, borrows its assumption that the individual will make rational choices based on full information.

Free market: an economic system achieving an equilibrium of supply and demand by unconstrained interplay of market forces guided by the rationality of ***homo oeconomicus.***

Gender: a set of cultural identities, expressions, behaviours and roles that are assigned to people based on how they read or interpret their bodies. The World Health Organisation (2021) defines gender as the "socially constructed" characteristics, norms, behaviours and roles associated with being a woman, man, girl or boy which "[vary] from society to society and can change over time. [...]

Gender awareness: "a person's readiness to recognize how gender differences and privilege are deeply embedded in the assumptions, expectations, practices and manifestations of organizations and society" (Van den Brink 2015, 485).

Gender bias: a tendency to give differential treatment to people based on their perceived or real gender identity. Gender bias can be conscious or unconscious.

Gender identity refers to a person's deeply felt, internal and individual experience of gender, which may or may not correspond to the person's physiology or designated sex at birth. "[...] Rigid gender norms also negatively affect people with diverse gender identities, who often face violence, stigma and discrimination as a result" https://www.who.int/health-topics/gender#tab=tab_1

Gender mainstreaming: a globally recognised strategy of "promotion of gender equality through its systematic integration into all systems and structures, into all policies, processes and procedures, into the organisation and its culture, into ways of seeing and doing". Its adoption "comprises one of the entry conditions for admission to the European Union" (Rees 2005, 555).

Gig economy: a system where businesses hire independent workers for specific tasks, usually for low pay with no job security.

GILT (Globalisation, Internationalisation, Localisation, Translation): A standardised process, often discussed in translation studies, of four distinct strategies that companies may use when expanding to international markets.

Glass ceiling: an invisible barrier that prohibits *promotion* to positions of leadership and responsibility, for example, a lack of women or minorities in CEO positions.

Glass door: an invisible barrier that prohibits access to certain jobs, for example, women in STEM.

Global South: collective term for those countries—not necessarily in the geographical south—that do not belong to the dominant economies of the North Atlantic realm.

Globalisation: is the process of cultural exchange and increased trade in goods across the globe. It manifests in increased interconnectedness and interdependence of the world's cultures, peoples and economies.

GLOBE Project: Global Leadership and Behaviour Effectiveness Project. A large-scale study of cultural practices and leadership ideals. https://globeproject.com/results#country

Great Depression (the): the huge economic decline experienced globally in the 1930s.

Hearing workplaces: workplaces in the mainstream that are dominated by people who hear and cannot sign.

Hegemonic masculinity: a form of masculinity that reflects normative behavioural ideals for males in a culture and legitimises their dominant position in society. In contemporary Western cultures, hegemonic masculinity promotes stereotypical masculine heterosexual values and is implicated in the subordination of women and marginalised masculinities (e.g. gay men).

Historical School (in economics): an approach to political economy that pays close attention to historical and cultural factors; geographical base in Central Europe; strongly shaped by Roman Catholic social ethic.

Homo oeconomicus (literally: Economic Man): the rational individual idealised in neo-liberalist economics; invariably male.

Impairment: physical or psychological limitations of the individual, which can be temporary or permanent.

Imperialism: policy of expanding power and dominion by direct acquisition of, or gaining control over, another territory.

In-groups/Out-groups: social groups of people where individuals identify psychologically with other members (in-group/"us") or where individuals do not identify psychologically with other members (out-group/"them").

Indigenous languages: this is often used to refer to a language which is native to a particular region.

Indigenous psychology (IP): generally tends to involve "obtaining a descriptive understanding of human functioning in cultural context" through the study of "knowledge, skills, and beliefs people have about themselves and how they function in their familial, social, cultural, and ecological context" (Kim et al. 2006).

Informal economy: sphere of economic activity not complying with the way the economy is supposed to work according to mainstream theory.

Institutionalist economics: perspective on the economy acknowledging the significance of institutions in the anthropological sense of established modes of thinking and doing.

Institutions: in an anthropological sense, the totality of ideas and processes that create the fabric of a socio-cultural system through which individuals pursue their goals

Integration is a contested concept in cultural and migration studies because of its frequent conflation with assimilation. It describes a possible end result of the process of acculturation, where the minority feels included in a group or a workplace. Integration needs a fertile ground in the form of an inclusive dominant culture. Integration is not the responsibility of the minority culture alone, and this is a dangerous misconception. Acculturation processes may not always lead to integration if the dominant culture does not encourage or foster it. Integration may be described as *additive multiculturalism* (Triandis 1994, 241) because the acquisition of the dominant culture occurs without losing one's own cultural identity.

Integrity is one of the dimensions of trustworthiness in the model developed by Mayer, Davis and Schoorman (1995). It relates to responsibility, adherence to principles and ethical behaviour.

Intercultural competence is the ability to move away from ethnocentrism and its perils by adapting well to a new cultural context or a given cross-cultural situation. The self-transformational dimension of this process is crucial, and indeed the term intercultural competence has been criticised for implying a static notion, fixed end state or an attained goal.

Intercultural dialogue involves interaction, dialogue and contact between cultures beyond simple co-existence or mere tolerance, towards recognition of dynamic identities, promotion of respect and shared values. Intercultural dialogue is instrumental to implementing the aims of interculturalism, such as fostering understanding and empathy with others.

Intercultural responsibility in the workplace goes beyond the static notion of intercultural competence. It refers to "a conscious and reciprocally respectful, both professional and personal, relationship among the team/group members, assuming that they have different ethnic backgrounds, whether national or sub-national" (Guilherme 2012). Its constituent elements are coherence, empathy and solidarity.

Intercultural sensitivity: the "ability to have (a) more complex personal experience of otherness" to the extent that perception, experience and ability to communicate of and across cultural difference may ultimately become as complex as in a person's own culture (Bennett 2017).

Interpersonal dynamics refers to the ability and the way people interact with each other in a specific context, in a way that they can build meaningful relationships and effective communication. It also describes the way that people relate to each other in a specific context.

Interpreting/Interpretation: the process of transferring one spoken or signed language to another form of spoken or signed language contemporaneously in real time.

Intersectionality: originally coined by Crenshaw in 1989, intersectionality refers to "the critical insight that race, class, gender, sexuality, ethnicity, nation, ability, and age operate not as unitary, mutually exclusive entities, but rather as reciprocally constructing phenomena" (Hill-Collins 2015, 1).

Intersubjectivity refers to a distinct common world shared by people when they communicate. Individuals may have their own worldviews and their own experiences, assumptions, values and meanings that *they* consider 'common sense' and *they* take for granted (e.g. that the manager is always right, that the manager is always a man, that your colleagues are also your friends, etc.). But to reach understanding and communicate meaningfully and constructively, we need to move beyond our own subjective world into a shared, intersubjective world, which consists of shared meanings and interpretations.

Keynesianism: the school of Economic Thought inspired by the work of J. M. Keynes. It greatly influenced economic policy in the Western World from 1945–1970s and to a large extent during 2020–2022. The school encourages active government economic intervention and policy in periods of economic downturns, especially very severe ones (e.g. 1929, 1937, 2009, 2020).

L1 speakers: L1 refers to the first language that someone has acquired from birth.

L2 speakers: L2 is not the first language of the individual but one that is learnt later.

Leader: a team member who initiates change, creates vision, provides answers and convinces team members to follow this vision. Often (but not always) the leader in the group is directing and coordinating task-relevant activities.

Leadership: a reciprocal process of mobilising by persons with certain motives and values, independently or mutually held by leaders and followers.

Leader-Member Exchange (LMX) Theory: a relationship-based approach to leadership that focuses on the two-way relationship between leaders and followers.

Medical model of disability: focuses on the individual, with the aim to treat or cure the disability (Oliver 1996).

Mentor: an individual with professional experience who supports and advises others with less experience to achieve their professional development.

Misgendering: intentional use of pronouns other than those specified by the individual.

Modes of transaction: umbrella term covering modes of production, consumption and exchange from a relational perspective.

Moral economy: concept developed by British Marxist historian and activist E. P. Thompson, seeing economic activities in moral rather than just material terms; considered a Western-centric concept by some.

Negotiated culture is "an ongoing, emergent, working arrangement of imperfectly shared rules and routines" (Brannen et al. 2006, 45). A negotiated culture involves new meanings, new understandings and, ultimately, a new culture altogether (Clausen 2007).

Neurodivergence: differences in brain function and processing, which leads to, for example, Autism, Dyslexia or Dyspraxia.

Nonverbal communication may include contextualisation cues, such as body language, facial expressions, gestures, movement, posture, eye contact and proximity. Gabbott and Hogg (2001, 6) identify four categories of nonverbal communication:

a. *Proxemics* also referred to as 'personal space', proxemics refers to the amount of physical space that people feel appropriate or necessary to exist between themselves and others.
b. *Kinesics* refers to body movements and gestures.
c. *Vocalics* aspects such as pauses, volume (speaking loudly or softly), intonation, speed, stress and pronunciation. This category is also called paraverbal communication.
d. *Oculesics* refers to eye behaviour such as gaze and movement, e.g. rolling your eyes, staring or making eye contact in general. In many Asian cultures, for example, direct eye contact is prohibited between persons of differing status. Some employees on the autistic spectrum may avoid eye contact, finding it stressful or invasive, or may overcompensate by attempting to mimic 'neurotypical' interaction (Trevisan et al. 2017).

There are other categories of nonverbal communication, such as *haptics*, which refers to touch. Some cultures are more tactile than others, e.g. in some cultures kissing or hugging friends regardless of gender, while in others it is offensive to touch someone (especially their hair) who is not a relative. Some forbid physical contact between genders, which would prohibit handshakes, for example.

OECD countries: these are the 38 member countries in The Organization for Economic Cooperation and Development. These countries are represented by ambassadors at the OECD Council.

Occupational gender segregation: the dominance of one gender in a particular occupation; the tendency of men and women to work in different professions.

Organisational communication refers to any kind of communication between organisations and their stakeholders.

An **organisational crisis** is a sudden and unexpected event caused by internal or external factors that impacts stakeholder trust in an organisation and has the potential to damage the organisation's image, reputation and financial performance.

Organisational culture refers to the established norms, rules and ways of working in an organisation or a workplace that reflect the organisation's values, what is meaningful and important. There are many theories and models of organisational culture. In this volume, we focused on Schein's (2010) description of organisational culture as comprising (visible) artefacts, espoused beliefs and values and basic underlying assumptions.

Othering is the categorisation that takes place and is established by the dominant group when coming into contact with other cultures or individuals. What is fundamental in processes of othering is that the dominant group constructs group boundaries and assigns subordinate characteristics to other groups, devaluing and demoting them to a lesser category, thus establishing a hierarchy (Strani and Szczepaniak-Kozak 2018). This hierarchical categorisation leads to the assumption that difference from the dominant group signifies weakness or subordination.

Personality Theory studies how an individual develops their personality, whether they believe human traits to be fixed or to be capable of growth.

Personality Traits: an individual's dynamic collection of psychophysical systems that creates their characteristic pattern of behaviour, thoughts and feelings.

Pluricentric Language: a language with more than one formally standardised version. This often corresponds with the country in which the language is spoken. There are many standardised forms of English. This includes British English, American English, Hiberno-English, etc.

Prejudice: a pre-conceived negative opinion that is not based on fact or actual experience, but on biased information.

Prototypical Leadership: when a group perceives their leader as more effective due to a set of similar attributes that they both hold, e.g. attitudes, behaviours.

Racism is the belief that certain races are naturally or biologically inferior to a dominant race. Racism holds that "race is the primary determinant of traits and capacities and that racial difference produces an inherent superiority of a particular race" (Ying Yee 2008, 1118). In the workplace, this can be expressed as an assumption that certain groups are only good at manual work, others are particularly good at problem-solving, and others (usually the dominant ones) are born leaders. When racism has become embedded and represented within the culture and structure of institutions, we refer to it as institutional racism (Ying Yee 2008, 1118–1119).

Reasonable adjustments: changes an employer makes to remove or reduce a disadvantage related to someone's disability, e.g. making changes to the workplace, changing someone's working arrangements, finding a different way to do something, providing equipment, services or support. Reasonable adjustments are specific to an individual person's needs. Employers in the UK must make reasonable adjustments by law (ACAS https://www.acas.org.uk/reasonable-adjustments)

Reciprocity: non-market exchange, ranging from barter to forms of gifts.

Redistribution: form of reciprocity involving centralised gathering of certain goods from group members with subsequent division of these among the same.

Remote interpreting: a type of interpreting in which the interpreter is physically located in a different place from some or all parties involved and communicates via telephone, video, or other technologies.

Sex: The World Health Organisation (2021) defines sex as "the different biological and physiological characteristics of females, males and intersex persons, such as chromosomes, hormones and reproductive organs " https://www.who.int/health-topics/gender#tab=tab_1

Sign language: visual languages that are used by deaf people and are natural languages that are separate from spoken/written languages. Sign languages have their own grammatical rules, and every country has its own sign language.

Signed language: a way to focus on the modality of languages, by distinguishing between spoken and signed languages.

Simultaneous interpreting: a type of interpreting in which the interpreters deliver the speech into a different language while the speakers talk at the same time.

Small talk: polite social conversation about uncontroversial or unimportant topics, particularly between people who are not close acquaintances.

Smith, Adam: Scottish philosopher (1723–1790) widely regarded as a founding father of modern economics.

Social class: a dimension of the self that is rooted in objective material resources (via income, education and occupational prestige) and corresponding subjective perceptions of rank vis-a-vis others (Côté, 2011, 1).

Social Identity Theory: theory proposing that a person's sense of self is based on their social group membership, e.g. social class, gender, occupation. Through social categorisation, we put people into groups ("them" and "us"), and promote the in-groups made up of those with similar attributes, and criticise the out-groups made up of those with different attributes.

Social-relational model of disability: model that regards people as being disabled by a society that is designed for able-bodied people who can walk, talk, see, hear and are not neurodivergent, rather than any 'impairment' that they may have, which is the focus of the medical model of disability). Distinguishes between impairment, the physical or psychological limitations of the individual, and disability, the loss or limitation of opportunities to take part in normal life due to societal factors such as exclusion or stigmatisation. The social-relational model of disability puts the onus on society to accommodate the disabled person and does not focus on treatment or cure.

Soft Power: a concept coined by American political scientist Joseph Nye in 1990. Soft power refers to power that is manifested through cultural rather than military or economic means. It results in influence rather than military prowess or domination. See Nye, (2004) and Mackie and Strani (2023).

Stablecoin addresses the volatility issue of first-generation cryptocurrencies in that the system is more centralised and the privately created coins are tied to other cryptocurrencies, fiat currencies or regulated by a smart contract to maintain a stable value over time.

Stakeholders are any group affected by the behaviour of an organisation. They may be internal to the organisation (e.g. employees, shareholders) or external (e.g. media, regulatory authorities, customers, the general public).

Stereotyping: an often untrue, generalised, reductionist and fixed opinion about a group of people with particular characteristics. Stereotypes are the most common form of bias and constitute a very limited view of the average characteristics of an imagined group. They focus on simplified distinctive features, which ultimately results in undifferentiated judgements about people, cultures, races, genders and social categories (O'Sullivan et al. 1994, 222). Stereotypes can also be positive, but equally harmful because they are still homogenising the target groups and are based on reductionist premises.

Substantivism refers to how human beings make a living by interacting within their ecological setting, presupposing neither rational decision-making nor conditions of scarcity

Sustainable Development Goals (SDGs): UN-agreed set of 17 interconnected objectives through which sustainable development is expected to be achieved.

Sukuk: a sukuk is an Islamic bond that complies with Islamic Sharia law.

Terminology management: a multilingual process of extracting terms from written texts, storing and organizing the terms, identifying key terms from the source text and suggesting or automatically inserting the translation from a terminology database.

Tokenism: keeping the dominant group intact while only nominally fulfilling diversity requirements by "ticking boxes". For example, hiring the minimum number of disabled, female or other minority employees to meet equal opportunities legislation, without offering real opportunities for progression or positions of leadership. To combat a box-ticking approach to diversity management, less focus on numbers is needed and more on "the assumptions, micropractices, social relations, and power dynamics that define our collective cultural common sense about the nature of social difference and the practices of inequality" (Gray 2016, 246).

Translation: the process of conveying meaning from one language into another, or more commonly the process of producing a translation product from a written/signed text in one language into a written/signed text in another language through a process of reviewing, editing and revising.

Translation memory allows translators to operate under standardized work processes, and automatically saves all the translations into the database. On subsequent projects, if a similar segment or sentence comes up, the tool will automatically suggest or insert the translations into texts. This function increases the ease and efficiency of quality control of translated projects.

Trust is a multifaceted concept that has been examined by many disciplines (ethics, philosophy, politics, cultural studies, management, information systems). It is the belief that an individual or group or organisation has our best interests at heart and will act in such a way that respects or furthers those interests or, at the very least, will not act in such a way that harms them. It relates to "expectations and cognitive judgments of the motivations of others […] that would make them trustworthy" (Hardin 2006, 27), and it also involves reliance on a person, an institution or on certain rules. Trust is vital for team working, particularly when teams are remote, virtual and/or multicultural. It is also crucial for the sustainability of systems, workplaces and companies. Mühl (2014) distinguishes ten dimensions of trust in multicultural teams: competence, compatibility, goodwill, integrity, well-being, reciprocity, predictability, accessibility, inclusion and openness towards information. The trust attached to domestic financial institutions is vital in determining the effectiveness of their policies. Intercultural and cross-border trust greatly influences the effectiveness of international organisations.

Turn-taking refers to the length of time people normally wait before responding to the other person in a conversation ('taking their turn to speak'). Conventions on turn-taking vary considerably across cultures, resulting in ample scope for misunderstanding. For example, Northern Europeans are more likely to wait until the other person finishes their 'turn' before responding, while people from Mediterranean cultures may be more tolerant of overlapping, interruptions, increase in volume, rising intonation or even simultaneous speech. This is sometimes called **turn appropriation** (Clyne 1999).

Ubuntu: a widely practised value system and deep ontology that underlies ways of being in Africa. As a paradigm, Ubuntu is based on the experience of a person existing in a web of interrelations and is often translated as "I am because you are".

Vernacular (models): local styles, e.g. dialects or architectural designs; in economics: location-specific *modes of transaction.*

Visibility or invisibility doctrine: this refers to the extensive literature discussing the visible or the invisible role that the interpreter is mandated occupy while at work as well as the strong beliefs of scholars for the active participation or passive conduit-like role that interpreters employ.

Weber, Max: German sociologist, historian, jurist and political economist (1864–1920). One of the most important theorists of modern Western society.

Women's Empowerment Principles (WEPs): A set of Principles offering guidance to business on how to promote gender equality and women's empowerment in the workplace, marketplace and community. Established by UN Global Compact and UN Women, the WEPs are informed by international labour and human rights standards and grounded in the recognition that businesses have a stake in, and a responsibility for, gender equality and women's empowerment. WEPs are a primary vehicle for corporate delivery on gender equality dimensions of the 2030 agenda and the United Nations Sustainable Development Goals. By joining the WEPs community, the CEO signals commitment to this agenda at the highest levels of the company and to work collaboratively in multistakeholder networks to foster business practices that empower women. These include equal pay for work of equal value, gender-responsive supply chain practices and zero tolerance against sexual harassment in the workplace. https://www.weps.org/about

References

Bauman, H. D. L. 2004. Audism: Exploring the Metaphysics of Oppression. *Journal of Deaf Studies & Deaf Education* 9 (2): 239–246.
Bennett, M. 2017. Development Model of Intercultural Sensitivity. In *International Encyclopedia of Intercultural Communication*, ed. Y. Kim. Wiley
Byram, M. 1997. Teaching and Assessing Intercultural Communicative Competence. Multilingual Matters.
Chin, C. 2019. The Concept of Belonging: Critical, Normative and Multicultural. *Ethnicities* 19 (5): 715–739. https://doi.org/10.1177/1468796819827406
Clausen, L. 2007. Corporate Communication Challenges, p. A 'Negotiated' Culture Perspective. *International Journal of Cross Cultural Management* 7: 317–332.
Clyne, M. 1999. Variation in Communication Patterns and Inter-Cultural Communication Breakdown in Oral Discourse in Inter-cultural Communication at Work. Cultural Values in Discourse, Cambridge University Press.
Côté, S. 2011. How Social Class Shapes Thoughts and Actions in Organizations. *Research in Organizational Behaviour* 31: 43–71.
Gabbott, M., and G. Hogg. 2001. Non-Verbal Communication in Service Encounters: A Conceptual Framework. *Journal of Marketing Management* 17 (1): 5–26.
Guilherme, M. 2012. Critical Language and Intercultural Communication Pedagogy. In *The Routledge Handbook of Language and Intercultural Communication*, 366–380. Routledge.
Hall, S. 1996. The Question of Cultural Identity. In *Modernity: An Introduction to Modern Societies*, ed. S. Hall, D. Held, D. Hubert & K. Thompson. London: Blackwell Publishing.
Hardin, R. (2006). *Trust*. United Kingdom: Wiley.
Hickman, M.J., and N. Mai. 2015. Migration and Social Cohesion: Appraising the Resilience of Place in London. *Population Space Place* 21: 421– 432. https://doi.org/10.1002/psp.1921.
Johansson, G., and I. Lundberg. (2004). Adjustment Latitude and Attendance Requirements as Determinants of Sickness Absence or Attendance. Empirical Tests of the Illness Flexibility Model. *Social Science & Medicine* 58 (10): 1857–1868.
Kim, U., K-S. Yang, and K.-K. Hwang, eds. 2006. *Indigenous and Cultural Psychology: Understanding People in Context*. NY: Springer.
Lucas, K. 2017. Workplace Dignity. In *The International Encyclopaedia of Organizational Communication*, 1–13.
Mackie, A., and K. Strani. 2023. On the Soft Power of Values: The Scotland is Now Campaign. In *The Routledge Handbook of Soft Power*, 2nd ed., ed. N. Chitty, L. Ji and G. Rawnsley. London: Routledge.
Mayer, R.C., J.H. Davis, and F.D. Schoorman. 1995. An Integrative Model of Organizational Trust. *Academy of Management Review* 20 (3): 709–734.
Mühl, J.K. *Organisational Trust*, Springer Cham. https://doi.org/10.1007/978-3-319-04069-1
Nye, Joseph S. 2004. *Soft Power: The Means to Success in World Politics*. Hachette UK.
O'Sullivan, T., J. Hartley, D. Saunders, M. Montgomery, and J. Fiske. 1994. *Key Concepts in Communication and Cultural Studies*. London and New York: Routledge.
Schein, E.H. 2010. Organizational Culture and Leadership, vol. 2. Wiley.
Strani, K., and A. Szczepaniak-Kozak. 2018 Strategies of Othering Through Discursive Practices: Examples from the UK and Poland. *Lodz Papers in Pragmatics* 14 (1): 163–179. https://doi.org/10.1515/lpp-2018-0008

Trevisan, D.A., N. Roberts, C. Lin, and E. Birmingham. 2017. How Do Adults and Teens with Self-Declared Autism Spectrum Disorder Experience Eye Contact? A Qualitative Analysis of First-Hand Accounts. *PLoS ONE* 12 (11): e0188446.

Triandis, H.C. 1994. Culture and Social Behavior. New York: McGraw-Hill.

Ying Yee, J. 2008 Racism. In *Encyclopaedia of Race, Ethnicity, and Society*, ed. R.T. Schaefer, 1118–1119. NY: SAGE.

Index

A
ability, 101
acculturation, 32, 275, 283
adjustment latitude, 222
anchor currency, 148
Anglo-Saxon model, 135
assimilation, 32, 283
audism, 243, 245, 246

B
belonging, 17, 125, 149, 156, 215, 217, 220, 235, 276, 279, 280
benevolence, 101
bias, 217–219, 221–223, 232, 235, 238, 280, 281, 288
body language, 285
business, 52–54, 57–61, 120, 124, 127, 138–140, 142, 156, 163–165, 167, 169–175, 179, 182, 185, 186, 190, 193–203, 205, 206, 213, 215, 217, 219, 222, 224, 228, 244–247, 249, 259, 261–266, 269–271, 276, 277, 280, 289
business case for diversity, 5
business communication, 171, 172, 196, 200, 263, 266

C
Central Bank Digital Currencies (CBDCs), 154
coaching, 79, 277
Cognitive Behavioural Therapy (CBT), 70
communication, 1, 15, 16, 49, 51, 52, 54, 127, 164, 169, 171–173, 180–186, 189, 194, 196, 199, 206, 212, 216, 235, 242–244, 248–251, 257, 259, 261–263, 265, 266, 271, 275, 277, 278, 283, 285, 291
communicative, 15, 171, 175, 184, 197, 201
complexity, 50, 54
conflict, 31, 124, 126, 127, 198
cross-cultural, 183, 196, 199, 200, 206, 212, 214, 257–259, 261–266, 269–271, 283
cultural awareness, 199, 200, 266
cultural intelligence (CQ), 91
cultural literacy, 89
cultural values, 18
culture, 15, 16, 31, 51, 53, 54, 56, 58, 60, 115–118, 124–128, 134–136, 138, 142, 143, 169, 193, 195, 199, 201, 205, 206, 216–219, 227–229, 245, 250, 251, 258, 259, 261, 265, 268–271, 275, 278–286, 291
currency, 147, 148

D
deaf, 1, 188, 194, 203–205, 220, 241–252, 258, 270, 271, 275, 276, 278, 287
deaf people, 1, 203–205, 241–251, 258, 270, 271, 275, 276, 278, 287
deaf workplaces, 248
dialogue, 182, 283
dignity, 211, 278, 291
disability, 212, 220–224, 243, 267, 279, 284, 286, 287
discrimination, 167, 211, 217–224, 235–237, 243, 244, 267, 268, 280, 281

© The Editor(s) (if applicable) and The Author(s), under exclusive licence to Springer Nature Switzerland AG 2023
K. Strani and K. Pfeiffer (eds.), *Intercultural Issues in the Workplace*,
https://doi.org/10.1007/978-3-031-42320-8

diversity, 49–51, 56, 116, 175, 179, 182–185, 187, 211–213, 215–218, 221–224, 236, 241, 250, 258, 267, 268, 271, 276, 279, 288

E

economy, 116, 117, 121, 122
emotional intelligence, 92
empathy, 42, 102
entrepreneurship, 244
equity, 220
essentialist, 3, 127, 213
ethnicity, 212, 215, 217, 223, 266, 279, 283
ethnocentrism, 5, 258, 261, 283
exchange rate policy, 149
executive coaching, 85
externality, 149

F

face, 39
finance, 126, 133–138, 140–143, 148, 152, 157, 188, 237, 262, 265
firestorm, 105
fixed exchange rates, 150
flexible exchange rates, 150

G

gender, 212, 213, 219, 220, 223, 227–238, 258, 260, 261, 266, 279, 281, 283, 285, 287, 289
gender awareness, 220
gender bias, 232
gender mainstreaming, 219, 281
glass ceiling, 219, 235, 245
glass door, 219
global, 1, 15, 115, 116, 118, 121, 124, 126, 133, 135, 140–143, 149, 152, 153, 165, 167, 169–175, 181–183, 187, 190, 194, 195, 206, 219, 222, 228, 229, 242, 258, 259, 261, 277
globalisation, 133–136, 143, 164, 167, 169, 171, 173, 175, 181, 182, 202
Global South, 116, 281
GLOBE Project, 282

H

haptics, 35
hearing workplaces, 244, 245, 251
hegemonic masculinity, 236

I

identity, 147, 287, 290
impairment, 220
indigenous psychologies, 88
in-groups and out-groups, 75
integration, 33, 141, 147, 151, 156, 173, 219, 250, 251, 281, 283
integrity, 101, 102
intercultural, 1, 51, 52, 54, 56, 59–61, 125, 127, 133, 134, 141, 143, 147, 151, 204, 257, 262–264, 266, 269, 278, 283, 289, 291
intercultural competence, 31, 41, 262, 283
intercultural dialogue, 33
interculturality, 15
intercultural responsibility, 43
intercultural sensitivity, 89
international, 119, 136, 143, 147–152, 154, 155, 157, 164, 169, 171, 172, 174, 180–182, 184, 185, 187, 189, 194–196, 199, 206, 211, 212, 214, 243, 257, 260, 289
interpersonal dynamics, 108
interpretation, 194, 248, 275
interpreting, 1, 180, 193–198, 201, 203–206, 247, 248, 250, 258, 264, 266, 271, 276, 277, 287
intersectionality, 212, 224, 283
intersubjectivity, 22
invisibility doctrine, 107
Islamic Finance, 140, 142, 261

K

Keynesianism, 149

L

language, 164, 168, 172, 181, 188, 200, 203, 216, 269, 279, 286
leadership, 1, 15, 49, 74, 79, 189, 219, 228, 232, 235, 257–261, 267, 268, 270, 280–282, 284, 286, 288, 291
leisure, 49–52, 54–56, 59–61, 128, 258, 263, 268, 269

M

management, 52, 56, 180–182, 195, 202, 204, 206, 212, 213, 221, 224, 231, 251, 259, 267, 288, 290
medical model of disability, 220
mentor, 84
misgendering, 220

multicultural, 31, 49, 50, 61, 143, 182, 216, 258, 289
multicultural teams, 31, 216, 258, 289
multilingualism, 1, 179–184, 186, 189

N

national culture, 134
negotiated culture, 31, 33, 259, 284
negotiation, 194, 195, 258, 262–265
neurodivergence, 221
nonverbal communication, 34, 285
    kinesics, 35
    oculesics, 35
    proxemics, 34
    vocalics, 35
norms, 17, 278

O

occupational gender segregation, 232
OECD countries, 137
organisational communication, 99
organisational crisis, 101
organisational culture, 19, 229, 259, 270, 285
othered, 32

P

paraverbal communication, 35
personality theory, 72
politeness, 198
positivist, 3
power, 55, 117, 120, 124, 125, 165–167, 169, 195, 198, 217, 229, 232, 234, 237, 238, 259, 282, 287, 288, 291
productivity, 53, 55, 57, 60, 141, 181, 183, 211, 214, 221, 222, 224, 237, 276

R

race, 168, 212, 215, 217, 223, 279, 283, 286
racism, 215, 216, 221, 286, 291
reasonable adjustments, 222
religion, 52, 53, 116, 125, 212, 217, 218, 223, 260, 266, 267, 280

S

sequential time, 57
sex, 213, 229
signed languages, 203, 287

sign language, 203–205, 220, 241–243, 245, 248–250, 287
sign language interpreters, 197, 203
small talk, 54
social class, 219
Social Identity Theory (SIT), 75
social model of disability, 220
social-relational model of disability, 243
stakeholders, 100
stereotypes, 217, 218, 222, 223, 227, 232, 233, 235, 236, 238, 259, 270
sukuk, 142
synchronic time, 57

T

teamwork, 214, 216
time, 49–61, 79, 117–119, 124, 136, 138, 140, 151, 153–156, 166, 173, 174, 181, 182, 195, 197, 198, 201, 202, 205, 206, 213, 214, 219, 220, 229, 251, 258, 259, 262, 263, 265–269, 278, 281, 283, 287, 289
tokenism, 221
training, 133, 157, 173, 196, 203, 204, 218, 221–224, 235, 237, 250, 251, 257, 260, 261, 265, 268, 271, 275
translation, 1, 180, 194–196, 199–206, 242, 243, 258, 264, 266, 271, 275, 288
trust, 20, 33, 101, 147, 151, 263, 265, 266, 288, 291
turn appropriation, 36
turn-taking, 35, 250, 289

U

Ubuntu, 91
uncertainty, 74, 140, 168, 221, 270

V

values, 49, 51–54, 59–62, 116–119, 122, 124, 135, 141, 143, 150, 169, 174, 185, 200, 212, 217, 228, 229, 235, 243, 260, 265, 275, 278–280, 282–285, 291
virtual teams, 258
visibility doctrine, 107

W

Women's Empowerment Principles, 219
work, 49–52, 54–57, 59–61, 79, 117–120, 122, 125, 134, 136, 139, 147, 169,

174, 180–185, 187–189, 194, 197, 199, 202–204, 211, 213, 214, 216, 218, 219, 222, 228, 230, 232–236, 238, 241–252, 258, 260–263, 266–271, 275–278, 282, 284–286, 289

workplace, 1, 15, 31, 49–52, 54, 59, 61, 157, 171, 173, 175, 180–182, 184–190, 203, 204, 211–216, 218–224, 227, 228, 230–232, 234–236, 238, 241–247, 250–252, 258–261, 267, 268, 270, 271, 275, 276, 278, 283, 285, 286, 289, 291

www.ingramcontent.com/pod-product-compliance
Ingram Content Group UK Ltd.
Pitfield, Milton Keynes, MK11 3LW, UK
UKHW022344140125
453680UK00001B/15